THE RI[SE AND FALL OF]

EMI
RECORDS

Brian Southall

THE RISE & FALL OF

EMI RECORDS

Brian Southall

OMNIBUS PRESS

London / New York / Paris / Sydney / Copenhagen / Berlin / Madrid / Tokyo

CONTENTS

With much love and thanks to Pat, who saw me through the EMI years and knows where to put a comma

FOREWORD

I THINK it's fair to say that almost everyone I know who ever worked for EMI Records, EMI Music or any of its other music-related offshoots retains a soft spot for the great British music company. Even if you were paid off – as I was in 1989 after 15 years' service – the sense of affection, appreciation and pride in having worked for Electric & Musical Industries never disappears.

It was always the first lady of the UK music business and while it was often compared to that other great British institution, the BBC, as an unwieldy, occasionally ham-fisted and often bureaucratic organisation, EMI was the first and undoubtedly the greatest music company ever to emerge in this country or, for that matter, anywhere in the world.

It's a story that goes back over 110 years and involves some of the finest artists, both classical and popular, ever to put their music on a cylinder, wax disc, vinyl record, cassette tape or compact disc.

During its long history the company has occasionally hit troubled waters, had to suffer short-sighted management and overcome the concerns of investors and shareholders. At its worst it was even dubbed Every Mistake Imaginable, but the fact that it survived all this and more is testimony to its staff, its artists and its reputation.

But things change and right now EMI is a company in a state of flux. It has new private owners and is trying to rebuild itself in an industry that, globally, is suffering decline and disinterest in equal measure.

Former EMI chairman Sir Colin Southgate sums up his sense of disappointment with these words: "In the last five years – except for music publishing – EMI has fallen apart."

When I was asked to write this book, which focuses on EMI's performance and standing in the world music market over the past 12 years (since it separated from Thorn), I spoke with a friend and former EMI colleague who is still involved with the record business as, according to him, "a design and creative guru".

I was, perhaps appropriately, in the music department of Foyles book shop in London's Charing Cross Road when he called my mobile phone

1

to ask what I was up to. I told him that I had just been asked to write a book tracing EMI's recent history, its fall from grace and prospects under its new owners.

He said simply, "What a shit show that is." How things have changed for the business we once dubbed "the greatest music company in the world".

There is no question that EMI is right up there in the pantheon of great British companies – it signed The Beatles, owned the HMV Dog & Trumpet trademark, opened and ran the world-famous Abbey Road Studios, sacked The Sex Pistols, and released records by Cliff Richard for 30 years while also developing high-profile defence, medical, leisure and film divisions.

In fact there was a time when you could walk down London's Oxford Street and give your hard-earned cash to EMI at every turn. You could stay in a hotel, visit a coffee bar, buy an album in a record shop, lunch in a restaurant, see a movie in a cinema and finally dance the night away in a disco – and EMI would own it all.

Meanwhile, outside London, there were opportunities to do most of the same things with the added bonus of playing squash or bingo in a leisure centre, purchasing a television set, radio or record player and enjoying the delights of the Blackpool Tower, not to mention yachting in the company's marina or buying some night radar equipment or even a brain scanner.

EMI owned or was involved in all these things, but it was its music business that caught the imagination and interest of millions of record buyers the world over; its roster included many of the world's leading recording artists assigned to world-famous labels ranging from HMV to Parlophone, Capitol to Columbia and Angel to Harvest.

From 1931, when the company was founded, until the late 1970s, EMI stood at the forefront of British enterprise and creativity. The fact that it had been founded over 30 years earlier as the Gramophone Company and acquired by Thorn in 1979, could not take the focus away from EMI as it discovered talent, made and released million-selling recordings, spread its wings internationally and became one of the great British institutions.

But in recent years – arguably following its demerger from Thorn – the company has suffered a steep decline and this book charts that regression with interviews and comments from some of the most important players, from company executives and artist managers to financial analysts and music industry journalists.

Their suggestions as to how and why it went wrong and their solutions to the problems are varied, fascinating and illuminating in equal measure, for even now, as a privately owned company, with no shareholders or public investors, EMI still captures headlines and divides opinion.

While the company's former leading executives Sir Colin Southgate, Jim Fifield and Eric Nicoli spoke candidly to me about EMI and its trials and tribulations, its new owner, Guy Hands, was more cautious and gave his views to me off the record and as background information. Nevertheless, he still displayed an awareness of EMI's great history and tradition, even though they are probably the least of his concerns as he fights to maintain a future for the company.

And in talking to managers, analysts, commentators and ex-staff members it became clear that the historic rise and recent fall of EMI involves a host of good intentions coupled with a myriad of mistakes and poor decisions, plus a smattering of bad luck.

Two essential elements of this book – and of any music company's business record – are market share figures and financial information. While the market share data comes as relatively obvious and easy to read information, the financial reports are sometimes less clear.

So I think it only fair to point out that, while reporting the 'numbers' chronologically, there are occasional discrepancies as figures reported at one year end are often later adjusted to reflect amended calculations by the 'money men'. Even so, you will still get an overall feel for EMI's performance in any one year compared with an earlier or later year.

It has to be acknowledged that on occasions EMI's past glories have masked its present troubles, as the music editor of *The Daily Telegraph* suggests. "Nostalgically we are clinging on to the idea of EMI being this great British institution," says Neil McCormick. "There is this wonderful notion of EMI being built up around The Beatles, George Martin and Abbey Road but these companies have had a vampiric relationship with music culture all along. They've never been the gate-keepers, they've always been the bouncers on the door."

Nevertheless EMI is a famous name, a historic company and, even if its past may be greater than its future, the place it holds in people's affections is based primarily on its musical heritage – its extraordinary and unique contribution to an art form that moved the hearts and minds of music lovers around the globe.

People might argue – in the wake of the success of emerging independent companies – whether EMI was the last great British record company.

Right now, as it slips to last place in the league table of majors and indies, it cannot claim greatness on any international scale, but the fact that its fall from grace evokes more sadness than satisfaction suggests that EMI is bigger than the people who own it or run it.

Alison Wenham, head of the UK's Association of Independent Music and someone who fought against EMI's plans to strengthen itself through a merger, derives no pleasure whatsoever from the company's current perilous situation. "I am sad about EMI's decline because EMI has been with me, on both a personal and professional level, for as long as I can remember and it is one of the great record companies. I like to think all this has been a rather protracted blip rather than the beginnings of a terminal decline."

If you worked in music at EMI as I and many thousands of others did, you were treated to arguably the best apprenticeship you could get. Being poorly paid went with the territory, but then so did learning about every aspect of the music business, and it's no coincidence that many of the most successful executives in the British music industry over the past 50 years began their careers at EMI – and they were proud of it and never slow to tell you about it.

The first head of EMI Music, when it was established as a global division of EMI Limited in the late 1970s, was Bhaskar Menon, whose career with the company embraced EMI in India and Capitol Records in America. Since he retired as chairman of EMI Music and as a director of Thorn EMI in 1990, he has kept a fatherly eye on the business he helped to develop and now speaks with sadness of EMI's current situation.

"I am personally deeply saddened that a great British company involved so much with the serious arts and the popular culture of our times has been reduced to being paraded as a comic and pathetic joke in the very industry which it so dominated globally for many decades."

Talking to people about EMI only served to re-emphasise what an extraordinary company it was – and it may be again one day – but its new masters will have their work cut out to make it any more than a faded former star reduced to playing a bit part in a drama that, despite falling attendances, is still played out under the spotlight.

The music industry faces changing times with record companies forced to cope with new technologies, falling sales and increasing piracy. The antics of the big four – Universal, Sony BMG, Warner and EMI – are assessed, analysed and scrutinised as much as, if not more than, any number of anonymous groups or singers unearthed by countless TV talent shows.

Things in the music business have changed dramatically with the emphasis and interest switching from the talent to the suits. In the words of one commentator, "As the story has gone on into the 21st century, it turns out that [it] is more and more about the record industry and the record companies, and that has become more interesting than the artist's story."

Here then is one of those 'interesting' stories about one of the most famous and most troubled record companies of modern times – EMI.

TIMELINE

1897 – Original Gramophone Company is founded in London.

1898 – Company officially incorporated. First British recordings made by EMI in Covent Garden studio.

1899 – The HMV Dog & Trumpet trademark and painting acquired for £100.

1900 – Business briefly renamed Gramophone & Typewriter Ltd.

1902 – Tenor Enrico Caruso signed for £100 to record ten songs.

1904 – Dame Nellie Melba signed for £100 and paid a 5/- (25p) royalty on each recording.

1907 – Work started on company's new factory in Hayes, Middlesex.

1909 – HMV 'Nipper' logo appears on UK release for first time.

1914/18 – Gramophone Company factory used to produce munitions during WWI.

1917 – Companies in Germany and Russia lost because of war.

1918 – The Gramophone Company sells over 5 million records in UK.

1921 – First HMV store opened by Sir Edward Elgar in London's Oxford Street.

1926 – Ernest Lough recording of 'Hear My Prayer' sells over a million copies and company introduces its first mobile recording studio.

1929 – Company reports profits of £1.2 million and assets valued at £5.3 million.

1931 – Gramophone and Columbia Graphophone companies merge to create Electric & Musical Industries – EMI.

1931 – Abbey Road studios opened by Elgar in St John's Wood while EMI scientist Alan Blumlein patents technology for stereo recording.

1933 – EMI company posts a loss of £1 million in face of economic depression.

1939 – New HMV store in Oxford Street opened by Sir Thomas Beecham.

1939/45 – EMI's business restricted during WWII by conscription and a shortage of raw materials.

1946 – EMI joins forces with MGM to release records in America.

1948 – EMI celebrates 50th anniversary of the founding of The Gramophone Company.

1952 – Maria Callas signs to EMI as company releases its first 33⅓ and 45rpm records.

1954 – Joseph Lockwood named EMI chairman. Eddie Calvert's 'Oh Mein Papa' is the first UK number one single from Abbey Road studios.

1955 – Company buys US Capitol Records for $8.5 million.

1956 – Elvis Presley's UK releases issued by EMI on HMV label.

1957 – EMI Records created to oversee company's UK record business.

1958 – Cliff Richard signs to EMI.

1960 – EMI moves into Manchester Square offices.

1962 – The Beatles signed to EMI by Parlophone boss George Martin and Capitol signs The Beach Boys.

1964 – The Beatles' single 'I Want To Hold Your Hand' sells over 15 million copies worldwide.

1966 – EMI buys Grade Organisation for £9 million.

1967 – Beatles release *Sgt Pepper's Lonely Hearts Club Band* album and Pink Floyd sign to Columbia.

1969 – Associated British Picture Corporation acquired to make EMI the UK's largest entertainment business.

1970 – Lockwood replaced by Sir John Read as chief exec of EMI.

1971 – First clinical trials of EMI's CAT 'brain scanner' take place in UK.

1972 – EMI Music Publishing division established, Queen signed and T.Rex have first hits on newly formed EMI label.

1973 – Pink Floyd release *Dark Side Of The Moon*.

1976 – EMI acquires Screen Gems and Colgems publishing companies.

1977 – Sex Pistols fired from EMI and The Rolling Stones signed.

1978 – EMI Music created with Bhaskar Menon as chairman.

1979 – US company Paramount offers £75 million for 50% of EMI Music.

1979 – EMI Music buys United Artists record company and Thorn acquires EMI for £165 million to create Thorn EMI.

1983 – EMI releases its first compact discs. EMI and Virgin combine to launch *Now That's What I Call Music* compilation series.

1985 – Thorn EMI announces music, rental and retail as it new core businesses.

1986 – Company sells EMI Screen Entertainment for £128 million while EMI Music opens its first compact disc manufacturing plant in Swindon, UK.

1987 – Colin Southgate becomes chief executive of Thorn EMI.

1988 – Jim Fifield appointed as president EMI Music.

1989 – SBK Entertainment World company acquired for $295 million and Chrysalis Records bought for £79 million.

1992 – EMI Music acquires Virgin Music from Sir Richard Branson for £560 million.

1995 – Spice Girls sign to Virgin Records and Blur set new record with four BRIT Awards in one year.

1995 – EMI Records leaves famous Manchester Square offices.

1996 – Separate EMI and Thorn companies created as Thorn EMI demerge.

1997 – Ken Berry appointed president EMI Recorded Music and 50% of Motown's Jobete music publishing business acquired for $132 million.

1997 – EMI celebrates centenary of creation of The Gramophone Company.

1998 – Fifield leaves with a reported £12 million pay-off.

1999 – The possibility of a sale of EMI to Seagram ends when the US company acquires Polygram for $10 billion.

1999 – Southgate retires as chairman of EMI to be replaced by United Biscuits chief Eric Nicoli and Hikaru Utada sells 7 million albums to become biggest-selling artist in Japanese history.

2000 – First plans for merging EMI and Warner Music are abandoned while Garth Brooks passes 100 million sales mark.

2001 – EMI and Bertelsmann merger talks collapse while Ken Berry is replaced by Alain Levy as head of EMI Music.

2002 – Mute Records bought by EMI for £42 million, Mariah Carey is dropped as Robbie Williams signs a new long-term deal.

2002 – Norah Jones' Come Away With Me is year's biggest-selling album and she wins record-breaking eight Grammy awards.

2003 – EMI's attempts to acquire Warner Music fail.

2004 – EMI buys remainder of Jobete and also acquires Hit & Run company while closing CD plants in UK and Europe.

2004 – EMI announces its third profit warning in three years.

2006 – EMI and Warner Music once again fail to reach agreement on a takeover amid reports of an offer from an unnamed organization, while company takes control of Toshiba-EMI joint venture in Japan for £93 million.

2007 – Levy and sidekick David Munns let go as company announces another profit warning and Jason Flom appointed as head of new Capitol Music Group in US.

2007 – EMI signs new iTunes digital download deal with Apple.

2007 – Private equity company Terra Firma acquires EMI for £3.2 billion and Nicoli is replaced by Guy Hands as head of EMI.

2008 – Veteran EMI UK boss Tony Wadsworth leaves while Coldplay's *Viva La Vida* becomes year's biggest-selling album.

2009 – EMI Records UK moves from Hammersmith to join Terra Firma in Kensington HQ.

2009 – EMI Music announces a pre-tax loss of £1.7 billion and Terra Firma boss Guy Hands moves his business (and himself) to the tax haven of Guernsey.

2010 – After nearly 40 years with EMI, Queen leave the company to join Universal while Abbey Road Studios is granted English Heritage Grade II listing.

2010 – Roger Faxon named CEO of the EMI Group and Terra Firma loses the law suit it brought against CitiGroup.

2011 – Pink Floyd sign a new long-term deal with EMI ahead of bankers CitiGroup taking control of the company from Terra Firma's Maltby Investments arm.

2011 – Rivals Warner Music are acquired by Access Industries and Robbie Williams leaves EMI to join world leaders Universal.

2011 – Universal Music pay £1.2 billion to acquire EMI Recorded Music while Sony Corporation announces the purchase of EMI Music Publishing for £1.3 billion.

CHAPTER 1

Start Me Up

(The Rolling Stones, EMI 1981)

JUST one year before it was due to celebrate its 100th birthday, Electric & Musical Industries, known throughout the world as EMI, was separated from its mother ship, the corporation that was Thorn EMI, and left to make its own way in the world as a stand-alone music company.

So, almost a century on from when it was launched in 1897 as Britain's first and only major music company, EMI found itself without the financial or creative support of any sister or subsidiary company that might step in and help out when the going got tough in the potentially rewarding but notoriously unpredictable international music business.

The decision to de-merge EMI out of Thorn EMI in 1996 was the beginning of a calamitous new chapter in the story of the company that had seen off all challengers to its crown as the UK's foremost major player in the global music business.

While famous and important operators such as Decca and Pye fell by the wayside in the early 1980s and energetic, successful upstarts such as Island, Chrysalis, Virgin and Zomba capitulated and sold out between 1989 and 2002, EMI soldiered on to the point where, in 2009, it is struggling – even under new owners – to stay in touch with its competitors.

To fully chart the momentous story of not just this country's but one of the world's most important and influential companies, we have to go back to its origins in the back streets of London's Covent Garden where two men – one an American salesman and the other a British lawyer – laid the foundations of EMI. It was the summer of 1897 and the two leading players were Massachusetts-born William Barry Owen and Trevor Williams, the son of wealthy Welsh landowners.

While it was Owen, a gambler and lover of the highlife, who actually established the original Gramophone Company as an unincorporated business run from the Hotel Cecil in Central London, he needed the financial backing of his legal advisor, Williams, to fulfil the dream and launch the business that would eventually be known the world over as EMI.

And, just as EMI in 2009 is simply and solely a music company, so The Gramophone Company began life as a business determined to take advantage of the latest inventions in recorded music and the public's growing interest in the new-fangled sound machines.

To understand how The Gramophone Company came about, it is necessary to go back to the late 19th century and the first stirrings of the recorded music industry. These beginnings were convoluted to say the least, largely because of complex patent laws in effect at the time and the eagerness of those involved to secure the rights to their inventions. Twenty years before Owen and Williams joined forces in anticipation of blazing a trail in the burgeoning recorded music business, Thomas Edison had created and quickly patented his machine for the storing and reproducing of sound – and he called it the phonograph.

Bizarrely, within three years he abandoned work on his sound recording invention, turning his attention to the development of the light bulb, and it fell to Alexander Graham Bell to pick up the needle and, over the following five years, transform Edison's phonograph into a machine with genuine commercial possibilities. By 1887 Bell and his engineer, Charles Sumner Tainter, had moved on from the phonograph, and their development of the wax cylinder as the "software" required a new playing machine, which they dubbed the graphophone. Such was the importance of Bell's work with recording and sound reproduction that the word we use today to measure sound levels – decibel – was created in his honour.

In the same year six of their master patents were acquired by The American Graphophone Company, the manufacturers of the new mechanism. The company's owner, Edward Easton, then created a new company, based in Washington D.C., which he called The Columbia Phonograph Company, despite the fact that it was established to act as a sales operation for the new graphophone.

One of the companies to come out of this mish-mash of phonograph and graphophone businesses was The Columbia Graphophone Company, which emerged as part of Easton's growing empire and would eventually play a significant role in the creation of the company known today as EMI. By 1887 the slightly renamed Columbia Phonograph Company General had spread its wings and expanded into Europe, with its debut French company offering the citizens of Paris American-made cylinder records.

One of the other physicists involved with Alexander Bell – and the man who developed the microphone for the first telephones – was Emile Berliner, and he too saw a future in sound recording. One year after Columbia's first venture into Europe, Berliner created a significant buzz with the introduction of his new gramophone and the revolutionary recording process that saw flat zinc discs replace wax cylinders.

Turned down by rival phonograph companies, Berliner decided in 1895 to create his own Berliner Gramophone Company with noted recording engineer Fred Gaisberg, who was in charge of the artists and their repertoire, effectively the world's first A&R man. By the end of the year, the Berliner catalogue of 7in records, mostly made by American Gaisberg, numbered 100.

Berliner was joined by two other important figures in his new music business. William Owen was hired to lead the push into Europe, and affluent New Yorker Alfred Clark, who had once worked for another of Easton's operations – The North American Phonograph Company – was put in charge of the important Philadelphia retail outlet with a brief to sell Berliner products throughout the USA.

To add further confusion to the story of the phonograph, the graphophone and the gramophone, Delaware-born engineer Eldridge Johnson, who had spent years improving Berliner's machine, elected to register patents covering his own inventions and, in the ensuing conflict, established The Victor Talking Machine Company in 1901.

However, during the period Johnson and Berliner were working together to improve the gramophone, Owen and Williams – thanks to the latter's generous £5,000 investment plus an exclusive licensing deal with Berliner – began their business in London with Williams as chairman, Owen as managing director and Berliner as a director.

Combining the best of the two gramophone options, the new British Gramophone Company imported machines from Johnson's US factory and discs from Berliner's American agent. When this arrangement proved unsatisfactory, Owen and Williams decided to turn to the company Berliner had established in his native Germany in 1898.

Deutsche Grammophon was able to manufacture discs for its British sister company and in return The Gramophone Company soon bought a controlling interest in the German business in order to guarantee a regular supply of discs.

Even though The Gramophone Company had opened for business in

1897 and Gaisberg had made the company's first British recordings a year later, it wasn't until 1898 that the company was formally incorporated. By this time it was located in offices in Maiden Lane, a side street in Covent Garden that runs parallel with the Strand. It was here that Gaisberg supposedly recruited a barmaid with aspirations as a singer to test out the company's recording studio. Her name was Syria Lamonte, who worked at the nearby Rules restaurant*, and she was persuaded – apparently for no fee – to sing 'Comin' Thru The Rye' and so establish The Gramophone Company as a new home for British talent.

Having artists signed to the company meant that the resulting records would need to be issued on a label, and The Gramophone Company introduced the Angel trademark in 1899 as its major, and first globally registered, imprint.

In the same year the company was offered the opportunity to add a second label when an artist named Francis Barraud offered The Gramophone Company his painting of a dog listening to a phonograph. The dog, a fox terrier, was called Nipper and the painting was titled *His Master's Voice*. Before acquiring the new trademark, the company requested that Barraud paint over the phonograph, by now an old-fashioned listening device, and introduce instead a new gramophone. This done, it paid £50 for the copyright and a further £50 for the exclusive reproduction rights. The original painting, now the most iconic record company trademark in the world, was also part of the £100 deal.

However, the Gramophone Company's rights were not global and when Berliner saw the new design his British outlet had purchased, he set about acquiring the rights to the HMV logo for North America. Ultimately, when the Victor company took over Berliner's business, the trademark was included in the deal and it added the rights for Japan in 1904. As a result of these deals, the HMV label and logo, which were officially registered in Britain in 1901, remained the property of EMI throughout Europe and in various other international territories while RCA, which later bought Victor, owned the rights to the image in the USA, Canada and Japan.

In the same year as the company acquired the famous HMV painting, The Gramophone Company signed the biggest music-hall star of the day to the first ever royalty-based recording contract. Under his October 1898

---

* Rules, established in 1798, is still in business at 35 Maiden Lane and advertises itself as 'London's Oldest Restaurant'.

contract, Albert Chevalier was to be paid one old shilling (5p) for every 12 records sold. Keen, even then, not to be accused of ripping off the artist, the company also offered his agent "ample opportunity to inspect our books for such verification".

Around this time serious consideration was also given to the merits of actually merging The Gramophone Company and The Victor Talking Machine Company to create what would have been the first multi-national gramophone and recording company. When nothing came of these discussions, the two companies settled on a series of trading agreements, which resulted in Victor focusing on America and the Far East, while the Gramophone business was left with the rest of the world.

Expansion was now very much the name of the game for The Gramophone Company as machines and records began to attract interest around the world. New companies were formed in France and Italy, throughout Central Europe and in Russia, while the remaining shares in Deutsche Grammophon were also acquired. Williams and Owen also decided to invest in another new invention that appeared on the market at the turn of the century, the typewriter, and in 1900 they went into partnership with Lambert Typewriters and formally changed the name of their two-year-old company to Gramophone & Typewriter Limited.

Nevertheless music remained at the heart of the company. Gaisberg, its celebrated master of recording, travelled the world in search of talent, picking up opera singers, soloists, conductors and music-hall stars along the way. The likes of Nellie Melba, Peter Dawson, Edward Lloyd, Feodor Chaliapin, Edward Elgar, Dan Leno, Adelina Patti, John McCormack and Ignacy Paderewski were all signed to the rapidly expanding British-based company's roster of superstars.

Gaisberg's enthusiasm to seek out and record the best performers he could find resulted in him signing an agreement in 1902 with the legendary tenor Enrico Caruso, even though it was an expensive three-figure deal. The Italian star asked for £100 to record ten songs and also insisted that the recordings were all made in a single afternoon. Gaisberg's efforts were well rewarded as profits for the company from the ten records exceeded £15,000. Music hall superstar Harry Lauder was another major signing and, by 1909, sales of his records in Britain were reckoned to be in excess of 90,000, which by today's standards would make him very nearly a certified gold best-seller.

In 1904 Gramophone Company founder and managing director Owen resigned and returned to the US, and in the same year the company gained its first listing on the London Stock Exchange and issued its first £1 ordinary shares. Owen's successor as managing director was London-born sales and marketing high-flyer Theodore Birnbaum, who had been responsible for creating and running the company's Central European and Russian operations.

Birnbaum came with the highest credentials. A cultured man, he was friendly with many of the day's top recording artists, most of whom were represented by his lawyer father-in-law, who was also solicitor to King Edward VII. One of his major achievements during his period as head of the company was signing the Australian superstar singer Nellie Melba. In 1904 Birnbaum wrote, "If we can secure Melba, we shall have done something far beyond what we have up to now achieved," but securing her was neither easy nor cheap.

Dame Nellie asked for and was given a £100 advance, her 12 in records were issued on a special mauve label with a copy of her signature and sold for a guinea (£1.05p) each. After recovery of her advance, she was then paid a royalty of five shillings (25 pence) per record and, flushed with this success, she was eventually persuaded to put her name to a top-of-the-range gramophone.

Sadly Birnbaum's tenure lasted only until 1909 when ill health forced him into retirement. He was replaced by an American who had previously worked for The North American Phonograph Company before launching The Gramophone Company's French operation. Alfred Clark was named managing director of the London-based Gramophone Company at just 36 years of age and, over the following four decades, he would have an enormous impact on the fortunes of the fledgling company.

In 1907 there were more changes as the typewriter business was abandoned and the company reverted to its original name as The Gramophone Company. At the same time it moved to larger and plusher new offices in City Road, London, while singer Edward Lloyd cut the first sod to launch construction work on a new manufacturing and distribution plant in Hayes, a western suburb of the capital in Middlesex.

This development went hand in hand with new factories being built in Germany, Spain, France and also Russia where, in the midst of a huge upsurge in business, EMI established new headquarters in St Petersburg. Meanwhile in India, where the dog was considered 'unclean', EMI's records were manufactured with a new and distinctive HMV logo featuring a cobra listening to a gramophone instead of the traditional 'Nipper'.

The early years of the 20th century were something of a golden period for the British record business. By the time World War I broke out, a third of all British households owned some sort of gramophone and a total of 13 million discs had been sold – a quarter of them coming from The Gramophone Company.

This performance saw the value of an ordinary £1 Gramophone Company share shoot up to £4, while the company's sales in 1914 climbed to £300,000 compared with £116,000 ten years earlier. But, not surprisingly, the war put an end to this period of growth and the industrial site EMI had opened in Hayes in 1907 became a munitions factory for the duration of the conflict.

Even so The Gramophone Company still had its successes on the record front during the Great War, not least its 1913 recording of 'It's a Long Way To Tipperary', which was adopted as the theme song of the British Expeditionary Force as they left for France. This sat alongside 'Till The Boys Come Home', 'Take Me Back To Dear Old Blighty' and 'Roses Of Picardy' as songs that brought relief and release for those at home and at war.

However the war also brought an end to the career of The Gramophone Company's London recording chief and brother of the great producer Fred Gaisberg. William Gaisberg had undertaken the task of recording for posterity the actual sounds of the war and, to this end, he spent time on the Western Front capturing the noise of gas attacks and gun fire. Tragically he was gassed during the recordings in October 1918, contracted pneumonia and died a month later.

While The Gramophone Company was benefiting from the public's pre-war love affair with gramophones and recorded music, the UK arm of its arch rival, The Columbia Graphophone Company, was also reaping significant rewards. In 1915 its business was valued at £182,000 with profits of £36,000, while its purchase in 1917 of the UK assets of German record manufacturer Carl Lindström brought it access to the famous Parlophone and Odeon labels and trademarks.

Within a year of the end of WWI in 1918, The Gramophone Company reported sales of five million records in Britain but, at the same time, the company suffered two serious setbacks. As a result of the war it lost its successful German Deutsche Grammophon business, and the 1917 revolution then brought to an end its business interests in Russia.

Some five years later, in 1922, in America, the US Columbia business went into receivership, but the upside of this development was that the board of the British-registered Columbia operation was able to buy the shares originally owned by their American masters. As a result, in 1923, the British Columbia Graphophone operation issued 400,000 10 shilling (50p) ordinary shares and created a new public limited company on the British Stock Exchange. Those who invested saw a good return on their money, for in the same year it reported sales of 6.7 million records and by the end of the decade this figure had jumped to more than 15 million. Profits in the last year of the 1920s reached £500,000 and the value of its original 10/- shares peaked at £15.

With the war over, The Gramophone Company returned to manufacturing records and gramophones to meet a post-war demand for music that now reached new heights, but the glory years came to an abrupt end with the major recession of the 1920s.

Investment from the American Victor Company gave the British business a much-needed lifeline, which not only saw it through the bad times but enabled The Gramophone Company to embark on plans for expanding its business.

The newly formed International Artistes Department put the company on a global footing when it came to pursuing talent, while the first HMV store was opened in Oxford Street, London in 1921. The move into retailing – even though the store only stocked and sold its own goods – was such a major development for the company that the country's leading artist of the day, the composer Sir Edward Elgar, was persuaded to perform the opening ceremony.

Despite reporting a net loss in the first year of £874 on a turnover of £42,000, the idea of a series of HMV music shops was part of The Gramophone Company's plan for future growth, as was the creation in 1925 of Electrola – a brand new wholly owned company in Germany to replace the previous Deutsche business – plus new operations in Holland, Italy, Turkey and Australia.

On the technical front, the major new development in the 1920s was the advent of electrical recording, which, in return for a royalty of a penny for every record sold, was made available to The Gramophone Company by Western Electric.

This move in 1925 brought to an end the era of mechanical engineers and introduced skilled electrical recording engineers to the business and gave them the opportunity to make 'live' recordings. Within a year the company was using a mobile recording studio based in the back of a customised Lancia van and soon after it was rewarded with its first ever million-selling record.

Schoolboy chorister Ernest Lough was recorded singing 'Hear My Prayer' at London's Temple Church and within six months the HMV release had topped the 650,000 sales mark in the UK. By the end of 1926 the 15-year-old treble soloist had a global million-seller to his credit.

If classical and music-hall artists had been the first stars of the gramophone, it was the turn of jazz to dominate record sales in the 1920s. Created in America, jazz bands led by the likes of Paul Whiteman brought the new music to Britain and gave the record industry a much-needed boost. Soon after, Bert Ambrose and Jack Hylton were leading successful British jazz bands on the HMV label and, in the ten years from 1923, Hylton sold over seven million records in a golden era for The Gramophone Company.

In 1928 it reported profits exceeding £1 million; these increased to £1.2 million the next year when the company, with assets valued at £5.3 million, rivalled the BBC and its music competitor Columbia Graphophone on the list of major British businesses.

In 1930, The Gramophone Company's founding chairman, and the sole survivor from its inception in 1898, decided to retire. Trevor Williams remained a director of the company until 1946, but he handed over the running of the business to managing director Alfred Clark on the eve of the Great Depression, which was to hit both the US and Europe.

Such was the impact of this huge financial downturn on the music business that in 1930–1931 the combined profits of The Gramophone Company and Columbia Graphophone totalled a measly £160,000. It was a performance that was to lead directly to the formation of a brand new company – EMI.

CHAPTER 2

EMI

(Sex Pistols, Virgin 1977)

ELECTRIC & Musical Industries was formed in the summer of 1931 as a direct result of the economic depression, which saw consumer spending on recorded music in Britain fall by over 50% during a four-year period. By the end of 1932 spending on records, gramophones and sheet music stood at £2.6 million compared with £5.4 million in 1929, and things were not going to get any better in the short term.

In 1929 the joint Gramophone and Columbia operations had sold over 30 million records in the UK but by 1931 sales were down to 20 million. Despite the new EMI business structure the downward trend continued until 1937 when sales reached an all-time low of five million.

By combining the assets, executives, artists and operations of the Gramophone and Columbia Graphophone companies, the newly created EMI gained £2.7 million in cash and investments from the sale of shares in the American Columbia business. Even so, by 1933 EMI had lost half its sales and had losses of over £1 million.

Despite the falling sales, EMI managed in 1934 to somehow report its first profits – totalling £500,000 – with a dividend of 12.5% paid on new EMI company shares. From then until 1979, when the company was taken over by Thorn, EMI never failed to declare a profit and pay its shareholders a dividend.

But such was the impact of the depression, together with the new-found popularity of radio and talking pictures, that by the end of the 1930s there were only two companies manufacturing records in the UK – EMI and its arch-rival Decca.*

---

* Decca Records was established in 1929 by Edward Lewis, later Sir Edward. The name "Decca" dated back to a portable gramophone called the Decca Dulcephone patented in 1914 by musical instrument makers Barnett Samuel & Sons. That company was eventually

The new EMI company boasted The Gramophone Company's Alfred Clark as chairman with Columbia Graphophone boss Louis Sterling as managing director, but the rivalry between the two men resulted in an arrangement that was destined to fail almost from day one. Sterling wanted to be chairman of the new company and, according to reports, his resentment of Clark was apparent until he left in 1938. A future chairman of EMI, Sir Joseph Lockwood discovered evidence of their strained relationship: "They weren't on speaking terms despite being chairman and Managing Director of a major public company. They used to send letters to each other but they never spoke to one another."

If having senior executives who weren't on speaking terms was not enough of a problem, the advent of radio put extra pressures on EMI and the record business in general. During the 1930s the public embraced this newest form of in-home entertainment in a big way, with 80% of British homes owning a radio set by 1939. At the start of the decade the figure was around a third. As the radio market grew and competition increased so hardware prices fell, and while music remained the most popular form of entertainment it was now being heard more often on the radio than on the family gramophone.

Part of EMI's salvation in the years after its formation was that the company also produced radios and radiograms, so while sales of records fell, it was able to find some solace in radio sales. The fact that it was able to sell them through its growing chain of six HMV stores – spread between London, Wolverhampton and Harrogate – brought it further relief.

In an effort to stimulate record sales Sterling came up with the bright idea of introducing a cheap gramophone that sold for under £2. Apparently dealers bought them from EMI for 26s 4d (£1.32p) but, as they cost EMI 26s 6d (£1.35p) to make, the company lost 2d (1p) on every machine. However, as was later explained by L.G. Wood, then a salesman and later managing director of EMI Records, "The company lost money on every machine but they did generate a lot of record sales so overall it was a successful move."

Wood, who joined The Gramophone Company in 1929, later revealed that during his time on the road visiting record stores as an HMV sales rep,

renamed The Decca Gramophone Co. Ltd. and sold to former stockbroker Lewis in 1929. Within years Decca Records was the second largest record label in the world, calling itself 'The Supreme Record Company'. After Lewis' death in 1980 Decca was acquired by Polygram and is currently part of Universal Music.

he was required to wear a hat and always carry a packet of cigarettes, even though he never smoked. "You wore a hat in order to be able to take it off when you greeted the retailer and you could also then offer him a cigarette."

In the same year that EMI was formed, the company also invested in new custom-built recording studios in the fashionable St John's Wood area of London, close to Lord's cricket ground. Abbey Road Studios was constructed inside a nine-bedroom house* that had cost The Gramophone Company £16,500 – it had been bought before the new company was officially formed – and a condition of the sale was that the exterior of the house should never be changed . . . and to this day it never has been.

As it had done a decade earlier with the opening of the first HMV store, the company once again called on Sir Edward Elgar to start things off at the new studios, which he did on November 1931 with a recording of 'Land Of Hope And Glory'.

Soon Abbey Road Studios was attracting to North London the finest artists of the day, including conductors Arturo Toscanini, Sir Thomas Beecham, Sir Adrian Boult and Wilhelm Furtwängler alongside pianist Artur Schnabel and a teenage violin prodigy named Yehudi Menuhin. There they mingled with non-classical stars of radio, music hall and theatre such as George Formby, Gracie Fields, Joe Loss, Ray Noble, Victor Silvester, Al Bowlly and Noël Coward together with visiting American stars such as *basso profondo* concert singer Paul Robeson and jazz pianist Fats Waller.

These musicians shared this dignified and expensive area of North London with a host of young ladies who were found homes there by their aristocratic or parliamentarian 'friends', and a common phrase at the time was that the only people you saw in St John's Wood were "whores and artists".

One of the recruits to the new EMI company was Columbia's electrical engineer Alan Dower Blumlein. He had earlier worked for Western Electric, which had provided EMI, for the fee of a penny per record, with an early electric recording system. Blumlein, whose pioneering work in television, stereo and radar was a feature of EMI's Central Research

---

* The estate agent's particulars listed "two attic bedrooms on the second floor, seven bedrooms on the first floor and bathroom on the half-landing, a dining room, 'handsome' drawing room, library, morning room, study and w.c. on the entrance floor, and kitchen, scullery, servants' hall, pantry, two servants rooms, larder and wine cellar in the half-basement, with a large garden at the rear".

Laboratories, was able to create a new EMI process of electric recording that was not only better than the Western version but also cheaper. In the ten years from 1925 The Gramophone Company and EMI had handed over more than £500,000 in royalties to the American Western Electric operation.

As Europe headed towards World War II, so EMI opened a new HMV store in Oxford Street to replace the original, which had been destroyed by fire on Boxing Day 1937. This new store – costing £42,000 and opened by Sir Thomas Beecham in 1939 – featured records on the ground floor plus a lower ground floor (the word basement was an Americanism that was banned) displaying HMV household and electrical kitchen appliances. On the first floor there was a radio showroom and a recording studio, which, some 23 years later, would play a major part in EMI and Britain's pop music history.

In 1935, in the face of increased Japanese nationalism, EMI sold its wholly owned Nipponphone record company to a collection of local entrepreneurs for £482,000, although, until 1941 and the outbreak of war in Asia, the company's recordings were still pressed in Japan.

In the year before war was declared, EMI's managing director, Louis Sterling, finally resigned, leaving his arch-rival Clark in sole charge of a business that was in danger of suffering substantial war losses throughout its global operations. Though, somewhat surprisingly, sales of recorded music increased immediately after the start of the war – by a million in EMI's case – it was a short-lived success story, as the introduction of purchase tax on records coupled with a serious shortage of pressings took their toll on the business.

With recordings from Europe nigh-on impossible to obtain, EMI turned its attention to America and forged new licensee links with Columbia Records and RCA Victor. By the end of the war EMI's sales stood at 6.3 million, thanks in part to recordings by the likes of Fred Astaire, Bing Crosby and the duo of Jeanette MacDonald & Nelson Eddy.

After the war EMI appointed Australian Sir Ernest Fisk as its fourth managing director and he created a costly structure of wholly owned operating sub-companies, putting them under the banners EMI Studios, EMI Factories, EMI Sales & Service plus the Columbia and Gramophone operations.

The company was also intent on resurrecting its operations in countries involved or occupied during World War II. In the mid-1940s it reclaimed the Pathé Marconi company in France and around the same time the two companies it owned in Italy were also returned. However, things took a little longer in Japan where contact with Nipponphone was not restored until 1950, and eventually a partnership was formed in 1953 under the banner Toshiba-EMI. In the same year EMI's two German businesses, Electrola and Lindström, were restructured and merged to create EMI Electrola.

EMI's first full year financial reports immediately after the war showed a post-tax profit of £165,000 on a turnover of £7 million and by 1949, with music pushed into the background and the company focused on new electronic businesses, it announced pre-tax profits of £1.2 million.

New artists signed after the war, such as opera singers Elizabeth Schwarzkopf, Joan Hammond and Victoria de Los Angeles plus esteemed Austrian conductor Herbert von Karajan, teamed up with popular acts such as Arthur Askey and Josef Locke to help bring EMI out of the shadows.

Fisk's controversial move to divide the company coincided with the news that America's record business was on the up, and in order to survive as a truly global business EMI had to find a way of entering the biggest music market in the world. Fisk's proposal in 1946 was to get into bed with MGM and form a new licensing agreement, but chairman Clark was so opposed to this plan that he apparently threw his papers across the boardroom table and stormed out of the office, never to return . . . bringing to an end a career in the recorded music business that had begun in 1889.

It was Fisk who also delayed EMI's introduction of the 33⅓ rpm long-playing album and the 45rpm single. As Columbia and RCA Victor in America – both EMI licensees – forged ahead with these new album and single formats for records, which would make the long-standing 78rpm redundant, evidently the short-sighted EMI executives remained unconvinced by the concept of producing records in two new formats playing at two different speeds.

In 1950 Fisk issued a press release that confirmed that EMI would continue to produce standard (78rpm) records in "undiminished quantities to meet the needs of the millions of gramophones already in use throughout the world". He then went further and announced, "It is in the public interest for the gramophone industry to continue to develop on the sound principle of a common turntable speed."

Soon after, Fisk left EMI and in October 1952 the first EMI 33⅓ rpm long-playing albums and 45rpm singles were issued. At the same time

Columbia ended its long-standing licensing agreement while RCA Victor – whose recordings accounted for 50% of EMI's total sales – signed what would be its final five-year agreement with EMI.

Still chasing the pot of gold that was the American record market, EMI created Electric & Musical Industries (US) Limited as a marketing outlet for its fast-growing classical catalogue. This was launched using the Angel Records trademark, which had been replaced internationally by the HMV 'Dog & Trumpet' logo which was not available to EMI in North America.

The ploy worked and within the first year Angel Records captured 6% of the US classical market. Nevertheless, there was still much ground to make up in the company's popular music activities in America.

This was all to change under the chairmanship of Joseph Lockwood, who joined EMI in 1955, succeeding Sir Alexander Aikman. Speaking in 1988, Lockwood, who considered Alfred Clark "a great man who really created the company", was less complimentary about his predecessors Aikman and Fisk. "They were both dead losses," he said. "You can forget about them and they should not be mentioned in the history of EMI."

On assuming the chair of EMI, Lockwood's first job was to visit the City of London and secure funds to keep the company afloat. It has been claimed that his first success was to borrow £2 million to pay the company's wage bill.

Convinced that the board and management of EMI were "very ineffective", Lockwood set about making important changes in the company's operations. He started by insisting that the HMV stores sold records from other companies, and by playing down the rivalry between the people employed on the HMV and Columbia labels. He also insisted that the HMV label dropped its exclusive arrangement whereby only shops with a franchise were allowed to sell HMV records, and made its records available through the likes of WH Smith and other independent stores that already stocked Columbia releases.

The biggest and boldest move however was in America where, in 1955, EMI paid $8.5 million for Capitol Records, the country's fourth-largest record company. Housed in a 13-storey circular building, the Capitol Tower, in Hollywood, designed to look like a stack of records, Capitol was the only major located on America's West Coast where it had been founded in 1942 by retailer Glenn Wallichs, songwriter Buddy DeSylva and singer/composer Johnny Mercer. The deal meant that suddenly EMI acquired a roster of artists that included Frank Sinatra, Nat King Cole, Stan Kenton, Peggy Lee, Dean Martin and Gene Vincent.

The acquisition of Capitol brought rapid rewards for its new owners. In the first year sales reached a new high of $35 million – up 37% – and by 1957 Capitol was merged with the existing EMI US Ltd to create a single powerful company that added considerable strength to EMI's already impressive global presence.

The only sour note in an otherwise rosy state of affairs was Frank Sinatra's decision to leave the Capitol label. Between 1955 and 1961, when he formed his own Reprise Records label, Sinatra notched up a total of 17 US hit albums plus 14 chart albums in the UK – and he hit the top spot three times on each side of the Atlantic. Despite this success, however, the self-styled 'Chairman of the Board' was less than happy when he discovered that a fellow Capitol artist was getting a royalty of 6% while he was only receiving 4%. Sinatra's demand for an equal royalty, coupled with his legendary rudeness to staff at the label, convinced Wallichs, who had continued as chief executive, to let the great singer out of his contract.

Sitting in London, Lockwood was also less than happy with the outcome. "I told Wallichs it was a big mistake and if I had had a word with Sinatra I could have solved it in five minutes," he recalled some years later.

"Sinatra was quite a friendly chap and was fond of anyone who was nice with him, but then he left and formed Reprise. He had a model of the Capitol Tower which he brought out in front of friends, pressed a button and the whole thing collapsed – that was what he thought of Capitol after he left."

In the event the loss of Sinatra was not quite the catastrophe it seemed at the time, for on the horizon was a new style of music that in time would come to dominate the record industry and bring about the slow demise of Sinatra and his fellow crooners. "The most brutal, ugly, degenerate, vicious form of expression it has been my displeasure to hear," Sinatra wrote of rock'n'roll at the time of Elvis Presley's emergence in the mid-1950s, no doubt hoping to turn back the tide. He had no more chance of succeeding than King Canute.

CHAPTER 3

Opportunities (Let's Make Lots Of Money)

(Pet Shops Boys, EMI 1986)

IN the late 1950s the introduction of the new 7in 45rpm single and 12in 33⅓ album formats, coupled with a rapidly developing interest in pop and rock'n'roll music, saw massive changes in the buying habits of music lovers. Between 1956 and 1958 sales of the new LPs rose from 1.7 million to over 2 million but the biggest boom came in the sales of 45rpm singles, which shot up from just 1.3 million to 7 million.

Much of this enthusiasm for recorded music came from the intro-duction of sales charts. In America *Billboard* magazine had introduced its Music Popularity Chart in 1940, but it was its more pop-orientated Hot 100, which was introduced in 1958, that proved decisive. In the UK, the first singles chart was launched in November 1952 in *New Musical Express*, a music paper launched the previous March and designed to appeal to young pop fans. *NME*'s main rival, the longer-established *Melody Maker*, published the first album version six years later.

Ironically the first UK number one single was a hit from Capitol in its pre-EMI days – Al Martino's 'Here In My Heart' – while Sinatra's Capitol collection *Songs For Swingin' Lovers* was the first long-player, as they were called in those days, to top the British album charts.

Trumpeter Eddie Calvert's 'Oh Mein Papa' was EMI's first British chart-topper in January 1954 (and the first of countless number one records to come out of Abbey Road) and alongside the likes of singers Shirley Bassey, Alma Cogan, Ruby Murray and pianist Russ Conway represented EMI's new and successful investment in UK pop talent.

This influx of home-grown talent was partly the result of losing the licensing deals with RCA and Columbia, which had forced EMI to find a roster of new British artists. With this in mind four label managers cum producers were handed a unique opportunity, a challenge to revitalise the fortunes of Britain's premier recording organisation.

Norman Newell, Norrie Paramor, Wally Ridley and George Martin were the modern-day 'four musketeers', working for the HMV, Columbia and Parlophone labels. With Newell having a roving brief and not directly linked with any label, they went in search of singers and groups who would rival the best America could offer.

One American artist, however, already stood head and shoulders above all the aspiring young rock and pop singers emerging from the US and the UK – and he was briefly linked to EMI.

Elvis Presley was signed to RCA in late 1955, arriving on the scene while the label was still licensed to EMI. Thus, between May 1956 and January 1958, 15 hit singles by Elvis were issued on the pale-blue HMV Pop label – complete with the famous Dog & Trumpet logo that was owned in America by RCA and consequently also used on his US releases.

The first Elvis hit in the UK was 'Heartbreak Hotel', which was sent to HMV producer Ridley for consideration. Even though he was sceptical and later admitted he didn't understand more than a couple of words of the record, he decided to release it. "The people at RCA in America told me the singer was going to be an absolute giant so I put it out," he said. "We got the worst press we had ever got for an HMV release. People said it was disgusting and even Radio Luxembourg wouldn't play it."

EMI's short-lived association with Presley came to an end when RCA left to set up its own UK business, thus adding another name to the list of rival record companies that for so long had been dominated by just one – Decca – but now also included the likes of Britain's Pye and the Dutch-owned Philips. Since establishing Decca in 1929 Sir Edward Lewis was way ahead of his main UK rival when it came to establishing a business in America. More than 20 years before EMI bought Capitol, Lewis had opened up an American Decca operation and, after selling it to MCA (Music Corporation of America), he introduced London Records into the US market in 1947.

EMI and Decca were rivals for British talent – both classical and pop – for over three decades and Lockwood saw the signing of guitar-toting Tommy Steele by Lewis' company in 1955 as a particular setback. "I was very mad when I found that he had got engaged by Decca, he was almost the first pop star that appeared on our UK scene."

Somewhere around the same time Lockwood apparently made an approach to merge EMI with Decca but, according to L.G. Wood, the two major executives were the biggest stumbling block. "Lewis and Lockwood were never the best of allies and when the merger was suggested there was the issue of who was to run it. Lockwood's idea was for him to be chairman with Lewis as president, but Lewis refused to do business and the deal faded away."

Lockwood's response was to create EMI Records in 1957 as the division to oversee and manage the company's UK record business including signing, recording, manufacturing and marketing. This meant that The Columbia Graphophone Company finally ceased trading in Britain although it held on to the Columbia trademark for a further three decades.

Although rock'n'roll and pop records were now dominating sales and the airwaves, classical music was still considered an important and lucrative part of the music business, and one of EMI's greatest signings was the singer Maria Callas. She joined a roster of conductors, soloists and orchestras that was the envy of the world; by the beginning of the 1960s, EMI's classical catalogue boasted close to 2,000 albums with, on average, a further 400 being added each year. While sales of serious music would never match the emerging pop business – only 16% of the company's record turnover came from classical – the high retail price of these premier recordings ensured their profitability.

If EMI missed out on Tommy Steele – apparently George Martin did not see the singer's appeal but instead signed his backing group, The Vipers – the label did hit gold with Norrie Paramor's new Columbia discoveries Cliff Richard and Helen Shapiro as well as Parlophone signing Adam Faith.

These three singers, together with Cliff's backing group, The Shadows, were at the forefront of Britain's new rock'n'roll and pop movement and between them they delivered over 50 UK hit singles between 1958 and 1962. As Richard's sales topped 5.5 million by the end of 1960, EMI accounted for 40% of Britain's pop record sales.

While admitting to being aware of labels such as Columbia and Parlophone, Richard has acknowledged that the name EMI meant very little to him at the start of his career. "Ironically Decca turned me down early on and I only became aware of EMI when I got started with my band and we began thinking what it would be like to be on a record label. Before then it was just the small print on discs I had at home and didn't really hit home."

Under Lockwood's astute leadership, by 1962 EMI had grown into a truly international corporation that traded in electrical appliances, defence equipment, retail outlets and even early computers in addition to its core music business. Its operations stretched across 30 countries and the long-standing Central Research Laboratories were the vanguard for the development of new ideas and technologies.

The early 1960s was a period when EMI reported extraordinary growth, with turnover in 1962 reaching £82.5 million and pre-tax profits totalling £4.4 million. In the same year the British record market was valued at £20 million and album sales reached 17 million while sales of 45rpm singles peaked at over 50 million.

But still it was EMI's American business interests that were the biggest contributors to its profitability and there was still more to come as British pop geared itself up to invade and conquer the largest market in the world.

Having discovered and elevated Elvis Presley to the very pinnacle of rock'n'roll stardom, while at the same time sending out the likes of Chuck Berry, Jerry Lee Lewis, Little Richard, Buddy Holly, Eddie Cochran, Roy Orbison and The Everly Brothers as ambassadors of US pop music, America seemingly had no great need for what Britain had to offer at the start of the 1960s.

This was an attitude that existed within Capitol Records and that became apparent to EMI chairman Lockwood, who was knighted in 1960. "The people who ran Capitol were very limited. They had very well-known people in their orchestras and bands and they thought all the other people were second rate."

Certainly with the likes of Tennessee Ernie Ford, The Four Freshmen and The Kingston Trio emerging in the US charts, Capitol seemed well positioned until rock'n'roll reared its head. "We are in a most discouraging revolution in the pop singles field," commented Capitol A&R manager Dave Dexter, who bemoaned the fact that records were being bought by children "strictly for the beat".

Capitol's attitude at the start of the decade reflected a mind-set that was rife within the US record industry. As a result, both the label and the industry were caught napping when the UK became immersed in a wave of new music and new acts as the "beat boom" broke across the country.

And at the very centre of the storm was a four piece group from Liverpool that EMI had initially turned down. Rivals Decca followed suit with its rejection slip in 1962, and instead signed a group from Essex simply because they were more conveniently located to attend recording sessions in London. However in June the same year EMI, thanks to the foresight of

Parlophone artist manager and producer George Martin, finally offered The Beatles a contract.

Within 18 months John Lennon, Paul McCartney, George Harrison and Ringo Starr had racked up four Top 10 singles and a number one album. Over in America, however, Capitol remained unmoved and unconvinced by the phenomenon that was taking Europe by storm.

A&R man Dexter told his colleagues: "I got 'em (Beatles) in, they're a bunch of long-haired kids. Forget it. They're nothin'." This was the attitude that led to Capitol passing on the first batch of Beatles' singles, which were then licensed by manager Brian Epstein to Vee Jay Records and Swan Records, minor labels with insufficient resources to promote The Beatles properly, which probably explains why they failed to dent the US charts during 1963.

It took a year for Capitol to finally relent – "They didn't believe in them but they came round slowly with our persuasion," recalled Lockwood some years later – and when they did they were rewarded with an immediate number one in February 1964. 'I Want To Hold Your Hand' – with global sales of 15 million – opened the floodgates as single after single and album after album topped the charts not just in the US and UK, but all around the world. In April 1964 The Beatles held down the top five places in *Billboard*'s Hot 100, an unprecedented achievement that has never been equalled, let alone bettered.

Thanks to the lads from Liverpool, EMI's companies and licensees enjoyed hitherto unheard of levels of success and profitability. In the mid 1960s, £1 million was earned from overseas sales of EMI recordings made in Britain – this equalled 50% of the record division's profits. Within three years, sales of The Beatles' first ten single releases had reached nine million while their first five albums notched up close to four million sales – and that was in the UK alone. But it wasn't just The Beatles who helped to keep the EMI books in the black.

In their wake came fellow Liverpudlians Gerry & The Pacemakers, Billy J Kramer & The Dakotas and Cilla Black, Manchester's Freddie & The Dreamers, Herman's Hermits and The Hollies, The Animals from Newcastle and London's Manfred Mann and Dave Clark Five. All were signed to EMI labels and all made important inroads into the US pop market but, as was initially the case of The Beatles, it was not always with the help of Capitol. Dave Clark, Herman and The Animals, all of whom reached number one in America during this heyday of British pop, were shunned by Capitol and allowed to go to Epic and MGM Records.

Despite these lapses, by the end of 1964 – thanks almost entirely to The Beatles, local discoveries The Beach Boys and with a little help from fellow number one acts Peter & Gordon, Glen Campbell and Bobby Gentry – Capitol's gross income had grown close to $70 million from around $50 million in 1963.

At the same time EMI's profits overall grew to over £9 million, an increase of 80% on the previous year. And they grew further to £11 million by 1966, by which time the company's cash reserves exceeded £16 million.

Elsewhere in its fields of endeavour, EMI's expansion had included the 1960 purchase of household appliances manufacturer Morphy Richards for around £12 million, but the company had bigger fish in its sights.

In 1966 the Grade Organisation, which included an artists' agency, theatrical, film and music publishing interests in addition to a chain of cinemas, was acquired for close to £9 million although negotiations had apparently begun at around £4 million. Included in the Grade deal was its chief, Bernard Delfont, who joined the board of EMI and became head of its leisure division, which he expanded throughout the next decade.

By the end of the 1960s the important Associated British Picture Corporation, with its major interest in Thames Television and Elstree Studios, had been added to the company's portfolio – the massive £56.6 million price made it the company's largest acquisition to date – making EMI by far Britain's largest entertainment organisation.

In America in 1967 – the year in which The Beatles released their ground-breaking album *Sgt Pepper's Lonely Hearts Club Band* – Capitol celebrated its 25th anniversary by topping the $100 million sales mark for the first time in its history.

However, throughout the decade that was dubbed the Swingin' Sixties largely because of them, it was The Beatles who dominated proceedings in the media, in the charts and in the offices and studios of EMI. After the group ceased touring in 1966 they virtually took up residence at Abbey Road Studios, where they had carte blanche to record as and when they desired to do so. This was without doubt a prudent business move for between 1966 and 1972 Capitol calculated that it had sold 35 million Beatles albums, while EMI announced in 1967 that worldwide sales of The Beatles had topped 200 million.

But to company chairman Lockwood the Fab Four were occasional visitors who usually arrived in his office with problems to resolve. "They only came to see me when they couldn't get any sense out of the other people below," he said in a 1988 conversation.

"They were pretty tough down below and often told The Beatles they couldn't use this or that and then they came to me. I had to find a solution to the *Sgt Pepper* cover and the picture of Lennon naked with Yoko Ono that was brought to me. I couldn't keep out of it because they created great problems."

In 1970, the year when Paul McCartney's public defection prompted the formal end of The Beatles, Lockwood stepped down as chief executive to be succeeded by Sir John Read, who would later become chairman. He inherited a company that boasted sales of £225 million together with pre-tax profits of £21 million. With this amount of cash in hand, Read led EMI on a new round of investment, adding the legendary Blackpool Tower, restaurant chains, hotel and public houses, sports centres and bingo and dance halls to EMI's corporate portfolio.

But the departing Lockwood, who had spent over 15 years steering EMI out of the doldrums and into financial stability, was less than impressed with the new expansion. "It wasn't a good idea to move into so many areas of business," he said. "Read took over from me and suddenly he started buying all over – anything he could – and eventually he had to sell them all because he nearly bankrupted everything through the scanner."

The 'scanner' was a major medical development that had been invented at EMI's Central Research Laboratories by senior engineer Godfrey Hounsfield during Lockwood's period as chairman. The Computerised Axial Tomography (CAT) scanner was a revolutionary machine that could be used for taking X-rays of the brain, and during the 1970s EMI allocated huge resources towards developing the technology and also its manufacturing and marketing strategies.

All of this required money and lots of it, and much of it was siphoned from the company's profitable recording division, which itself was being hit by falling sales and a reduced market share. Despite the huge success of The Beatles, The Beach Boys, The Band and others throughout the golden period of the 1960s, Capitol in 1971 reported a loss of £6.2 million on the back of a £7.6 million profit the previous year.

The 1970s heralded a period of economic instability and despite the success of acts such as Pink Floyd, Queen, Deep Purple, the individual Beatles, Helen Reddy, Bob Seger, Cliff Richard, T Rex and Kate Bush, EMI's music divisions faced major problems. Its position in America was further weakened by the non-appearance on the famous Capitol label of huge-selling acts signed to the British arm of the company. Pink Floyd jumped ship to Columbia after two albums, Queen went with Elektra and Deep Purple were snapped up by Warner Brothers.

According to music fan-cum-media analyst Mark Beilby the great British company's problems in America went back as far as the 1960s when the company was riding high on the back of The Beatles, The Beach Boys and even Frank Sinatra. "You would have thought they had the ammunition in the 1960s to get American bands to sign up, but Doors aide Danny Sugarman recounted in his book [*No One Gets Out Of Here Alive*] that people at Capitol thought The Doors were 'the work of the devil' and that, for me, was the root of the problem."

It certainly seems as if an innate conservatism and an underlying fear of the unknown – and an unwillingness to take a chance on it – was at the root of EMI's problems. Perhaps this was why in 1977 former head of EMI Records and EMI main board member L.G. Wood said the competition facing the EMI Group throughout the world, but principally in the USA and the UK, "is now becoming intense and extremely serious".

That same year the company also went through a very public and – for the corporation – a very embarrassing divorce from The Sex Pistols after just three months and one record. The Pistols' behaviour – swearing on national TV, vomiting at airports and mocking the royals – was evidently just too much for Sir John Read and his fellow board members to stomach. It was therefore slightly ironic that around the same time EMI should put out the welcome mat for the previous decade's bad boys, The Rolling Stones, whose singer, Mick Jagger, now fully incorporated into the establishment, complete with a seat at Lord's, told the world: "In this Silver Jubilee year I feel it is only fitting we sign to a British company."

Despite newer star names such as Andre Previn, Daniel Barenboim, Jacqueline Du Pre, Ricardo Muti, Placido Domingo, Itzhak Perlman and Kiri Te Kanawa, EMI's classical business also suffered as its market share fell by 6% to 20% in 1975. With the added problems of home taping and piracy, the entire record industry – not just EMI's classical and pop businesses – faced a daunting future.

Throughout all this the brain scanner was being fine-tuned by EMI's top engineers while the company's medical division was taking orders and preparing to build factories to manufacture the revolutionary and potentially life-saving equipment. EMI's initial investment in the scanner was £6 million and it protected its invention with seemingly watertight patents, although it faced competition from the American giant General Electric, which was developing its own version.

In the end the issue boiled down to whether EMI should license its scanner in America and sign a franchise deal with a royalty on each machine, rather than pursuing its aim to build and sell them in America through EMI-owned companies.

However, the final chapter in the saga was written by US President Jimmy Carter, who in 1976 introduced new regulations covering spending by hospitals that was underwritten by the government. Items costing more than $100,000 (and scanners came in at around $250,000) would require a special certificate and this very quickly brought to a halt orders for EMI's brain scanners.

EMI board member Lord Delfont later charted the situation. "We made the mistake of rejecting an American franchise deal on the grounds that we wanted a British invention to stay British. This prompted our competitors to lobby Washington for import restrictions to give them time to produce a superior scanner."

As a result EMI's medical division suffered a 30% slump in sales in 1977–1978 plus a further 35% drop the following year, which accounted for combined losses over two years of £30 million. In the end this finished EMI's global plans for the brain scanner, brought EMI Medical to its knees and put the very survival of EMI in serious jeopardy.

The company's music division was for the first time in its history assembled as one global operation in the late 1970s. Under the banner EMI Music, it was headed by long-time Capitol chairman Bhaskar Menon but, between 1977 and 1979, profits from the music division fell from £33 million to just over £2 million.

The music division was accused of adopting a lavish operating style, a trait that was actually widespread throughout the industry, paying imprudently high advances and royalties to artists and, most importantly, not investing in new talent. Its leaner and fitter rivals CBS, Polygram and Warner were making serious inroads into EMI's position as the preeminent global music company.

In his statement to the annual meeting in 1979, Read confirmed the reality of the situation, which saw world record sales fall by 22% in the same year. "The record industry worldwide suffered a severe setback from January 1979 with a marked reduction of sales of recorded music." The impact on EMI as a whole was to reduce the corporation's pre-tax profits for the years 1977 to 1979 from £75 million to £29 million.

At the same time EMI was planning a major move involving all its operations based in Central London. A site in fashionable Tottenham Court

Road was acquired as the new headquarters of EMI but the financial crisis saw it sold to the Prudential Assurance company and then leased back, a move that raised some £33 million.

However, there were other more important moves in the pipeline. It turned out that Lord Delfont had been in discussions with the American company Gulf & Western – known to many as Engulf & Devour – about the purchase of the newly created EMI Music business by its subsidiary, Paramount. In exchange for £75 million, Paramount, a major player in the film business but with limited experience in music, would get a 50% interest in EMI Music.

There were those who thought that getting half of a company that two years earlier had made a profit of £33 million, and still owned the rights to some of the world's most valuable recordings and songs, for just £75 million was bordering on corporate theft. And there were those who saw the sale of 50% of EMI Music – which was still at the very heart of the company's future – as sounding the death knell for the whole of EMI.

It's perhaps hard to believe but the interest from Gulf & Western represented the first and only genuine approach made for EMI's music activities in the near 40 years since the company's inception in 1931. More importantly it also signalled for the first time that EMI might be prepared to 'do a deal' such was the perilous state of its cash flow and corporate standing following the brain-scanner problems.

While Gulf & Western was perhaps the first serious and publicly confirmed bidder, former EMI Music chief Menon was involved in talks as far back as the early 1970s. He recalls "endless conversations" in 1971 with MCA, which, according to the man who headed Capitol Industries at the time, believed that Capitol's poor performance would "provide them with an inexpensive acquisition opportunity". This unsuccessful sortie by MCA was followed soon after by what Menon describes as "an absurd RCA corporate initiative to merge EMI Music with a weak and exhausted RCA Records, under their leadership".

By September 1979 the Gulf & Western deal had been called off as neither side could agree on some of the more basic details, such as how much it was all worth and whether EMI or Paramount would hold a majority on the board. But the press reports of EMI's problems and possible positive reaction to a deal of some sort brought Thorn Electrical Industries into the picture.

There had been talk of merger between the two British companies some years earlier but, despite a long-standing friendship between Sir Jules Thorn and Lockwood, nothing ever came of the discussions.

Now, however, it was a different scenario. Thorn could acquire the whole of EMI, merge it with its already successful lighting, consumer electronics, domestic appliances and engineering businesses and at the same time save its great British rival from bankruptcy.

But even before any deal with Thorn could be completed, EMI Music brought the United Artists record company into the fold and with it the Liberty and Blue Note imprints. Alongside the British new-wave band The Stranglers and the million-selling Electric Light Orchestra, it also brought American singers Don McLean, Crystal Gayle and Kenny Rogers who, in 1980, achieved the rare feat of having three separate million-selling albums in a 12-month period.

Finally, before the year was over Thorn, whose own performance leading up to 1979 showed pre-tax profits that had risen over a four-year period from £79 million to £122 million, made a successful bid that valued EMI at £165 million. Under the lead of new Thorn EMI chairman Sir Richard Cave, EMI directors Read, Delfont and Menon would all join the new board.

Among Cave's first moves was a serious rationalisation of the new company and within five years he had got rid of EMI's hotel and restaurant interests, the leisure businesses (including Blackpool Tower), a chain of social centres and the ill-fated EMI medical division.

For one EMI artist the purchase of EMI by Thorn brought his career full circle, as Cliff Richard's only other job before becoming a recording artist was working for a subsidiary of Thorn lighting. "I left school and went to work for Atlas Lamps and it seems strange after all these years that they (EMI and Thorn) have joined forces. Now I can actually say that I've worked for the same company ever since I left school."

Music, despite Thorn's complete lack of experience in the business, remained a core element of the new Thorn EMI company, which, in those early days, decreed that in all media reports and correspondence its name should be spelt out in capital letters as in THORN EMI. This brought a mixed response from both insiders and outsiders, and dissenters were regularly taken to task by the company.

At the start of the new relationship Thorn EMI stood as a corporation with literally hundreds of different companies under its belt and a total pre-tax profit in 1981 of £129 million. However, things changed dramatically in 1985 when Sir Graham Wilkins and Colin Southgate took over as chairman and managing director and quickly established the company's core activities as music, rental and retail.

Interestingly Southgate describes as "an absolute farce" the linking of Thorn and EMI. "EMI should never have been merged with Thorn. It goes back to there being too many things in the EMI company. Back in the 1970s there was too little money chasing too many things – steak houses, bingo halls, Blackpool Tower – and the whole thing was bloody nonsense."

While a host of engineering, technology and television subsidiaries were disposed of – including the high-profile EMI Screen Entertainment for a massive £128 million (the total number of sell-offs would eventually top the 100 mark) – record companies were acquired around the world alongside music retailers and international rental operations.

One of the record companies EMI bought in the early 1980s was producer Mickie Most's famous RAK Records, which, although it had very few album artists, was a powerhouse of hit singles thanks to the likes of Hot Chocolate, Suzi Quatro, Mud, Smokie and Kim Wilde.

Most was a long-time associate of EMI who had brought acts such as The Animals and Herman's Hermits to its labels in the 1960s and regularly used Abbey Road studios. When it came to selling his own multi-million pound record company he took a philosophical view, saying, "Everything's for sale isn't it? Just the right price at the right time really, it's just a question of business. It's not an emotive thing."

In its first year – 1986 – the newly structured Thorn EMI reported pre-tax profits of £154 million, a drop from £172 in 1985, while music turned in a pre-tax profit of just £9 million. For internal accounting purposes it was linked with Thames TV but separated from HMV, which was re-branded as the HMV Group with over 40 shops and an annual turnover of around £40 million.

Without Thames TV, which was floated as a public company in 1986, and with a new-found enthusiasm for music within the Thorn EMI management, EMI Music's performances showed signs of improvement and pre-tax profits more than doubled from £19.4 million in 1987 to over £44 million two years later.

Ultimately much of this improvement was down to the arrival of a revolutionary new record format called the compact disc and an increased investment in music publishing, but in both cases EMI made negative decisions that impacted on its performance and long-term standing in the music business.

The invention of the CD by Philips and Sony in 1982 – arguably as important as the arrival of both electric recording and stereo – offered the music business a new digital format for its releases. But, as had been the case with the new 33⅓ rpm long-playing record some 30 years earlier, EMI did not immediately embrace the new format.

The sticking point was the royalty it would be required to pay to Philips for every CD manufactured but, as its rivals gradually adopted the disc and agreed to pay the royalty, EMI finally relented, its concerns allayed to some extent by the fact that the increased retail price of each CD would more than cover the royalty due to Philips.

Very soon both classical and pop titles were issued by EMI on CD and in the first 18 months the company shipped over 2.5 million CDs, including 140,000 copies of Pink Floyd's already monster-selling *Dark Side Of The Moon* and 25,000 copies of Beethoven's Violin Concerto featuring Itzhak Perlman.

New recordings by the likes of Tina Turner, David Bowie, Bonnie Raitt, Diana Ross, Duran Duran, Pet Shop Boys, Heart, Crowded House, Sheena Easton and Iron Maiden were all placed in music stores alongside classic catalogue items from Pink Floyd, Queen, Kate Bush and Cliff Richard in both the old vinyl and new CD formats.

One group who stayed away from the new format for longer than most were The Beatles, who used the enormous potential demand for CD versions of their albums as a major weapon in their negotiations with EMI. With the relationship between artist and record company already at a pretty low level as a result of audit claims and EMI's plans to issue previously unreleased material, the group held out for better terms and it wasn't until 1987 when the first Beatles CDs became available.

But, despite their in-store availability, not all these releases made an impact in the vitally important American marketplace as David Munns, in charge of marketing, A&R and promotion at EMI Records UK during the introduction of the CD, recalls. "America was a problem back then . . . they got nowhere with Kate Bush, and the Pet Shop Boys was always a struggle."

Such was the overall demand for the new CDs that EMI Music eventually invested in a joint Toshiba-EMI manufacturing plant in Japan alongside wholly owned factories in the USA, UK and Europe, and by 1988 world sales of the compact disc had overtaken the traditional vinyl album.

During the mid-1980s EMI Music boss Menon had, by his own admission, been involved in a number of "interesting exploratory conversations" with Steve Ross and the Warner Communications Group, all of which came to nought. A bizarre tale circulating within the industry concerned a day in New York when three or four senior EMI Music executives, including Menon, decided that the best course of action was to call the Warner boss from the lobby of his building and talk to Ross directly about a possible deal . . . only to discover that none of the senior men had any change for the phone call.

Also on the table at around the same time was the ambitious but highly improbable idea of a management buyout of EMI Music from Thorn EMI. It was raised in my presence during a dinner following an EMI Music management board meeting in Los Angeles, when everybody round the table was asked their opinion of what was referred to in a clandestine manner as "the MBO".

As it was my first management meeting since being appointed head of PR for the company, I had no idea what 'MBO' stood for and went through all sorts of permutations from Manhattan Black Orchestra to the 'many Beatles' offences' we had been accused of over the years. Fortunately before it got to me, a colleague went into a lengthy address about the merits of a management buyout of the music division from the parent company and then, like everyone else around the table, I was able to give my support.

To this day I have no idea whether Menon was the instigator of the plan, who was going to fund it or how Thorn would have reacted to the news, but I never heard another word of a buyout during my time with the company.

More established were EMI's music publishing interests, which dated back to around 1902, just after the start of the original Gramophone Company, and which had been expanded over the years with major acquisitions such as Ardmore & Beechwood – publishers of the first songs written by Lennon and McCartney – Keith Prowse Music and Affiliated Music Publishers.

In 1972 EMI Music Publishing was formed to oversee the international business and the Screen Gems and Colgems catalogues were added in 1976, but in 1983 Thorn EMI denied its music division the opportunity to acquire one of the world's greatest and most valuable music catalogues.

ATV Music was being sold by Australian entrepreneur Robert Holmes à Court, head of the Associated Communications Corporation (formerly ATV and run by Delfont's brother Lew Grade), and after Paul McCartney, Abba's manager/publisher Stig Andersson and the Japanese music company

Shinko Music had all dropped out, EMI Music stepped into the picture.

Over a two-month period in the autumn of 1984 EMI held talks about possibly acquiring the ATV Music catalogue, which included the all-important 250+ songs written by Lennon, McCartney and George Harrison for The Beatles and others and published by their Northern Songs company, which had been bought by ATV in 1969.

The executives of EMI Music knew that by acquiring the rights to these songs while already owning the rights to records by The Beatles, the company's earnings from sales of Beatles' recordings reissued on the new top-price CDs would be substantially boosted, as would the music publishing division's performance.

With EMI Music proposing that an official bid of $42 million be offered to Holmes A'Court, parent company Thorn EMI – in the words of one EMI executive – "started to wriggle" and to nobody's great surprise eventually pulled the plug on the deal. Within days a new bidder arrived and ATV Music was sold to Michael Jackson for $47.5 million, much to the disappointment of Thorn EMI's incoming managing director.

Colin Southgate was not in a position to influence the bid for ATV Music but years later he confirmed that had he been around: "I would never not have bought Northern Songs as I believe music publishing was and is a great asset."

On being appointed as chief executive of Thorn EMI in 1987, Southgate quickly determined which of the company's operations were genuine international businesses. "I decided then that the only truly global business was EMI Music. It was the only thing worth developing and that was when I started pouring money into it." As the only business in the corporation's portfolio that could boast at least 10% of every major international market, EMI Music was the envy of all its rival operations within Thorn EMI.

By 1988 changes were in the air at EMI Music as American businessman Jim Fifield, a veteran of General Mills and video company CBS/Fox, was named as president and chief operating officer and, more importantly, as successor to long-time Capitol and EMI Music chief Bhaskar Menon who would retire a year later.

It was Southgate who recruited and appointed Fifield as his man in EMI Music and he is clear about why he did it. "It was very difficult to have a conversation with the people in music and think you were getting the whole story. They were very secretive and there was a group within the group of music executives who met secretly."

Despite his lack of music business experience, it was Fifield's knowledge of entertainment and international distribution that attracted him to Southgate, who somewhat scathingly observed, "Frankly, finding an executive with music knowledge who could add up was quite difficult."

As the man responsible for the first major change at the very top of EMI Music in the decade since it started, Southgate knew exactly what he expected of Fifield. "I asked Jim to get to grips and sort it out from a business point of view while I got rid of the rest of the stuff in Thorn."

Among the first deals Fifield oversaw was the purchase of SBK Entertainment, a major publishing business with over 275,000 songs, run by Martin Bandier and Charles Koppelman who, with their original partner Stephen Swid, had bought CBS's music publishing business in 1986. The renamed SBK company cost EMI a reported $295 million and the deal also saw Bandier and Koppelman, who had been beaten along with EMI in the race to purchase ATV Music, take over the enhanced EMI Music Publishing arm and also joint ventured, their own SBK Records, with EMI.

For London City analyst Beilby the purchase of SBK would make up in no small way for EMI's failure to acquire even one of the important independent US labels that were apparently available, including A&M and Motown. "They did buy SBK, which was smart," he says, but even then there was criticism of the deal.

"Everybody said it was mad and that Swid, Bandier and Koppelman had 'legged them over' but they hadn't," explains Beilby. "When it was CBS Music it had gone for $125 million and EMI paid $295 million, but it was worth a lot more. They did that right and they showed over the next decade that they understood publishing much better than they understood recorded music."

Soon after, half of the legendary UK independent label Chrysalis was acquired by EMI for what some thought was a generous £79 million, followed by the Ensign and IRS labels.

While Southgate acknowledges that Fifield was the man behind the deal to buy Chrysalis – although it had been talked about as a potential EMI acquisition (alongside the likes of A&M and Island) in the years before he joined – he is keen to take credit for the purchase of SBK. "I did that deal with the third original partner, Stephen Swid, because EMI Music Publishing needed to be strengthened – it was a mega move as it made the company number one in the world."

The music division's investment in music publishing was something that not only delighted music journalist Emmanuel Legrand but also moved him to suggest that it was an award-winning strategy. "One amazing prize of excellence that could be awarded to somebody was for growing the publishing side of EMI."

Recognising the time it took both CBS (after its sale of SBK to EMI) and Polygram (after the sale of Chappell to Warner) to regain positions of strength in music publishing, Legrand compliments EMI's management. "Understanding the value of publishing when it was not really sexy – and in the process gaining an amazing management team led by Marty Bandier – was brilliant."

However EMI's failure to acquire either of the major independent record labels A&M or Island contributed significantly to the company's move down the market-share listings, as both labels were eventually snapped up by the rapidly expanding Polygram group. Having acquired Decca UK in 1980, in 1989 it bought Island for $300 million and A&M for £500 million and then added Motown in 1993.

While Fifield purged some of those he considered part of the old guard of EMI Music – this author included – he left those remaining in no doubt as to what he expected of them. In order to cultivate a much-needed 'winning culture' and succeed in business he pronounced that "constructive conflict is far more productive than passive disagreement".

Looking back on his appointment as president in 1988 and promotion to chief executive officer a year later, Fifield confirms what he had to do to make EMI Music work. "There were issues in all areas of the company: A&R needed to be strengthened, global priorities were not part of the culture, the infrastructure was in need of investment and team management didn't exist. Once we developed a plan and received board approval I was given pretty much a green light to execute the plan."

For David Hughes, who was in charge of EMI UK's catalogue exploitation division at the time, Fifield's arrival heralded a new era and attitude within the company. "He was not remotely interested in the past and his main criticism of the company was its inability to change," he says.

Hughes, a former music journalist, was also impressed with his new boss's way of doing business. "It was a revelation to see him in a meeting, he took no prisoners. There were people who thought this was just another guy they could deal with but he caught a few people out and they were gone."

And while Fifield was not considered by Hughes to be Southgate's man, there was a belief that he was a man on a mission. "I was impressed with the man in that he recognised the value of catalogue and instigated a major worldwide push, and also by the fact that he was a music lover who wanted to help down-and-out old musicians who had been ripped off by their record companies."

Over the next four years EMI Music's worldwide performance reported increased turnover from £663 million to £1,016 million in 1990–1991, with profits growing from £38 million in 1987–88 to £103 million. And between 1989 and 1991 the company's own estimated share of the world music market went up from 11% to 13.9%.

In a major focus on Fifield, published by *Music Business International* in September 1991, the now-defunct magazine posed the question, "Can Jim who? do the impossible and make EMI a superpower?" and pointed out that "almost as soon as he arrived Fifield was on a collision course with the old guard".

The reaction to Fifield of some of EMI Music's 'old guard' was illustrated during a secret breakfast meeting this author was called to attend by two fellow executives. So angered were they by Fifield's style and his behaviour towards existing staff members, they were planning on calling Thorn EMI chief executive Southgate to ask for his (Fifield's) removal.

Ironically, I was the one least in favour of the move, sensing that Southgate was not going to admit to any mistakes regarding Fifield. The plan was eventually dropped . . . only for me to be let go by Fifield within a few months while the other two executives continued with their successful EMI careers for many years after.

Despite the fact that leading US entertainment lawyer John Branca warned him early on, "Good luck – EMI is the last place I'd go to get one of my acts signed," Fifield and his 'new' team set about improving things. A range of new American acts emerged including MC Hammer, Richard Marx, Wilson Phillips and ultimately Garth Brooks, the first country performer to debut at number one on the American album chart and an artist who, by 2000 when he announced his 'retirement', had sold a staggering 100 million albums.

Sadly for EMI, despite limited international success, few of these acts – including Brooks, whose sales were limited almost solely to the US and Ireland – became huge global super-sellers and for former CBS Sony UK and Europe executive Paul Russell that was a bonus. "The EMI companies internationally were very strong competitors," he says. "They were our major competitors not only in finding UK talent but also in marketing and selling that talent internationally – but with the exception of the US."

In America, according to Russell, EMI suffered from not having a strong roster of artists with genuine international appeal. "You are only as strong as your release schedule and when you have artists – as we had – like Barbra Streisand, Neil Diamond, Bruce Springsteen, Billy Joel, Boston and Michael Jackson delivering significant releases it was a huge advantage."

The American three-girl vocal group Wilson Phillips did manage some UK success with two Top 10 albums and a Top 10 single in 1990 with 'Hold On'. This was one of two US number ones for Carnie and Wendy, the daughters of Beach Boy legend Brian Wilson, and Chynna, daughter of Mamas And Papas stars John and Michelle Phillips, but the fact that it stalled at number six gave birth to an EMI legend.

Not since former EMI managing director L.G. Wood had sat with notorious Mafia-connected Roulette record label boss Morris Levy in the late 1960s and decided that he was "not a nice chap to do business with", had the British major been confronted by threats of violence – either spoken or unspoken.

However the story goes that when Wilson Phillips' single did not make it to its expected position at the top of the charts – apparently because there was not enough stock to meet demand – an American SBK executive is said to have arrived at the company's distribution centre in Leamington, in the West Midlands, waving a gun and demanding to see the man responsible for the error.

For Legrand, it was the arrival of Fifield that signalled a major culture change for the grand old lady of the British music business. "With Bhaskar Menon you had a sense that EMI was like the Foreign Office, then Jim Fifield comes in and turns it into an American-driven business with the added twist that it was still quite British but with a different style."

To the writer, formerly editor of the pan-European magazine *Music & Media* and previously its French correspondent, it was apparent that Fifield was "shaking the tree while also holding the cheque book".

"He rejuvenated the company, grew the market share mostly through acquisitions and turned it into a modern company. EMI used to be like the old lady on the bench who you approached only if you had to," said Legrand, "but it became a more sexy company in the Nineties."

In fact in the year up to April 1991, EMI acts held the number one spot on *Billboard* magazine's US album chart for a total of 46 weeks thanks to Bonnie Raitt, MC Hammer, Sinead O'Connor and Vanilla Ice – and they were followed by 18 weeks of Garth Brooks from September 1992.

In the UK during the same period, EMI claimed the album top spot for a total of just seven weeks thanks to Queen, Bowie, O'Connor, Carter The Unstoppable Sex Machine and Iron Maiden, while their joint venture *Now That's What I Call Music* compilation series (launched with Virgin & Polygram in 1983) notched up three more number ones alongside three EMI-only collections.

Even so EMI's share of the UK album market in 1990 and 1991 – when it came in at 15.9% and 15.7% – was the highest in the years between 1985 and 1995 and, while it never beat Polygram to the top spot, EMI did hold second spot in eight out of the 11 years.

The influence of Fifield and his management team, which still included a number of former Menon-men, was apparent even to Tony Wadsworth, who was then a marketing man in EMI's UK company. "He concentrated on return on sales, he made people focus on getting their overheads in order and he was a respected business figure and brought business disciplines to the company."

One of Fifield's less spectacular but nonetheless significant decisions was to order the scrapping of the strap line the company carried on its corporate adverts and official stationery. Since its inception in 1979, EMI music had termed itself "The greatest music company in the world" and the word 'greatest' had been chosen carefully as it signified neither the biggest nor the most successful. To Fifield it was a wholly inappropriate word and one that would not be used until it could be justified by the figures.

While they missed out on acquiring Geffen Records from American music entrepreneur David Geffen – there was talk of personality clashes and requests by Geffen for an enhanced role and an equity share in Thorn EMI – the next target soon came into Southgate and Fifield's sights.

Richard Branson's famous Virgin Music company, which had risen since its founding in 1972 to a position where it had operating profits of £21 million in 1991 and sales of over £330 million in 1992, was considered a sensible fit with EMI Music as it had a reasonable stable of acts plus a valuable music publishing catalogue.

It had come a long way from its famous beginnings with Mike Oldfield's instrumental *Tubular Bells* album to build an artist roster featuring the likes of Neneh Cherry, Peter Gabriel, Phil Collins, Genesis, Bryan Ferry and Simple Minds, and its operations in places like Australia, Canada, France, Germany, Hong Kong, North America, Scandinavia and Spain gave the label a significant international spread.

Despite the fact that Branson had intended to launch a bid for Thorn EMI back in 1987 following the Virgin Group's flotation on the London

Stock Exchange – he abandoned it a year later – the entrepreneur had personally completed expensive deals with both Janet Jackson and The Rolling Stones in 1991 in order to bolster the company in advance of its possible sale.

By the end of the same year Thorn EMI's interest in Virgin Music was common knowledge and in early 1992 the corporation's intentions – an offer of £425 million up front with an earn-out kicking in during the second year – became clear. Negotiations took the deal up to £510 million in cash and, with Thorn EMI taking on £50 million of Virgin's debts, a final announced purchase price of £560 million.

One of the key Virgin Music executives was Ken Berry, who had been with Branson since the very earliest days and, according to the Virgin founder in his autobiography *Losing My Virginity*, he was determined to stay with the label after its sale. "Ken told staff that he would be staying with EMI to ensure Virgin's independence," wrote Branson, who also assured his staff that Ken "would look after them in the new EMI company".

For Southgate, buying Virgin was "a long haul" with Branson taking 13 months to agree terms. "That's Richard for you – slow to get to the word yes" was Southgate's summing-up of the negotiations, which ended with EMI and Virgin sitting side by side as separate operations under the control of Fifield with Berry remaining in charge of Virgin, while Joe Smith controlled Capitol in America and Rupert Perry was head of EMI Records UK.

However, it was clear to everyone involved in the music business that the cultures that made EMI and Virgin work were poles apart. "We bought it (Virgin) in 1992 but it went wrong after that because the people running Virgin in the 1990s had the same attitude as the people running EMI in the 1980s," says Southgate. "They were totally independent and even more laid-back than EMI, there was no sense of urgency."

For Southgate it was also important and relevant to keep EMI and Virgin as separate record companies in the major music markets, but not necessarily in America where "Virgin had no presence".

But even if the top man was adamant that the two labels would remain as independent as possible, there was a feeling within the company that merging them made the most sense. "The presumption was that EMI and Virgin would be run as one company," said one senior EMI executive. "But it didn't happen and we never knew whether that was Southgate's decision or not but it caused all sorts of problems."

At the early stage in the relationship between the two companies Fifield was in complete agreement with his boss. "Part of the operating philosophy when acquiring Virgin was to maintain the label's personality and autonomous label identity. This worked extremely well at the beginning but had diminished returns over time."

This idea of keeping Virgin apart from EMI while they shared the parent company's manufacturing and distribution facilities was apparent to Ray Cooper who, together with Ashley Newton, was head of Virgin Associated Labels before becoming deputy to Virgin UK head Paul Conroy just after the purchase.

"Richard [Branson] had a need to sell and the deal with EMI seemed to make sense – two British companies, one young and one nearly 100 years old by then, working together," says Cooper, who now runs his own music management company in Los Angeles. "My understanding was that the person who decided not to merge EMI and Virgin was Jim Fifield, who liked the qualities he saw in Ken Berry such as his patience, the way he did negotiations and his artist-friendliness, and we were told he liked the idea of Virgin being apart. And business was robust so it wasn't necessary to merge the operations."

Virgin's head of international at the time of the deal with EMI was Jon Webster, who joined the company as a shop assistant in 1975 and knew exactly how Berry would react to EMI's takeover. "He very much wanted to protect his people, he felt responsibility to his staff and what was 'his company' but there was still some trauma as people knew what was coming and, in many cases, expected the worst from the deal."

Although Webster left just months after the EMI deal to become a consultant to Berry – "I didn't want to be part of the EMI Virgin, which I knew was going to be different" – he was surprised at the fact that everything was kept separate. "In any deal you expect the back-room stuff to be merged but it didn't happen for some reason."

So despite the potential for making significant savings by merging areas such as royalties and accounting, sales and distribution, the companies were kept almost entirely separate and that led to a bigger problem – the way in which the companies operated and the relationship between the staff at the two labels.

"The guys from Virgin despised the other guys from EMI," says journalist Legrand, who also saw another reason why no merger took place. "There were two digit margins year on year so there was no need to merge even back-room operations – don't fix something that isn't broken."

But the animosity that existed between EMI and Virgin staffers was obvious to almost everybody involved in the music business. "There was a snobbery from the Virgin side, saying that EMI was mainstream and old fashioned while they were the cool guys," adds Legrand, and his sentiments are echoed by artist manager Ed Bicknell, who signed Bryan Ferry to the Virgin label in the late 1980s. "The whole Virgin thing was very much part of the sex drugs rock'n'roll myth. They were a very disrespectful bunch and then it got linked with EMI, which was monolithic and had a kind of imperiousness about it."

Another commentator who was a regular visitor to both the EMI and Virgin offices in the years after the acquisition was *Music Week* journalist Martin Talbot, who analyses what he saw as "a big difference in culture" between the companies.

"When you went to visit EMI in Manchester Square* it was a quiet, upstanding place, rather old school in context of the wider record business, especially compared to Virgin, which still wore its independent spirit on its sleeve, and its headquarters in Kensal Green straddled a canal and felt much more bohemian."

Irrespective of whether the people within the two companies got on or not, there was no arguing with the fact that together EMI and Virgin were a powerful force from the outset. Thorn EMI's financial figures for 1993–1994 showed that Virgin's profits had reached a record level of £90 million and this achievement, the last year in which Virgin would be reported separately, added to EMI Music's improved performance.

With Thorn EMI reporting turnover down to £4,292 million from the previous year's £4,452 million but profits up (to £382.5 million from £379.3 million), the music operations notched up a sixth successive year of record results.

Sales topped £1,760 million (from £1,507 million in 1992-1993) and profits rose 25% to reach £246 million, thanks to Virgin finishing as the top UK label with six number one albums from the likes of Genesis, Lenny Kravitz, Janet Jackson, UB40, Meat Loaf and Phil Collins. And, like it or not, these Virgin successes were listed alongside EMI best-sellers from the Pet Shop Boys, Diana Ross, The Beatles, Paul McCartney, Iron Maiden and newcomers Radiohead.

Oxford-based band Radiohead arrived at EMI in 1991 and signed what

---

* The building in the north-west corner of the square was famously featured on the cover of The Beatles' debut album, *Please Please Me*, and their later 62–66 & 67–70 compilations.

co-manager Chris Hufford describes as a "worldwide classic old-school deal for six albums". Together with partner Bryce Edge – both had been signed to EMI a decade earlier as members of a band called Aerial FX – he signed the five-piece group to a deal with EMI UK without even knowing that Capitol was the company's American label.

But being unaware of EMI's US business operation seemingly did the band's prospects in America no harm as they broke through in the world's largest music market in 1994 with the album *Pablo Honey* and the single 'Creep'. "We did it the wrong way round to most acts and broke in the US first," says Hufford, while his partner remembers what success meant to Radiohead and their Courtyard Management company.

"I lived in the US in the early days of 'Creep' taking off," says Edge, "and I realised that it's only when you have a hit that doors open and then you get to see how it all works."

The two managers also had both respect and regard for EMI despite some reservations about its size and structure. "In those days visiting EMI was like going to a branch of the Foreign Office," explains Edge, while Hufford contends that, even in the 1990s and despite being an institution, "There was a weird sort of feeling of security about EMI."

The company's business methods also engendered a sense of fair play according to Edge. "For good or worse EMI did play by a set of rules; people knew where they stood, which was not always the case as time went by."

Meanwhile over in the less exciting world of music publishing, EMI Music Publishing was still leading the world under the control of Bandier and Koppelman, being voted 1993 Publisher of the Year in both the UK and US and signing deals with the likes of Aerosmith, Depeche Mode, Rod Stewart, Nirvana and Pet Shop Boys, in addition to a short-lived global administration deal for the ATV catalogue, which included the prestigious Beatles' Northern Songs copyrights.

Unfortunately for EMI, ATV owner Michael Jackson abruptly ended the EMI deal in 1994 and merged his ATV catalogue with Sony Music to form a billion-dollar allegiance as Sony ATV.

For Legrand it was, in many ways, the difference between EMI and Virgin that contributed to the corporation's strength and success. "Having these two totally different companies in major territories was one of EMI Music's new strengths as it catered for different artists and different music.

"With EMI you had classical and jazz plus a fantastic catalogue, which you didn't have with Virgin where there was the likes of The Sex Pistols,

Genesis and Peter Gabriel. The combination of the two, with the growth of the CD market, made it a very strong company."

In the midst of EMI's continuing success story in the early 1990s, a new face appeared among the list of EMI non-executive directors. Eric Nicoli had been chief executive of the United Biscuits Group for two years when he was invited on to the EMI board in July 1993.

He brought with him a lifelong passion for music and a detailed knowledge of EMI's labels and artists although, by his own admission, he knew little about how a music company was actually run. And it soon became clear to him that he was not about to learn very much from the person who ran EMI Music on a day-to-day basis.

Fifield was the only person from music management who attended EMI Group board meetings and, according to Nicoli, he had made some obvious improvements. "At that time I thought the whole music industry was lacking a certain amount of business discipline although there was no doubt that Jim Fifield introduced some."

But it seemed to Nicoli that the flow of information about the company's music division came directly from Southgate or his chief financial officer, Simon Duffy, and the new non-exec director was never encouraged to meet and discuss matters with any EMI Music executives.

However, even from his position on the edge of the music business, Nicoli reached some interesting conclusions. "By all standards the executives in the music industry were paid well. Only some of them were competent as business managers and there was a lack of general management skill in the industry and in our company," he noted – and there was worse to come.

"Communication was apparently not high on anybody's agenda and there were quite obviously many silos and signs of internal warfare within the company, but as a non-exec I was largely insulated from that."

The man who one day would become head of the EMI corporation accepts that Fifield, as the only music man on the EMI board, was the obvious person to approach for more information but this, Nicoli recalls, was never that easy. "Any interest or any challenges we may have had were channelled through Jim Fifield and I haven't met anybody less open to challenge than Jim," says the man who joined United Biscuits in 1980. "He did not like anyone interfering in his business but he clearly brought discipline and delivered results."

A decade on, and while in part acknowledging Nicoli's observations, Fifield puts his poor relationship with fellow board members down to the attitude of his own boss. "The one thing I did wrong was that I didn't develop personal relationships and interface with board members. Colin [Southgate] wanted to control all contact with the board so I basically went to meetings and only spoke when spoken to; that was how Colin wanted it to be. It was clearly understood that this was Colin's board."

Somewhat chastened by this experience, the man very much responsible for the upturn in EMI Music's fortunes admits he could and should have handled things differently. "I never had any one-on-one conversations about the business with board members, and looking back it was one of things that I didn't do well," says Fifield.

One man who actually made the switch from Virgin to EMI and forged a rare link between the two companies was Jeremy Silver, who moved from his original role as Virgin press officer to become EMI Music's first ever vice president of interactive media in 1995.

With the music business entering a new age of technology, Silver, as early as 1993, started talking up the infant internet business. "I told people that there were bits of music up there on the internet and that this would change our business and transform things forever."

His observations met with scant response until he created the first Virgin websites in late 1994. They impressed his Virgin bosses and got him the role within EMI Music, but even then it was still hard work. "I was the future for quite a long time until I got fed up with being told I was the future and decided I ought to be the present. But the EMI people were even less receptive to the idea of the internet business than the Virgin people – they were completely baffled by it all."

This then was EMI's first step into the new world of websites and downloads, although in those early days it had little or no impact on a global music industry that was losing an estimated \$2 billion to good old-fashioned piracy and counterfeiting.

By 1994 EMI Music had 64 record companies and 22 music publishing operations in 38 countries around the world where the French, German, Spanish, Japanese, Australian, South East Asian and Latin American markets demonstrated the value of having a roster of successful local artists.

Until the member companies of the International Federation of the Phonographic Industry (IFPI) agreed on a format for calculating global market share figures by company in 2001, there was no official breakdown of the worldwide performance of each of the major music companies.

EMI claimed it had a 13.9% global share in 1991 and reckoned this had increased to over 15% in 1995, thanks to 30 albums achieving sales of over

1 million, when once again sales were up (by 24.3%) and operating profits increased by 19.8%.

And while the company boasted of the success of US acts Smashing Pumpkins, Beastie Boys, Megadeth and Jon Secada plus UK signing Blur, there was a host of older and more established artists who dominated the sales figures and once again emphasised the importance of having a history and a catalogue.

The Beatles, Pink Floyd, The Rolling Stones, Bob Seger and Frank Sinatra all delivered million sellers, while respected tenor Placido Domingo was a top ten hit in Latin America and EMI Music Publishing UK won a coveted Queen's Award for Export Achievement.

And for the first time Southgate, in his chairman's report in the 1995 Thorn EMI annual report, gave a clue as to how things might look in the near future. He confirmed that the company's divestment policy (which included selling security, sensors, defence, microwave and retail operations) left "a clear field for the future development of our three businesses – EMI, Thorn and HMV".

The year 1995 also saw the rise of Berry within the EMI organisation, which he had joined somewhat reluctantly three years earlier. He was appointed as head of all music operations outside the US, where Koppelman had reigned as chairman EMI Music Group North America since 1993, and coincided with the departure of long-time executive Joe Smith.

This meant that all executives within both EMI and Virgin operations outside the US reported to Berry and according to one veteran EMI executive this led to "the dismantling of the EMI management as Berry got rid of senior EMI people and put Virgin people in their place". This was also the time when EMI's UK operation was moved out of its historic home in Manchester Square to take up residence in an old ice-cream factory in Hammersmith, where the original balcony The Beatles had leant over on their famous album cover photos was installed in the in-house restaurant. Outside the front door were two pillars made from old black vinyl albums.

The same person, who saw time with EMI operations in both the US and UK, reckons this move shaped much of what was to follow. "Fifield was sort of out of our lives as Berry took day-to-day control of the music business."

One of the things that Berry oversaw was the signing of an all-girl group, which would change the face of the international music business through to the new millennium. Despite dissenters, there was competition within the music industry to sign The Spice Girls and that included rivalry between odds-on favourite Virgin and its sister company EMI.

Virgin UK executive Cooper was never in any doubt as to where Ginger, Scary, Baby, Sporty and Posh were going to end up. "We were first in for The Spice Girls and you couldn't counter-bid within the same company, and as Ken was at heart a Virgin man there was never any real argument as to where they were going." However, the story that went round EMI Records was that Berry instructed the senior company to back off in favour of his former label.

The success of The Spice Girls in 1996 was followed by Virgin breaking The Verve and The Chemical Brothers while, over at EMI, Supergrass, Queen and classical violinist Vanessa-Mae joined US stars Garth Brooks, Bob Seger and Bonnie Raitt in the list of best-sellers, and the late Latin superstar Selena topped the four million sales mark.

With sales of their debut album passing the 14 million mark, The Spice Girls dominated Virgin's performance but, according to Cooper, details of their success were never shared with the staff. "At that time we never got told how successful Virgin was in financial terms, but at a sales conference we did ask the financial director how well The Spice Girls had done and he said, 'We've made £49 million net out of them this year'."

Even with their success, staff at Virgin, according to the company's former head of communications Robert Sandall, still viewed their sister company EMI in exactly the same way as they looked at genuine rivals such as Sony or Warners. Writing in *The Daily Telegraph* in 2008, Sandall, a respected music critic, looked back on his six-year Virgin career, which ended in 2002, and recounted the fierceness of the in-house competition.

"I vividly remember the jubilation in the Virgin building when EMI's great white hope Robbie Williams failed to make number one with his first solo single, 'Freedom'." He then went on to recount the joy that was felt at Virgin when a senior EMI executive left the company.

Equally he recounted that the people who ran the Virgin subsidiary label Hut – home to The Verve and Placebo – were desperate not to be considered as part of Virgin, while confirming that the division that looked after big-name signings such as The Rolling Stones and Janet Jackson was a "law unto itself, answerable only to a charismatic . . . lady who worked out of LA".

While this was an obvious reference to Nancy Berry, wife of EMI international boss Ken Berry, Sandall confirmed that it was EMI that bore the brunt of the Virgin staff's displeasure. "We sneered when those cloth-eared fat cats at EMI signed a band we considered to be feeble Radiohead-soundalikes called Coldplay."

Either unaware of or undaunted by the internal strife within his company, Southgate, in addition to announcing the best ever results for Thorn EMI, confirmed in his chairman's statement for the 1996 annual report that a major change in the company's structure was on the cards.

Part of Thorn EMI's success was EMI Music's operating profit being up over 23% – to £365 million – and HMV, with 231 stores in seven countries, showing a 40% increase in operating profits totalling £187 million.

This then was the company that Southgate was on the verge of reorganising, and its music division – comprising operations in 78 countries and claiming a 15% world market share (although media estimates put it closer to 11%) – was basking in the glory of eight consecutive years of record results.

With the phrase, "This is likely to be my last annual report statement to you as chairman of Thorn EMI in its present form," Southgate gave advance notice of the creation of Thorn plc and a brand new EMI company – on the eve of the centenary of its founding as The Gramophone Company.

CHAPTER 4

I Want To Break Free

(Queen, EMI 1984)

THE irony of Thorn EMI announcing its plans to demerge and establish the EMI Group as a major force in the global music business was that it also made the new stand-alone company an attractive proposition for rival music and media companies.

Eight years of record-breaking results were enough to catch the eye of any of the world's leading media companies and, according to *Variety* magazine, in 1996 there were a host of them with an existing interest in music including Disney, Time Warner, Bertelsmann, Viacom, Sony, Polygram and Seagram.

From this list, EMI's main rivals in the international recorded music business during the mid-1990s were BMG, MCA, Polygram, Sony and Warner, and each had its own – or had a parent company with – interests in media, electronics and entertainment.

Bertelsmann Music Group emerged out of German media giant Bertelsmann – which was founded in 1830 – and its ownership of the Ariola label and acquisition of US label Arista in 1979. The addition of the world-famous RCA Records in 1986 made BMG a substantial player in the world market, pitching the likes of Elvis Presley, Eurythmics and David Bowie alongside Barry Manilow and Whitney Houston.

The Music Corporation of America (MCA) was founded in 1924 as a booking agency but quickly went into management, music publishing and films before starting MCA Records in 1962, boasting the likes of Lynyrd Skynyrd, Neil Diamond, Tom Petty and, for America only, The Who, Olivia Newton-John and Elton John.

In 1990 the MCA corporation was acquired by the giant Japanese Matushita organisation, but six years later Canadian drinks company Seagram bought MCA for a reported $5.7 billion and created the Universal Music Group.

Polygram's history can be traced back to 1962 and the merger of Phonogram, the music arm of Dutch electronics company Philips, with Polydor and Deutsche Grammophon, which were part of the German corporation Siemens.

The businesses were merged under the name Polygram in 1972 and in 1987 Philips bought Siemens' share of Polygram. The new publicly owned music company – with acts such as The Jam, The Osmonds, Bon Jovi, Tears For Fears and Luciano Pavarotti plus major interests in films and television – then expanded to add Island Records, A&M Records and Motown Records.

Sony Music was created following the Japanese electronics corporation's acquisition in 1988 of the CBS Records Group from the film and television giant Columbia Broadcasting System for $2 billion.

Boasting the Columbia and Epic labels, Sony Music's roster of front line acts included artists such as Bob Dylan, Simon & Garfunkel, Barbra Streisand, Bruce Springsteen, Billy Joel, Michael Jackson, Celine Dion and Wham!

Warner Music was a division of major television, film and publishing corporation Time Warner, which oversaw the activities of the established Atlantic, Ayslum, Elektra, Reprise and Warner Bros. record companies. These labels were brought together between 1963 and 1974 and boasted a roster of acts ranging from Ray Charles, Aretha Franklin and Led Zeppelin through Joni Mitchell, The Doors and The Eagles to Madonna, Fleetwood Mac, Red Hot Chili Peppers and R.E.M.

But, amid all the rumours of the EMI Group being at the heart of one of the music industry's biggest ever auctions, News Corporation chief Rupert Murdoch was quick to rule himself out of the equation. Speaking at a music convention in America in February 1996, the Australian media entrepreneur, while admitting that music was a gap in his company's portfolio, ruled out a bid for EMI on the grounds of cost.

He told UK industry magazine *Music Week* in advance of the demerger, "At the price we are expecting, it is just too expensive." And while the industry saw Canadian distiller Seagram as favourite to acquire EMI and link it with its MCA music operation, Southgate offered up the insider's view on the rumoured bidding war.

While confirming that he had held talks with some companies about a possible sale, he still pronounced, "Obviously people talk and I've said, 'Come and have a chat, we are not for sale [but] if you want to buy us make me an offer'. It would need to be a lot [of money] and music is still growing."

Speculation about the demerger saw Thorn EMI's shares increase in both 1995 and 1996 with the price in February 1996 settling at £17.20 compared with a 1994 price of £10.35. And six months ahead of the expected August shareholder approval of the demerger, City analysts were anticipating a price of £20 per Thorn EMI share.

Having declared that his life's work has been all about "saving EMI from the knacker's yard – that's my service to British industry", Southgate sat through all the speculation and continued to hold his consistent line that while it was not his intention to sell EMI Music, he could not stop people making overtures.

"It never entered my head that what we were doing with EMI was putting it up for sale," says the man who was knighted in 1992. And while one anonymous senior executive with a rival US music company told *Music Business International (MBI)* in April 1996 that, "Southgate is being less than frank if he says he is not looking to sell EMI Music; he's not telling the truth", the man himself expresses surprise at the City's reaction to his decision to split Thorn EMI.

"£18 a share was ridiculous but they thought someone was going to come across the horizon and bid a huge amount of money. It [£18] was a nonsense price but the company could have been bought then if someone had paid the right price," states Southgate, who also confirms that one of the suitors he met was the mighty Disney Corporation. "I had meetings with them but I always thought they could have built their own music business."

As the head of EMI Music, Fifield was obviously aware of the activities of potential buyers but confirms that there was little in the way of serious interest. Confirming Disney's interest he also acknowledges that there were conversations with both Gulf & Western and Bertelsmann. "They kicked the tires but nothing came of it," he said.

But even as the potential suitors circled, impressed by what EMI Music had achieved since 1988, the man destined to be chairman of both Thorn and EMI before focusing solely on EMI Group from midway through 1997 acknowledges that the lack of American superstar acts remained a problem.

Southgate's assertion was that while the company did surprisingly well out of the non-mainstream areas of jazz and classics, "The real problem was never getting North America to deliver the right number of big artists on a regular basis – one major act a year is not enough." This was borne out by an *MBI*-sourced market-share ranking for 1995 that put EMI in fifth place with just 9.8% of the world's biggest music market.

And while EMI's American operations failed to deliver the 'big arena acts' that consistently came out of main rivals CBS and Warners, David Munns, who worked for EMI between 1972 and 1987 before rejoining the company in 2001, reflected on their performance with British acts. "They had let Queen and Pink Floyd slip through their fingers in the 1970s, which was not good."

Finally in August 1996, with the rumours of potential bidders for EMI still linking Sony, Paramount, Dreamworks and MCA, the Thorn EMI shareholders were asked to give their support to the demerger plans and approve the combining of EMI Music and HMV (including the Dillons chain of book stores) under the banner EMI Group alongside a separate Thorn company.

With Southgate predicting, "EMI is very strong. It is a pure music player and I'd assume it will be highly rated," the offer to shareholders was two shares – one for each of the two new companies – in exchange for an existing Thorn EMI share. With EMI shares expected to be the more valuable, analysts predicted a price of between £13 and £15 for the music business and just £2 to £4 for a Thorn share.

And the analysts got it just about right as, in its first week of trading as the EMI Group, the company's shares peaked after three days at £14.80; the same analysts put a value on EMI of £8 billion.

In September, respected analysts Deutsche Morgan Grenfell joined in the speculation with a 16-page report headed "EMI: What's The Story?" Warning that in the medium term the music industry should not expect the level of growth some were suggesting, the report confirmed that "consolidation between the majors makes sense since it can generate profits growth through costs savings, particularly in the areas of distribution and A&R (artists & repertoire)", and they plumped for a deal between EMI and the Seagram-owned MCA.

They reckoned that a deal with Polygram would be "difficult"; linking with Warners could be "slightly difficult"; an EMI and Sony deal looked "problematic"; while EMI and BMG was "OK"; but EMI and MCA "looks snug".

They based this assertion on a combined US market share of 22% – "the US has always been difficult for EMI" – and MCA's problems outside the US being improved by EMI's strong international business. But while the analysts saw logic in Seagram buying EMI, they also hedged their bets by warning that the market was "overestimating that chance".

While the company he worked for reckoned that Seagram was ahead of the game as far as rival record companies were concerned, analyst Beilby reckoned there were other potential bidders waiting in the wings. Speaking a decade on, he says, "My understanding was that it was never really going to be another record company that bought EMI," and adds, "Disney were on the bench but British Telecom and Microsoft were names that came into the frame as they were about convergence and the growing value of content."

The decision to demerge Thorn EMI and create the EMI Group as a stand-alone music company was one that, not surprisingly, attracted substantial speculation and opinion among artists' managers, analysts, commentators, competitors and people who worked for and ran the company. Why was it done, was it the right move and what would it lead to? Plenty of people seemed prepared to offer an opinion . . .

"It was the final step in the overall strategy and it involved selling about 100 companies and was a lot of effort"

– Thorn EMI chairman Colin Southgate.

"In my view there was never any synergy between the various parts of Thorn EMI and the only thing that being part of Thorn EMI did for music was protect us from being acquired"

– EMI Music CEO Jim Fifield.

"It was the sensible next step for the company. It was the long-term objective when I joined. At the end of a 10-year unbundling exercise Thorn EMI was transformed from having 80-plus largely unrelated businesses to having just a rental business and a music business"

– EMI non-executive director Eric Nicoli.

"In principle I thought the demerger was a very good idea particularly since it had become quite apparent that the parent corporation was incapable of managing effectively the mix of disparate Thorn and EMI businesses, which the 1979 merger had brought together without any real industrial logic"

– EMI Music founding chairman and Thorn EMI board member Bhaskar Menon.

"At the time of the demerger there were constant rumours that the music business was for sale but it never happened"

– EMI Music UK managing director Rupert Perry.

"There was a feeling that this had to be the start of something rather than the end of something"
– EMI UK corporate PR David Hughes.

"The demerger was absolutely the right thing to do. Trying to marry film companies with record companies is tough enough but to mix and muddle things like Rumbelows and Kenwood Chef with music is even harder. To be subsidised by some other form of retail business doesn't make any real sense"
– Sony Music Europe president Paul Russell.

"The demerger was probably not a bad thing but where EMI became exposed was in being the only [music] company which [sic] was completely stock floated – it was the only company with such transparency during a pretty tough period for the music industry"
– *Music Week* and *fono* writer/editorial executive Martin Talbot.

"There was a perception from the outside that wondered what the hell they were doing with that sort of conglomerate that had light bulbs, rental, defence contracts and music – it wasn't a good fit. What Southgate did was probably right for the image and strength of the company but the mistake was that he kept EMI as a public company"
– *Music & Media* and *Billboard* writer/editor Emmanuel Legrand.

"Demerging did expose them as a stand-alone music company and over a ten year view that probably told on EMI in the end, and it affected their reputation and their share price. But any of the majors trading solely as a public music company at that time would have had just as bad a time"
– *The Times* media editor Dan Sabbagh.

"The demerger meant that EMI had to go to the City and demonstrate that intellectual property was as valuable as bricks and mortar – and they did that remarkably well. There came a time when all those various arms of Thorn EMI didn't make sense and they had to streamline, and the major thing was that out of it came EMI, which was a successful company"
– *Music & Copyright* editor Phil Hardy.

"Comparing the relative performance of the two [Thorn and EMI] in the two to three-year period post-merger, Thorn was a disaster. Should EMI have demerged – yes; should it have merged with a bigger entertainment group – yes; and it should have tried to do that at the time of the demerger"
– Dresdner Kleinwort Benson/ABN-AMRO/UBS and PMM analyst Mike Hilton.

"At the time the demerger of EMI was a good move but with hindsight it was not a good move to expose a record company to the scrutiny of the financial markets, and it was never a good idea for EMI to be the only record company that was listed and competing with other companies that were not having to go through the same kind of financial disclosures"

— Market Tracking International/Dresdner Kleinwort analyst
Helen Snell.

"The share price reaction in the short to medium term to the demerger was very positive and it was probably the right thing to do. However the problem was that a sense of complacency crept in at top management in part because the demerger was so well received from a stock market perspective"

— SG Warburg/Deutsche Bank/Dresdner Kleinwort analyst
Mark Beilby.

"I don't think it [the demerger] was a bad move. While the music industry was still flourishing EMI, as I recall, got fairly good price/earnings multiples and being the only stand-alone company with some good cash flow characteristics would have been an advantage relative to the TV leasing businesses, which had declining prospects"

— Schroder/ABN–AMRO/North River financial analyst
David Londoner.

"I think the music business in 1996 was strong enough to justify making EMI a stand-alone public company dealing in music but it was probably still too corporate. EMI had shareholders, which meant it didn't have that flexibility that the small companies have and the City didn't understand music anyway"

— Pink Floyd, Syd Barrett, Roy Harper and Billy Bragg manager
Pete Jenner.

"I don't think the demerger made any difference to managers; it doesn't really matter to a manager who owns a record company. The only advantage is if you get synergy as a result but in reality you never do"

— Jamelia and Mylene Klass manager Jonathan Shalit.

"I think from the point of view of the people in the music arena it probably made no difference, although EMI probably did become more exposed. Most artists don't think in these terms but managers have had to start to think about them in recent years"

— Dire Straits and Bryan Ferry manager Ed Bicknell.

"I had a view on the demerger and I felt it was going to be jolly difficult for EMI to compete. I felt it was going to be incredibly hard because you need very deep pockets and without having the likes of Universal, Sony or Time Warner they [EMI] were without a cushion"
— Robbie Williams and Craig David manager Tim Clark

"The day that EMI demerged from Thorn and became a stand-alone shareholding music company was the beginning of the end"
— Radiohead and Supergrass manager Bryce Edge

"EMI should have gone independent and private and not remained a publicly owned company when it demerged; it would have been brilliant if that had happened"
— Blur, Gorillaz and Damon Alban manager Chris Morrison

"The demerger that allowed EMI to remain as a stand-alone music company on the public market – and pretty much the only stand-alone music company – was a terrible thing and it probably sowed the seeds of most of the difficulties that came later"
— Beggars Group director/chair UK Music Andy Heath.

Speaking over a decade later Southgate confirms that the privatisation of EMI in 1996 was not something that figured in the business equation, although there were some other ultimately unfilled plans. "It was never a consideration to take it private at the time of the demerger. We were doing very well at the time but I thought there was a need to broaden the media base from just music.

"I didn't see films as the right fit . . . we did talk very hard about a book publishing business but it was never pursued."

While the demerger was approved by the shareholders, Bhaskar Menon, the former head of both EMI Music Worldwide and America's Capitol Industries whose EMI career began with The Gramophone Company of India in the 1960s, had his doubts about how the executives would make it work.

Menon's concerns were focused on the way in which the newly created EMI Group was going to be managed. "It was puzzling and diffi-cult to understand why, after demerging EMI Music, it was decided to retain the same duplicated corporate management structure as before by keeping the business under the direct overall executive chairmanship of Colin Southgate, reporting to virtually the same pre-merger board, together with the expensive two-tier superstructure of corporate staffs in place just as before."

The Indian-born music executive and one-time head of the International Federation of the Phonographic Industry (IFPI) also holds the view that the management structure put in place after the demerger was largely to blame for what followed. "I think this extraordinary organisational miscarriage was really the genesis of EMI Music Group's subsequent collapse as a serious force in the world music business."

Although he retired from EMI Music in 1990, Menon has remained an interested observer of his former employer's fortunes and compliments his successor Jim Fifield on his leadership of a "well-motivated and strong, direct management group" within EMI Music. He is, however, not quite so complimentary about his own boss during the earlier Thorn EMI days. "As a matter of personal judgement I do not think that Colin Southgate was the 'right man' to head the newly demerged EMI Music in 1996."

Undaunted by any criticism or speculation surrounding his company, and revealing the new EMI Group's first set of figures three months after the demerger, Southgate dismissed reports of a global music slump and announced half-year figures up to September 1996 that showed EMI Music profits up 5.9% to £131.9 million, but sales up just 1.6% to £1,095 million.

He was pinning his future hopes on a strong finale to the year with The Beatles' *Anthology 3*, the first Spice Girls album and The Artist's (Prince) EMI debut album, plus some big titles in the first quarter of 1997 but, as is so often the case in the music business, there were some 'delivery' problems.

With Southgate putting forward albums from the likes of Robbie Williams, Blur, Duran Duran, Supergrass, Richard Marx, Megadeth, Gary Moore and Simple Minds as major items, it turned out that Blur was the only one of these acts to actually deliver a new album in early 1997. However the end-of-year figures still showed a 2.7% increase in profits for EMI Music – up to £374.9 million on slightly reduced sales of £2,491 million, compared with £2,705 million.

Alongside news of George Michael signing to Virgin for the world outside US and selling five million albums, EMI's German operations delivering seven million albums and America offering up Deana Carter, Crowded House and Selena, there was confirmation of the company's interests in US independent labels Priority, Matador and Java, plus the acquisition of American Christian music label Forefront to go alongside EMI's purchase of Sparrow Records five years earlier.

There was also – under the heading of exceptional item – the news that

Berry was all set to become president of EMI Recorded Music whereby he would assume responsibility for EMI Music International, Capitol and Virgin operations.

For industry writer Martin Talbot it was a move that made perfect sense in the circumstances. "Ken Berry was seen to be artist-friendly and therefore possibly the best choice they could have made. He came from the Virgin bloodline and carried memories of that entrepreneurial spirit, the independent ethos."

Although he would still be reporting to Fifield, this move, which took effect in June 1997, saw Berry take Koppelman out of the picture and with him went EMI Capitol's expensive New York offices, plus most of the staff, at a cost of £117 million, and the move would, it was claimed, reduce annual operating costs of between £35 and £40 million.

Included in the £117 million, according to informed media reports, was a one-off £30 million pay-off to Koppelman, while Southgate took the opportunity to give the clearest indication that his successor as chairman of the EMI Group would be Berry and not company president and CEO Fifield.

Even though he publicly acknowledged Fifield's part in EMI's improvement since his arrival in 1988 – "Jim has turned EMI into a very professionally run business worldwide" – Southgate seemed to clear the way for Berry to take the helm. In June 1977, confirming his own plan to retire, he apparently sealed Fifield's fate by explaining, "Jim and I are not very far apart in age and over that period we aim to lay the foundations for the next generation."

Talking ten years later Southgate was at pains to point out that even though he promoted Berry there was no clear decision regarding the next chairman of the EMI Group. "I did not see him [Berry] as my successor," says the man who went on to become chairman of the Royal Opera House.

At the same time he also gave an insight into the behind-the-scenes boardroom machinations. "Jim Fifield saw himself as my successor but the board didn't feel that Jim was the right sort of guy to run a public company." So while Berry took over recorded music, he still reported to Fifield, who was in charge of both music and publishing but, according to Southgate, had loftier ambitions.

"I was due to retire in 1998 and he wanted to become chairman, but the board did not want him as chairman. He started to play politics. It was nothing to do with him being American – Jim was just being Jim and he was very much concerned with putting himself first."

For his part Fifield is quick to point out that he had no problem with Southgate being chairman of what was essentially a music-only company, but confirms that he did have a "major problem with him [Southgate] trying to run it as opposed to acting as chairman".

The man who joined EMI Music in 1988 was now nearing the end of a decade in charge and the main reason for things falling apart was his worsening relationship with the company chairman. "From the beginning Colin [Southgate] was my partner and we did really well together for the first eight years, but after the demerger things started to unravel," he recalls before adding, "Colin would push and I would push back and eventually it unwound itself."

Despite the obvious internal wrangling at the very top of the company, media-business analyst Mike Hilton saw the overriding issues for EMI as the possibility of a deal and what the future held for the music business. His summing-up of the likelihood of Southgate actively seeking a partner for his company is as follows: "In any situation of corporate activity it's quite a strange CEO who thinks, 'I'm going to push for a merger which will almost certainly mean I'll lose my job'. It's only out of absolute necessity that you would do it."

But while it wasn't a necessity for Southgate to do any sort of deal – merger, sale or acquisition – there were issues looming large on the horizon that Hilton thinks EMI and its senior management could and should have anticipated.

He believes that, while it should have begun looking for partners soon after the demerger, the company could also have looked forward four years and forecast the decline of the CD replacement cycle while at the same time noticing that technology was on the march. "EMI should have predicted some of the technological innovations that were coming but they were head in the sand about it all."

The speculation about EMI's future post-demerger from Thorn had refocused the City's interest in the company and the music industry. What was its future, were companies going to have to merge to survive, how would the new digital age impact on the business? They were all questions that the people in the financial, investment and analysis communities were asking the music companies . . . and each other.

City analyst Mark Beilby, who confirms that the City "swallowed wholesale" the de-merger, was concerned about the impact the compact disc had made on the music business and how EMI and other companies analysed the CD boom, which had begun in earnest around 1989. "CDs masked the growth rate in the industry and artificially inflated recorded music profits," he points out.

Beilby was worried by the fact that the CD was not a recordable device but simply a new and improved version of the old vinyl disc, and in replacing vinyl was responsible for a period of artificial growth that was further boosted by the buoyant economic conditions of the 1990s. "I think there wasn't a proper analysis by any of the record companies of that situation," he says.

According to industry journalist Phil Hardy, EMI's demerger and the boom in CD sales were always going to bring renewed interest from the City and potential investors. "EMI had to convince the City that intellectual property mattered and they did this very successfully," says the editor of *Music & Copyright*.

"It was at a time when record sales were going up and everything looked jolly good but, when you have convinced the City that intellectual property is valuable and that you are good at that business, and then record sales stumble and your share price stumbles, you discover that the relationship with the City is very cold."

EMI's performance was not helped in early 1997 by concern in financial circles over the state of the global music industry. Difficulties in the US retail market, caused by a combination of overexpansion, heavy discounting, a dearth of major-selling albums and a drop in the CD replacement cycle, saw the company's share price fall to £11.15.

However a number of positive analysts' reports saw it rise 47p within a week or so and by May, on the back of new rumours of a merger with Seagram, it rose to £12.15. While EMI officially denied the reports – a spokeswoman stated, "We have never had merger talks with anybody and we are not in talks at the moment" – City analysts were recommending EMI shares as a good buy, as they had fallen £3 since the demerger and a deal with Seagram was seen as a positive move.

Worries about how the City might react to EMI's new-found freedom also concerned experienced artists' manager Pete Jenner who says quite simply, "You can't hide from the City the peaks and troughs that the music industry goes through when you are a big company. Music was exposed, and having major ups and downs with your constant overhead is a disastrous situation for any large company."

The fluctuating delivery of product by artists has been an ongoing problem for record companies over the years and Jenner senses that the business community doesn't see it as a positive. "If you have ten bankers [major releases from major artists] and five of them come through in one year then you have a huge year, and then if you only have one [banker] the next year, you have a catastrophe and the stock market has a hysterical reaction."

These are sentiments echoed by Radiohead and Supergrass manager Bryce Edge who says the music business is cyclical, with a year of great results being followed by a less successful period. "Artists can be in a fallow period and albums are not being delivered, but shareholders want continual growth in profits," he says before adding that there have been times when the record company has put pressure on him, his partner and their acts to deliver a new album.

"A couple of times we were told, 'If you can get the record out before the end of March [EMI's financial year end] we'll give you blah blah.'" While he refuses to explain the details of these offers, Edge is clear about his response to EMI's approach. "Well fuck that – it's not about that, it's about the music and making the right album. And the other irritating thing is knowing that part of the pressure is the executives looking to get their bonuses – they only want the record out to make their numbers."

One of the emerging answers to the problem of the 'peaks and troughs' lay in new opportunities that were developing apace through the ever-expanding internet business. Even though EMI's new business ventures made no money for the company in the mid 1990s, things were at least being talked about in a positive manner according to the company's interactive media executive.

"By the end of 1997," according to Jeremy Silver, "we were talking about things like who owns an act's domain name – is it the label or the artist? – and we started having conversations with people who wanted to do celestial jukeboxes or in-store CD burning."

But despite these developments there were those who remained unconvinced about EMI's commitment to new technology. "EMI was very conservative and very conservatively run," says Phil Hardy, adding, "The money was flowing and it was much too overstaffed with middle and top management and their interests were not in embracing technology."

He also holds the view that as they had always controlled the distribution of their own product, "which had been terribly good for them", they were uncomfortable with a new system that would control distribution of these recordings. "They saw it as a threat and for me there was always a sense of desperation about the way EMI did deals. I think that stemmed from the fact of being a stand-alone company and not having big pockets compared with some of their rivals, who had strategies regarding the internet that at least made sense."

Hardy goes further to suggest that standing alone as the EMI Group and focusing simply on the music business after the demerger also made the company desperate in its search for a potential suitor or partner. "It was always going to be the altar place or the cemetery for EMI," he says.

This argument that EMI was left isolated as a music-only company is not one that sits comfortably with Nicoli, who contends that a business should be able to stand on its own two feet, and that EMI plc – as it became in 1996 – was still a very big company. "It had extraordinary record growth in the previous ten years," says the man who eventually led the company for nearly a decade, "and I would argue that not being part of a multimedia conglomerate was an advantage and not a disadvantage."

In the immediate aftermath of the demerger another problem facing EMI became abundantly clear, according to Hilton. While he holds the view that investors who held EMI stock were quite happy to see Thorn go, his overriding concern was in the ability of the City and its plethora of financial experts to actually understand the business that EMI was now concentrating on. "The City has never understood the music industry because there was only one British company in the industry – EMI. The City works on a sector-by-sector basis, and in utilities or house-building for instance there are a number of companies operating, but that wasn't the case with music."

Because of this, financial institutions and companies never employed specialist music people to do the job full-time and usually linked EMI alongside companies in the media sector. "This meant," explains Hilton, "that the analytical skills in music were lower than they would have been had there been six or seven companies to follow. You never really truly understood the music business . . . it was only people who worked in music who truly understood the whole mechanics."

One of the few specialist music analysts was Helen Snell who worked for Market Tracking International, which produced industry data for publications such as *Music Business International* and *Music Week*. She subsequently moved into the City, and arrived on the scene just as EMI was demerged from Thorn.

"It had just demerged when I started looking at it and EMI was a suc-cessful and profitable operation, and sitting in the UK you always had a perspective of EMI being very strong because it was so very dominant in the UK market. You really had no perception of it being weaker than its peers, although from the SoundScan* information you knew they were always the weaker player in the US."

Andy Heath, experienced 'indie' music publisher and board member of the Music Publishers Association, takes the view that Southgate's lack of understanding of the business he was now involved with played a major part in EMI's fortunes. "I don't think he ever really got it in terms of EMI being a creative company.

"If you are a stand-alone music company you stand or fall on your creativity – or the poetry – and all the rest, to paraphrase Lord Stephen Carter[†], is just plumbing," says the man who launched the Momentum and 4AD publishing companies. "It doesn't matter what you do to the plumbing if the poetry is not working, and the poetry can't work in a stand-alone corporation that is disciplined by quarterly performance requirements. Southgate knew enough about the company and he should have known that."

EMI's performance in America had been a constant thorn in the company's side and its failure to develop, break and market American artists on a truly global basis continued in the late 1990s.

The genuinely big world superstars established in or coming out of America at the time were Madonna, Celine Dion, R.E.M., Shania Twain, Mariah Carey, Bruce Springsteen, Eminem, Britney Spears and Bon Jovi, and EMI was significant by its absence from the list of international best-sellers. In addition, its lack of profile in the important and hugely successful rap market mirrored EMI's reluctance to embrace disco music two decades earlier, and despite linking with a number of urban labels neither Capitol nor Virgin was able to attract major artists such as Puff Daddy, Public Enemy, NWA or Dr Dre. The importance of having successful American artists who can sell records around the world becomes obvious when you realise that in most of the world's major music markets US repertoire accounts for a huge share of sales.

In Britain it has traditionally been between 30% and 40% during recent years with domestic (UK) repertoire averaging out at just over 50% with, by comparison, repertoire from Canada, Ireland and Australia very occasionally reaching a combined total that was just in double figures.

---

* Nielsen SoundScan is the company that analyses and reports US music-industry figures.
† Labour peer and Minister of Communications.

Former music-business journalist Martin Talbot sums up the situation: "The EMI company in America was much less successful and has remained so ever since. In a sense the UK company had to perform well in developing new talent because of the US underperformance. Unlike many of its competitors, [EMI] had no American repertoire to speak of."

The year 1997 will be remembered by many for the celebrations that surrounded EMI's centenary but, despite the significance of the anniversary of the company's founding in 1897 as The Gramophone Company, it was, according to EMI's UK head of PR at the time, a tough sell.

David Hughes had eventually moved into the PR position, though it was now somewhat grandly retitled director of public affairs, following my own departure from the company and the 100-year party fell under his control, although he was seemingly supported by only one executive. "Colin Southgate was the instigator of the centenary celebrations," he says. "It was his idea. He fought against opponents from within the music division as nobody in the record company was really interested."

While there were special concerts involving Paul McCartney and Nigel Kennedy plus a classical evening at Glyndebourne, the centrepiece of the birthday was a major exhibition, which cost over £2 million to assemble and operate and was supposed to tour the country as a historic music spectacle.

But problems finding appropriate venues restricted the show to an opening four-month stint in Edinburgh followed by a six-month stay in Canary Wharf between June 1997 and January 1998. Funded by Southgate and Thorn EMI until its demerger, the EMI Centenary exhibition was deemed something of a success by the few people who saw it in Scotland's capital city and London's Docklands development.

For Hughes, who was the driving force behind the project, it was probably a missed marketing opportunity for the most senior British music company but as he says, "We had very little cooperation from within the company, we worked almost in isolation, but nevertheless I was proud of what we achieved."

In July 1997, as the company claimed an extra 1% on its 1996 global market share – taking it to 19% – the share price was significantly boosted by a further major development in EMI's music publishing division.

The acquisition of 50% of the last major US independent publisher, Jobete Music, and its sister operation, Stone Diamond Music, added 44p to the EMI share price, taking it up to £11.23. The 15,000 songs covered by the deal included a host of hits written for and by the roster of Motown

71

acts that included Marvin Gaye, Smokey Robinson, Stevie Wonder, The Supremes, The Temptations and The Four Tops.

The City generally applauded the $132 million deal and while EMI's publishing boss Bandier told the world that it was EMI's respect for the songs that attracted Motown founder, Berry Gordy, to the company – "We won't diminish its value for a fast buck" – Merrill Lynch media analyst David Chermont told the music press, "It's very rare to be able to acquire such a large and quality publishing outfit."

While the deal for Jobete was global, and in time would benefit EMI Music Publishing's overall standing in the world marketplace, its domination of the UK publishing industry was already well established by 1997 when it reported a massive 26.9% market share, while its three major competitors managed 31.8% between them thanks to Warner Chappell (11%), Polygram (10.8%) and BMG (10%).

The various unofficial and often estimated global market-share figures for EMI during the mid-1990s continued to vary enormously. While EMI itself was claiming 19% for 1996, music industry publication *Music & Copyright* – at the time a *Financial Times* title – reduced its share to 11.2%. This put EMI in fifth and last place among the majors, way behind Polygram on 23% and trailing Sony (15.7%), Warner (14.5%) and BMG (14%).

However in the UK, EMI's historically strong position had been significantly strengthened by the addition of Virgin's market share. In 1996, according to figures compiled by the British Phonographic Industry (BPI), it was the top music company with 22.5% of the British album market . . . the split was 11.8% EMI and 10.7% Virgin.

The following year EMI triumphed again with 24.5%, ahead of Polygram (19.6%), Sony (12.1%) and Warner (7.2%), and boasted albums from two Virgin acts – The Verve (number 2) and The Spice Girls (numbers 3 & 5) – in the list of top ten best-sellers for the year.

If Virgin artists were leading the way in the UK, Nielsen SoundScan's figures for US album distribution shares in 1996 only emphasised EMI's problems in America. They trailed in fourth place with 12.6%, ahead of BMG on 11.8% but behind Polygram (25.1%), Warner (18.9%) and Sony (13.7%).

For the company that, thanks to The Beatles, had led the way for British acts in America, its position in the mid-1990s was worrying and not just to the people who ran and worked for the company. An unnamed analyst took the view that the heyday for EMI's Capitol Records was during the

1960s and the company's US market had been in decline ever since those heady days came to an end.

A former EMI executive who would later return to the label was of the view that the company's US problem stemmed from a lack of major 'arena acts' to compete with the likes of U2, Bruce Springsteen, Celine Dion, Madonna, R.E.M. and Bon Jovi, while former Sony chief Paul Russell says that, although his American colleagues were never dismissive of EMI's standing in the US, he saw a major flaw in their operation.

"They had and continue to have a major structural problem about the way they operate in the US and until that is solved – which would involve headquarters in New York with an experienced music man in overall charge – I don't think EMI will ever have a significant American company."

While he might not have fully embraced the centenary of EMI – and indeed was well-known for being critical of what he saw as the company's obsession with its history – Fifield nevertheless steered the business through to a position of financial stability that, according to long-time EMI executive Rupert Perry, might have surprised some people.

"He was probably more successful than Southgate and the board ever imagined he would be, even in their wildest dreams," says Perry, who was also aware that life under Fifield was not always comfortable. "He was not always easy to work with but he brought business disciplines to EMI and put in a sparkling performance with eight years of record profits."

However, the financial figures for the first six months of 1997 (up to September) showed a 4.5% drop in operating profit despite a near 5% increase in sales. But there was still good news with million-selling albums from Radiohead, The Rolling Stones, Paul McCartney and US new-comer Meredith Brooks, supporting The Spice Girls' eight million debut album sales.

Radiohead's continued success through *The Bends* and *OK Computer* made them the standard-bearers, alongside Blur, for the Parlophone label, which was undoubtedly the jewel in EMI's crown.

For co-manager Chris Hufford, the success of Radiohead and their stablemates Supergrass meant greater access to the powers-that-be at EMI. "We could certainly get meetings now and we also realised that once you are in the position of having a hit, there are a brand new set of rules. Then *OK Computer* kicked off and the rules changed again," he says. His partner Bryce Edge confirms their increased significance to the record company.

"We were incredibly important people at that time in the world of EMI and we sold records in America, which nobody else was doing."

At the same time the second album – *Spiceworld* – from the company's favourite all-girl group, The Spice Girls, arrived to further boost EMI's coffers and also make the girls the first UK act to have two albums in the US top 20 chart since Elton John in 1975. And, perhaps not surprisingly, the combination of a reduced financial performance and a handful of million-selling releases resulted in more takeover rumours.

Once again the speculators had Seagram and its Universal music division as the favourites but also named Walt Disney, News Corporation and British Telecom as interested parties. Talking to industry publication *Music Week*, music business analyst Cliff Dane posed the question, "Whether EMI is a more attractive proposition when it is high and frothy or its value has dropped a bit?"

Even if all the talk in and around the music industry about EMI "doing a deal" was just rumour and gossip, it still had an unsettling effect on those close to the company. Even though experienced artists' manager Chris Morrison – he has looked after the likes of Thin Lizzy, Ultravox and Paul Hardcastle over the years – had no real concern as to whether EMI was part of Thorn EMI or not, he was unsettled by what he saw happening to the company.

"The gradual demise more or less occurred when Colin Southgate first of all demerged it and then put it on the 'for sale' block," he says, adding that in his view the chairman of the company seemed to be promoting its sale. "My thought then was, 'Why would I want to buy it if someone else is selling it?' If somebody else wants to keep it then I may want to buy it."

Acknowledging that there may never have been any firm offer for EMI in the months following its demerger, Morrison, who took over the management of Blur in 1992 after they had signed to EMI, believes the whole period was still damaging. "Even if there wasn't an actual bid for EMI, rumour was rife and that was not good for anybody. It caused uncertainty and there was disquiet about who you might be dealing with and what changes might be made."

Either way another year was about to pass without any formal bid being made for the 100-year-old granddaddy of British music companies. However, the company was about to undergo a major change in the management of its Virgin Music operation in America as Nancy Berry, the wife of EMI's Recorded Music president Ken, and two Virgin UK executives, Ray Cooper and Ashley Newton, took over the running of the business in the US.

American-born Mrs Berry began her Virgin career when she teamed up with her future husband in New York at the very start of Virgin's initial assault on the US market in the late 1970s. Eventually Nancy Myers and Ken Berry returned to the UK and worked together for Virgin before marrying in 1985, after which they both rose through the ranks of Richard Branson's growing music empire.

Finally in September 1997 she was named vice chairman of Virgin Records America at the same time as she became vice chairman of Virgin Music Group Worldwide.

All that company chairman Southgate says on the subject is "appointing Nancy Berry in America was a huge error", while his chief sidekick Fifield observes, "She put herself in charge of all the marketing and promotion of what you would call superstars; she was in charge of the approvals of the monies for the whole nine yards involving those major acts," adding, "That's where Colin had a blind eye to what was going on there."

Veteran American music executive Phil Quartararo left the company soon after Nancy Berry arrived, and his role as president of Virgin Records America was taken by co-presidents Cooper and Newton, who were formerly joint managing directors of Virgin UK.

These moves did not sit comfortably with long-time music executive Bob Mercer, who watched all the coming and going at EMI with interest from his position in America with rivals Universal. Having sensed a feeling of "desperation" about the promotion of Berry, he saw the arrival of Mrs Berry, Cooper and Newton as "reflecting Ken's need to Virgin-ise EMI".

Early in 1998 rumours began to circulate that Southgate was not prepared to give up his power base as chairman of EMI Group and was insistent that Fifield would continue to report direct to him rather than succeed him in the top job. Whether the stories of a power struggle were true or not, things finally came to a head for Fifield at EMI in early 1998 when he left despite, he says, being offered a new contract to stay on. "I could no longer work with Colin and I informed members of the board. My contract was not renewed and I was asked to leave."

Looking back on it all a decade later Fifield maintains that his departure was "not in the best interest of shareholders, but that's what happens when you have too many cooks in the kitchen".

As the man who oversaw Fifield's departure after an eight-year period of growth in the music company's fortunes, Southgate acknowledges the role his president played but also admits that he made an error along the way. "It needed a period with somebody like Jim [Fifield] in charge but the mistake I made with Jim was renewing his term."

Somewhere in the midst of his tenure as president of EMI Music, Fifield's contract had come up for renewal and Southgate reflects that he should have made a change at the top at that time. "I think when he had restructured the thing and got it talking about forecasts and planning, then was the time to find a more creative person, somebody more in tune with the music business."

But, as Southgate admits, "they don't grow on trees", and perhaps the constant rumours about EMI's ability to remain as a stand-alone music company made rival music executives reluctant to take up the challenge of steering EMI Music through a period where the outlook for music sales was described by one major analyst as "not attractive".

Within the senior ranks of EMI Music the breakdown in the relationship between Southgate and Fifield was common knowledge. Things were seemingly brought to a head by Southgate's suggestion that he was going to have to get involved in the music business because, as one unnamed EMI executive claims, "Berry was not delivering and there were problems on the horizon".

At a meeting in January 1998, described by the then head of EMI UK, Rupert Perry, as "crucial", Fifield called his EMI and Virgin executives together for the first time. "He gave a state of the nation address in front of Southgate and Berry," says Perry, who saw the speech as a "tour de force presentation that outlined the future and a vision for the future of the company."

But, according to Perry, not everybody was impressed by Fifield's performance. "EMI people were 'buzzed' about seeing Jim back in action and bringing some direction but the Virgin people took a different view and Berry admitted to me that his people were 'uncomfortable' with it, which didn't really surprise me."

Irrespective of what EMI or Virgin people felt about Fifield's rallying call, the feeling persisted that Fifield was going to succeed Southgate. Perry's view was that Fifield's appointment as CEO of EMI Group was very much on the cards and it "all looked pretty clear about what was going to happen".

A major part of Fifield's concern over the company's future was a structure that would see EMI and Virgin continue to operate as separate entities at a time when he was less than optimistic about what lay ahead. "Our business was slowing down and the 1998–1999 release schedule was looking weak. In addition I had no idea the negative impact that the internet and file-sharing would have on the industry," admits Fifield before adding, "All I knew was that we were facing a company slowdown and we had to look to alternatives to deal with it."

With shareholders and board members expecting continued growth from the music division, part of Fifield's plan involved merging the company's two major operating divisions. "One alternative was my recommendation to combine Virgin and EMI in territories that didn't supply repertoire to the rest of the world, which would exclude the UK, North America and France. But I got no support from Colin or Ken Berry."

Berry's reluctance to sanction any change that would impact on the company and label he grew up with was a major talking point within both EMI and the industry. For Fifield, however, it was a major problem. "One of the management issues I was dealing with at the time was the inability to do anything that affected Ken Berry's view of Virgin in a negative way. For him Virgin was an independent label within EMI and I was fighting that view towards the latter part of my tenure at EMI."

Years after he left EMI, Fifield still believes that Berry never really became a bigger team player and admits, "I grossly underestimated the size of the abyss between EMI and Virgin and Ken's bias on the whole subject."

As a long-time colleague of Berry at Virgin in both the UK and US, Ray Cooper was closer than most to the man who was to succeed Fifield as the boss of EMI Music, and even he has doubts about Berry's thinking. "Maybe Ken's management style wasn't suited to being corporate head of EMI Music," says the man who thought his own move to head Virgin US was "something of a present" from Berry.

"He wouldn't have a number two who was maybe the bad cop," says Cooper. "He liked the culture of Virgin and he liked working with all of us at Virgin. I think he found the EMI culture a bit hard to deal with and he always got swept back to Virgin because it was successful and we weren't political."

Another colleague from the original Virgin days was Jon Webster, who saw Berry's management style at first hand. "He had a particular style and skill. When managers came in annoyed and about to bang the desk he would simply ask, 'What do you want?' and then say, 'I think we can do that' before pointing out what we'd like from them in return . . . 'if at all possible'."

Confirming that he never saw Berry change his management style after he took over as head of EMI Music, Webster simply suggests, "Maybe he should have done."

Finally in April 1998 it was announced that Fifield was leaving EMI Music with, according to press reports, compensation of £6.2 million for early termination plus a pension contribution of £6.1 million. Confirming the departure of EMI Music's president and CEO, an EMI spokeswoman said, "There is no replacement for Jim Fifield. We are basically two divisions [recorded music and music publishing] and Ken [Berry] and Marty [Bandier] are both chiefs of these."

She also stressed that not having a chief executive of EMI Music would not create a power vacuum and added that neither Berry nor Bandier was being tested as a potential successor to Southgate. All the activity saw the EMI share price drop from 482.5p to 465.5p overnight.

For Bhaskar Menon, who had retired as head of EMI music and given up his seat on the Thorn EMI board two years before the company acquired Virgin, the appointment of Berry as head of the record division of EMI Music was another step in the wrong direction. Even though he did not know Berry, Menon remained a most interested observer of his former company's fortunes.

From what he heard from various EMI Music insiders about life during the reign of Southgate and Berry, Menon concluded, "It would seem that the departure of Fifield, his partial replacement by Berry with responsibility for recorded music only, and the strengthened hegemony of Southgate were crucial management fault lines that significantly accelerated the decline of the company compared to its competition."

While the decision to let Fifield leave brought some reaction from the City and the media, for long-time EMI executive Perry it represented a major mistake. "I thought it was the worst decision that the EMI board had ever made. It was a horrendous decision as has been borne out by what has happened to the company since then."

Perry's view is supported by his former EMI Music colleague Menon, who suggests that Fifield's EMI career was brought to an end in a "Byzantine manner", which, irrespective of the huge financial cost to the company, "illustrates the forces and characters dominating the leadership struggle at the time".

The respected music industry magazine *Music Week* made its feelings clear in an editorial written by editor Steve Redmond, which stated, "Much of the criticism of him [Fifield] and his pay packet is complete and utter nonsense", before going on to add, "The sums that EMI have paid to him may have been fantastic but no one can deny that he has done a fantastic job."

At the same time former EMI marketing and PR director David Hughes noticed a change in the media's reaction to EMI boss Southgate, who had overseen the change in his company's music operation. "EMI's image in the media was as good as it ever had been and Colin could do no wrong," says the former music journalist. "Then suddenly overnight the press was anti him and it was probably because of getting rid of Fifield and the huge pay-off, which they viewed badly."

But even before news of management disputes at EMI leaked out there were indications that there was trouble in store for both the company and the recorded music industry in general. In January 1998 Southgate warned that EMI's profits would be slashed by £25 million as a result of a slump in the Japanese and South Asian music market.

The announcement that "consumer confidence in these countries has suffered a severe setback and this is being reflected in music sales", drove the EMI share price down from 447.5p to 434p.

On the back of the Asian crisis, which would carry over into Latin America, and a strong pound that affected exchange rates, EMI struggled to meet expectations when it came to announce its figures for the year 1997–1998.

In the final months leading up to the end of the financial year to March 31, 1998, the company completed the sale of its HMV retail business to the newly created HMV Media Group – while retaining a 45.2% interest in the new company – and netted around £500 million. This came at about the same time as EMI Music completed the acquisition of American urban/rap label Priority Records, one year after Virgin had bought an initial 50% interest.

Even so, while turnover was down marginally (to £2,352.7 million from £2,511.5 million), the EMI Group profits before tax fell by over £73 million to £307.1 million despite strong million-selling performances from The Spice Girls, Garth Brooks, Janet Jackson, The Rolling Stones, Radiohead, The Verve and Meredith Brooks.

While the company claimed that at 1997 exchange rates both turnover and profits would have increased, it also indicated that its global market share had increased by 0.5% to 14.8%, making it the third-largest music company in the world.

However, while Southgate claimed that increased A&R resources would allow the company to "aim for Sony just above us and then climb to Seagram", the music industry put EMI in fifth place in the global music market behind both Warner and BMG as well.

Speaking in June 1998 Southgate described EMI as an independent and added that the company would "always want to stay that way". This statement came on the heels of more speculation that EMI was once again a target for prospective buyers.

Just as Tony Wadsworth was being appointed as president and CEO of EMI UK – after a number of years as head of the company's Parlophone division and in the wake of an offer from rival Warner Music to become head of its UK operation – the company confirmed an approach had been made.

While EMI refused to name the interested party, the City was quick to put its money on Canadian company Seagram with Bertelsmann, Disney and Sony the next three favourites. For its part Seagram dismissed talks with EMI as "merely speculation" and added that there was "absolutely nothing" to rumours of the company also bidding for Polygram.

Mere speculation or not, the talk of a deal took EMI shares up from 465p to 511p in three days while Seagram shares, in the last week of April 1998, reached a year-long high of $59.75 on the Toronto stock exchange. Within a fortnight – as talk of auctions and bidding wars fascinated the financial community – EMI's shares shot up a further 20% to finish at a high of 607.5p

In its official statement to the stock exchange, which was also distributed to staff, EMI talked of receiving "an approach about a possible offer for the company". While EMI's share price had dropped from over 700p at the demerger from Thorn, the City reckoned rumours of a 580p offer were way off the mark, with 650p being tagged as the price that could prompt a deal.

While he refused to reveal the identity of the suitor for the hand of EMI in a marriage of the music companies, Southgate did finally admit that he met with Seagram president and CEO Edgar Bronfman in both London and Los Angeles, but denied that he had set a minimum takeover price of £7 a share.

Speaking 20 years after the event Southgate confirms that he always suspected that Bronfman had "other fish to fry", a reference to the Canadian executive's interest in Polygram, the music division of the Dutch-owned Philips corporation.

"We always knew the alternative for Bronfman was Polygram and we also knew that Philips had decided to sell recorded music – which EMI was not allowed to buy," says Southgate, who understands why Bronfman would be attracted to Polygram. "I think in many respects that Bronfman might have preferred to have bought EMI but Polygram was an easy step to become the biggest record company in the world virtually overnight."

As Bronfman's interest in EMI began to wane – put off by either the asking price or the possibility of acquiring Polygram – EMI responded by calling time on all takeover talks in mid-May, three days after Philips announced it was prepared to sell its majority 75% interest in Polygram.

Within EMI the story doing the rounds was that Bronfman had suggested a price of £6.25 a share, considerably less than the £7 share price that, it was suggested, Southgate was holding out for. It was also rumoured that when Bronfman went back to his bankers, who had advised him that EMI would want £7 a share, he was alerted to the possibility of acquiring Polygram.

Analysts, commentators and managers generally considered EMI's decision to call time on takeover talks as a mistake. According to expert music analyst Helen Snell, who says the story going round the City at the time was that Southgate actually refused to entertain an offer of 780p a share, there is no doubt that the EMI chairman got it wrong. "Without question Southgate not doing the deal [with Seagram] was a mistake and a lot of investors – who do not take kindly to not being shown offers – thought so at the time."

Fellow analyst Mark Beilby says simply that "it probably was a missed opportunity" and music journalists Phil Hardy and Emmanuel Legrand both agree that a deal with Seagram would have benefited EMI in America.

"Had EMI done the deal [it] would not have been in such deep shit in America," says Legrand, who adds that, with the two companies' combined US market share reaching around 17%, "you are a real player with close to one fifth of the US market." For his part Hardy believes it would have been a "wonderful deal" that would have given EMI better access to American repertoire.

While Rod Smallwood, long-time manager of veteran EMI act Iron Maiden, takes the view that any deal would have been a mistake – "We didn't want EMI to end up as part of MCA or anybody else because it would change the company's worldwide structure" – fellow manager Pete Jenner suggests that while MCA was "a useless company" it would have delivered "some all-important US repertoire" to EMI.

Former Sony executive Paul Russell also believes that EMI combining with Seagram would have definitely made a difference but "how much of a difference one will never know", while Eric Nicoli, still an EMI non-executive director at the time of the talks, also views it as a missed opportunity.

"With hindsight a sale to Seagram at between £6 and £7 [a share] would have been a good move and we might have been the Universal of today. I believe it would have been a good combination," says the man who would later oversee a number of failed merger bids.

One man who is less than convinced about the wisdom of major music companies trying to buy or merge with each other is long-time manager Ed Bicknell. "I used to watch these things with considerable interest," says the man who was an executive with the renowned William Morris Agency until 2008, "and I'm not sure if any of the mergers turned out how the people involved thought they would."

While he agrees that the big-money deals have nothing to do with the artists signed to the various companies, Bicknell suggests that what he calls "the corporatisation of the music process" does eventually impact on the artistic community. "Acts did begin to think they were being bought and sold and no act – no matter how big they are – had any impact on what was going on."

The talk of a deal with Seagram, and the potential linking of its MCA operation with EMI, rekindled the issue of EMI's performance in America for Bob Mercer, who joined EMI in the UK in the early 1970s and became managing director of its Group Repertoire Division before relocating to America in the 1980s.

Now retained by EMI, Sony and Universal to oversee the successful *Now* compilation series in the US, he is of the opinion that from the mid 1990s EMI was "not viewed as any sort of competent company". Despite having hits and experiencing "the whole Garth Brooks phenomenon", Capitol, according to Mercer, did gain much-needed industry profile . . . but at a cost.

"They had done a deal whereby they could potentially lose money on almost every Brooks' record they sold," says Mercer, who contends that the deal was general knowledge throughout the US music industry. Apparently Brooks' contract, which included a sliding royalty rate that reached close to 40% at the top end, gave the singer control of the marketing spend on his albums while Capitol collected its money from the distribution of the records.

However, when the marketing budgets controlled by the hugely successful country singer ran into millions of dollars per album, the company struggled to cover these costs and ended up making little or no profit. "So, despite the fact that Brooks was selling more records than The Beatles, everybody's feeling was 'big fucking deal' if you're not making any money out of it."

Mercer, who worked closely with Kate Bush, The Rolling Stones, Pink Floyd, Queen and the individual members of The Beatles, and briefly headed up Paul McCartney's MPL company, says quite simply that EMI "never figured it out in the US and that's the reason they're in the position they are in right now".

Echoing those concerns about EMI's American operations is Iron Maiden co-manager Andy Taylor, who even turned down the opportunity to switch his band from Capitol to Virgin in America. "That seemed like an out-of-the-frying-pan-into-the-fire situation to us. In fact we had so many problems with Capitol after all the good years in the 1980s that we left."

For fellow manager Jenner, America was "the fundamental problem EMI always had" and it meant that acts that consistently sold well in the UK and Europe failed in the US. "The company never forced it through in America so the smart people did deals with EMI but excluded America from the deal."

It is also Jenner's view that EMI was never going to be bought by Seagram, Disney or Sony, who reportedly went after the company in the years following its demerger from Thorn. He believes that a business involved in the emerging new technologies of the 1990s would have been a better bet. "I always thought the dot.com people would buy EMI. As we got into the dot.com era it made sense for one of them to own a record company," says the member of the executive board of the Music Managers Forum.

The media too were far from impressed by EMI's performance in America despite the company claiming a US market share of over 12%, which was backed up by the Nielsen SoundScan album distribution shares for 1997 allocating EMI fourth place with 12.6%.

These figures emerged on the back of Brooks becoming the all-time highest-selling American artist in the US and The Spice Girls' album *Spice* coming in as the biggest-selling album in America with sales of 5.3 million. But according to journalist Hardy, "Capitol Records was never a great calling card for EMI", and this was compounded by a distinct lack of big-selling international acts from America. "US repertoire was the one thing that EMI could not bring to regions like Europe and Asia."

Concerns about the company's performance in America saw Capitol Records' president, Gary Gersh, lose his job after five years in charge. He was replaced in June 1998 by Roy Lott, who took on responsibility for EMI's flagship US label alongside his role as deputy president EMI Recorded Music North America.

It wasn't a move that pleased everybody as the team at Courtyard Management is quick to point out. Bryce Edge and Chris Hufford went to great lengths to get to know Berry and promote the future of their acts Radiohead and Supergrass, and they quickly spotted a difference in his attitude as the US business struggled.

"Ken changed and we knew something was going on," says Hufford before adding, "After Gersh went it all turned weird." For Edge, Gersh being replaced by Lott represented a major change. "You couldn't necessarily believe what Gersh said but as a president he did inspire people and he was the best pitcher of a project I have ever seen."

Compared with his predecessor, Lott, who had moved to EMI Music three months earlier, was, according to Edge, "the worst president of a record company you could ever meet" and the managers showed their displeasure by having Lott banned from Radiohead's next album launch in 2000.

"At an EMI conference where we were launching *Kid A* we had to beg the EMI UK people to ban Roy Lott from the meetings, because we did not want him involved in the marketing of the record," explains Edge. "He was the head of the US label and we had just sold millions of copies there but we did not want him involved."

The manager of million-sellers Blur was no more impressed with EMI's US management structure. From the outset Chris Morrison had opted for Virgin as the label for his band in America rather than the long-standing Capitol imprint – "The industry knew that Capitol was not a successful company and I saw Virgin as more maverick" – but even he wasn't prepared for a system that brought him four different label chiefs in little over ten years.

And, despite the changes at the top, both Blur and Damon Albarn's offshoot Gorillaz still managed to come through with million-sellers and hit albums, which prompted Morrison to explain to the company's leaders, "I don't need your fucking presidents, just give me your company. It helps if you've got good presidents but it isn't necessary."

Former music journalist Martin Talbot believes that EMI had set its sights firmly on the British music market during the 1990s. "My perception of EMI was that it was rooted in the UK business rather than international. It was a UK company that, while not the biggest in the market, was certainly widely respected. It was the company that everybody aspired to be, particularly its Parlophone label."

And for Talbot, one-time editor of European music magazine *fono*, it was the success of Parlophone that led directly to its chief Tony Wadsworth – "one of the most admired executives in the UK business" – eventually being named head of EMI UK.

Within nine months of Southgate abandoning talks, and the possibility of any potential deals with Seagram or anybody else, a new corporation was created that promptly became the biggest music company in the world. Bronfman finally took the plunge and succeeded in acquiring Polygram from Philips in a deal worth over $10 billion.

The world's most expensive music purchase created a new, giant Universal Music operation with an estimated 25% of the world music market – nearly 10% ahead of its nearest rival Sony – and led to a new round of EMI-bashing in the media.

Southgate was compared to Charles Dickens' Miss Havisham, who was left standing at the altar by a man who married someone else. The questions in every story were whether there would be another suitor and what price they would be prepared to pay for EMI. The speculation was that potential buyers were thin on the ground, EMI was overvalued and the company's share price – down to 523p on news of the Universal/Polygram deal – would, according to one unnamed analyst, "go down the toilet".

Accepted wisdom was that a fair price for an EMI share was now around 450p, which, analysts claimed, made a mockery of Southgate's rumoured demand for 700p a share. "EMI wanted to play clever and has come unstuck," said one broker, while respected industry researcher and analyst Cliff Dane suggested that EMI did not have to link with anyone to survive.

The man who heads up Music Research Publishing saw an amusing side to Seagram's acquisition of Polygram. "Wasn't it funny how it came about? Bronfman didn't seem to care whether it was EMI or Polygram. It was a bit like asking, 'Do you want to go out with me? No, OK, well have you got a sister?'"

After missing out on a deal with Seagram and its Universal Music division, Southgate surprised everyone in September 1998 by expressing an interest in buying Polygram Filmed Entertainment, which was put up for sale by Bronfman following his acquisition of Polygram Music. However, just 24 hours before the final deadline for bids for the company behind *Trainspotting* and *Lock, Stock And Two Smoking Barrels*, EMI was reported to have pulled out, which seemed to please the stock market as its shares rose 9p on the news.

But the increase was short-lived as EMI warned that its results for the first half of 1998 would suffer from falling sales in Asia Pacific (down 15%) and Latin America (down 6%), alongside "flat" sales in major European markets including the UK. A 9% increase in EMI's US business was not sufficient to halt a 20% drop, to £91.2 million, in operating profits for the year up to September 1998 from reduced sales of £994 million.

These numbers came despite the company releasing two of the UK's biggest-selling albums, from The Verve (*Urban Hymns*) and Robbie Williams (*Life Thru A Lens*), and followed Southgate describing EMI, at the company's annual general meeting, as "the most profitable business in the music industry".

Around the same time as the AGM – in July 1998 – EMI reportedly settled into negotiations with Ken Berry and Martin Bandier, who had both joined the board in the aftermath of Fifield's departure. The company's remuneration committee was looking to improve on record music chief Berry's basic $1.3 million salary and music publishing head Bandier's basic $2 million deal.

With Seagram out of the picture there appeared to be no obvious prospective buyer for EMI and while there was talk of Murdoch's News Corporation still holding a candle for the British major, the Australian entrepreneur settled for a smaller catch when he took a controlling interest in independent music label Mushroom, to add to the Rawkus label started by James Murdoch.

However Michael Dornemann, head of the German media giant Bertelsmann, stirred the flames in October 1998 when he announced that he would be prepared to buy EMI if the share price became "attractive".

His comment brought a stinging response from Southgate, who told *The Los Angeles Times*, "Dornemann sure talks a lot of rubbish doesn't he? What makes him talk like that, where are his company results? We never see them. Why don't you ask him how his record club is going at the moment? From what I hear it's in the toilet."

Throughout 1998 Southgate and EMI were plagued by media stories concerning Mr & Mrs Berry. The Ken and Nancy show was making headlines and in the main they weren't the sort that the company was looking for.

In December 1997 *The New York Times* carried a short item that began with news of The Rolling Stones' Bridges To Babylon tour being the top-grossing tour of the year, and then went on to declare that Nancy Berry was "one of the most talked-about topics in the music industry", before suggesting that allegations of nepotism regarding her promotion were rife. The short piece ended by mentioning that her husband denied all the allegations against her.

The following February the prestigious *Wall Street Journal* printed a lengthy feature entitled "Ken and Nancy's rock'n'roll circus", which was reprinted in a number of major British newspapers and added to the discomfort of both the Berrys and EMI.

The article suggested that Mrs Berry's "high-profile appointment only cranked up the negative buzz about her in the music industry" and mentioned allegations of favouritism and that she was difficult to work for.

It was also suggested that Southgate had looked into the matter and even reportedly asked Richard Branson to talk to Berry about "getting his wife under control", and was evidently so incensed by an article in *Forbes* magazine that carried unsubstantiated allegations about Nancy Berry that he reportedly wrote to editor in chief Steve Forbes describing the article as "malicious innuendo".

The stories were understandably all denied by Mrs Berry, who defended her forthright management style. Even the success of acts like Lenny Kravitz, Janet Jackson and Smashing Pumpkins didn't begin to placate those who questioned publicly how the husband and wife team shared their executive responsibilities, while *Billboard* magazine dubbed Mrs Berry "the Hillary Clinton of the global recording business".

For his part Berry claimed to be bewildered by the attacks on his wife and commented, "If we knew people were going to write malicious articles we wouldn't have made the change."

One of those closest to the action within Virgin America was Ray Cooper and the head of Virgin Records US outlines how things were run on Mrs Berry's watch. While he focused on marketing and his co-MD Ashley Newton was in charge of A&R, Mrs Berry ran her own separate division.

"She ran special projects and we ran the label," says Cooper, who still lives in California. "Some acts didn't want to be special projects, like The

Spice Girls who always went through the label, but if you were, it meant that Nancy would throw the black AmEx card at you, which was a weird way of doing business although it wasn't necessarily dangerous."

According to fellow Virgin executive Jeremy Silver, artists such as Lenny Kravitz, The Rolling Stones, Janet Jackson and David Bowie were "vehicles of Nancy's famous special projects department and were subject to a totally different set of rules from anything else the label dealt with".

The company's former new technology executive goes on to explain, "Nancy cherry-picked the most expensive, most valued artists plus the new acts she wanted to engage with. In theory there was also an element of the big button about it all – a global operation at the centre rather than the federated efforts that were distributed among the territories."

Describing Mrs Berry as "a socialite whose business became her life", Cooper still believes that the media and the industry's treatment of her bordered on sexist victimisation. "There have been a lot of people who have run record companies who have dilettante lives but because they were men they were never fingered. In the end she tripped over herself but sexism was against her."

While Cooper admits that Berry did react to his wife's executive behaviour – "he would take her aside from time to time and talk to her" – he concludes that unless Berry was going to be there all the time, it was going to be hard for the top man in EMI Music to control his other half. "She was so passionate about what she did."

Although he left Virgin at the time of the takeover by EMI, Jon Webster remained as a consultant to Berry and admits that his boss didn't deal with the problem called Nancy very well. He confesses that he was one of those ex-Virgin people who sat on the outside looking in at it all in astonishment. "There was a whole issue about the way that she rose through the company; the great dichotomy was that you were never sure what he [Ken Berry] knew and approved of when it came to Nancy, who was a great driver of things but created a climate of compulsion and fear within the company."

Close to the end of 1998 analysts Dresdner Kleinwort Benson published a 68-page report on EMI, detailing the possibilities of a takeover bid and the company's potential for the future. The headline news was its front-page banner "EMI Time To Bail Out", with its recommendation to shareholders to SELL their shares rather than HOLD them.

It also forecast profit warnings, increased piracy, problems in the US market and reduced popularity for The Spice Girls, estimating that the group made £64 million for EMI in 1997–1998 but were expected to make only £15 million in 1998–1999.

The document concluded that "the balance of probability weighs against a bid for EMI at present", while forecasting that the company's sales would be flat for three years and profits would decline by 23% over the same period. The report gave EMI a D on its five-point CRAM (comparative risk assessment measure), which translated as "weak/below average".

The report also acknowledged the growing importance of digital online distribution in the international music business but warned that "technology is a double-edged sword", with piracy likely to increase while record companies faced a major issue over the protection of their copyrights on digital sales.

For Silver, EMI's investment in the emerging digital business was all-important as its companies around the world opted for local websites that ultimately had to be reined in and brought under control from the centre. "It all felt terribly anarchic – there was no hard product and there were no rules about what you made available," recalls the man who was in charge of EMI's new technology business in the late 1990s.

According to Silver, the whole business was run on a shoestring and the only way for EMI to make any money was by licensing its content to the wide range of new-technology companies that were emerging from the woodwork on an almost daily basis. "These new companies were popping out all over the place, being venture-backed by private investors, and basically we worried less about whether they would make money or not and thought more about the cash handouts we could get from them up front."

But while Silver was busy trying to build a business, there were those who felt that EMI's efforts left a lot to be desired. "I think it's fair to say that in the late 1990s EMI, along with most of the record industry, lost the plot with digital technology," says Tim Clark, manager of Robbie Williams who released ten hit singles and two million-selling number one albums in the run-up to the new millennium.

"Digital drove a panzer division through copyright law and copyright law was what allowed record companies to exist in the first place," says Clark, a partner in the IE management company. "But if a law is un-enforceable it ain't a law and I think EMI were slow to realise that, plus I don't think anybody realised how quickly CD sales were going to drop off."

Agreeing with Clark's concerns, music business analyst Helen Snell acknowledges that the industry faced a problem in solving the issue of rights in the new digital age. "The record industry was shockingly slow to react but the major issue was a complete unwillingness to accept that this was a reality."

Comparing the new record industry to the old days of Tin Pan Alley – "the music business originated on a song-by-song basis" – Snell concludes, "This was all about unbundling the CD model and people cherry-picking the three or four songs they wanted to download and share. The only way any record company was going to get anything from the internet was by radically changing the way they operated, changing the way they went about selling music to consumers."

While there were people who believed that EMI stood by the established bricks and mortar business of selling music through shops for longer than its rivals, it was also apparent that all record companies faced a dilemma in trying to work out the right business model for both the industry and the consumer. "The record industry took a confrontational stance," says Emmanuel Legrand, "rather than thinking that maybe there was something out there we should investigate."

Supposedly testing the market and trying to prove to shareholders and the City that it was proactive in the new digital arena, EMI was guilty, according to Phil Hardy, of not understanding "the transformation that was taking place around it".

In his 2008 article about EMI that appeared in *The Daily Telegraph* under the heading "A giant at war with itself", writer Robert Sandall observed that the company could and should have invested more in the digital download market, which, "like all the other majors [EMI] chose initially to view as a threat rather than an opportunity".

Davin McDermott worked in finance at EMI from 1997 until 2002 and recalls that the company's attitude was to go for a share of the equity. "[It] wanted to share in what was going on around the dot.com bubble but I don't think there was any real regard that this was a long-term business."

He goes on to explain EMI's attitude to the new digital music business in the late 1990s. "[It] wanted equity share and [it] did quite well – [it] did a few big deals going back as far as 1997 and 1998 where [it] pocketed some good returns."

One of the most lucrative deals from that period came in June 1999 when Silver met up with a company called musicmaker in New York just as they were about to go public. "We got them to pull their initial public offering (IPO) of shares on the stock market and quickly licensed to them all the EMI catalogue we could," explains Silver. While this deal excluded The Beatles, The Rolling Stones, Janet Jackson and a number of other major acts who had not agreed a digital deal with the company, it still enabled EMI to take 50% equity in the company.

This new business model involved tracks being made available to the public, who chose their favourites to be burned onto a CD by music-maker. The new disc was then mailed out to the customer.

After the initial public offering was delayed, the musicmaker company went ahead with its IPO in early 2000 and the stock shot through the roof. "EMI netted $30 million in profit by trading the stock on day one," says Silver, who also confirms that the business was short-lived. "We were never able to fulfil the digital commitment we made and the company folded a year or so later."

Silver views this as possibly the "original dot.com black box revenues" deal. "There was lots of money on the basis of all the catalogue but none of it was ascribable to any one act so no distribution of revenues was required . . . or so went the internal argument with acts and managers."

The year 1999 arrived with the departure of Southgate as EMI chairman – and the identity of his successor – as the main talking points within both the company and the industry. The music business's global village was alive with rumour and counter-rumour, but by focusing their attention on Mrs Berry, the media had reduced her husband's chances of landing the top job as head of the EMI Group.

And, as the company's financial year came to an end, so the name of Eric Nicoli emerged from the pack as the new boss of EMI. Recruited from United Biscuits (UBS), 48-year-old Nicoli was named in early March as the man to take over on August 1, 1999, with Southgate retiring a year early from the role he first took up at Thorn EMI in 1985 and con-tinued in after the demerger in 1996.

It was also announced that EMI non-executive director Sir Dominic Cadbury and finance director, Simon Duffy, would serve as joint deputy chairmen, with Berry and Bandier remaining as the heads of recorded music and music publishing respectively.

In a statement EMI told the media and the music industry that, "They [the board] have unanimously concluded that the appointment of an executive chairman who brings complementary skills and experience would provide the most effective structure for EMI."

This announcement came despite the fact that one member of the EMI main board apparently advised his colleagues that naming Nicoli as chairman "was the biggest mistake you've made".

While UBS shares rose slightly – just 2p – on the news of Nicoli's appointment, EMI's dropped 8¼p to 440p and slowed to 430p by the end of the week, but the chairman expressed no dismay at the City's reaction to his new role. "I would have expected some mild surprise bordering on disappointment because a music industry big hitter was not appointed."

This came on the back of the *Financial Times*' Lex column pulling no punches and proclaiming that, after overseeing the fall in the UBS share price, "Mr Nicoli will certainly not have the problems of having to live up to high expectations."

For former EMI Music chief Bhaskar Menon, the appointment of Nicoli represented a new name in the history of the famous British company and it wasn't one that inspired confidence. "Nicoli seemed to share his predecessor's lack of familiarity with the music/entertainment/media business."

Speaking in mid-March 1999 Nicoli told the world that "organic growth" was his first priority but broadening it to include related entertainment or media areas was a "potentially attractive option". And in answer to his critics he announced, "I much prefer to be underestimated than the opposite."

Close to the end of March, EMI's share price was back up, this time to 436p as City investors and analysts were treated to an outline of the company's plans at a day-long conference. One fund manager described the mood as upbeat and added, "There was a very strong sense that this was a very powerful business which [sic] has a very powerful potential future, particularly with the way technology is changing."

Followers of the music business were quick to come forward with a variety of ideas to assist the new boss of EMI in his job, with the long overdue merging of the EMI and Virgin operations at the top of the list followed by the possibility of getting into bed with a rival company to combine distribution, although the issue of a takeover or merger was not far behind.

Nicoli was quick to put a damper on all ideas of a sell-out or even a link with a rival operation such as Bertelsmann or News Corp. "It's a definite 'no'," was his reaction in April 1999, although *Music Business International* editor Ajax Scott came up with another proposal in an editorial in the same month. "Perhaps the most radical strategy for Nicoli to pursue would be to take EMI private, thereby bypassing the need to produce six-monthly results to please shareholders."

Recalling the events surrounding the appointment of his successor in 1999, Southgate confirms that none of the major music players – Universal's Alain Levy or Warner's Michael Fuchs or Ramon Lopez – were ever in the equation, but he does admit approaching one experienced executive. "I did try to get Clive Calder from Zomba but he said he'd got this extraordinary option to sell his company and wasn't going anywhere."

With that being the case, the board of EMI plumped for Nicoli who, in Southgate's words, was "a suit – a me, if you like – not a rock'n'roller". While suggesting that not staying on as non-executive chairman was a mistake, Southgate easily defines the brief that was handed on to Nicoli.

"He was to carry on and find the merger. EMI needed a partner and he was put in as the suit to find a deal," he says, before going on to acknowledge the major shortcoming of his chosen successor as the new head of a global music company. "Eric has no knowledge of music, no history and knows nothing about it – absolutely nothing."

For his part Nicoli claims that he had good skills as a communicator and that was one of the things that EMI needed most, plus he was a good general manager, but he denies being installed to follow a predefined course of action. "If Colin [Southgate] said his idea of my role as his successor was to be 'a suit and do a deal' it was never discussed with me."

Speaking nine years after his appointment, Nicoli defines how he saw the role he took on in 1999. "I saw my job as being to maximise shareholder value with or without major deals. There had been rumours that we were being taken over. I had different audiences but I was always mindful of the people who worked for me and in March 1999 it was absolutely not in my mind to sell the company."

But it has to be said that Southgate was not the only person who had doubts about Nicoli's suitability for the role as chief executive of Britain's largest and most famous music company. Music writer Phil Hardy confirms that the debate at the time was focused on what Nicoli knew about music, "and what came out of that was the fact that he hadn't been a terribly good businessman at United Biscuits". The long-time editor of *Music & Copyright* also concluded that there was only one thing on the new man's mind. "It was clear from his actions that his concern was to sell or buy."

These concerns are echoed by experienced analyst Mike Hilton, who says that describing Nicoli's naming as EMI chief executive as a surprise is an understatement. "You were thinking, 'Where did this come from?' You could understand it if he had a great track record running a media company with talent; he was in the food business and his record at UB wasn't great."

EMI PR director David Hughes – who dealt with the City and media on a daily basis – was more aware than most of the jibes that were being hurled at the new EMI boss. "Sadly the City didn't like or respect Eric and from the outset the media branded him with biscuit connotations – Mr Wagon Wheel, Yorkie man or Jammy Dodger."

Hughes also noted the difference between the old and new guard. "The City's view of him was that he was not serious or effective, while Southgate was a very dominant man. It was probably a privilege for the media to interview him."

The annual report for 1998–1999 boasted that EMI was the world's third-largest recorded music company, operating in close to 50 countries and employing 10,000 people. Its recorded music division had a roster of over 1,500 artists, while as the world leader in music publishing it owned over one million songs.

The continuing success of EMI Music Publishing did not go unnoticed, and the operation that Southgate headlined as a highlight of his EMI career – "We created the biggest publishing company in the world, which is a wonderful business and has been very profitable" – also had its supporters outside the company.

Former rival music executive and current partner in his own publishing company Paul Russell believes it is "a fantastic publishing company", while commentator Martin Talbot recalls that the company that was consistently crowned publisher of the year throughout the 1990s, "dominated the business throughout that period". His assessment of the highly successful UK publishing division was that "they were the ones who had ambition and wanted to be biggest; they didn't shirk when it came to signing the cheques".

In terms of recorded music, while its global market share fell from14.2% to 13.5%, EMI could lay claim to the biggest-selling album in Japanese history thanks to Hikaru Utada's seven million sales, while Robbie Williams was the UK's best-selling solo artist and Virgin the most successful UK label for the fourth year running.

But despite these successes the company's balance sheet showed a 26% drop in pre-tax profits to £227 million, which Southgate described as "in line with expectations". He opened his final chairman's report by describing EMI as "a jewel of a business" and concluded by confirming that "the independent EMI is in good hands and good shape".

When he finally brought his EMI career to an end after the July 1999 AGM, Southgate was generous in his praise for the man who was taking over the helm. Despite his later criticism of the new EMI boss, he said at the time that Nicoli had impressed him with his ability to get to grips with the business and "developed an excellent working relationship with his team".

The two men at the forefront of Nicoli's EMI team were Ken Berry and Martin Bandier and the chief executive felt that both men were comfortable with him – as a non-music man – taking over the reins. In the City, however, there were still some mutterings of discontent. "We put it in a flowery manner," explains Mike Hilton, "but we pointed out that nobody in the City knows what these two guys are doing and you've got this new guy over the top. Berry was kept in a dark room until Nicoli and was brought out because Eric didn't know the first thing about music."

For Hilton this situation posed another problem for the British music company as Berry and his cohort from publishing, Bandier, took on new importance in the management structure. "All the money went to these two guys because the other people didn't know the industry and if they lost these two they were screwed," he says. He also suggests that talent industries are notoriously fickle and, as a result, another possible scenario was looming. "I have no doubt that these two executives were saying 'I'm key to this whole thing – if I go, the team goes.'"

As an outsider closely involved in the digital operations of rival company Warner Music International, Pete Downton looked at EMI's digital strategy and saw something that "had no consistency in terms of the kind of deals they were doing". Initially he considered EMI's downfall to be their inability to manage the new business on a regional level, but this went hand-in-hand with another concern – the need for money up front.

"From the outset EMI were always advance focused. Once they got themselves organised it was then all about the advance and they didn't look at recurring revenues and building a long-term business . . . it was very much about getting the cheque and moving on to the next deal."

Before the end of 1999 the chief executive of EMI Music, Berry, proclaimed that the company's revenues from new media in the coming few years would be balanced by investment in the business and added, "We are going to make it so much easier for people to get new music."

At the same time as Nicoli took over the reins at EMI so Jay Samit was joining as senior vice president New Media. Recruited by Berry, the American executive says that his new boss knew things had to change in order for the music business and the company to survive. "Ken had the wisdom to see that the business had a different future and we bought in a ton of money and modernised the business at the same time."

Claiming that pursuing the new digital business was "a colossal thing to do" as piracy impacted on the traditional business, Samit set about preparing his plans for the future. He presented to the EMI board the details of various dot.com companies that were dedicated solely to music. "Instead of doing a traditional deal, I favoured partnering with these companies and making some of that upside – and it proved very effective."

Unconcerned whether these upstart companies were likely to stay the course, Samit and EMI took the view that whatever they did and however long they did it for, these new outfits would do their business "on the back of our artists".

Unfortunately for EMI its existing artists' contracts did not give it the rights to uncouple songs and sell them individually to the burgeoning digital download operations. However, taking the view that if it did not supply tracks to the public then consumers could steal them, it took a bold decision, according to Samit, to, "do as many deals as we can and then see what happens".

Anticipating the reaction from artists and their managers, EMI then divided its roster of acts into two camps. "The ones who were going to sue us or audit us and then everybody else," explains Samit, whose job it was to meet up with artists and managers of artists on the excluded list, which included many of the company's most successful acts like The Beatles, The Rolling Stones, Pink Floyd, Garth Brooks and The Beach Boys.

Samit eventually persuaded all but five of the 'excluded' acts to be part of EMI's digital download strategy – both The Beatles and Brooks were among those who remained uncommitted – and nowadays reflects proudly on the job he did for EMI. "We did 120 deals and made $200 million in profits for EMI and at one point we did a deal every nine days."

However, for UK-based media analyst Helen Snell the new media business plan put in place by Samit was seriously flawed. "EMI's internet model of doing deal after deal was a ridiculous strategy, but then I don't think any record company had a decent strategy." And Snell is also quick to explain how the companies should have reacted to the internet business when it arrived on their doorstep. "They should have been much more forward looking and the minute it came along they should have thought, 'This is going to change our business' and adopted it much more quickly."

At the same time as EMI announced its interim results for the half-year up to September 1999, analysts ABN AMRO issued a 12-page company report that acknowledged the extraordinary impact on the figures of Japanese artist Utada – they reckoned her sales alone had boosted the company's Japanese market share by 3% – and the £24.8 million reaped from the sale of the company's 10% stake in musicmaker.

Overall the figures showed a 10% increase in pre-tax profits to £75.4 million, however EMI's UK market share was down nearly 3% to 18.8% and the drop in America was an even more worrying four points to 10%. Globally, according to official IFPI figures, EMI stood at third place with an 11.8% share, behind Universal (21.7%) and Sony (17%) but ahead of rivals Warner (11.4%) and BMG (10.1%).

In fact EMI were not market leaders in any of the world's major regions during 1999, finishing second in Europe and Japan (behind Universal and Sony respectively) and fourth in Latin America, just 0.3% ahead of last placed Warner.

EMI's poor performance in the US was brought home in the IFPI's 1999 yearbook, which showed that not a single EMI release figured in the lists of the ten best-selling albums and singles for 1999, and this came on the back of the 1998 list, which showed only one EMI title among the American best-sellers – Garth Brooks' double live album, which made number seven.

While the general consensus was that EMI did well in exploiting local repertoire through its raft of companies around the world, the spotlight was always focused on its performance in America. And, according to Emmanuel Legrand, that's just as it should be. "When you have a market that is about a third of the global market and you are not a major player there, then it's a major problem on a worldwide basis because that repertoire can also travel further afield."

The French-born music journalist concludes that it was the lack of US repertoire that forced EMI's companies in places like France, Germany, Spain and Italy to promote and sell their own local artists and rack up million-selling hits along the way.

While admitting that he has never really understood EMI's problems in the US, Legrand puts forward an interesting suggestion involving the shape of its Capitol Records office in Los Angeles. "I have a theory that when you have a circular building then you never see the angles and never have a straight view on anything – I believe it does affect your psyche."

Although he was never based in the legendary Capitol Tower, former

Virgin US executive Ray Cooper still looks back on the company's overall performance in the biggest market in the world and asks, "Why didn't EMI ever get it right in America?" He settles for the argument about perception being more important than fact.

"In an industry where perception is 95% of the business then the perception about EMI is that the US has always been a negative, that they'll never get it right because they compromised."

As the old millennium drew to a close, ABN AMRO's experts concluded in their November 1999 report that, with both new media and CD piracy posing an increased threat alongside ongoing depressed sales in Asia and Latin America, EMI was a "low growth consumer cyclical" company and the best advice they could give to shareholders was to sell.

The London-based media section of the international analysts, with offices throughout Europe in addition to Australia and America, also announced that while they considered Bertelsmann the most logical suitor, "the well of potential buyers for EMI is now drying up".

While their assessment of the situation regarding a possible deal involving EMI made perfect sense – after all nobody had come forward with a bid when the company's shares hit a rock-bottom price of 312p in October 1998 – both the financial world and the music industry were in for a surprise with the dawning of the new millennium.

CHAPTER 5

Rock The House

(Gorillaz, EMI 2001)

WITHIN the first two weeks of January 2000 two major media deals made headline news and, while one impacted almost solely on the music industry, the other was a truly global landmark merger that, it was predicted, would change the face of the whole entertainment industry . . . and another blockbuster deal was soon to follow.

In a deal worth a rumoured $200 million, Warner Music Group chairman Roger Ames announced the sale of his London Records operation to Warner Music International, the company responsible for Warner Music's activities outside the US.

Following nearly two decades in charge of London Records – which he is rumoured to have gained control of via an escalating share basis after it was revived by Polygram in the early 1980s – Ames sold up to focus on his role as head of the New York-based Warner Music, the division of the mighty Time Warner corporation that oversaw Warner Music International (WMI).

However, Time Warner's attention was firmly focused on the deal that saw them being acquired by America Online (AOL) for $183 billion. In what was claimed to be the biggest merger in business history, the combined value of AOL and Time Warner was reckoned to be a staggering $350 billion (£220 billion) and it left the traditional Time Warner company with a minority 45% share of the new company, which perhaps reflected the importance of new media and the potential digital delivery of music to a mass market.

The AOL/Time Warner deal also had an extraordinary impact on EMI's share price across a seven-day period either side of the announcement. It closed at 591p on Friday January 7, rose to 683.5p on the following Monday and then on Tuesday January 11 – the day after the deal was announced – rocketed to a three-year high of 721.5p.

By the end of the week it had slipped back to 686p and analysts speculated that it was still too high to bring out a potential bidder, even though the proposed AOL/Time Warner deal was deemed to have made EMI a more attractive proposition. Bizarrely the organization that found EMI most attractive was in fact Time Warner, which was keen on merging its Warner Music Group with the EMI Group in a £12 billion deal that would create the world's largest music company.

News of the deal was broken in *The Sunday Telegraph* on January 23, 2000, one day ahead of the announcement to the Stock Exchange of the proposed merger. While the *Sunday Telegraph* article suggested that the City would be "stunned" by the news, it also came as a complete surprise to both members of staff and those closely associated with the companies.

At the time I was retained on a consultancy basis as head of corporate communications for WMI, and the first I knew about the proposed deal was when I read the Sunday newspaper story. This was followed closely by a call from the head of WMI who told me to be at the offices of London investment bank Warburg Dillon Read at 6.30 a.m. on Monday, January 24, when the official announcements would be made.

The *Sunday Telegraph* story, written by Damian Reece and Neil Bennett, suggested that EMI would become a majority-owned subsidiary of Time Warner with Eric Nicoli giving up his role as chairman of EMI, while music chief Ken Berry was tipped to be a senior executive in the new business.

The speculation was that while the new company's combined sales would exceed £5 billion, their joint overheads would be over £3 billion and these could be reduced by as much as £500 million. There was also mention of secret talks taking place in London over the weekend prior to the official announcement between an EMI team led by Nicoli and Time Warner's senior staff including music chief Ames.

In fact the first conversation about a possible EMI/Warner Music merger had taken place over three months earlier, just over a month after Nicoli had taken over as head of EMI. "Fairly early in my tenure, in mid-September 1999," recounts Nicoli, "I met Dick Parsons [a senior Time Warner executive] and Roger Ames together with Ken Berry in London and we discussed the possibility of a combination of the two businesses."

The conversation took place at a time when the whole industry was faced with a flat market for recorded music as opposed to one that had been predicted to grow. By merging their operations it was clear that EMI and Warner would be buying time and gathering together its firepower in order to invest in the new technology that was going to boost the music business in the future.

"I thought there was a compelling strategic case for combining those two businesses," says Nicoli, "and so fairly quickly we put together our deal, which would have created spectacular value for our shareholders."

Despite newspaper speculation, the official plan was for Nicoli and Parsons to be joint chairmen of the new company, which was to be 50.1% owned by Time Warner, with Nicoli fulfilling the role on a full-time basis while Parsons also continued to act as chairman of Time Warner.

The day-to-day running of the number one music company would revolve around Ames as chief executive officer and Berry as chief operating officer, and the thought process from within EMI was that while the new structure would give Time Warner management control, EMI's shareholders would be part of what was described by one senior executive as "a much, much better business".

While acknowledging that the power base in the new company would shift to the American conglomerate, Nicoli is adamant about the advantages for EMI and its shareholders, who would receive £1 per share if the deal went through. "Technically we were selling the company to Time Warner for a premium but our shareholders would be retaining 50% of a much bigger and better entity."

According to reports, the combined EMI/Warner Music operation would command a global market share of 27.5%, giving them a 6.4% lead over Universal, while the combination of Warner Chappell Music and EMI Music Publishing, already the two leading music publishers in the world, would mean a 30% share of the world market.

And even as details of the merger were being digested around the world – and staff at the two companies were receiving e-mails from their chief executives telling them the news – there was speculation that, whatever happened to the EMI, Parlophone, Capitol, Atlantic, Elektra and Warner Brothers labels, Virgin – reflecting Berry's senior role – would remain autonomous.

Speaking a few days after the official announcement both Ames and Berry insisted that no decisions had been made as to the future structure of the combined business. "We're going to try and make it, in so far as we can, non-political in what the selection and what the structure is," was Ames' view. "I'm sure it will be a real challenge and inevitably we will get parts of it wrong but this is how we are setting about it."

For his part Berry told media, "We are not trying to make our deal work by dropping lots of artists and firing lots of staff. We want to try and preserve and protect the labels." With that said, it was confirmed that Ames and Berry were off on a whistle-stop world tour to meet with EMI and Warner Music executives in an effort, according to Ames, to calm nerves and offer reassurance. "We are going to say to them, 'Stay focused, don't get nervous, we're going to be sensitive to people's needs, it's going to take a while.'"

While the two top men gave nothing away as to how the new Warner EMI (this was how the industry referred to the new business) would operate, the music biz was quick to give its opinion to trade journal *Music Week*.

Walt Disney co-chairman Michael Eisner said, "I liked it when there were five big players. I liked it even more when there were six. When you are a content company you want to be able to move around different companies," while Zomba founder Calder commented, "Whatever the PR spin put on this by Time Warner and EMI, this 'merger' is clearly a defensive move by both of these once great music companies."

Co-manager of Robbie Williams, David Enthoven, added, "I wasn't surprised, but I'm delighted it wasn't Cable & Wireless they did the deal with," while UK Culture Secretary Chris Smith warned, "The potential change in ownership of the last major British player in the music industry of real global size must be a disappointment. On the other hand if this merger does proceed then let's look at how it will be able to happen in a way that benefits the UK music industry."

While the influential *Financial Times* said the deal made "industrial logic", it was left to a former Warner UK chairman, Rob Dickins, to sum up the historical and creative significance of the deal. "Time Warner and EMI together is a fabulous record company because you're combining the history of pop music. EMI has the most glamorous history of UK artists such as The Beatles and Pink Floyd and Warner has Neil Young, R.E.M., Madonna and the Eagles."

On a more contemporary note it would also bring together the likes of Radiohead, Blur, Robbie Williams, The Chemical Brothers and The Spice Girls under the same roof as Red Hot Chili Peppers, Alanis Morissette, The Corrs and Missy Elliott in a combined enterprise that, it was estimated, would be the number one company in seven of the world's top ten markets.

The City was equally split on the rights or wrongs of the proposed merger. In New York Michael Nathanson of brokers Sandford Bernstein argued that it was great deal for EMI shareholders. "People should open their eyes and face up to where EMI was likely to be heading in the next three years. With Time Warner they've got access to some of the best marketing platforms in the world."

On the other hand an unnamed broker described the deal, with EMI ceding control, as "rubbish" but admitted that it was probably EMI's best and possibly only option. "There was no one else out there," he said.

In the immediate aftermath of the announcement of the deal, the world was subjected to endless photographs of Ames and Berry hugging each other, but some were not convinced about the relationship. "The deal looked a bit odd because everyone was aware that Ken Berry and Roger Ames didn't like each other," says analyst Helen Snell before adding that in the circumstances the picture of them hugging each other was also "a bit odd".

There were certainly rumours of friction and resentment between the two strong but usually silent music industry giants who share a dislike of personal publicity. However, other sources suggested that there was a close personal friendship between the two men who had built up the fortunes of the London and Virgin companies respectively. An unnamed industry observer took the view that, "It took the only guys in the record business without egos to put this thing together."

As the excitement surrounding these potential major changes in the global entertainment and media businesses continued unabated, the media was left to speculate that Bertelsmann and its worldwide chief Thomas Middelhof were the biggest losers in the scenario that was unfolding. Any plans he had to link with AOL to become a force in electronic business or with EMI to create a new music major were now sunk without trace, as he watched AOL try to buy Time Warner and EMI and Warner Music attempt to merge.

The only issue on the agenda that could prevent the deals going through was the small matter of obtaining approvals from the world's anti-trust authorities, and the most rigorous of these were going to be the regulators within the European Commission.

Certainly the situation was not helped by AOL seeking approval for its purchase of Time Warner at the same time as the proposed merger of EMI and Warner Music was put on the table. Experienced rock manager Peter Jenner was convinced that trying to do a double deal was "just a prescription for a total monopoly operation".

But the overall feeling within the music business was one of optimism, with a senior EMI executive being assured by the world's top anti-trust advisers that the merger would not just be approved but approved in the first phase of the European Commission's review, which could have meant everything was done and dusted within just one month.

For Jenner a merger between EMI and Warner was "a marriage made in heaven", which was exactly the reaction of former Sony man Paul Russell. "Warner had such heritage and was a fabulous American company but traditionally was weak internationally, whereas EMI had a very weak American company and was very strong internationally."

Reflecting on the proposed merger eight years later, the head of EMI UK at the time of the deal, Tony Wadsworth, recalls, "We convinced ourselves that the merger with Warners would be a good thing because our perception was that Warners are great in America and we're not; and we're pretty good everywhere else so it looked like a complementary fit."

At the same time Chris Hufford, co-manager of Radiohead, who had racked up million-selling top ten albums all around the world for EMI, took the view that, "There was an absolute logic to the move", while his counterpart in the Blur management camp, Chris Morrison, was less enthusiastic and would have preferred a different course of action.

"I had a view that EMI should get their ship in order, stop all the deals and stop trying to merge or sell – there were other answers. The company had remarkable people, remarkable talent and you just needed to look at the bones of the skeleton and rearrange them."

Looking back at the proposed deal Virgin US chief Ray Cooper still believes the merger would have been a "brilliant" move personally, although he had some professional concerns. "Personally it would have been great because all of the things that we were bonused on would have been paid out, but while they complemented each other very well, the Warner big shots might have wanted to kick the Virgin culture a little bit or even absorb it."

With a combined Warner/EMI operation boasting a global recorded music market share of below 30%, there was little or no concern among the people who created the deal that the regulators would come up with any insurmountable problems or barriers. Even the dominant share of the world music publishing market that Warner Chappell and EMI would command – it would run to over 50% in some territories – was not considered an issue as this accounted for only about 20% of mechanical and performing rights revenues.

However, it was these figures that caused UK trade body the Association of Independent Music (AIM) to worry about the merger of the two majors. While stating that it was not fundamentally against music mergers, AIM had a concern that mergers without "behavioural, commercial and legislative remedies" would damage the whole market as well as the independent sector, according to CEO Alison Wenham.

"We were concerned about the emergence of market shares that would exceed 30% [and] 50% in smaller territories or even more," she explains. "It has always been a feature of this industry that market share buys you market power because you can dictate terms, command more of the media and manipulate the supply chain to your advantage."

While the European Commission set about running the rule over both the AOL Time Warner and Warner Music/EMI deals, there was further speculation about another deal – this time involving Bertelsmann and Sony merging their music interests. Unsurprisingly both corporations officially denied the story, which was fuelled by the German media giant's chief Middelhoff telling the *Wall Street Journal* that he could see that a match with Japanese-owned Sony would strengthen his company's global position.

In the midst of the merger talks EMI released its figures for the year ending March 2000, and while they showed an improvement on the previous year it was EMI's music-publishing division that took the honours. Thanks to a roster of writers that included Janet Jackson, Robbie Williams, Diane Warren, Sting and Puff Daddy, plus the acquisition of the important Windswept (£126 million) and Hit & Run catalogues – the latter featuring Phil Collins and Genesis songs and costing £17 million – music publishing improved its turnover by 11.8% (up to £354 million) and operating profits by 9.1% (to £95.5 million).

This corresponded with EMI's recorded music division reporting a 1.2% drop in sales (down to £2,032.5 million) alongside a 7% increase in operating profits (to £195.1 million) and the news that – according to the company's own estimates – EMI had increased market share in every region except the USA, where it slipped 3.3% to a lowly 9%, while the company's global share dropped from 13.2% to 12.5%

Boasting 30 albums that had each sold a million copies – including releases from Backstreet Boys, George Michael and D'Angelo – EMI was also bullish in its plans for the future with new releases from Robbie Williams, Spice Girls, Richard Ashcroft, Radiohead, Utada Hikaru and Snoop Dogg apparently on the schedule, along with the £24 million purchase of US label Blackground Records as part of the Virgin US operation.

Alongside announcing plans for a digital download launch in July 2000, which involved "digitising 100% of the company global content, developing business models and exploring marketing and promotion opportunities", EMI Group announced a slight increase in sales, to £2,386.5 million, and an improvement in operating profits to £290.6 million.

Writing in his chairman's statement Nicoli described the strategic and financial rationale for the proposed merger with Warner Music as "compelling", and confirmed that the date for closing the transaction "continues to be targeted for the second half of 2000".

Throughout the spring and summer months there was a seemingly never-ending round of meetings aimed at finding the best way to merge the two music majors at the same time as one of the parent companies was being acquired by a giant third party.

While there were those who saw AOL's bid to buy Time Warner as a distraction in the midst of the music merger, the senior management remained confident of getting the right result at the end of the day. Speaking off the record, one of the main players in the unfolding drama suggests that things might have been made easier by the double whammy of putting two proposals before the European Commission at the same time.

He says, "We decided that if anything it was an even better idea now because we had the world's biggest internet service provider working together with what would be the world's best music content bank. And the legal advisers were still saying there would be no problem in getting regulatory approval."

But, as time went by, a growing sense of unease spread through both companies and the fear was that the EC's directorate general for competition was not convinced of the logic of either the AOL/Time Warner deal or the EMI/Warner Music merger.

There was talk of somebody, somewhere having to make a sacrifice and it seemed that disposing of Virgin Music would convince the regulators to approve the music deal, but that was never to going to happen with Berry involved in the talks. "Nobody ever officially mentioned that Virgin might be sacrificed in the merger," recalls Cooper, who adds that when people within the company began asking questions about their future, it became an issue for Berry.

"He flew about 20 Virgin managing directors from around the world into London and told us all that it was possible that Virgin might have to be sold off. Then the rumours started that he might buy it and take it independent again."

City analyst Mark Beilby watched as the proceedings unfolded but still had questions of his own about the merger. "I was not quite clear what the structure of a merged EMI Warner company would look like and that's where the regulator would have his say," says the man who followed EMI for over a decade and was now worried about the bigger picture.

"A lot of the Commission's concerns would have been with the integration of Warner into AOL, which was going on at the same time. It was absolutely extraordinary that the EMI/Warner deal was announced in the same month as AOL bought Time Warner."

However, for manager Pete Jenner, the problem about the proposed Warner/EMI merger was more to do with making it work as opposed to getting it cleared. "It was the natural merger but I don't think it would have worked because the EMI people would still be running Europe and the Warner people would still be running America, and they would spend their time fighting each other."

Analyst Mike Hilton had much the same concerns about the merger even though he acknowledges that it came at exactly the right time. "It was at the absolute peak of the dot.com bubble when content was king," he says. But it was how the new company would operate that worried him most. "From a management side nobody could really understand how this whole thing was going to work. There was Warner over there, EMI over here – nobody really understood how it would work and not only did you have cultural differences, you had a chain of command that affected a lot of people."

Slowly it began to dawn on those involved that clearing the deals with the European Commission would not be as easy as the various legal advisers were suggesting. Hilton also sensed it was not all going to plan. "I think they [EMI] were a bit naïve on the regulatory front and the market did begin to understand how difficult the deal was becoming. It was dragging on and on and the share price began to fall and then pessimism replaced optimism."

One of the issues facing EMI was the value of intellectual property and, ironically, with EMI having spent time convincing the City of its value, the European Commission's regulators took a new interest in the evolving business of selling intellectual property rights in the music business.

As writer Phil Hardy points out it was unlucky for Nicoli and EMI that the EC had become aware of the value of rights, but it wasn't the only bit of bad luck. "He [Eric] was doubly unlucky that Warner was committed to the silliness of the AOL deal at the same time as the regulators had a better knowledge of the music business."

All this, according to Hardy, made EMI's proposed link-up with Warner more difficult, although he believes Nicoli made the biggest error by not seeking another buyer. "The real mistake Nicoli made was, if you were going to sell EMI you would do much better selling it to an outsider. Certainly Microsoft had a survey done on EMI at around that time but nobody ever came in with a bid."

It's Hardy's view that by this time EMI could no longer stand alone and survive as a major music company, and they were being forced "to find someone to get into bed with".

June 2000 brought the first serious indications that the Warner/EMI deal might be in jeopardy, and there were also doubts about AOL's bid for Time Warner being approved. It also seemed likely that the EC Competition Directorate, under the leadership of Commissioner Mario Monti, would take up to four months investigating the proposals.

A spokeswoman from Monti's office pointed out that the merger task force would decide whether the music deal would "create a dominant market position or a strengthening of an already dominant position". All this was at a time when objections to Warner and EMI becoming one company were raining down from the Independent Music Publishers and Labels Association (IMPALA); the confederation of songwriters and composers from Scandinavia, Denmark and Iceland; the British Academy of Composers and Songwriters; and the UK's AIM, while over in the US one-time interested bidder for EMI, Universal Music, also launched an objection through its music-publishing division.

For AIM chief Alison Wenham, the problems for the independents, caused by mergers and acquisitions among the majors, began before EMI and Warner started talking. "They started in the Eighties with Polygram gradually acquiring significant independents such as A&M and Island and then merging with MCA in the late 90s to become Universal, before the European Commission took any real notice."

Speculation about the list of concerns facing Warner, EMI and the EC revolved around the size of the combined music-publishing operation, the high market share of the merged recorded music operation in various European territories, a potential manufacturing and distribution overlap, the involvement in major joint-venture compilation albums with rival labels and possible dominance in digital delivery in light of the AOL/Time Warner link.

As the EC looked more closely at the details and possible ramifications of allowing Warner and EMI to merge, so the two companies launched a new campaign to persuade the regulators that the new bigger Warner EMI company would not dominate the European market either in terms of publishing or recorded music. By late June 2000 it seemed that there would be at least two months of fact-finding, statements and hearings before a decision was reached.

However, no deal could be approved or completed until the EMI share-holders actually voted in favour of the merger and on June 26, 2000, at an extraordinary general meeting, this was what happened. Less than 1% of EMI's investors voted against the proposal even though Nicoli conceded that Time Warner having a majority on the board was "not absolutely ideal but we think it's the best thing to do".

In a detailed report circulated to investors EMI explained how the new company would work. "EMI and Time Warner have agreed to create two entities to conduct their music businesses throughout the world. One, WEM US, will be a Delaware [registered] general partnership that will operate principally in the US, Japan and Canada. The other, WEM UK, will be a company incorporated and registered in England and Wales that will operate principally in the UK and other countries outside the US, Canada and Japan. Both EMI and Time Warner will indirectly own 50% of the equity in each of WEM US and WEM UK."

At the same meeting Nicoli adjusted the number of likely redundancies as a result of the merger, suggesting that it would be 2,000 over three years rather than the 3,000 Berry had announced in January 2000.

There was also activity on the AOL/Time Warner front during the last week of June as 97% of the AOL shareholders approved the company's plans to purchase Time Warner while its rival Seagram, owner of Universal Music, also announced its merger with French media, utilities and transport company Vivendi in a deal valued at £20 billion.

Following the release in early September 2000 by the European Commission of its "statement of objections", EMI and Time Warner were expected to deliver their responses in time for a further EC meeting set for October 4. An EC competition spokeswoman also announced that a final decision on the merger would be delivered on October 18 with an announcement on the proposed AOL buyout of Time Warner set for October 24.

For experienced music industry executive Paul Russell the message coming out of the EC meant only one thing. "You can't take two of the biggest music companies in the world and merge them. It was not going to happen because the rest of the industry would be screaming the place down . . . and the Commission was giving out those signals," says the former Sony European chief who saw music publishing as the main problem, coupled with some ego issues.

"They weren't going to go to Brussels and say, 'Guess what, we're going to sell one of the publishing companies as part of this deal' because the egos at the top couldn't decide which one was to go."

Russell goes further and points out that while Warner and EMI wanted to merge they couldn't agree on how to do it. "But if you dropped the man with logic from Mars into the situation he would have looked at it and said, 'You merge the two record companies and toss a coin to see who runs it – because it doesn't really matter as they are all good on both sides – and you sell Warner Chappell because EMI Publishing is such a strong company.'"

Former EMI chairman Colin Southgate also saw publishing as the main stumbling block along the path. "EMI and Warner Chappell were not only one and two but they dominated the business and it was always the case that they would have to sell one or the other," he says, while confirming that during his time in office he had spoken to Time Warner's Dick Parsons about a possible EMI/Warner Music deal but nothing came of the talks.

During a hectic September 2000 executives from both companies faced a two-day grilling behind closed doors in Brussels. Nicoli and Berry from EMI were joined by Warner's Parsons and Ames and they seemingly offered the EC Competition Directorate a number of concessions that were not made public.

This meeting was followed by a further confrontation with Commissioner Monti during which, it was rumoured, further concessions were offered in an effort to keep the deal alive. However, the cause was not helped by a leaked "internal document" from Brussels, which, it was reported, suggested that the merger would not be allowed to proceed because it would create an oligopoly capable of fixing prices.

Watching in the wings, journalist Emmanuel Legrand spotted a flaw in the arguments that had nothing with market shares. "They were all very, very arrogant in their approach to the European Commission," he says, and it was an observation that was confirmed in part by one of EMI's most senior people, who believes that the attitude of AOL's negotiators, in their efforts to get their bid for Time Warner approved, rubbed up the Commission the wrong way.

"My impression was the regulators were really pissed off with AOL's arrogance in all this – not Time Warner. AOL was the major problem. I think EMI did as good a job as it was possible to do in the circumstances," says the anonymous EMI executive, who spent some considerable time in Brussels arguing his company's case.

Legrand also saw some truth in the leaked document that threatened to pour cold water on the deal. "The guys in the competition department at the EC have dogmas on prices and on dominant position and they applied the dogma in the EMI/Warner case, where it would almost certainly have to have been a sale of one of the publishing companies."

As one of the main objectors to the proposed merger, AIM was concerned that the EC seemed to understand very little about the music business and might be swayed by the majors' tactics. "The armies of economists, lawyers and academics employed by EMI and Warner in 2000 were playing to that [lack of understanding] and put forward all sorts of rather complex economic models that showed there would be no damage to the independents," recalls Alison Wenham.

But, says the CEO of the UK indies' organisation, the EC was not convinced. "The Commission understood enough to conclude that the merger would have been damaging because it marginalised the independents."

Still determined to get the deal through, EMI and Time Warner continued making concessions through to the end of September 2000 with apparent promises to give up the physical distribution of product, pull out of joint-venture agreements and even sell four record and four music-publishing companies.

Further concessions were reported to have been made a week later and this time the disposal of Virgin Records and a share of Warner Chappell were offered up as sweeteners, although one media analyst suggested that "getting rid of jewels like that wouldn't make the deal worthwhile".

While the EC confirmed that "new proposals" had been received, the City reacted badly to the concessions and EMI's shares dropped 15p to 540p and it now seemed that the writing was on the wall – the proposed merger between EMI and Warner Music was sinking fast and would very soon be dead in the water.

Sensing that the European Commission's regulators were not inclined to approve the deal – certainly not at the same time as they were also debating the question of AOL buying Time Warner – EMI and Time Warner finally withdrew their application for approval on October 5, 2000, the same day as the EC advisory group was due to issue a ruling.

As EMI shares dropped to 528p on the news of the pull-out, there was still talk of the two companies returning with a revived proposal before the year end. But there were also those who believed it was all doomed the moment AOL and Time Warner began negotiations. One City analyst said at the time, "The issue is that the AOL/Time Warner deal had to go through and it was not worth jeopardising for the sake of this merger," while a spokeswoman for the EC competition group confirmed, "The concerns over the AOL/Time Warner deal refer to concerns over the music sector. Now EMI is no longer on the table then draw your own conclusions."

And the conclusion was obvious – with EMI and Warner off the table there was nothing to stop AOL acquiring Time Warner. Before the end of October, the EC gave the plan regulatory clearance and in the week before Christmas 2000 the deal was given the green light by the US Federal Trade Commission.

The failure of the EMI/Warner Music merger was seen by some as the price the bosses of AOL and Time Warner were prepared to pay to get their corporate marriage sanctioned, but Time Warner president Richard Parsons was adamant that a music merger was still possible. "We will continue to explore ways to structure a combination that will make sense for the two companies and be acceptable to the Commission."

EMI's Nicoli added, "We continue to believe that a joint venture with Warner Music can create substantial value for our shareholders and benefit our artists, consumers and employees."

However, while the City was critical of EMI for a lack of communication over the reason for the EC's objection, there were those in the media who believed that the top players from both EMI and Time Warner had misread the signs coming out of Brussels. *Music Week* editor Ajax Scott wrote that Parsons, Nicoli, Ames and Berry all "attempted to play a game of brinkmanship in order to give away as little as possible".

But for Nicoli there was only one bad guy and that was the EC's Competition Commissioner. "They didn't reckon for Mario Monti, they didn't reckon for the regulators' paranoia," is his assessment of events some eight years later.

"And it was AOL's acquisition of Time Warner that represented a major spanner in the works. Regulators didn't know what to make of it. They knew they couldn't block it on competition grounds so they decided to block the music merger, because they didn't fancy this potentially dominant internet player having ownership of the world's biggest music-content bank," is his explanation for the failure of a deal that he spent 10 months trying to pull together.

In his analysis of the talks and the problems he and his fellow executives faced as they attempted to get the merger through, Nicoli recalls that there were times when the disposal of either Virgin, EMI Music Publishing or Warner Chappell were all possibilities. "Because the regulator just didn't want it [the merger] to happen they set the bar so high that we wouldn't want to do it. Whatever we did would not have made economic sense.

"The hurdles they were setting got higher and higher as the thing progressed; every time they put up an obstacle and we knocked it down and satisfied them, they put up another one even higher," he says and cites music publishing as an example of his frustration. "There were no issues on publishing until we had satisfied all of their demands on recorded music and then suddenly there were huge issues on publishing."

Believing that the EC was not going to approve the deal and that time was running out, Nicoli concludes, "It was not the Commission's finest hour – nor was it ours."

But there is another story that perhaps had some impact on the outcome of the merger discussions and maybe explains the Commission's reluctance to approve the deal.

Observers in Brussels during the presentations recall the day when, as a female EC lawyer outlined various objections to the EMI/Warner partnership, an executive linked to one of the music companies leapt over the table, grabbed her in a headlock and said, "Are you going to let this fucking deal go through or do I have to rip your fucking head off?"

No matter which side he came from, it was a move that was not likely to have impressed Monti or anyone else involved in the decision-making process.

For AIM, in association with IMPALA, the failure of EMI and Warner to complete their merger was a major victory and they fully recognised the part they played in the final outcome. "We believe we were the largest contributor to the failure of that merger," says AIM's Alison Wenham. "I think we astounded our 'opposition' by the strength of our argument and we fought very well indeed – we had a collective platform and we argued our case very well."

Not only did it take EMI close to ten months to get nowhere in their search for a partnership with Warner Music, it also cost them a lot of money. This was detailed in the 2000–2001 annual report as a £42.9 million exceptional charge covering "full formal shareholder and regulatory approval processes and covers advisory fees incurred over a 12 month period".

For Nicoli, the non-deal remains the ultimate strategic disappointment during his time as head of EMI and he remains convinced that the people in high places still have a lot to answer for. "If the regulators – and the ones who made the decision are not around any more – look back now and see what happened to the industry and what has happened to AOL, they ought to be embarrassed."

Looking back he concludes that while most people now agree that the EMI/Warner Music merger was the best deal, it wasn't always that way. "I was, at the time, fairly lonely in promoting the notion that these two businesses should be put together and I had to work hard to get share-holder approval," he says.

And while he accepts that people's perception at the time was that he was selling a great British company to an American business, he holds an opposite view. "That wasn't how it would have worked out and I hope all the critics back then take just a minute or two to reflect on how they felt then and whether they still feel the same."

Nicoli's disappointment at the failure to merge with Warner Music was shared by executives, analysts and managers, some of whom chose to blame him for one of the most embarrassing moments in EMI's long history.

Back in the 1990s Southgate had spoken to Time Warner about a link with Warner Music, but the first positive signs of a possible merger came on Nicoli's watch as the former EMI chairman confirms. "I would have loved to have got together with Warners. That was the brief for Eric, that was what he had to do; he tried but he did spend a lot of money not getting to the altar."

At the outset of the negotiations Helen Snell had her reservations about Roger Ames and Ken Berry working together – "You can't have two people running one company" – but was still essentially in favour of the merger. "It would have been a good deal with the benefits of aggressive cost-cutting and some revenue synergies on top of that."

However when the deal was finally pulled she foresaw a bigger problem for EMI. "Having told everyone it was a fantastic deal, then to have to say it wasn't going to happen but it was all still fine, was massively damaging to investor sentiment around EMI. Having convinced investors that a deal makes sound strategic sense, it's very difficult to come back and convince them that not doing it is equally as attractive a proposition."

Having succeeded in their aim of halting the EMI and Warner merger, the UK independents showed no sympathy for their larger British competitor. "It wasn't on our radar that EMI was in any trouble in 2000 – it was trading very well and all EMI and Warner were doing was putting together a super-sized company to aggressively compete with other majors," explains Wenham. "Why would the independents have any sympathy towards that?"

On the management front Jonathan Shalit took the view that EMI merging with Warners was a "win-win for everybody because clearly the company will become bigger and stronger", but suggests that discussions about mergers create a lack of morale among staff.

His biggest concern was the length of time it took to not do a deal. "I think for both companies to spend so long trying to negotiate a merger that didn't happen demonstrates a certain degree of incompetence on both sides. Eric [Nicoli] was too nice a guy – he's not a killer."

Andy Taylor, a partner in the management of long-time EMI act Iron Maiden, also saw the negative impact of EMI's failure to complete the deal with Warner Music. "Everybody saw as a negative situation the fact that the company was trying to change and it hadn't happened. The fact that the deal did not happen ended up as a bad thing because they had tried and failed rather than not tried at all. It created massive uncertainty and that was harmful."

The final word on the failed attempt to create the world's largest music company goes to Tim Clark, manager of EMI superstar act Robbie Williams, who was also annoyed by how long it took for things not to happen. "An awful lot of executive time was taken up with this and it was not doing the company itself much good. A lot of people were worried about their jobs and it was just not a good thing to go through."

He also had wider concerns about his and his artist's relationship with their record company. "I think by this time we become fairly cynical about major record companies and we really started to think seriously about how we could extricate ourselves from being part of this."

This concern about record companies was shared by the team who looked after Radiohead, as, according to Bryce Edge, being part of a large corporation rankled with leader Thom Yorke. "Thom has reminded us of what we got him into ever since we signed with EMI. It is a lot of what Thom kicked against."

So as 2000 came to an end EMI found itself standing alone, having been forced to abandon its first attempt at a merger. According to Clark, however, there were alternatives that Nicoli should have pursued. "I'm astonished that Eric did not look for a deal with a non-music company — absolutely he should have been exploring those options."

While she agrees that it was "bizarre" that EMI did not search for a non-music company as a potential partner, Alison Wenham suggests that "companies in the technology industries probably see no real need to be content owners".

But, as it became clear that EMI was not going to get into bed with a non-music company and its one very expensive effort at a music merger had failed miserably, it didn't take long for another prospective suitor to appear on the scene.

Just a few weeks after embracing the internet company Napster — which was being taken to court by the music industry for copyright infringement through its file-sharing operation — and investing a multi-million sum in order to make the American company legitimate, Bertelsmann stepped up with a plan to combine its Bertelsmann Music Group with EMI.

According to IFPI figures, a combined BMG and EMI operation would have claimed a global market share in 2000 of 21.9% (BMG 8.4% and EMI 13.5%), just one percentage point behind market leader Universal.

But even as it confirmed that an approach had been made by Bertelsmann, EMI also acknowledged that it was locked into a contract with Time Warner that precluded it from soliciting a deal with any other company until after January 31, 2001. And this was at a time when EMI and Time Warner were still making positive noises about revisiting their proposed merger and had reopened discussions with both the EC and the US Federal Trade Commission.

Speaking in late October, an EMI spokeswoman confirmed that the company was in talks to "devise solutions that address the regulator's concerns while preserving the economic merits of the merger".

But within a month — and with no real developments involving Time Warner — Bertelsmann arrived on the scene and overcame the 'no talks' contract with Time Warner by making the first approach, although it was made clear at the time by the British company that the deal being proposed by Bertelsmann "does not involve an offer being made for EMI".

The approach by Bertelsmann, owner of the RCA and Arista record labels, came as EMI Group announced half-year figures up to September 30, 2000 that showed a 5.9% increase in turnover but a 6.9% drop in pre-tax profits to £110.9 million, with music publishing once again steadying the ship. Its 25.5% increase in operating profit (£51 million) was offset by recorded music's operating profit falling by 23.5% to £59.9 million.

While Berry was telling media that it was "still far too premature to know if there are any prospects of something happening" with Bertelsmann, Nicoli was stressing that EMI's strategy and plan for its business operations "have excellent prospects with or without a merger".

At the same time the EMI chairman, in light of the company's failure to convince the EC regulators of the merits of a merger with Warner Music, was keen to stress exactly what needed to be done first regarding Bertelsmann's interest. "We need a rigorous assessment of the synergies and we need to evaluate each other's businesses but far and away the most important issue is anti-trust."

Despite the unrest caused by a year of merger talks, EMI still came out of 2000 with the year's first and second best-selling albums in the UK – The Beatles' hits collection *1* and Robbie Williams' *Sing When You're Winning* – which brought it a 21.7% UK market share behind Universal's 23.9%.

Meanwhile in America the company increased its US market share by 1.8% to 10.8% despite not having one album or single in the list of ten best-sellers, while its prospective partner, BMG, could lay claim to the fourth best-selling album in America during 2000 thanks to Santana's *Supernatural*, and four top ten singles from acts such as Kevin Edmonds, Lonestar and Christina Aguilera.

In the run-up to Christmas 2000 executives from EMI and Bertelsmann met to compare notes and prepare the paperwork for a presentation in the new year to Mario Monti and his EC competition office. Anxious not to repeat the £42 million costs incurred during the ultimately fruitless attempt to merge with Warner Music, it was clear that EMI and BMG were talking to EC officials first in an effort to work out a deal that would get official approval.

Three months into 2001 and the talk was still of EMI and BMG getting together in some way, although a statement by the EMI board made their position clear. "The transaction proposed by Bertelsmann does not involve an offer being made for EMI." While EMI was also thought to be still in discussions with Time Warner, which might lead to the resurrection of the previously abandoned merger, the suggestion was that the German company would inject its music operation into EMI in return for a stake in the enlarged company, which was being valued at over £7 billion.

Even as the talks went on, Berry commented that EMI did not need to do a deal with Warner but "if we can do a deal and cut all the costs it will create an enormous amount of value", while Nicoli added, "The challenge is to find a combination that can excite shareholders without alarming regulators in Europe or the US."

However in May 2001, when it became clear that it was going to be impossible to complete a deal that would benefit EMI's shareholders and also clear the EC's regulatory concerns, the proposed merger was called off as the companies admitted that they were unable to offer a merger proposal that had a "high likelihood of approval from anti-trust authorities".

While Bertelsmann chairman Thomas Middelhoff confirmed, "Our companies will now continue along their respective paths", Berry explained that doing a deal with Bertelsmann would have destroyed value for EMI's shareholders. "I think it says of mergers between the major music companies that it's very hard to make them happen and create value."

The head of EMI's recorded music division also denied rumours of a rift with Nicoli over the merger, saying, "Eric and I have been on the same page through this rather difficult process," while the EMI chairman dismissed as "nonsense" stories of his own departure from the company because of the two failed mergers.

While he suspected that any teaming of Middelhoff and Nicoli was "potentially combustible", analyst Mark Beilby's recollection of the reasons for the failure of the EMI/BMG deal was once again focused on Virgin. "The feedback I heard from the EC was that the deal would be fine if Virgin was unloaded, which created a problem with Ken Berry," he says before going on to consider Nicoli's position at the time. "The fact that Eric had not completed two deals within eight months of each other was pretty damaging for him."

Beilby's colleague in the City Helen Snell was similarly concerned about EMI's reputation in the business community, where she says the company was already "out of favour and looking like a bungled management for failing with two deals and then they issue a profits warning, which compounded the problem – it was considered to be in a downward spiral".

However, for music writer Emmanuel Legrand there was never a question of Nicoli being ousted from the company in the event of a merger. "The Warner and Bertelsmann deals had to go through with him in it, he was always there in the deal and it's interesting that nobody seemed to have called his bluff and said, 'We don't need you.'"

He also takes the view that Nicoli got "trapped into the flashing lights of rock'n'roll very quickly" and was very much the new kid on the block. "He had no real experience – what would he bring to the table?"

If confirmation were needed that the Virgin operation was not going to be merged with the EMI business, even though it was considered by many to be the major reason for the two failed deals with Warner Music and BMG, it came in the middle of 2001 when Berry proudly pronounced, "Speculation that we might put together Virgin and EMI is so crazy that it's ridiculous. Those are real assets and you don't destroy assets in the name of synergies and back-room savings."

There was undoubtedly a sense within the City of London that, after failing to complete two deals that they considered important for the future of the company, EMI's management would have difficulty convincing anybody that the company could survive on its own. "If you are going to do these things you have to make damn sure they are going to happen because aborted mergers have a knock-on effect," explains business analyst Mike Hilton.

But according to EMI UK chairman Tony Wadsworth that knock-on effect did not spread as far as the people within his own part of the company. While he was aware of "the slings and arrows" he insists that there wasn't a feeling of demoralisation. "The people in the company were just immersed in what they thought was a very dynamic time," he says, citing the initial success of Coldplay and other developing artists, alongside strong UK figures, as the criteria for his team. "The rest of it was external noise, which the UK staff did not get distracted by."

On the other hand, for former EMI Music boss Bhaskar Menon the failure of the deal with Bertelsmann represented a third missed opportunity for the company in a matter of just five years. "Despite being the most vulnerable major EMI was unable to close a deal with the Bronfman-led Universal or with Time Warner or to merge with BMG, or even to convince the regulatory authorities in Brussels of its desperate circumstances.

"External pronouncements during those years always reflected a sense of bravado, not often backed by reason, that EMI could indefinitely hold out for better terms for its shareholders."

On the management front Sam Feldman, who helped steer his artist Norah Jones to record-breaking success through EMI's Blue Note label, believes that if either of the mergers had gone through it "would cause chaos and a larger infrastructure that is easy to get lost in".

But he was able to take shelter within the New York–based Blue Note operation, run by industry legend Bruce Lundvall, and not worry about EMI's well-reported poor performance in the US or the merger speculation that was rife in London and Brussels. "I had no more concerns about EMI than I would about any other major label. We were very comfortable with the creative environment fostered by Bruce."

Similarly Tim Clark's view is that EMI joining forces with either Warner or BMG would "just have brought the same frustrations for us" and he adds, "I was not disappointed that either deal did not go through, but the concern still was that this company [EMI] was not going to survive on its own."

On the back of EMI's failure to ink a deal with either Warner or BMG, there was rising concern within the industry as to how the UK's biggest music company would survive as the internet began to have an impact on the business. "It became all the more compelling for EMI to find a partner," says Helen Snell, "and consolidation made sense within the industry as the spectre of the internet began to emerge."

The arrival of the internet as a provider of recorded music was just one of three forces that would adversely affect EMI's share price, according to Mark Beilby. "You had the technology media telecommunications bubble bursting after its period of euphoria; you had some reputational damage through two very public and long negotiations; and you had the growing realisation of the internet."

Ironically it was the acquisition of Time Warner by AOL that, for many, signalled the arrival of the new digital age and the internet as potentially serious competitors to the traditional music business. "The whole AOL/Time Warner thing gave this area some kind of credibility," says ex-EMI and Warner finance executive Davin McDermott. "An internet company and a multi-media company joining forces suggested to people that there must be something in this new business and that there was an internet world out there."

Coming on the back of early start-up companies such as MusicNet and Pressplay and followed by the likes of OD2, the internet was going to test the music industry's resolve, although there was still a feeling of optimism. The major players continued to convince themselves that the physical business of selling music through traditional outlets would stabilise after the initial switch to illegal downloading had plateaued, and the new legal

An early gramophone from the newly-formed Gramophone Company's 1897 range of machines.
(HULTON ARCHIVE/GETTY IMAGES)

In 1904, best-selling opera superstar Dame Nellie Melba was paid a royalty of 25p for every record sold. (REDFERNS/GETTY IMAGES)

An American record label featuring the famous Dog & Trumpet logo which was bought by Victor in around 1900. (HULTON ARCHIVE ARCHIVE/GETTY IMAGES)

A Columbia Records sales brochure produced to boost sales during WWI.

Italian Tenor Tito Schipa joined the work force to make his own records at the Gramophone Company's Hayes factory in 1927.
(HULTON-DEUTSCHE COLLECTION/CORBIS)

Posing with an HMV machine and Nipper model are Australian singer Peter Dawson (left), Gramophone Company chairman Alfred Clark (centre) and pianist Mark Hambourg. (HULTON ARCHIVE/GETTY IMAGES)

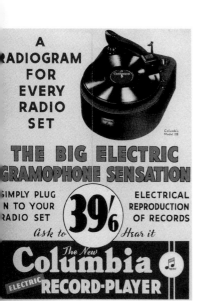

EMI launched the 'under £2' gramophone to help sales of its recording during the 1930s.

Opened in 1939 by Sir Thomas Beecham, the HMV store in Oxford St cost over £42,000 and sold records, gramophones – and kitchen appliances.

(HULTON ARCHIVE/GETTY IMAGES)

Recording on magnetic tape was developed at EMI's central research laboratories after WWII.
(POPPERFOTO/GETTY IMAGES)

Elvis Presley's UK releases appeared on EMI's HMV label between 1956 and 1958.

Britain's own rock'n'roll king Cliff Richard first hit the charts with 'Move It' in 1958.

Cliff Richard (second right) receives an award from EMI chairman Sir Joseph Lockwood (left), watched by managing director L.G. Wood (third from left), November 1959. (HULTON ARCHIVE/GETTY IMAGES)

To ensure the finished product was perfect, EMI factory staff checked 'mother' copies for faults before pressing could begin. (HULTON ARCHIVE/GETTY IMAGES)

The first copies of the Beatles' Parlophone debut single 'Love Me Do' were released in 1962 on a red label which was replaced by the familiar black version in 1963.

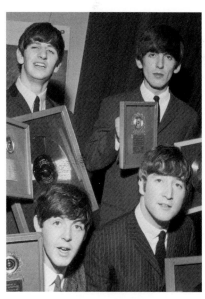

Ringo Starr (back left), George Harrison (back right), Paul McCartney (front left) and John Lennon (front right) show off their silverware from sales of their *Please Please Me* album and 'Twist & Shout' EP.
(HULTON ARCHIVE/GETTY IMAGES)

The production line at EMI's factory went into overtime in 1965 to produce copies of the Beatles' *Rubber Soul* album for the Christmas market. (HULTON ARCHIVE/GETTY IMAGES)

Ringo Starr (left) and George Harrison make their way into Abbey Road studios in November 1966 when 'Strawberry Fields' and 'Penny Lane' were recorded. (HULTON ARCHIVE/GETTY IMAGES)

EMI producer Norman 'Hurricane' Smith conducts future England manager Terry Venables during the Abbey Road recording of Tottenham Hotspurs' 1967 Cup Final song. (HULTON ARCHIVE/GETTY IMAGES)

The original Pink Floyd line-up of Roger Waters (left), Syd Barrett (centre), Rick Wright (right) and Nick Mason (front), jump for joy on the steps of EMI's Manchester Square offices. (DEZO HOFFMAN/REX FEATURES)

Legendary EMI chairman Sir Joseph Lockwood poses in front of the original Francis Barraud painting of His Master's Voice, December 1968. (HULTON ARCHIVE/GETTY IMAGES)

digital business would replace just a small percentage of the traditional business.

But in the midst of these developments there was still confusion and frustration for artists and managers according to Chris Hufford and Bryce Edge, who were steering their acts Radiohead and Supergrass into the new digital age with little or no help from EMI. "From our perspective they were always looking at the wrong thing," says Hufford. "It was this horrible protective thing to do with DRM [Digital Rights Management], as opposed to seeing where the positive things could be and trying to develop what iTunes eventually did fabulously well."

While he claims that EMI's labels spent much of their time "squabbling with each other and just wasted shit loads of money", Hufford also recalls a sense of complacency within the company. "Everybody assumed it was going to be exactly the same as CDs and they would be able to march in and it would be fabulous. Then piracy started happening and it just got bigger and EMI could never keep up with the young kids. The industry was always going to lose."

For his partner Edge the core issue was the record company's refusal to accept that control of its copyright was being eroded by technology. "If your copyrights aren't worth anything because people can copy it and get away with it, then the notion of you actually owning something becomes irrelevant."

Their frustration was compounded during regular meetings with EMI to debate the company's digital policy. "The fundamental thing was them banging on the table and saying DRM is the only way forward. EMI refused to accept that there was any other option in terms of the digital marketplace than having your copyright DRM-protected," says Edge before adding finally, "We said they were wasting their time – the horse had bolted and they had to accept that."

As partners – with AOL Time Warner, Bertelsmann and Real Networks – in the new MusicNet business due to be launched in late 2001, EMI claimed in its 2000–2001 annual report to be launching a "secure platform for the digital distribution of music through a variety of media including internet portals, dedicated internet music sites and other digital services".

It also listed 10 further new-media deals with American, European and Asian distributors and service providers, and added to that list in October 2001 when it signed a deal to license music to online file-sharing website Pressplay, becoming the first of the five majors to link with both Pressplay and its rival MusicNet.

121

According to EMI's new-media vice president Jay Samit it was part of the company's plan to "support as many innovative and competing music services as possible" while, for analyst Aram Sinnreich from Jupiter Media Matrix, the deal confirmed EMI's role as music producers. "They don't want to own distribution. They're just a record company."

Meanwhile the annual report showed increased turnover and profit for both the recorded music and music publishing divisions, resulting in overall figures for the EMI Group of £2,672.7 million turnover (up 12%) and an operating profit of £332.5 million (down from £290 million the previous year) plus a claim for a 14.1% global market share.

While confirming the exceptional charge of over £42 million relating to the abandoned merger with Warner Music, Nicoli pointed out to shareholders and investors that there were no "significant costs" from the failed talks with Bertelsmann. Among the company's best sellers was The Beatles' *1* album – which was dubbed the fastest-selling album of all time and reached sales in excess of 21 million – and multi-million sellers from Lenny Kravitz, Robbie Williams, Hikaru Utada, plus Coldplay's debut album, *Parachutes*.

Presenting the company's performance to investors and media, Nicoli claimed that the 2000–2001 year-end figures made EMI "one of the world's most efficient and profitable music companies", while analysts ABN Amro declared that although the short-term outlook for EMI was "reasonably positive" the long-term prospects for the industry as a whole remained "fundamentally cautious".

Despite the analysts' caution, EMI bucked the worldwide downturn in music sales in the early part of 2001 and returned a 3% sales increase, while albums by Radiohead, Gorillaz and Paul McCartney all made an impact internationally, including the all-important American market.

However within a matter of months the company was forced to issue a profits warning as business plunged in the wake of the terrorist attacks on America on September 11, 2001. EMI put the fall in business down to "a marked deterioration in conditions" as the first album from their new superstar signing Mariah Carey – released on the same day as the attacks on New York and Washington DC – registered disappointing sales amid concerns over the singer's health.

Predicting that his company's pre-tax profits would be 20% lower the following year, at around £208 million, Nicoli announced plans to cut 100 jobs and make total cost savings of £65 million. As the company's share price dropped 116p to 214p, analysts downgraded their estimates for the company and some even forecast that EMI would do well to hold the fall in profits to just 20%.

It was the delay in The Spice Girls' final album that brought things to a head for EMI, according to Mike Hilton. "It was only when *Forever* was delayed and we had a profit warning that people asked, 'How can it be that exposed to one act?'" Calculating that the all-girl group was responsible for 20% of EMI's profits in 1998, Hilton reckons the group's break-up, the delay in releasing their album and the company's dependence on one act was "an accident waiting to happen" as EMI relied on only five or ten acts – out of a roster of hundreds – to make money.

Fellow analyst Helen Snell takes a similar view – although she reckons Ginger, Sporty, Posh, Baby and Scary accounted for closer to 15% of EMI's operating profit in a single year – and suggests that, as it was never going to be possible to replicate that "phenomenal year", EMI's profits were certain to fall.

The drop in share price also brought a sharp reaction from former EMI chairman, Colin Southgate, who pointed out that the business was in "pretty good shape" when he left in 1999. "It was making decent money and suddenly my shares are worth a third of what they used to be worth."

It was little consolation to EMI that rivals AOL Time Warner and Sony also issued profit warnings in the wake of 9/11, alongside concerns about a downturn in consumer spending that included music products.

According to the *Telegraph*'s Neil McCormick, EMI's problems could still be traced back to 1996 and its decision to demerge from Thorn. "Clearly EMI should not have become a publicly quoted stand-alone music company," says the journalist, who believes that this move focused too much media attention on the company. "It became fair game for endless analysis in newspaper columns, picking over its returns, and EMI also became a game that analysts and the stock market could play."

Reflecting on the fact that the most boring newspaper section for the average reader is the business pages, McCormick says EMI was the perfect solution. "The hardest thing is to illustrate business pages – and this is a real factor. So if you can get a picture of Mariah Carey or Robbie Williams or Coldplay on your business page, then you make that page sexy and that became a driving force for the newspapers."

The media's coverage and treatment of EMI was something that also concerned Martin Talbot, a former *Music Week* editor and now managing director of the Official Chart Company, who claims that "perceptions about the music industry have caused EMI no end of harm over the past five or ten years".

Acknowledging that EMI was the company most exposed to the City's nervousness about the music industry, he adds, "Every time something negative happened to the music industry – from disappointing sales figures to worrying piracy statistics – it was flagged up about EMI and it reflected badly on the company, both in general terms and in terms of its share value."

And there was to be more analysis on October 13, 2001, when the influential *Financial Times* gave over two pages of its weekend magazine to assess the chances of EMI achieving the 15% global market-share target set by its top music man, Ken Berry.

The article suggested that the third-largest recording group in the world – and the biggest music-only company in an industry worth £40 billion – was "facing severe obstacles". Reflecting on an impressive back catalogue including The Beatles, David Bowie, The Rolling Stones, Frank Sinatra, The Beach Boys and Pink Floyd, the *FT* concluded, "but EMI is desperate to harness a new generation of hit-makers in the US".

As part of that process Berry closed the company's corporate offices in Los Angeles, wound up small unprofitable deals with various labels and announced the transfer of the company's global head office from London to New York. He also recruited music producer and artist manager Andy Slater as the new president of the flagship Capitol Records.

The man who produced hits for Macy Gray, Fiona Apple and The Wallflowers and also managed Lenny Kravitz, The Beastie Boys and Don Henley became the fourth head of Capitol in less than 10 years and, according to Berry, "his impressive track record in discovering exciting new talent will prove invaluable".

However just days after the *FT*'s feature appeared, Berry was out of a job. After over four years as chief executive of EMI Recorded Music, the man who joined the company when Virgin Music was bought by EMI in 1992 was sacrificed on October 15 on the back of the profit warning and the company's failure in America.

While he took home an annual salary of nearly £3 million, Berry saw EMI's share of the all-important American market slump to 10.6%. In a *New York Times* report, Snell commented that Berry "has to be held accountable to some degree for the underperformance of the recorded music division".

At the same time insiders and commentators saw the move as Nicoli flexing his muscles and stamping his authority on the company.

Acknowledging that 2001 was a bad year and that "sadly it did spell the end for Ken", Nicoli described Berry as both a "hugely respected and very decent man" who made some big bets. "And a number of them turned out badly. He did a number of urban deals – like Blackground, which turned out really nasty – and of course the famous Mariah Carey deal."

Nicoli wasted no time in appointing Berry's successor. In what *Billboard* magazine described as "his most decisive action since becoming EMI Group chairman in 1999", he named Alain Levy as chief executive for recorded music on the same day as Berry departed. Joining him at EMI with immediate effect as vice chairman was David Munns, who was Levy's trusty lieutenant during their time together at Polygram.

Nicoli heralded the duo as a "truly world-class team who helped make Polygram the world's most profitable music company". In fact during their period at the helm of Polygram prior to its acquisition by Seagram in 1998, the pair were credited with increasing the company's value from $2.5 billion to over $10 billion, and helping to develop the careers of artists such as U2, Texas and Sting while acquiring A&M, Island and Def Jam Records.

The French-born Levy switched from CBS to become head of Polygram France in 1984 and moved through the ranks until be was appointed president/CEO of the company's global operations in 1991. Englishman Munns had moved from EMI to the Polygram subsidiary Polydor in 1987 and became Levy's right-hand man as head of international marketing in 1991.

While Berry was reported to be leaving EMI with a compensation package worth around £5 million, Levy was apparently joining the company for just £700,000 a year plus a potentially lucrative share-option package based on performance and share-price targets.

While Levy made no immediate public comment about his new role, Nicoli announced that the EMI shareholders were "thrilled" about the arrival of EMI Music's third chief executive in five years. Reflecting in 2008 on his move to recruit the French executive he explained, "Alain Levy was available and excited about doing the job and came as a double act with David Munns. I felt it was absolutely the right move to bring in those two and relieve Ken of his duties."

Speaking during the week after his appointment, Levy, who admitted that he had told the EMI board "not to expect miracles", confirmed that time was not on his side. "We need to think through our approach fairly quickly because we have another job to do, which is to push A&R and create artists," he said before setting off on a world tour of EMI's key territories, during which he and Munns would "both go to evaluate people in the company and to be evaluated by them".

It seemed that most of the industry also applauded Nicoli's move, with journalists, analysts and EMI colleagues generally agreeing that if anybody could salvage the reputation and performance of EMI it was the two executives who had continued to work together in their own partnership after leaving Polygram.

> *"Because they were known by the business, people felt that these guys could possibly do it for EMI – there was a real sense of optimism. Whereas Ken was seen by some as just too nice for his own good, Levy and Munns would be hard arsed and they'd just make it happen"*
>
> – former *Music Week* editor Martin Talbot.

> *"It was a bold move by Eric to bring in Levy and Munns, who were an amazing management team and they proved that at Polygram. Their way of managing – which is always to duplicate functions wherever they can to create a tension between people – works very well when you are on a roll and there is growth"*
>
> – former *Billboard* international editor Emmanuel Legrand.

> *"Bringing them in was definitely seen to be a positive move. A lot of investors would have remembered Levy from his Polygram days, were familiar with him, felt he had a track record and understood the concept of having a record company listed on the stock market"*
>
> – analyst Helen Snell.

> *"At the time it was a very well-regarded move for them to replace Berry. After the massive pessimism of the failed merger, profit warning and artist write-offs, it became more optimistic again. Eric could say he had taken steps, 'Look at these two fantastic people I'm bringing in – they've got clout, they've got vision' "*
>
> – analyst Mike Hilton.

> *"They are aggressive characters and things had to happen quickly. What they brought into the company was a new injection of energy, a sense of urgency, and that worked. It came at a time when a couple of signings – Coldplay and Norah Jones – were starting to work."*
>
> – former EMI Record UK chairman Tony Wadsworth.

But there were also detractors and those who were concerned about what the two 'super' executives would contribute or could achieve for the beleaguered British giant.

"*The arrival of Levy and Munns did not fill me with great hope for the future. I did not think their style of management was great and actually I didn't think they knew very much about marketing. In periods of great change you need a real entrepreneurial spirit and they had shown during their time between leaving Polygram and joining EMI that they were failures as entrepreneurs*"

– artist manager Tim Clark.

"*I would not describe hiring them as a coup for EMI – neither of them had a job at the time. Clearly it was a positive move at the time but I'm not sure how well managed it was*"

– artist manager Jonathan Shalit.

"*The round of changes of executives at EMI – Southgate/Fifield/ Berry/Nicoli/Levy and Munns – did have an impact; it was a period of great unrest. It didn't work when Levy and Munns came in and I don't know why, but EMI changed its character when they came in – it just all changed*"

– artist Manager Chris Morrison.

"*Levy essentially has always seen music as part of a lot of other things but he was given a company that had no other interests and unfortunately wanted a short-term solution. They certainly got a good reception but the prime problem was America – Levy had no great track record in America – and they could not bring much to improve it*"

– music journalist Phil Hardy.

"*I think the move that Eric made from Ken [Berry] to Levy achieved nothing for EMI*"

– former EMI chairman Colin Southgate

"*The hiring of Levy and Munns was very surprising. Nobody broke into a round of applause when they were appointed; you struggled to find any grown-up in the music industry who thought that the declared plan was a powerful proposition*"

– Beggars Group director Andy Heath.

For Munns, who had spent part of his time since leaving Polygram managing Bon Jovi, rejoining EMI as a senior executive over 15 years after he left was seen by one close friend and former colleague as a chance to make up for an earlier disappointment.

Currently an employee of Universal/Sony/EMI in the *Now* Series partnership in America, Bob Mercer was Munns' boss at EMI Records UK during the 1970s. "Munns was as pleased as punch to get the job at EMI. He wanted to be managing director back in the mid-1980s and never got it so he left for Polydor. But EMI always beckoned," says Mercer. He also believes that while his former charge "was one of the best marketing people in the music business", he was "not a chief executive".

When he and his long-time ally Levy took over EMI, the task that faced them was, according to Munns, like "backing the ship off the rocks without getting a hole in it". Acknowledging that the first year was all about damage limitation and trouble shooting, Munns points out that Nicoli was primarily concerned with stemming the losses.

"In truth he didn't really have a vision for the company, he just wanted it to be sorted out," he says before going on to reflect on the state of the companies they had inherited. "The old EMI guard felt like second-class citizens really and actually the Virgin company wasn't doing that well – it had a few bits and pieces."

Among the "bits and pieces" were of course Janet Jackson, Lenny Kravitz and The Rolling Stones. "All expensive deals but not all loss-making deals," says Munns, who adds that it was five girls from the UK who dominated activities at the label in the late 1990s. "The Virgin people and the whole company got consumed by The Spice Girls – nothing else came along in those years and when the bubble burst they had nothing else to replace it."

While acknowledging that they were there "just to sort out the record labels" and not to seek out potential partners or buyers, Munns accepts that the shadow of the failed deals with Warner Music and BMG still hung over the company when they arrived. "The subject of merger, acquisition or being bought was always on the agenda," says the man who took over responsibility for EMI's operations in America where, he reflects, "Virgin was absolutely haemorrhaging money, with Blackground and RapaLot and some other deals that were just awful."

Accused by highly placed insiders at EMI of "running rampant round the company" and having "no concept of the money being spent", Nancy Berry's reign lasted less than two weeks longer than her husband's.

While Levy's public statement described her as "a talented record executive who has made great contributions to the development of Virgin Records", there was no doubting that she was the first major victim of the new EMI regime. But while the departure of the Berrys came as no real surprise to most people in the industry, it was still greeted with some disappointment by others.

For the artists most closely linked with Mrs Berry there were big changes on the horizon. The days of her free spending came to an end, and according to sources close to the likes of Mick Jagger and Lenny Kravitz, they apparently understood what had gone on and, more importantly, knew why it had to stop.

And for former Virgin and EMI executive Jeremy Silver it was all down to management skills. "Ken should have changed his style after becoming head of EMI because his strength was in personal relationships rather than a corporate environment," he says before adding, "He should also have probably reacted to Nancy's adventures in America, which undoubtedly contributed to his downfall – but it was still a surprise when he was fired."

While he believes that the teams of Ken and Nancy Berry and Levy and Munns were seen by many as the last of the untouchables – "People who could not be fired because they had a reputation" – Andy Heath says that the departure of the husband and wife team was "inevitable".

On the other hand the welcome given to Levy and Munns by financiers, investors and analysts served only to confirm Heath's opinion of the financial community. "The fact that the City thought it might be a good idea is another indication of why the City and the music industry just do not get on."

Former EMI boss Bhaskar Menon does not know Ken Berry, but even so he believes his appointment was "the result of a political game and was not intended to be an inspired management move" and came at a time when be believes Fifield should have stayed and Southgate retired.

Menon's view on Berry's departure is that "everyone inside the company and throughout the business seemed to know that the delay in taking this action was inflicting irreparable damage".

Whether the damage was irreparable or not, music writer Emmanuel Legrand certainly believes that Berry's reluctance to make any structural changes involving Virgin even when the market was showing signs of difficulty was his downfall. "I am not sure that Berry was a bad manager, but he probably didn't have a strategic view and was blinded by the fact that he was a Virgin person. He probably became head of EMI quite reluctantly when he would have been happy being head of an independent Virgin company."

For industry high-flyer Clive Calder, the founder of Zomba, the news of Ken Berry's departure came as a disappointing shock. Speaking to industry magazine *Music Week*, he said, "It is difficult for me at this stage to say anything other than express my distaste for this extremely unfair turn of events," adding, "I couldn't care less about whether this turns out to be a good or bad move for EMI."

Claiming that the signing and ultimately disappointing performance of Mariah Carey was a "catalyst" for both Virgin and Nancy Berry, former Virgin US chief Ray Cooper explains that despite all the bad press, "which ultimately made the shareholders go, 'What's happening here?'", Mrs Berry enjoyed her notoriety, particularly when things were going well. "But when the big things broke, like the *Daily Mail* story or the decision to sign Mariah without hearing a note of her new music, that was a dangerous ploy because there were already stories circulating that Mariah was not very well."

He recalls that the news of her departure prompted Nancy Berry to throw a party at her house in Los Angeles and also that she wasn't particularly surprised when the axe finally fell. "Maybe Ken, who had gone a few days earlier, was telling her to brace herself for it," says Cooper who, with his partner as joint MD of Virgin, Ashley Newton, was fully expecting to follow Mr & Mrs Berry out of the door.

"We were given a lifeline by Munns who came in, looked at the company, saw what was going on and then upped our deal. He didn't have to do it and it wasn't for very long but we were right on the edge of going with nothing," says Cooper, one of the very few Englishmen ever to run a US-based record label.

However their departure wasn't delayed for long and Cooper takes a philosophical view that their leaving – "which we read about in the *LA Times*" – was a straightforward knock-on effect. "It was a case of if the main man gets fired then eventually everybody else gets fired," admits the man who helped Gorillaz to their first success in America and Janet Jackson achieve the distinction of becoming the first act in pop history to have a single added to every US pop, R&B and urban radio station in the same week with 'All For You'.

But it wasn't just the Berrys or Cooper and Newton who were let go as the new regime began to make an impact in an effort to improve EMI's troubled situation. Between 50 and 60 people were released from the US Capitol, Virgin and Priority labels in the run-up to new boy Levy joining Nicoli and Bandier to announce the company's half-year figures up to September 2001.

Speaking to the City for the first time as head of EMI's music division, Levy admitted that there was scope for cost savings and increased efficiency by combining the back-room operations of EMI and Virgin, which Berry had so steadfastly refused to do. "I think that they're not having enough co-ordination of Virgin and EMI," he explained

In the light of the company's earlier profit warning, expectations were not high among analysts, investors and shareholders as EMI revealed total turnover down to £1,067 million, while operating profit dropped over 67% to £43 million, with the recorded music division actually posting an operating loss of £8.1 million.

On the news of the company's half-year performance, City brokers Merrill Lynch were quick to react and revise their own forecasts for the full year by reducing pre-tax estimates from £286 million to £195 million, although they were buoyed by news of anticipated cost savings in the region of £65 million.

While EMI's ultimate target was to report year-end figures in line with the previous 12 months, Nicoli did not sound overly confident when he conceded, "The target's the same but it's ever more challenging."

CHAPTER 6

Land Of Confusion

(Genesis, Virgin 1986)

FROM day one in their new top jobs at EMI, Alain Levy and David Munns made an impact on EMI UK chief Tony Wadsworth, who was called to meet with his new bosses at the very start of their reign.

Among other things, they were interested to know how the label's British-based, Australian superstar Kylie Minogue was doing in America. When Wadsworth told them that EMI's US companies had passed on the former TV soap star's latest album, the new team went into action.

"It was rescheduled within days and went on to be a platinum album in America," says Wadsworth, who believes the success of Kylie Minogue helped make a point about his roster of acts. "It showed that the music we were producing in the UK had the potential to cross over and do well worldwide if it was given the opportunity."

Kylie Minogue was the latest artist to join the line of British acts signed to EMI and Virgin – which featured Coldplay, Radiohead. Blur, Gorillaz and Chemical Brothers – who were in effect supporting the company's US labels as they struggled to discover and break major new American artists.

For manager Chris Morrison this partial success in America was something that EMI should have made more of, rather than keeping it hidden. "When Eric got rid of Ken he issued a statement that apologised for the company's performance in America," says the London-based manager involved with both Blur and Gorillaz.

As, according to his calculations, UK repertoire accounted for 9% of US top 100 sales at that time and EMI was responsible for half of that, there was some good news to spread. "That was a huge achievement and if I had been Eric I would have been standing there shouting about signing to EMI if you want to break in the US. Take advantage of your strengths and don't apologise for your weaknesses," is Morrison's view.

In fact EMI's continuing impressive performance around the world with artists signed to its UK company brought official recognition in April 2002, when EMI was awarded a Queen's Award for Enterprise for sales of UK repertoire overseas. It was the third such award for EMI Records UK, but came in a week when the *Billboard* Hot 100 US Singles did not feature a single British act.

Munns' long-standing reputation as a leading global marketing executive was one of the attributes that made him attractive to EMI, even though his appointment was sometimes lost in the coverage of Levy's role. "The perception among some was that EMI was buying Alain, but that Munns simply came along as part of the deal," comments Martin Talbot. "That proved to be a little unfair on Munns, who is a real record professional, and once he got his feet under the table and got things moving, there was a real sense that they could make it happen in the US in a way that their predecessors hadn't been able to."

While, by his own admission, he operated as a double act with Levy – "We had a deal where if we didn't agree we didn't do it" – the duo, according to Munns, also complemented each other. "The things he's good at, I'm not particularly good at and the other way round." And they were also tough and, according to some, even ruthless in their dealings with EMI operations and personnel.

The business maxim that good managers in good times don't always make good managers in bad times could be applied to Levy and Munns' search for the best people to put into place around the various EMI companies. At the same time they were also keen to change the way in which EMI's personnel behaved, which Munns puts under the heading of morals and transparency. "The morals in the company were just terrible. People saw what some senior people did and got away with, and they just didn't give a shit."

One of the first issues to which the new management team turned its attention, as predicted by Levy in his November comments to the City and the media, was the overlap of EMI and Virgin services, particularly the support and back-room areas such as accounting, royalties and technology.

"It was low-hanging fruit for Alain and David," is how Wadsworth describes the unnecessary duplication in overheads. "They came in to say you can still keep the labels but surely we don't have to have two sets of absolutely everything else. It was just a case of how to rationalise it all."

In its end-of-year review trade publication *Music & Media* carried figures for the major's European album chart shares over the six-year period between 1996 and 2001, and they showed that EMI's performance had begun and ended at about the same level – 21.1% in 1996 and 21.9% in 2001. In between EMI had reached a peak of 24.5% in 1997 and dropped to a low of 14.4% in 1999, but they still stood in second place in 2001 behind Universal's 26.4%.

While these were encouraging figures they came on the back of a hugely disappointing, and in many ways devastating, six months, which also saw the publication of the latest 16-page report on the global music industry from analysts ABN AMRO and their team, which included media experts Mike Hilton and Helen Snell.

While their advice to shareholders was to hold onto their EMI shares, they retained a "negative stance" with regard to the music industry's future, which they described as "extremely gloomy", but still managed to come up with some encouraging news for EMI.

Via figures from Nielsen SoundScan in America, they showed that EMI had gained 1.5% (up to 10.5%) of the important US album market for the first nine months of 2001, the biggest rise of all the majors. The estimated figures for the UK album market in the same period showed EMI down 0.7%, while in continental Europe, estimates put EMI among the winners with an album market-share increase of 6.8% to a high of 22.5%, just over 3% behind leaders Universal.

ABN AMRO's "implied global sales trends" up to October 2001 suggested that number one company Universal had dropped 2.5% in world-wide sales, which was nothing compared to the −11.5% figure for BMG and still above Warner's −3.5%. Sony was given a 4.2 % increase while EMI was the big winner with a 7.7% increase, even though the analysts were quick to point out that their study was limited to album volume only, plus European chart-share information.

They summed up their findings by suggesting that Universal's golden era appeared to be coming to an end, while BMG's negative trend would continue and Warner's decline reflected flat sales. For Sony they reported sales that were at odds with the company's own forecast downgrading full-year expectations, and they concluded that their positive figures for EMI were not in line with the company's profit warning or internal sales information.

Despite their initial 'hold' recommendation, the analysts still suggested that there was a "further downside risk to EMI forecasts" and they also decided that EMI's under-performance in the US was in part to blame for Ken Berry's departure. While that was undoubtedly true there was another Virgin problem from Berry's reign that was about to come to a head.

Speculation began about the future of megastar Mariah Carey as first Ken and then Nancy Berry left EMI and the singer's *Glitter* album managed sales of only 400,000 in its first month. While the former CBS/Sony artist with career sales in excess of 120 million albums, plus five US number one singles and 18 UK top ten hits, was saying that she was looking forward to working with the new team of Levy and Munns, there seemed to be less enthusiasm in the company for songbird Carey, who was signed by the Berrys.

Former EMI boss Southgate looks back on the decision to sign Carey as "the final straw for Ken", and sure enough by early 2002 the music industry was awash with rumours that the biggest-selling female singer of the 1990s was about to be dropped by EMI after just one album.

Writing in *The Daily Telegraph* on January 10, 2002, Neil McCormick reckoned that EMI's treatment of the singer was "an extraordinarily bad piece of business that has got nothing at all to do with music". Even though, by his own admission, he was not a fan of the multi-octave-range singer, McCormick calculated that though EMI's deal to sign Carey (reported to be £70 million for five albums) was expensive – and made even more so by an apparent marketing commitment of £5 million per album – there was still hope for the company because, as he pointed out, "the pop market is notoriously fickle".

His concern was that, despite sales of *Glitter* eventually reaching two million and the singer notching her sixth US number one single, the company had put itself in a position where in order to simply break even, sales had to exceed 10 million – and that applied to the next four albums as well. He summed it up by suggesting that, given that EMI was in the business of making music, "It might be best served taking its losses on the chin and considering what it can do to improve the commercial performance of this undoubtedly talented asset."

Talking six years on, he holds to his original view that it was a moment of bad business for EMI. "What a signal to send out – we are going to pay this incredible singer who's hugely popular millions of dollars to go away."

And there was the additional concern about the media's reaction to the news. "So Mariah Carey with her big breasts and her big voice, plus the EMI share price falling because she has been dropped, becomes a big business story," says McCormick, whose views are echoed by Mike Hilton.

"People were very aware of the excesses of the music industry and the Mariah Carey and Ken Berry pay-offs, while the industry was completely in denial about the fact that the good times were over," he explains with an added warning for investors. "Shareholders should never invest in football clubs or music because the money is siphoned off along the way – the talent takes it and if the talent doesn't take it, then the management and the corporate machines will take it."

For many the Carey/EMI scenario conjured up memories of 1977 when EMI famously dropped The Sex Pistols, who then, ironically, moved on to Virgin where they sold more than a million records.

With executives at EMI describing the Carey deal as "a big may-day" and efforts to renegotiate the financial terms – which were seen as "a monkey on our back" – not working out, the company took the view that there was only one route open to it. There were also concerns among the senior staff that, while the advance on the deal was "absurd", the marketing commitment "was just lunacy".

According to reports, the massive guaranteed spend by Virgin on the marketing of each Carey album, prompted Nancy Berry to ask each of the Virgin companies around the world to come up with ideas for 'money no object' campaigns for *Glitter* – and it seems the French and UK companies duly obliged. Apparently a plan from France involved closing and re-tiling Paris Metro stations with Mariah Carey and *Glitter* album tiles, while the UK operation offered up the idea of covering London's GPO Tower in a huge shroud advertising the singer and her new album.

However, for chairman Nicoli – who had to officially authorise the multi-million pound deal – signing Carey made sense in 2001. "Her track record up to the time we signed her was absolutely stunning, huge numbers," he says, before admitting, "It was an expensive deal and it became clear that we would incur losses for several years."

In the light of that calculation there was only one solution to the problem that was Mariah, explains Nicoli. "In 2002 we had an opportunity to cut our losses and I supported Alain and David in doing so." And by doing it in January the company could write off the loss before the end of the 2001–2002 fiscal year, which, as Levy commented, was "the most prudent course of action for EMI".

Bringing to an end what was described by the media as the biggest recording contract in the history of the music industry, cost EMI £20 million in a pay-off to the 31-year-old singer, in addition to the £15 million she had already received. The move saw the EMI share price drop 6½p to 340p and it also brought criticism from Carey's US lawyers, who were less than impressed with EMI's version of events.

Marshall Grossman of the firm Alshuler, Grossman, Stein & Kahan said, "The fact is that this contract was terminated amicably and the parties decided to go their own way. What EMI did was to unilaterally release its own statement, saying it terminated the contract itself. That is wrong."

In the midst of this corporate war of words, Carey – over £35 million richer as a result of the move – issued a statement that simply, and not surprisingly, said, "This is the right decision for me. I look forward to the many new and exciting opportunities which [sic] have been presented to me."

The arrival of the new management team at EMI brought a number of significant changes to the company's front-line executive team. Long-time head of Virgin UK Paul Conroy was ousted in favour of EMI chief Wadsworth, who assumed responsibility for Virgin in his new role as chairman and CEO EMI Recorded Music UK & Ireland.

At the same time, on the heels of Cooper and Newton's long-anticipated departure from Virgin US, record producer Matt Serletic was hired as chairman of Virgin Records America, with previous EMI Recorded Music North America deputy president Roy Lott reporting to him as president Virgin Records America. These moves came on the back of Munns officially taking added responsibility for America, as chairman and CEO EMI Recorded Music North America, and a decision that it was time for a change of name.

Levy announced in February 2002 that all EMI Records companies around the world would in future be known as Capitol Records, and sit alongside Virgin Records as the two dominant company labels. The name EMI was retained as the corporate brand for the EMI Group, plus EMI Recorded Music and EMI Music Publishing.

He explained his decision by saying, "Capitol, which has a long and rich musical legacy, and Virgin will be established as the two global brands for our creative activities that represent different identities with their own style and rich histories of creativity and great music."

Just as the industry was digesting the publication of *Billboard*'s analysis of the best-selling albums in the world during 2001 – which showed that EMI had only three titles in the top 20 (Janet Jackson's *All For You* number 12; Pink Floyd's *Echoes* number 16; Robbie Williams' *Sing When You're Winning* number 17) – there came news of a second profits warning from EMI.

Coinciding with the departure of Tony Bates, whose dual responsibility as chief financial officer for both EMI Group and EMI Recorded Music had caused some concern in financial circles, the company announced a further reduction in pre-tax profit expectations for the year ending March 2002.

Following the previous September's announcement lowering profit predictions by 20% to somewhere between £160 million and £207 million, the company was now estimating a figure no higher than £150 million. As a result the company's share price dropped over 6%, even though Levy gave details of a new EMI structure.

The moves to merge back-office operations such as sales, finance, IT, human resources and catalogue exploitation were expected to bring about annual savings in the region of £65 million, although initial plans to offload EMI's manufacturing business did not materialise. Company executives believed that these moves were well received by investors, who were considered to be impressed with Levy's tough reputation and skill at restructuring.

However, it brought a different response from the former new-media chief Jay Samit, who believes that EMI and Virgin were not exactly merged. "Levy and Munns purged them – by the time they got through there wasn't anybody left standing," he says, while Emmanuel Legrand takes the opposite view. "They [Levy and Munns] arrived when the business was already declining and they took some bold steps in merging the EMI and Virgin operations. They got rid of a lot of people and a lot of artists and people tend to forget that it was very violent in terms of what they did to the company, but it probably wasn't violent enough," he claims.

For ex-EMI Group chairman Colin Southgate a bigger mystery was the ability of his chosen successor to hang on to his job. "Why when he [Nicoli] put through his second profit warning in months didn't the board fire him – explain that to me. I've never heard of that in my whole working life."

There were also still question marks hanging over the company's future, its sensitivity to the market and its shortage of cash. Figures distributed internally in 2001 showed the company's "actual group net debt" as being £992 million at the end of the 2001 financial year, with the full-year net debt forecast to be £1,147million by March 2002.

"For EMI alone among the majors the release schedule drove the share price and when a big album slipped it affected the share price," says Davin McDermott, a member of EMI's global restructuring team under Levy and Munns. "EMI had no cash and cash management was a huge issue as, when they did some of their bigger deals, they had more commitments than they had facilities, which meant it was always tough on them to be competitive when it came to doing deals."

But for two City analysts the secret of Nicoli's survival came down as much to his style and personality as to any business acumen. "Eric is an incredibly good presenter and you can guarantee that every EMI analysts' meeting would be enjoyable; he could almost present a profits warning with a smile on his face," recalls Helen Snell, who adds that it might not always have been enough to convince everyone.

"However, no investor or analyst would be swayed by that – at the end of the day it is about 'show me the money' – but I do honestly believe that some of the major funds that stayed with EMI even when the writing was on the wall were swayed by Eric's presence."

Her view is echoed by Mike Hilton when he says that many in the City were prepared to give Eric a chance. "I don't recall a massive backlash against him. He's a funny guy, didn't have a bad reputation, he made people laugh and at the time the problems weren't so obvious that people thought you needed someone who was going to be more forward-looking and strategic."

Times media editor Dan Sabbagh, who has studied EMI for the past six years, also believes that Nicoli showed great skill when dealing with the company's investors. "One of the things Eric did well – possibly even better than people give him credit for – was to manage the shareholders," says the journalist, who also points out two things that EMI's boss was able to say "fairly convincingly" to any potential critics.

"Firstly, he said the problems are not my fault, so whether it was Napster or the EC or iTunes he could say 'it's the market', then add in that he was a player in the market and say that, for quite a while, EMI was much more profitable than its competitors."

Nicoli's people skills were also apparent to UK chief Tony Wadsworth, who saw the head of the company as, "A great figurehead as far as the staff at EMI Records were concerned because he could talk quite comfortably to people at all levels. Eric was a great believer in developing people."

One of the ongoing issues relating to Nicoli and his role at the top of the EMI tree was his love, knowledge and understanding of music and the music business. But did the man who ran the UK's only major music company have to be what was known as a "music man"? After all, why should it have been any more of an issue for Nicoli to have come from a non-music corporation than Southgate, with his background in the computer business, or Fifield, who spent 20 years working with food, fashion and toys at General Mills?

The *Telegraph*'s Neil McCormick says that Nicoli was viewed as a music man simply because he played a bit of music but adds, "I don't think he was a music man", while manager Clark says, "I never saw Eric as a record company man or a music man – and I like him!"

Acording to analyst Mark Beilby, having a background in the biscuit and confectionery business was perhaps what made Nicoli attractive to EMI in the first place. "There was a lot of talk about music being the classic consumer goods and him having experience in that area," he says. Artist manager Andy Taylor concedes that although he and his partner Rod Smallwood never really "got to grips with Berry", they did have an affection for Nicoli. "He was the first to admit that he wasn't a music person but he was a good businessman and a nice person, easy to deal with and honourable."

For Iron Maiden's management team, who took their own company, Sanctuary, public in 1997, Nicoli was not just the face of EMI but also a friendly face. "When Maiden played, Eric would always be there right through to the end of the show and he was one of the few people the band knew at EMI, although they took no real interest in what was going on within the company," says Smallwood, whose association with EMI goes back to the early 1970s and Cockney Rebel.

While he has been based in America for nigh-on two decades, experienced music industry executive Bob Mercer has kept in touch with the goings-on at his former company and observes that while Nicoli may not have been "a music man", there were plenty of other companies being run by experienced music industry people that weren't performing much better than EMI.

"I think the problem is not whether they are good music men or good businessmen or indeed good music businessmen, when you are talking about the Nicolis of this world the question is were they a good chairman?

"The chairman's job is a lot, lot different to that of a CEO, because the role he has to play is managing a company as opposed to managing a music company," concludes the man whose EMI career included a spell with the company's film division in the late 1970s.

But the bigger question surrounding the team of Nicoli, Levy, Munns and music publishing chief Martin Bandier was whether they could work together. According to Emmanuel Legrand there was "constant bickering among the company's top managers", while the traditional political feuding between management, regional chiefs and shareholders continued unabated.

"The real problem was that Levy should have been doing what Nicoli was doing, and Munns should have been running the company with only one of them in charge of strategy and the big picture."

By bringing in Levy and Munns, Nicoli had, according to Helen Snell, created what she called an interesting situation "whereby everyone knew that Eric had minimal impact on the running of the business – the power was all with Alain and everybody wanted to meet him." For Phil Hardy, however, the biggest problem facing EMI was the team of Levy and Munns, who each had particular skills that he found hard to see gelling at EMI in the same way as they had at Polygram.

"Munns is a tyre-kicker but he does understand artists because he has worked with a lot over the years in a way that Levy hasn't, but by the time they arrived, axes were starting to fall and it was hard for them to energise people," Hardy concludes before outlining what the two of them faced at EMI. "Levy had strategic plans but was confronted by short-term issues that he doesn't like dealing with, so Munns was left doing almost everything."

In Dan Sabbagh's opinion Nicoli could easily have changed how his company was run, but the journalist believes that the EMI chairman did not have enough power to get into the two divisions and "get a grip on costs". It seemed to the *Times* writer that Nicoli sat atop his empire dealing only with the City plus policy, lobbying and regulatory issues.

"Below him you had Levy and Bandier, neither of whom was going to tolerate much interference. They ran their own divisions as separate games of missile command," he says, which meant that in his view EMI was never run as a conventional company. "You had these big barons in Levy and Bandier and that caused some problems for Nicoli."

In March 2002 came the much-needed overhaul of EMI that had been promised since the arrival of Levy and Munns. Firstly the company closed its UK compact-disc manufacturing plant in Swindon with the loss of over 190 jobs, switching the business to the company's larger European facility in the Netherlands. This move came a year after EMI's historic UK record manufacturing operation at Hayes was closed in light of falling vinyl sales.

Before the end of the month Levy announced his plan to axe 1,800 jobs by September while at the same time slashing the company's dividend by 50% to 8p, saving the group £62 million. Levy's total restructuring – which he declared was aimed at "positioning EMI for the future" – included an exceptional payment of £240 million, including Carey's £38 million pay-off and a further £48 million to cover other artist and label write-offs.

In addition to the staff reduction, around 400 artists were also to be dropped from the company's worldwide roster of 1,600 acts; these included 49 artists in Finland, which prompted Levy to famously comment, "I think that's a bit too many; I don't think there are 49 Finns that can sing."

Explaining that "this is not a cost-cutting exercise for the sake of it", Levy added. "It is a reshaping of EMI for the future. It is about changing the values of the company." He went on to acknowledge that the company's dealings in America had not always made the best business sense. "Part of the US problem is that we have been trying to buy market share. We went into joint venture deals that don't make sense, in order to get a quick fix."

While the job losses being predicted in the US – some 27% of the total – would bring the largest savings (46% of £98 million), it was Europe that was forecast to bear the brunt of the staff cuts with over 600 jobs being lost. The announcements, which coincided with EMI predicting an increase in its global market share to 15% by 2005, raising its profit margin from 5.3% to 12.6% in the same period and boosting back-catalogue sales by 10% to bring in an extra £25 million in revenues per year, saw the company's share price rise 10p to 365p.

As *Music Week* concluded that "painful changes are healthy", its editor Martin Talbot declared EMI's move was "one of the most high profile streamlining processes we have seen within the UK music business in recent years", but it was needed in order to make EMI "fit to compete", while its rival companies would also have to face up to the very real possibility of future lay-offs.

However, for analyst Mike Hilton the changes represented a renewed sense of optimism within EMI following the pessimism that had surrounded its failed mergers, profits warnings and artist write-offs. "Through 2002 they put out some pretty aggressive forecasts for growth in the industry but had to instigate a massive restructure to take costs out," he says. "And by taking out costs they were less attractive to take over because the fat had already been removed."

EMI received a financial boost with the public flotation of HMV Group, the chain of music stores launched by EMI's predecessor The Gramophone Company back in 1921. Valued at £834 million, the HMV Group was bought by its management in 1998 and, under the terms of the deal, EMI was in line for a windfall of anything up to £180 million, depending on the value of the HMV shares at their mid-May 2002 launch.

The music company, which was still predicting operating profits of £150 million for year end March 2001, sought to calm investors' fears over the level of its debt by agreeing a refinancing with banks consisting of an £800 million facility spread over three years plus a £500 million bridging loan. Then, armed with this financial backing, EMI went shopping.

In early May 2002 it announced the purchase of leading UK independent record company Mute for £42 million. The deal, which saw EMI pay £23 million plus a further £19 million in performance-related payments spread over four years, brought artists such as Moby (excluding North America), Prodigy (US only) and Depeche Mode under the EMI banner.

Label founder Daniel Miller, who set up Mute in 1978, retained global responsibility for the label – which boasted a 20-year relationship with Virgin prior to the purchase – and explained the reasoning behind the deal. "The new agreement was carefully designed to preserve Mute's autonomy, stability and continuity into the future," and EMI commented that while it was "getting out of lots of businesses" it also "wants to get into businesses which work for us, like this one".

On the back of the IFPI's global market-share figures for 2001, which showed that EMI had slipped 0.5% to 13% – putting them in third place behind Universal on 23.5% and Sony with 14.7% – the company's figures for the year 2001–2002 made more depressing reading for employees, artists, managers and investors.

While turnover fell 8.5% to £2,445.8 million, and there was a much-reduced operating profit of £190.9 million (from £332.5 million), EMI overall reported a pre-tax loss of £152.8 million and even though these figures were in part predicted and expected, the company's share price lost 19p on May 22, 2002 to finish at 271p. Once again music publishing reported increased turnover and operating profit but the recorded music division showed an 11% drop in turnover (to £2,029 million) and a £144 million fall in operating profits to just £83 million.

A financial assessment of EMI in *The Daily Telegraph* valued the company at £2.1 billion and concluded that the major problem for the music industry was piracy, with the focus on illegal downloading from the internet. However the report stated that it was too early to write off the music industry as a lost cause although it did suggest that EMI represented a "risky buy on a long-term view".

In its annual report, EMI made much of the fact that it "is the only major company focused purely on artists and music", which of course was true but had also led to it seeking partnerships with two rivals in the previous two years.

On the sales front EMI's multi-million best-sellers ranged from Robbie Williams (*Sing When You're Winning*, 5.4 million) through to Kylie Minogue's *Fever* (3.6 million) – with Janet Jackson, Pink Floyd and Gorillaz in between – while music publishing picked out Alicia Key's five-million-selling debut album (for rivals BMG) as their songwriting highlight. The report also showed that Ken Berry received a £6 million pay-out after being ousted in October 2001.

Now there was a new worry for EMI as its share price and valuation put it in the "buffer zone" – for stocks ranked between 90 and 111 that were subject to analysis by the FTSE (*Financial Times* Stock Exchange) 100 committee for ranking. A negative decision could see the company drop out of the prestigious FTSE 100 for the first time since its inception in 1931.

That decision came in September 2002 when EMI was down-valued to just under £1.3 billion and found itself ranked at 114 on the FTSE index and, along with other blue-chip companies such as British Airways and International Power, was removed from the listing for the first time in its 71-year history.

And while the City was seemingly unmoved by this news – analysts Dresdner Kleinwort put out a "buy" notice on EMI stock – AOL Time Warner chief Dick Parsons was telling a Royal Television Society conference that the case for a merger between Warner Music and EMI was still strong, although sources at both companies denied that any talks were taking place.

EMI's half-year figures up to September 2002 made marginally better reading as operating profit increased to £79 million (compared to £43 million in the same period the previous year), even though turnover was down just under 10% to £961.5 million. And, while turnover for music publishing increased by just over 1% and profits dropped marginally to £51 million, it was recorded music that reported the biggest improvement with operating profit reaching £28 million from the previous year's £8 million loss.

Recognising that October 2002 heralded the first anniversary of the arrival of Levy as chairman and CEO of EMI Recorded Music, Nicoli concluded that "the magnitude of the change he and his team have made in that time has been enormous", and while he anticipated the global recorded music market would continue its decline in the second half of EMI's financial year, he expected it to be "at a reducing rate".

Meanwhile *Music & Copyright* was writing in September 2002 that the decline in soundcarrier (CDs, cassettes, records, music videos and DVDs) sales in the first half of 2002 was such that it threw into "serious doubt" EMI's ability to meet the sales, profits and market-share predictions it had made six months earlier.

The magazine was basing its findings on official US and UK industry figures, which showed that only France of the world's top ten music markets reported growth in the first half of 2002. In the UK the BPI reported a 6% decline in soundcarrier shipments, while in America the RIAA reckoned the fall was just over 10% in the US.

M&C calculated that EMI relied on soundcarriers for 84% of its revenues and that the downturn would have the greatest impact on the only stand-alone music company among the majors. On the upside it also concluded that EMI would also be the only company whose management was not distracted by non-music business matters.

If the market for soundcarriers was declining it was undoubtedly being replaced by the new technology of the internet and downloading – both legal and illegal – and EMI's own figures showed the legal monthly acquisition of tracks via downloads in the US to be 3.5 billion in 2001. The figure for pirated tracks (both physical and downloaded) was 1.2 billion tracks per month, a 22% increase between 1996 and 2001, while the total number of legitimate CD tracks consumed showed a 2% increase to 3 billion.

Overall the figure for monthly total track consumption over the five-year period was up from 5.9 billion to 9.3 billion, an increase of 9.4% but, according to former EMI new-media finance man Davin McDermott, between 1999 and 2001, there were "no major conversations about the digital business during our business reviews".

On the other hand a senior EMI executive claims that £75 million – "which we really didn't have" – was set aside to build new systems and make EMI, in his words, "a digital company". He admits that the digital business was started from scratch early in the new millennium and it quickly grew to encompass telephone company deals, fixed-line deals, subscription deals and ring tuners and ring-back deals on a global, regional and local basis.

Claiming that EMI sold digital music as well as physical music – "not the other way round because the primary business systems were shot" – the executive was adamant that EMI was the only company that could properly account its digital royalties to its artists.

Something like 500 deals were apparently put in place over four years and by 2006 EMI seemingly had more deals for just 15% of its business than they had traditional retail accounts for the remaining 85%. In fact just before the end of 2002, it announced deals with nine digital music distributors to sell music as permanent downloads in the US.

With both existing EMI partners MusicNet and Pressplay among the nine, the new deal was described by US boss David Munns as "an initial framework that is good for consumers, artists, customers and our business", while the company talked of plans to release more repertoire in the future. Artists being made available for the first time under this arrangement, which EMI hoped to expand into Europe, included The Beach Boys and Frank Sinatra alongside the likes of David Bowie, Coldplay, Joe Cocker, Duran Duran and Blondie.

Despite EMI's claims and their new multi-deals, Pete Downton, who was at the forefront of Warner Music's new-media business, suggests that there was another company that led the way in the digital music business. "Just by their pure scale as the biggest company around means that Universal are always towards the front of any new initiative. Anybody with half a brain who wants to build a digital music service needs to go and see Universal very early on as they have always been the most aggressive and the most organised when it comes to expanding rights and pushing them through their business."

One man who is also not sure about EMI's dealings in the new digital age is former company chairman Colin Southgate, who also has doubts about its ability to succeed in America. "Things had to change and while they got out of manufacturing – as did lots of other companies – in my opinion they hadn't got a strategy for the digital age and they also never found someone who was going to make Capitol a major force."

It was always Capitol that stood out in America as the flagship label and acted as a guide to EMI's development and success in the US. When Levy and Munns took over running EMI it was generally accepted – and confirmed off the record by insiders – that "Virgin was a mess and Capitol wasn't much better" and they both struggled in the highly popular mainstream areas of pop and rock.

In fact EMI means very little to anyone in America outside the music industry as ex-UK executive Bob Mercer explains. "EMI is still seen in America as the company that had The Beatles and if you asked people outside the business who owned the Capitol Tower they'd say Capitol Records. EMI is pretty meaningless to people outside the industry."

While the company itself might be "pretty meaningless", for the great American public the music being produced by EMI was hitting the right chord with music lovers and record buyers both in America and around the world.

The new management had a plan to grow market share territory by territory by continuing to invest in local repertoire while also exploiting international repertoire, but avoiding any involvement in licensed deals for product that was not owned by the company. However, there were still problems with the supply line of US artists.

For UK chart company boss Martin Talbot, EMI's poor performance in America in finding and delivering US repertoire actually benefited its UK-signed artists. "Even while there was chaos and the company was struggling globally, they were more consistent about breaking British acts in America than any other," he confirms before adding that this was partly due to a lack of US talent and also because the US arm of EMI "needed to, and had to, make the most of its British talent source".

But for EMI UK boss Tony Wadsworth, despite the well-publicised success in the US of a number of his UK-signed acts, there was still the problem of convincing people about those successes. "The reality was that nobody broke more UK music in America than EMI," he says but accepts that perhaps the perception that EMI had a troubled North American operation made it hard to sell EMI in the US to his artists and managers.

Certainly Jonathan Shalit, whose acts Jamelia and Mylene Klass were not considered priorities for the US market, echoes that perception. "They've tried a number of times to make EMI in America stronger, but have failed," he says. "Up until now UK artists signed to EMI have always found it hard to have a chance of success in America, because traditionally EMI in America has not been very strong," adds the man credited with discovering multi-million-selling singer Charlotte Church.

At the same time, Wadsworth struggled with the non-delivery of major US acts from EMI in America with which to boost his own roster of acts in the UK marketplace. Accepting that this lack of US repertoire was one of his biggest problems, he points out that this can represent between 45% and 50% of the UK market and "if you are getting no US repertoire you are dealing in about 50% or 55% of the market, which means you have one hand tied behind your back".

And, as Wadsworth's UK operation at times claimed close to a third of the market with its home-grown repertoire, there was an obvious problem. "We had a market share of UK music at times above 30% and a market share of non-UK music of about 4% or 5%, which is an imbalanced company," he says. "And we were being slaughtered."

One of the very few US-signed acts to break through and become a global best-seller was jazz singer Norah Jones whose debut album, *Come Away With Me*, released in 2002, topped the 10 million sales mark and charted worldwide.

Newly appointed EMI US boss David Munns recalls that it wasn't all plain sailing in the beginning. "Bruce Lundvall [head of Blue Note] signed her up and made a record but nobody liked it. Arif Mardin [legendary producer who served with Atlantic Records for over 30 years and worked with The Bee Gees, Queen, Aretha Franklin and Phil Collins before joining Blue Note] was around, so we got him to fix it and out of nowhere we sold millions of records," he says.

"That's why we are in the business – that's where the fun is and eight Grammys later we were hot for a while," recalls Munns.

The arrival and success of Norah Jones, daughter of Indian sitar legend Ravi Shankar, was heralded by the EMI management as a sign of better things to come, recounts Mike Hilton. "I remember Eric (Nicoli) playing me the Norah Jones album and saying that this was the first day of their recovery in the US. She was the vanguard, she sold loads of records and there was a little bit of optimism," he recalls, but bigger issues still lay ahead.

"A major failing of both the industry and EMI was not dealing with the issue of new technology. Everyone was in complete denial that anyone would want to pull it all together and give the companies any chance of getting any revenue and legitimising music downloads," suggests Hilton who believes that allowing this to happen without copyright protection was the biggest issue facing the record business.

Following the very costly departure from the company of Mariah Carey at the start of the year, EMI was again in the headlines in October 2002 over another expensive deal when it re-signed award-winning and chart-topping singer Robbie Williams. After months of speculation and negotiations that had begun with former EMI boss Ken Berry, the new deal was concluded in the face of competition from Universal, Sony and Richard Branson's V2 label.

While EMI rejected stories that the deal was worth £80 million, it was generally accepted that Williams received an advance in the region of £25 to £30 million for the new *Escapology* album and a planned *Greatest Hits* release. The downside of the deal was the apparent firing of Williams' successful songwriting partner Guy Chambers, whose contract negotiations broke down as the EMI deal, which included four studio albums and two hits packages, was being concluded.

According to Wadsworth the structure of the deal had much to do with a process developed by Levy and Munns during their time at Polygram. "It was based around Alain and David's experience with the Really Useful Group (RUG), which was a joint venture with Polygram, and was structured in the same sort of way."

Under the new deal EMI and Williams created a new company – owned 75% by the singer – to hold income from all of Williams' non-recording interests in the same way as Andrew Lloyd Webber operates his RUG partnership. "It was regarded as a ground-breaking deal and the template for future 360-degree deals, and it worked for both parties," explains Wadsworth – despite the media's attempts to brand it as a second piece of expensive mismanagement by EMI.

Taking income from areas such as merchandising, sponsorship and concerts, the deal was quickly branded as being worth £80 million – the media calculated £10 million up front, £15 million for the first album and £55 for the remaining three albums – despite EMI's protests. "We tried to control the PR in the lead-up to the Robbie deal," says Wadsworth, "but once the tabloids had decided it was an £80 million deal, then you can correct people until you are blue in the face . . . and it's still an £80 million deal!"

Even as a member of the media, *Music Week*'s Martin Talbot had some sympathy with EMI's plight over the deal with Williams, which, like everything else involving the UK's leading music company, was carried out in what he calls "the full glare of public scrutiny". "The Robbie deal was a good deal, but still it got criticised in the media," he says, adding that the scenario involving a certain American singer was also unfairly exploited. "The Mariah Carey situation was not exclusive to EMI – plenty of other companies have had difficult experiences with demanding artists."

Looking back on what he described at the time as "a very complex deal", Tim Clark, partner in Williams' IE Music management team, describes it as "a joint venture deal and it was the first of what has been called 360-degree deals, although we never really liked that term".

He prefers to describe it as an all-rights deal in which the financial investment was separated from the services, but explains that there was one crucial issue to the deal. "Rob himself made it clear that his main aim was to get a big pay-off. He wanted a lot of money, which was not unreasonable as he had worked very hard – he'd delivered four albums and had a great reputation."

While failure was a factor in the deal, loyalty to EMI's newly installed top brass was not, according to Clark. "I think all artists wonder when they are going to fail, so we said, 'OK we'll go and get the best possible cash deal we can.' It all came down to doing the best deal and we didn't have any sense of loyalty to Levy and Munns, although there were EMI individuals around the world we liked."

The fact that talks about the new deal had begun before the senior management changes took place at EMI was also something that Clark does not overlook. "There would have been a great sense of loyalty to Ken Berry – both David [Clark's partner David Enthoven] and I had known him for some years and his departure was a great sense of sadness for us, although we were not terribly surprised. We knew that some of the criticism of him was right, but we really appreciated him as a man of honour who worked incredibly hard for EMI."

And despite the concerns he has since expressed about the appointment of Levy and Munns to run EMI's recorded music divisions, Clark denied, at the time of the new Williams deal, that there was any rift with EMI even after nine months of wrangling. "We have had a brilliant time with them up to now. It has been a tough negotiation but it has been good-hearted," he said before adding that all the EMI people have been fantastic "in the past".

With album sales of over 17 million behind him, Williams was a hot property for EMI and re-signing him was an important must-do deal for the company. The fact that people within the company had already heard the new *Escapology* album and knew how successful a greatest hits collection would be made it easier to justify the numbers.

"We can afford to front load the deal; it makes absolute sense," was one insider's assessment of the situation. "We could very easily have walked away from this deal if it got ridiculous; for us there is no such thing as a must-have deal with no regard to costs."

While experienced EMI analyst Helen Snell believes that the Williams deal was a positive move for the company, she would have preferred to see more details made public. "I knew it wasn't £80 million and some people did not understand that it was including merchandising and tours," she says, adding, "but EMI didn't do themselves any favours by not disclosing more details although contractually they probably couldn't, which was a pity as it could have been seen as a positive for them if they had been able to show that they had done something smart."

One other aspect of the deal that caused some debate was how much it was dependent on Williams breaking in America. His two previous Capitol album releases had both failed to dent the US charts, with *The Ego Has Landed* (a special compilation of his first two UK albums) peaking at 63 and *Sing When You're Winning* (a five-million global seller) stalling at 110.

At the time Clark agreed that the US was a key part of the deal and he told media that, while breaking in America could never be a clause in any deal, "You don't do a deal this size if you don't intend to break America."

Speaking six years later Clark admits that the deal did not anticipate any sales in the US. "EMI would have been mad to have done that deal on the likelihood of breaking in America," he confirms before adding that there was at the time little chance of it happening. "We had tried and we hadn't given up on the US for Robbie, but we had to present a proper business plan for the deal, which had to have realistic forecasts covering all the streams of income."

For EMI, selling Robbie Williams in America was considered a bonus, and it even went so far as to forecast nothing in the way of US income from the former Take That singer. However, Tony Wadsworth believes that with the proper treatment Williams could have made it in the States. "I think America did like Robbie and with real serious focus and commitment from both the record company and the artist he could have broken America," says the executive who described himself as "comfortable" with the risk profile of the deal. "Unfortunately I don't think our American labels understood how to translate his appeal into the American market.

"I think they tried to remould him and make him appear different for America, when one of the reasons for UK acts succeeding in America is because there is nothing else like them in the US. They should have cele-brated that difference," argues Wadsworth.

Sadly little changed for EMI and Williams in America as the new *Escapology* release quickly became a European multi-million seller and the singer's fourth consecutive UK number one album, but peaked at just 43 in the US when it was released in April 2003.

The fact that it entered the *Billboard* 200 chart at 43 and within two weeks had dropped to 157 led Williams' co-manager, Enthoven, to complain that it charted too high. "I would have been happier if it had gone in at 70 or 80," he said, while Capitol Music marketing executive Mark Collen confirmed that breaking Williams in the US was going to be a "long haul".

As expected Williams did little to help EMI's performance in the US, where its 2002 market share, according to Nielsen SoundScan, dropped from 10.6% to 8.4% and its overall CD sales slipped by 28% to 58.4 million units. In the *Billboard* list of the Top 200 Album Distributors it was fifth with just 107 chart albums behind Universal (280), BMG (174), Sony (158) and Warner (163).

EMI's reaction to its drop in US sales was simply to announce, "There are no surprises in any of this. It's about getting our cost base tight and building from there."

Surprisingly, however, the now "rich beyond my wildest dreams" Williams and his multi-million sales, alongside those of Kylie Minogue, Coldplay, Moby, Blur and Radiohead, didn't improve things globally either, according to official IFPI market shares.

The EMI figures for North America (down 1.2% to 8.9%), Europe (down 1.3% to 16.6%), Japan (down 1.6% to 9.4%) and Latin America (down 1.8% to 12.4%) contributed to an overall drop of 1.1% (down to 12%) in its global share, with Asia (excluding Japan) the only real bright spot with a near 2% increase to 10.5%.

Of its rivals, Universal showed a 2.2% increase in its global market share (25.9%) while BMG was up 2% (to 11.1%) and Warner remained on 11.9%. The only other loser was Sony, which dropped half a percentage point to finish with 14.1%.

And as the year ended so BMG made up for its failure to link with EMI in 2001 by acquiring the world's most successful independent record company. Bertelsmann paid a mighty $2.74 billion for the 75% share in Zomba it did not already own. Founded by Clive Calder in 1981, Zomba Music included Jive Records – which brought artists such as The Back-street Boys, Britney Spears, Justin Timberlake and R Kelly to the fore – alongside the Silvertone, Brentwood and Music For Nations labels, plus UK distributor Pinnacle.

So while BMG was expanding its company and Universal was still growing as world leader, the talk again turned to EMI and its future. For music journalist Neil McCormick there was always a synergy between the record companies and the computer giants that could have produced something. "There was always an argument for a deal between EMI and somebody like Microsoft; possibly the people at Microsoft didn't need to own the software side, but it was probably a missed opportunity for them."

This is a view echoed by former EMI Music chief Bhaskar Menon, who believes that Nicoli could and should have sought a partnership with a technology business in the wake of profits warnings and a falling share price. "By then it was nearly all lost anyway and it should have been pretty clear that neither a miracle nor a quick sequence of new Robbie Williams, Coldplay or Radiohead albums would save the EMI ship on a stand-alone basis."

Other damaging rumours were also beginning to circulate, including the suggestion that Nicoli was becoming infected by the glamour of the music industry and the star names signed to his company. There was talk of him getting too close and too involved with the music at the expense of the money and, according to Bob Mercer, the general opinion was that "he went native and found rock'n'roll".

The danger, for outsiders who are asked to run music companies, is that they are "seduced by the business and also confused by it because it is different from anything else," suggests the former UK executive.

Manager Chris Morrison cautiously suggests that Nicoli "enjoyed aspects of the music industry but not necessarily the aspects he should have enjoyed", while the man who hired him to be chairman of EMI and "a suit" is less cautious. "It wasn't long before we saw a photograph of him at some music event in a suit and a black T-shirt, and I said then that the board had made a big mistake," recalls Colin Southgate.

Nicoli blames "mischievous commentators" for the stories that he was star-struck and had "gone native", and dismisses it all as "just bollocks". He believes that he got the balance just about right regarding the relationship between chairman and artist. "I was absolutely not star-struck. I devoted a part of my time to being with acts and I am genuinely interested in the music and respectful of the artists."

The fact that these stories were circulating at the same time as EMI was producing less than satisfactory figures served only to compound the company's problems. According to Emmanuel Legrand there was "a serious questioning about the overall strategy and where it would leave the company".

He suggests that the situation had a "disrupting effect on the whole eco-system – from artists to the people within the company who are trying to build something." He also believes that shareholders were unconcerned about morals or morale. "I think that throughout they were thinking about number one and never thought about the company."

For Phil Hardy the problem was the overall state of the company during the early years of the new millennium. "There was a general sort of malaise in EMI under Nicoli, when it seemed that the focus was on dressing up the company to do a deal," he says, while Nicoli himself accepts that the shareholders' interests centred around creating value in the face of a declining market and increasing piracy.

And if the large financial corporations with a vested interest in the future of EMI had any major concerns about his performance, Nicoli is quick to recognise the options that were open to them. "If the institutional share-holders were unhappy enough and the board was unhappy enough, I can assure you I would have been fired," he says, adding that the received wisdom when he fired Ken Berry was: "I was insane because this man was a guru and was admired by artists."

The long-time EMI chairman also recognises the importance of artists and managers in the mix and believes some of them "respected and even liked me", although being part of EMI in mid 2002 did not always repre-sent good news. "If you read every day that EMI is struggling, that affects everyone's morale. Then there's a sense of, 'Oh shit, I'm signed to a company that's doing badly.'"

The idea that EMI was a company doing badly was seemingly reflected on the FTSE 250 (EMI was still out of the FTSE 100) on February 4, 2003 when the company's shares fell to 131p – its lowest figure since 1985. Apparently influenced by 2002 sales and market-share figures, traders were still unhappy about the non-emergence of a potential buyer for the company and broker UBS Warburg issued a warning phrased in finance speak. "We believe medium-term lack of visibility with respect to revenue growth and an inevitable phasing out of cost savings raises the risk that earnings may come under pressure once more."

Within a week the EMI share price was down even further to 127p, with banker Morgan Stanley forecasting that the weakness in the music industry could last until 2006. And there was more bad news to come as, a year after trading at over 300p, the price dropped to an all-time low of just 80p.

All this negative action surrounding the EMI share price again served to set the rumour mill rolling with media stories once again suggesting that both AOL Time Warner and Bertelsmann had held exploratory talks with the British major in an effort to form some sort of joint venture.

While coverage suggested that talks were in the early stages, and officially EMI refused to comment on the rumours, the difference in value between EMI – reckoned by some to be worth only around £900 million – and Warner – estimated at approximately £2 billion – was considered a major stumbling block.

Nevertheless the speculation – which now included possible links with computer companies – helped the EMI share price to 113p by April 2003 when 19 million EMI shares changed hands in a single day, compared with an average of 10 million.

All this news came in the midst of EMI setting new records at the Grammy Awards where Norah Jones collected an unprecedented eight prizes alongside two for Coldplay. Meanwhile in the UK, BRIT Awards were also collected by Jones, Coldplay plus Robbie Williams and Blue.

In the words of new-media consultant Pete Downton "the digital business got real when iTunes was launched in the US and it all took off from there". The fact that EMI was one of the four majors to embrace Apple founder Steve Jobs' revolutionary online music subscription service – Sony was the exception – confirmed Mike Hilton's view that "it took an outsider – Apple – to pull them all together".

Bizarrely Apple's interest in music, its successful Apple Mac computers and its well-received iTunes music-managing software also brought them into the frame as potential buyer of the world's largest music company, Universal, for a rumoured £3.8 billion.

While Apple at this stage was aimed only at the US market, EMI announced its own online programme in the spring of 2003, which made 140,000 tracks from 3,000 artists available through a deal with UK company OD2, with tracks offered pre-release at the same time as they were delivered to radio stations.

Although The Beatles and The Rolling Stones were still missing from the list of acts, the new service would include most of EMI's artists who were signed to 'all rights' recording deals, which allowed the company to make their recordings available digitally without the need for specific clearances or agreements.

Early in the new 2003–2004 financial year the company announced the creation of new headquarters in London, where 300 staff employed in the group, global and European recorded music and classical music divisions would gather in fashionable Kensington. With leases on EMI's existing offices across London coming up for renewal, it was seen as a move that would bring improved communications and cost savings.

Another expense post-March year end was the decision to pay £70 million for a further 30% stake in the famous Jobete music publishing business formed by Motown Records founder Berry Gordy. Having bought 50% in 1997, EMI exercised an option to buy the remainder of the company, which features over 100 number-one songs in its catalogue, but agreed to Gordy's request that he retain a minority interest.

The deal was apparently funded through the sale of EMI's final 14.5% stake in HMV and it allowed the option to buy the remaining 20% of Jobete during the next two years. The news was well received in the City with one analyst observing that, with the company's balance sheet under pressure and question marks over the dividend, it was "a good move for the company".

Having suffered the indignity of recording a pre-tax loss of £153 million in the previous year, EMI bounced back into the black for the financial year ending March 2003 when it recorded a pre-tax profit of £319.3 million on turnover reduced by 11% to £2,175.4 million. And, for a change, while music publishing reported both reduced turnover and profits, the recorded music division increased its operating profit by over 80% to £150.5 million on turnover that was down 12.6%.

Even though Robbie Williams failed to break in the US, thanks to the multi-million sales success of Norah Jones, Coldplay and The Rolling Stones, the company's North American recorded music operation showed a profit for the first time in five years, and this was despite Nicoli's admission that the decline in the global music market was greater than the company had anticipated.

The figures brought about more merger speculation and while Nicoli viewed EMI's prospects as "good", he admitted that the combination of two music majors still made great sense. "Everybody understands the merits but such a combination is not without risk – both execution risks and regulatory risks."

The industry and media attributed EMI's improved performance to the severe cost cutting – involving job losses and reducing the artist roster – the company had undertaken during the year. Industry magazine *Music & Copyright* brought more good news when it declared that EMI was the most profitable of the majors despite, according to the magazine's own research, its global market share falling from 12% to 11%.

While EMI remained in third place in the league table it was the only major to lose global market share in 2002, and the gap between it and fifth-placed BMG was reduced to just 2.2% compared with 4.8% the previous year.

The speculation about merger talks reopening, plus Nicoli's admission that the "industrial logic . . . is unarguable" for two of the majors to join forces, brought new headlines in July 2003 – and these didn't involve EMI.

This time the talk was of Warner Music and BMG getting together, with insider sources suggesting that a deal would be completed during the summer and company officials admitting that a short-term exclusivity deal existed between parent companies AOL Time Warner and Bertelsmann precluding them from talking with any other interested parties.

As both Warner and BMG were smaller than EMI and because the EC had changed the role – and arguably reduced the power – of its merger task force, there was a strong feeling that this time a music merger might be allowed.

One analyst suggested that the merger of Warner and BMG – both weakened by cost cutting and industry problems – might be seen by the EC's Director General of Competition as not adversely affecting the rest of the business. He also warned that if the deal did go through, "EMI will be a lost soul who misses out again."

While talk of Warner and BMG getting together continued into August and September 2003, EMI was brought back into the frame, although rumours of a deal with US private equity group Blackstone and a possible bid for Warner, in the face of the BMG talks, were both dismissed. Mention of the powerful American company, which boasted assets of £116 billion in 2008, was the first suggestion of a move to take EMI 'private' and reports put the figure Blackstone was offering at £2.5 billion.

While any potential Warner/BMG link was further complicated by problems in reaching agreement on valuations of both companies, in the light of Warner's disposal of manufacturing and BMG's acquisition of Zomba and the non-inclusion of music publishing in that deal, the music industry heard news of possible changes involving Universal.

Following an agreement between Universal parent company Vivendi Universal and NBC, the broadcasting division of General Electric, to create a new $13 billion media group, there was immediate speculation that the successful Universal Music Group might be on the block, despite a company spokesman saying, "It is not for sale. I can say that loud and clear in two or three weeks and in six months."

September 2003 brought a new – and again unconfirmed – story that following the end of the exclusivity agreement between Time Warner (the AOL part of the company was now being phased out of the corporate identity) and Bertelsmann, EMI had offered $1.5 billion for Warner Music in a cash ($1 billion) and shares deal that would leave Time Warner with a 25% stake in the new company.

Creating a company that would boast the likes of Madonna, Norah Jones, Coldplay and R.E.M. on its roster alongside the catalogues of artists such as The Beatles, Queen, Ray Charles, Aretha Franklin, The Eagles and Phil Collins, would mean a global market share of close to 24% and, at the same time, reportedly generate cost savings in the region of $250 million.

It seemed that while Nicoli was expected to remain executive chairman of any new EMI Warner company, the American company's music executives would also figure in senior roles, although friction between Warner Music boss Roger Ames and EMI's Alain Levy – his former boss at Polygram – was always seen as a potential stumbling block.

Once again the perilous state of the international music industry, which the IFPI was forecasting to suffer a 5% to 8% fall in revenues in 2004 as piracy rose by 14%, was seen as a reason why the European and American regulators would not oppose the new merger.

Such was the strength of the rumours surrounding the possibility of EMI and Warner finally getting together that EMI issued a formal statement at the start of the last week of September. It said; "In view of speculation in the weekend press, EMI Group plc announces that it has now entered into non-exclusive discussions with AOL Time Warner Inc, with regard to a possible transaction involving the recorded music division of the Warner Music Group.

"Discussions are at a very preliminary stage and there is no assurance that they will result in an agreement acceptable to both parties. Any potential transaction would be subject to shareholder and regulatory approval."

Finally, close to three years after the two companies had held their first discussion about a merger, the EMI and Warner deal was back on – and it was official. Nicoli told the world that, while EMI was progressing as an independent stand-alone music company, his company "should explore every available opportunity".

Brokers and analysts in the City seemed to be swayed in favour of the deal and had no doubts that EMI could finance it either through a funding partner – and bizarrely the name Blackstone was near the top of everyone's list – a rights issue or by sourcing funds from an investment partner in the form of a loan.

The general consensus was that the deal was one that ought to be encouraged and supported for the sake of both EMI and the music industry, which needed to eliminate duplication and become tighter and more efficient.

With Warner Chappell – the music-publishing arm of Time Warner – excluded from the new deal, a large part of the problem that had caused the failure of the 2000 proposal was removed, but the European independent record companies' organisation Impala was still far from convinced.

Confirming its intention to oppose the merger – as it had in 2000 – and its concern about potential price fixing, the indie body said it believed that "any merger between the majors will have a seriously detrimental effect on the music market".

The highly respected music industry deal-maker Osman Eralp, who helped steer through EMI's purchase of Mute, said at the time that he believed the two majors had learnt lessons about presentation from the failed 2000 talks. Suggesting that both EMI and Warner would strive to keep the independents on side he commented, "Whoever delivers a merger needs to sit down with the independents, who are realistically looking for viable structures. They need to make it a win–win situation for both parties."

The view of *Music Week* executive editor Martin Talbot in October 2003 was that while the music industry could afford little excess fat and would probably benefit from being leaner, the independents could potentially gain from the wealth of mid to lower-selling artists made available by the majors.

He welcomed any deal that would bring greater consolidation and added, "The alternative, another year (or three) of failed attempts will do little for the music industry's image." And he was confident that would not be the case this time around.

One thing Talbot had not bargained for was four companies being involved in two mergers at the same time and therefore jeopardising each other's chances of completing a successful deal. And in November that was exactly what happened when Bertelsmann and the Sony Corporation announced plans to merge their music divisions.

At the same time there came the news that former Seagram and Universal music chief Edgar Bronfman was circling Warner Music and considering making a bid with the considerable financial backing of a private equity consortium. The possibility of a straight cash up-front deal was perhaps going to be more appealing to Time Warner than EMI's cash and shares option, which would also leave it with a 25% share of the combined EMI and Warner operation.

Nicoli was now standing on the edge of the precipice. Bronfman acquiring Warner Music would mean Nicoli's third failed attempt at a merger in four years and even the *New York Times* was moved to suggest that failure would raise questions "about whether Mr Nicoli is steering the company in the right direction".

But while the paper reminded its readers that Nicoli had been dubbed the 'Biscuit Bungler' by the British media, it also quoted Bear Stearns analyst Mark Harrington, who did not believe a merger was essential for EMI. "I don't think that it's necessarily a negative if EMI is left as a stand-alone company, even if there is another merger."

Given the unlikely scenario that both the Sony/BMG and EMI/Warner deals went through, the calculations were that three major music companies – Universal (24.2%), Sony BMG (23.6%) and EMI Warner (24.9%) – would control close to 73% of the global market. While the global figures showed little to choose between a 'big three', the European and UK markets highlighted individual company strengths and weaknesses.

Using figures for the three years from 2000, Europe showed EMI Warner with a 29.4% share, Universal with 26.3% and Sony/BMG on 22.9%. In the UK, EMI Warner would rise to a mighty 34.8% ahead of Universal's 27.5% and Sony BMG's 20%.

As the media began to plough through the details of the two possible mergers, it became clear that Bronfman buying Warner Music would do away with the expected drawn-out ritual of getting the shareholder approval needed for EMI to acquire Warner Music, and the Sony/BMG initiative might also complicate matters with the regulators.

It also became clear that the two major players at Sony and BMG – American Andrew Lack and German Rolf Schmidt-Holz – had formed a bond so quickly that by mid-November 2003 they were in a position to issue a joint statement confirming their intention to form a 50/50 joint venture called Sony BMG.

The new company would incorporate "the record company activities of the respective conglomerates", while all music publishing, manufacturing and distribution businesses would be excluded. BMG chairman Schmidt-Holz was named as chairman of the new company with Sony Music Entertainment chairman Lack acting as CEO, and it was agreed that the board would feature an equal number of representatives from each company.

The speed at which these decisions were made seemed to put Sony

BMG in the driving seat as far as gaining approval was concerned and it was expected that the merger proposal would be lodged with the EC's competition division within a matter of weeks.

There were also rumours that EMI was encountering problems in raising the finance for its proposed takeover of Warner Music and these were not helping the beleaguered British major's position. In late November 2003 things took a turn for the worse when Time Warner decided to consider a bid from a consortium led by Edgar Bronfman and billionaire television entrepreneur Haim Saban – known as the man behind cartoon character Inspector Gadget.

As Time Warner stopped to consider the offers on the table, Bronfman and Saban upped the ante and improved their bid to $2.8 billion – reportedly including $2.5 billion in cash – plus the assumption of some of the debt, and Time Warner having a 20% stake in the business.

It was an offer that Time Warner chairman Richard Parsons was said to favour and one that EMI was made aware of in late November, when it issued a statement saying: "Time Warner has tonight informed us that they are now considering a possible proposal from another party as an alternative to our own firm offer."

While EMI continued to make all the right noises about its deal with Warner still being alive, the arrival of Bronfman, coupled with the speed at which Sony and BMG were progressing their negotiations, made room for some doubt.

One EMI insider told the media, "We have been in this position so many times before we're used to the uncertainty," while Mark Picken, manager of EMI act Massive Attack, observed, "EMI as the last 'independent major' . . . is not potentially in one of the greatest positions if everyone decides to gang up." Meanwhile Rob Holden, the manager of Warner artists David Gray and Damien Rice, commented, "I'm a bit bored by it all. I wish people would spend their time doing their jobs rather than talking about this."

In the midst of all this takeover and merger frenzy, EMI's interim figures for the six months up to September 2003 showed that turnover was virtually unchanged at £960.3 million while operating profit was up marginally to £79.7 million. However, while both recorded music and music publishing increased their operating profit, exceptional charges including massive levels of returns in Japan (£16.9 million) reduced the group's overall pre-tax profit to just £11.9 million – a drop of 94% from the previous year's figure of £194.3 million.

In his chairman's report Nicoli confirmed the company's discussions with Time Warner about a "possible transaction involving the recorded music division of the Warner Music Group" and added that the talks "have progressed well and are at an advanced stage".

But even as Nicoli was announcing his company's figures, the general consensus was that his attempt to buy Warner Music was likely to result in his third failed deal. In his defence one analyst was quoted as saying, "It's a real shame because it isn't Eric's fault. There's no suggestion that he has negotiated badly. It just has not gone his way – again."

EMI eventually conceded defeat in the last week of November 2003 as Bronfman and his consortium won the battle for control of Warner Music. "We have concluded that it is no longer possible to reach an agreement on terms which would be acceptable to both parties and the interests of EMI's shareholders," said Nicoli.

The City's response saw EMI's shares rise by 1.75p to 164.75p on the basis that the company would not be involved in any further wranglings with the EC.

But for one long-time observer of EMI and the music industry, the company's failure to consummate their courtship with Time Warner was down to incompetence. "It's almost like EMI has forgotten the very nature of deal making," says Legrand. "A good deal is when both sides are happy and in this instance there was a sense that nobody was going to be happy."

For his part Bronfman, a man who was once a songwriter for Celine Dion, confronted those who doubted the wisdom of buying Warner Music in the midst of falling CD sales and increasing piracy – and with around $250 million of his own money. "There are those who would say it wasn't the world's greatest investment decision but as a manager I feel I have nothing to prove."

And within days of the Bronfman-led consortium claiming the prize of Warner Music, the music industry rumour mill was once again up and running with stories that he would quickly sell Warner Chappell music publishing in order to raise some cash . . . and attempt to buy EMI Music.

CHAPTER 7

What If

(Coldplay, Parlophone 2005)

S O 2003 ended with the creation of one new major music company and new owners for another, but the merger of Sony and BMG and the sale of Warner Music to a US consortium meant that EMI was still standing alone on the sideline. And despite some claims in the City that Nicoli was not to blame for the failure to complete a deal, he still stood to take some flak.

Media analyst Mike Hilton holds the view that the "two issues of management and regulations" were always going to make the EMI Warner deal a non-starter and adds, "There were some press articles around the failed merger saying it was time for him to go – once is unlucky, twice is careless and three times . . . But he was very good at saying, 'Yes, there's a problem but look I've done this and I'm dealing with it.'"

One of the journalists who believes Nicoli was fortunate not to lose his job is Emmanuel Legrand. "I never expected him to last that long – he was a lucky man. The smart thing that he did, that gave him a second lease of life, was sacking Berry and hiring Levy and Munns."

According to the experienced music industry writer this move probably bought the beleaguered company chairman some extra time in charge. "He probably told the board that now that I have a great new management team in place, give me three years to make things happen. He probably survived through that, but what should have been done was for the board to sack Nicoli and say to Levy and Munns, 'Now it's your turn'."

According to *The Times'* Dan Sabbagh, the new owners of Warner Music wasted very little time in approaching EMI about a possible deal and, although the talks remained secret for a while, they were seemingly doomed from the outset. "The discussions were about a kind of merger between Warner and EMI but Edgar Bronfman was very concerned to be chairman and chief executive and I think that was an issue. It eventually broke down for all the usual reasons – ego and price."

Watching in America while all this corporate toing and froing was going on was Sam Feldman, manager of Norah Jones, but it seems he was largely unconcerned about the profit warning, falling share price and failed mergers involving EMI. Making it clear that he does not speak for his artist, Feldman believes that although the record business, both then and now, is in a frightening state, "Artists and managers definitely can carry on in spite of all this and, in fact, control their destiny to a larger extent."

There certainly was an argument that the changing picture in the ownership of record companies, plus the reduction in the number of majors – and their obsession about savings and reducing staff and artist levels – alongside the increased opportunity this might give to the independents to make a new impression, meant that artists did have options and alternatives as and when their record deals ran out.

But the suggestion that the independent labels might gain from the majors trimming their artist rosters is one that UK indies chief Alison Wenham dismisses. "The idea that there would be a waterfall effect and smaller companies would benefit from the fallout of the merger because artists would be let go and could then sign to the independents is I think largely fiction."

The proposed merger of Sony and BMG – to create a new music company known as SBMG – was a major focus of the music industry's attention in early 2004 as the European Commission set about launching a phase-two enquiry. But despite the EC's concerns over market dominance, there were few who believed that the Japanese/German amalgamation would not be approved, despite an objection from Warner Music.

However, the newly created US independent's concerns that the new SBMG company could unfairly exploit links to its parent companies in areas such as television rights and music publishing was seen by many as confirmation that it was no longer interested in pursuing a deal with EMI.

Much of EMI's activity in the early part of 2004 was centred around its highly successful music-publishing operation, which finally completed the acquisition of Jobete by buying the outstanding 20% from founder Berry Gordy for £43 million, and then turned its attention to the Genesis and Genesis-related Hit & Run company, buying the remaining 49% for £11.5 million.

At the same time EMI music-publishing boss Martin Bandier was telling trade magazine *Music Week* that business was looking pretty good. "We may well have turned the corner in the US. If that is a sign of what is to come in Europe that can only be a good thing."

In fact the global success of EMI music publishing was something that former Sony executive Paul Russell believes EMI should have used to better advantage. "If you had someone who could leverage the tremendous credibility and size of EMI music publishing back into the record company, and if that person ran both, they could promise artists some very significant benefits."

Whether that was a claim for Bandier to be put in overall charge of EMI's entire music activities or not, the man who joined EMI when it bought SBK way back in 1989 did have a seat on the main EMI Group board, which, according to writer Phil Hardy, was a smart move. "When he was put on the board he suddenly had a responsibility for the whole company. When he was just head of publishing there was no possibility of any cuts in his area, but on the board he accepted things that were for the good of the company," he says, while one former senior executive suggests that Bandier was in fact disliked by the board of EMI and that Nicoli was "hell-bent on getting rid of him".

The company's much-vaunted cost-saving exercise continued into 2004 when it announced a further 20% cut in its workforce. Of the 1,500 people scheduled to go, around 900 were victims of the decision to close its CD plant in the US and sell its European factory. Both facilities were to be replaced by EMI outsourcing its manufacturing and further staff losses came from merging label operations in some European territories. The following year the outsourcing of CD and DVD manufacturing was completed in Japan where the joint Toshiba-EMI facility was sold for close to £12 million.

With the addition of a 20% cut in the artist roster – affecting what EMI described as "niche and underperforming artists" – the total cost savings were estimated to be worth £50 million, split over the next two years. And, according to Nicoli, the company had transformed its recorded music business over the previous two and a half years since Levy and Munns arrived, and he credited them with having "delivered over £100 million of fixed cost savings so far and also managed a dramatic turnaround in the performance of our US operations".

In fact when it came to the end-of-year results for 2003–2004, EMI reported a 1.4% fall in turnover to £2,120 million, while the group's pre-tax figure showed a substantial loss of £52.8 million against the previous year's adjusted pre-tax profit of £323.8 million. While these figures took into account exceptional restructuring charges of £138 million, the previous year's profit had included a one-off gain of £210 million from the sale of HMV.

Citing the likes of Norah Jones, Robbie Williams, Coldplay, Janet Jackson and Japanese star Hikaru Utada alongside newcomer Joss Stone and country star Keith Urban as the big sellers, EMI's recorded music division offered up operating profits of £147.4 million – against the previous year's £151.1 million – while publishing showed a small drop in operating profits to £101.9 million, with turnover down in both sectors.

However, the company was bullish about claiming a global market share of 13.2% (up from 12.7%) and its earning from the new digital music business. Citing 2003 as the year "that saw legitimate digital music take off", Nicoli's annual report reckoned that the company had achieved turnover of £15 million from sales of downloads and ringtones in the year up to March 2004, a three-fold increase on the previous year.

While the chairman described EMI as a "progressive music content company", music chief Levy declared that the figures had encouraged EMI to upgrade its previous forecasts for sales of digital music in five years' time from 5% to 25%. Conservative calculations estimated that if the trend continued, and piracy was brought under control, EMI could expect to earn between £30 million and £40 million in the next financial year.

The company's performance, including its position as the most profitable major music company, moved Nicoli to proclaim that it "proved that EMI's competitive position will not be affected by the proposed merger of Sony and BMG".

Certainly in 2003 EMI could lay claim to the best-selling album in the world thanks to over 10 million sales of Norah Jones' *Come Away With Me*, with Coldplay at number six in the list and The Beatles at 24, giving EMI three of the top 30 global best-sellers compared with BMG's 10, Universal with six and five each for Sony and Warner.

When the official IFPI market-share figures were published in June 2004, EMI found itself even better off with an improved 13.4% share of the world music market, which put it in second place behind Universal but ahead of Sony in the last year before its sales would be merged with BMG.

And while EMI increased its share of the market in Europe, Asia, Latin America and Australasia, it was the extra 1.5% it earned in North America during 2003 – giving the company a 10.5% share – that was most satisfying. This was coupled with the company's own improved financial performance in the important North American region where recorded music and publishing reported combined operating profits of over £99 million, up from £68 million.

Talking to *Hits* magazine in America in May 2004, David Munns said the company was "doing fine" in America and was starting to "build a nice little roster". And while he was keen for the company to be "stronger and stronger in America", he was unconcerned about the threat that a merged Sony/BMG might pose. "I think EMI has its own destiny worked out. EMI is prepared to move forward on its own without partners."

Under the management team of Nicoli, Levy and Munns, EMI moved forward slowly, although in addition to the cost cutting and staff and artist cuts there was additional pressure to simply keep the ship afloat. The people running EMI found it difficult to forecast what the music business would look like even two years ahead and, in the midst of continuing talk of mergers or takeovers, they were forced to focus on short-term thinking while restructuring for the long term. And even though they cut jobs and changed the shape of the company, they did it without losing market share.

For those in the media and financial communities, EMI was viewed as a company that was over-staffed with top executives and that this situation was unlikely to change. It had become apparent that Levy did not want to meet or talk to investors or analysts – saying it was Nicoli's job – and this meant, in the opinion of the experts, that Levy was never going to take on the top job and Nicoli was never going to be ousted in favour of his French colleague.

It seemed that when EMI did, as one analyst put it, "wheel Levy out", it caused even more confusion when he sat in investor meetings with Nicoli, Munns and financial head Roger Faxon. "Sometimes they even contradicted each other in front of investors," says one City person who sat through such a meeting.

There was also concern among the money people and the journalists about EMI's attitude towards financial reports and newspaper articles and the people who wrote them. "They were massively oversensitive to criticism and hated analysts and the media being negative about the company," is how one commentator puts it.

Talking to the influential business magazine *Management Today* in June 2004, at a time when the EMI share price was up to 250p – a pound higher than in the previous November – Nicoli gave some insight into his company's attitude to the media. Accepting that EMI, as a historic British public corporation and its only major music operation, was always going to be a focus of attention, Nicoli also conceded that his company had an appeal to the "tabloid audience". This he said was borne out in the headlines. "I can't get away from the celebrity nature of the business and there will always be headlines saying we're 'on song' or 'humming the right tune' or 'in a spin'."

And how right he was – just a month earlier *The Daily Telegraph* had carried the story of EMI's losses under the headline "Upbeat EMI see flipside to £52.8m slide into red" and the same paper went for "EMI makes overtures to rival groups" on its 2003 merger story.

Nicoli also defended EMI's global market share to *Management Today*. "We've got 13% of the global market. How many other UK companies in anything, anywhere, have a 13% global share," he told them before turning his attention to America. "The US has gone from 8% to 12% in three years and losses have been turned into profits."

While Nicoli and Munns were busy talking up EMI, its rivals Sony and BMG were still fighting their way through red tape in Brussels in an effort to get their merger cleared. While the US Federal Trade Commission was expected to give the union the official nod, the EC it seemed was still considering the implications of the merger and the objections of the independent labels plus Apple, Warner Music and Universal Music.

But a series of decisions by the European Union courts, overturning earlier merger rejections made by EC commissioner Mario Monti, seemed to suggest that Sony and BMG would get their way and become the world's second-largest music company.

Finally at the end of July 2004, Sony BMG came into being as a company with an estimated combined 2003 global market share of 22.1% putting it just 1.3% behind Universal. It also meant that the number one and two companies were around 10% better off than EMI and Warner in third and fourth place.

According to respected industry journal *Music & Copyright*, the merger left EMI as the sole music-only company with publicly traded stock and "even more susceptible than before to market forces and investor sentiment". It also pointed out that EMI was the only major not based in the US, which for many remained the hub of the recorded music business.

Among them is *Times* journalist Dan Sabbagh, who believes that EMI could and should have put an American – based in New York – in charge of the company's music activities. "All the other great music companies, while not ultimately American, do all feel like American companies."

Reflecting on the deal between Sony and BMG, Nicoli told *Music Week* that he remained focused on "building EMI as an independent, publicly owned music company", but even so there were those in the City who felt that with the EC approving one merger, there could be another one around the corner.

A briefing note from UBS Media made the point that, as the EC had failed to prove collusion on prices in the Sony BMG proposal, this could lead to "speculation that Warner and EMI now seek to resurrect their own merger". However, with both companies already deeply immersed in major reorganisations and sizeable cost-saving exercises, there was arguably little room for further benefits if they did merge. The sensible option, according to one analyst, was for EMI and Warner to "stick where they are for the moment".

However, irrespective of the company's position in 2004, analyst Helen Snell still held the view that EMI had missed the boat by not completing a merger in the four years since 2000. "The biggest mistake they made was not securing a deal. Whether it was with Warner or BMG they should have done it. That was their single biggest mistake as the music industry went through a round of consolidation and they weren't part of it," she says. "By not doing a deal they didn't buy scale."

As 2004 came to a close so EMI was cheered by the news that its share price had risen to 270p, an 80p rise over four months, following better than expected interim results for the six months up to September 2004. While the Group's turnover dropped from £960 million to £851 million, operating profit was up over 8% to £80 million and there were also increases in the company's digital business with sales of £6.5 million in the new technology arena accounting for 2% of the company's half-year revenues. And Levy – making one of his rare appearances at a brokers' meeting – told his audience to "enjoy Christmas because we will".

But it wasn't all good news. When the Nielsen SoundScan figures for the US in 2004 were totted up, EMI found itself trailing in last place with a meagre 9.9% share, nearly 5% behind third-placed Warner (14.6%) and close to 20% down on Universal (29.5%) and Sony BMG (28.4%). The fact that it had the second best-selling album in the US with Norah Jones' *Feels Like Home* and Coldplay had collected the Grammy for Best Record was little consolation.

In the UK it collected only five nominations at the BRIT Awards, compared with 12 in 2003, and had no winners to celebrate, as opposed to the previous year's five awards won by Coldplay, Robbie Williams, Blue and Norah Jones.

Since 1996 sales of over one million albums in Europe have been recognised by the official IFPI Platinum awards and during 2004 EMI saw Robbie Williams' *Hits* album reach the five million mark, followed by Norah Jones' *Feels Like Home* passing three million and, while both Massive Attack and Blue hit two million, newcomer Joss Stone saw both her 2004 releases, *The Soul Sessions* and *Mind Body & Soul*, qualify as single European million sellers.

These successes in Europe came on the back of Platinum awards in 2003 for Jones' *Come Away With Me* (×7 million), Coldplay's *A Rush Of Blood* (×4 million), Lenny Kravitz (×3 million) and Placebo (×2 million).

EMI's performance in international markets outside the US has for decades been a strong point in the company's armoury. It's something that has long been recognised by the industry in general and, more importantly, the managers of two of the company's biggest acts were equally impressed by what EMI achieved for them around the world.

"It would be hard to fault EMI," says Sam Feldman, the man who looks after Norah Jones and has seen his artist pass the 35 million sales mark globally. "They were extremely capable and if I had a criticism it would be that they were, at times, heavy-handed with the marketing when organic sales would have served everyone better."

Over in the Robbie Williams camp, Tim Clark picks out Germany – "He was the number one artist for a decade" – as the strong point of a successful European assault. "I think the EMI European companies did well, we had enormous success for Robbie and we enjoyed working with the very good people they had right across Europe," he says, before spelling out what was unique about the UK's major music company.

"I don't think that all record companies are the same and I think the culture that was at EMI was a very good one, and for years other companies stole EMI people because they were the best trained – and the worst paid. That continued right up until very recent times," says a manager who admits that whatever problems his company had with EMI they were always about the bigger picture rather than any local issues. "Our beef was always with head office," he admits.

Despite the success of Jones and Williams and a host of other artists, one cloud that loomed over EMI was the likelihood that it might lose one of its most prestigious and ground-breaking acts of the decade. Radiohead delivered the final album in their contract in 2003, *Hail To The Chief* following the group's five previous multi-million selling albums, including three UK number ones and a US chart topper.

According to manager Chris Hufford the album marked the end of a 10-year association with EMI for team Radiohead. "We knew it was a seriously changing business and we thought the band was never going to sign with anyone on a futures basis for a load more records," he explains. "That was never going to happen, so we were just going to sit back and see what happened."

What had already taken place in America with the Capitol label, which launched their US career with the single 'Creep' in 1993, saddened both the band and their management team according to Hufford. "When Capitol got thrown in with Virgin it was really sad for us – it was where our history started. Watching all that went on from 2003 onwards was all really sad and, as we still had Supergrass with the company, we were interested in what was happening."

Early in 2005 a change in the hierarchy of EMI's music-publishing division saw the group's financial chief, Roger Faxon, switch to become president and CEO under chairman Martin Bandier. As it was announced by EMI as "a succession plan for its music publishing division" and, with Faxon ultimately replacing Bandier on the main board, perhaps the rumours of a breakdown in the relationship between Nicoli and Bandier contained more than a grain of truth, although the move was negotiated by Nicoli as "a smooth succession".

The long-term plan was for Faxon to replace Bandier as chairman in 2008, although the man who took over as head of EMI's publishing operation in 1991 could remain involved with the company for a further three years unless he took the option to walk away after just 12 months.

As a leading music publisher, Andy Heath has no doubt about the strength of EMI's music-publishing business or the reason for its success. "It is unquestionably one of the great music-publishing companies despite all the other things going on at EMI, and don't underestimate the Marty Bandier effect in it all," he says. "He was perfect for the period but probably wouldn't be right for it now, while Roger Faxon is a good successor for now but in my view he might only be a caretaker if he doesn't understand the poetry as well as Marty seemed to."

For Nicoli, the decision to promote Faxon at Bandier's expense brought back memories of the time five years earlier when he opted to sack Berry as head of recorded music. "When I moved on Marty Bandier and appointed Roger Faxon, I got exactly the same reaction with many people saying I was nuts," he says, and talking in 2008 the former EMI chairman believed that ensuring that the company's music publishing continued to flourish and naming Faxon as its head were two of his most satisfying achievements.

Three years earlier, in January 2005, *Music Week* had invited a number of music industry bigwigs to debate the major issues involving new technology and how it was likely to affect the music business. EMI's Nicoli, Levy and Bandier were among the players invited and the company chairman gave his view on how long it would be before revenues from digital delivery rivalled the traditional business model.

"Digital revenues will certainly not overtake physical sales in the foreseeable future," he said before adding, "Even the most aggressive estimates have digital revenues at 25% of the industry's revenues mix in 2008."

For his part, Bandier took up the issue of pricing policies in new media with a warning that the industry needed to be careful and not presume that all music was worth the same to all consumers. "We can't put the same value on a McDonald's hamburger that we might for a great steak." Tactfully, Bandier declined to add which of EMI's music he compared with a Big Mac, and which was more filet mignon.

Tackling the subject of artist contracts in the face of the changing business model, Levy told *MW* that these contracts must always reflect the contribution made by the record companies and added, "All of these new expressions of value to artists will play in the evolution of new contracts over time."

However, even the prospect of increased revenue from the new digital arena could not save EMI from having to issue a further embarrassing profit warning in February 2005, its third in just over three years, and apparently it was all down to the failure of two acts to deliver their albums on time.

The postponement of albums by Gorillaz and, more importantly, Coldplay until after the March end of the 2004–2005 financial year, coupled with anticipated poor sales in the first three months of 2005, would, according to the company, result in an 8% to 9% drop in sales compared with the previous year. The company's share price dropped 40p to 241p as EMI forecast an end of year pre-tax profit of around £138 million, which was approximately £30 million below analyst estimates.

While some analysts were taken by surprise in light of the company's upbeat messages in the run-up to Christmas, EMI found itself in good company with its three main rivals – Universal, Sony and Warner – all warning of the late delivery of major releases.

Telling investors, analysts and the media that "creating and marketing music is not an exact science and cannot always coincide with our report-ing periods", Levy argued: "While this rescheduling and recent softness is disappointing, it does not change my views of the improving health of the global recorded music industry."

Using City-speak, his boss Nicoli added that the delayed albums and 'soft' sales were two factors that "have taken us outside our previously indicated sales range". This third profit warning, on top of the company's three failed mergers, certainly made Nicoli appear vulnerable with some industry commentators again suggesting that he was lucky to keep his job, while Tim Clark saw the whole affair as demoralising.

"EMI's problems and poor performance had an effect on us because it had an effect on the morale of the staff at EMI. When share prices are falling and there are big questions being asked about the company – which is making big reductions in staff – it absolutely affected us because you went to meetings and met with people with long faces."

Even though EMI upped its reduced profit forecast for the year ending March 2005 by three million to £141 million, it had little or no impact on Coldplay singer and highest profile member, Chris Martin, who reacted strongly to the company highlighting the delay of his band's next album as a reason for its reduced profits. On the eve of the company issuing its results for the 2004–2005 financial year, Martin told the world that he did not really care about EMI or its figures. "I'm not really concerned about that. I think shareholders are the greatest evil of this modern world. Dead-lines mean nothing to us," he said before warning, "We'll sink the whole company if we have to."

EMI's response was to confirm that the relationship between company and artist was "excellent" and while Nicoli believed that Martin "will have had a smile on his face when he said that", he did concede, "I suspect Chris said it out of some mild irritation at the suggestion that he might compromise his work to meet a corporate deadline."

While he also admitted that the band's postponement of their album *X&Y* until June was "unhelpful", Nicoli acknowledged that "Chris is an artist not a stockbroker", while Levy added, "Artists are not there to worry about shareholders. It's hard enough to be a worldwide talent."

Looking back on the situation with Coldplay, Nicoli views the post-ponement as a very public example of a major project not coming to fruition as originally planned. "The moment you start to distort the creative process in order to hit fiscal objectives you're asking for trouble," he said in 2008. "The alternative is you disappoint shareholders from time to time and get a different kind of trouble, despite the postponement being in everyone's best interests.

"My assertion was if it's going to take another six weeks to get a great product – and it was a great product with sales of over 10 million – then so be it and we'll take the punishment from the shareholders."

Three years later – and after the album had passed the 10 million sales mark – Coldplay's Martin looked back on the furore and confirmed, "Shareholders, stocks – all that stuff – it has nothing to do with me."

After the non-delivery of albums from Coldplay and Gorillaz plus reduced New Year sales, EMI managed to report a 2004–2005 operating profit of £232.9 million, down from £249.3 million, on sales of £1,942.8 million compared with £2,120.7 million the previous year. And while turnover for music publishing was up 4.9% but down by 7.4% for recorded music, the company was able to report tripled digital sales of £49.7 million, accounting for 2.5% of the total turnover.

Alain Levy summed up the year's performance by saying, "Overall we didn't have a great year but it's a temporary setback," while Nicoli's response to the figures was to claim that more over-40-year-olds were returning to buy physical music that made him optimistic about the recorded music market. "Over time the growth in digital will outstrip any decline in the physical market and the industry will return to growth," he said after watching over five years of constant decline.

In the lead-up to EMI's annual figures, its rival and one-time prospective partner, Warner Music, was expected to raise $581 million through its Initial Public Offering (IPO) after underwriters priced its shares at between $22 and $24. When the Warner shares finally hit the US stock market in early May they were actually priced at $17 and made an unsteady debut, dropping 3.5% on the first day to finish at $16.40.

The news that Warner Music was now also a stand-alone public music company was greeted with some caution by Nicoli who saw the development as "interesting" but confirmed, "We have no intention of doing any more speculation on the subject of consolidation."

During the company's financial year up to March 2005, EMI's top 10 best-selling albums sold a total of 22.5 million units – led by Robbie Williams' *Greatest Hits* (6 million), Joss Stone's *Mind Body & Soul* (2.7 million) and Tina Turner's *All The Best* (2.2 million) – and this compared with the 33 million Top 10 album sales the previous year.

By the end of 2005, the delayed Coldplay album, *X&Y*, had topped the UK and US charts and racked up sales in excess of six million, while

Demon Days by Gorillaz was a UK number one and a US Top 10 hit with sales close to three million. Robbie Williams' *Intensive Care* – despite mixed reviews – was Europe's biggest-selling album in 2005 and sold nearly four million, while newcomer KT Tunstall announced her arrival with her UK Top 3, two million-selling debut album, *Eyes To The Telescope*.

According to journalist Neil McCormick, EMI was a company with a high dependency on established best sellers, which left it vulnerable when things didn't go according to plan. "It became very dependent on superstar acts to deliver right out of the box and all it took was a couple of slips in delivery and a rather naff album from Robbie Williams [*Intensive Care*] to upset things," says the reviewer, who in fact believes that the problem with Williams' offering was in the marketing rather than the recording. "It was actually quite an interesting album but should not have been marketed as a major million-selling album because it was not that sort of record."

Despite the blip of *Intensive Care*, Williams was still a major international artist for EMI, but America remained a stumbling block that his management hoped might be overcome by a change of label. After years of being released through Capitol with little or no real success it was time, according to manager Tim Clark, for a switch.

"At our insistence we switched to Virgin in around 2005 but it didn't make any difference at all," he says, even though it got them away from the long-running boss of Capitol, who had never headed a record label before his appointment at EMI in 2001. According to Clark, "Andy Slater was the worst record company executive I've ever worked with," but the London-based manager lays the blame above the head of Capitol. "The problem has to start at the top and I don't think Ken Berry got to grips with America and certainly [David] Munns didn't – I don't think he had a clue about America."

Whether or not he got to grips with America, Munns and his partner Levy did take action in October 2005 when Virgin US chief Matt Serletic was let go three years after they had hired him. He was replaced by high-profile record company executive Jason Flom, who had launched his own Lava Records and ultimately become chairman of Atlantic Records, while Slater remained at the head of Capitol.

While nothing was ever said publicly, the music industry was awash with rumours that EMI spent many months searching for a music executive of the highest calibre to take over responsibility for North America from Munns, who was anxious to return to the UK. Headhunters were retained and it seemed that once or twice EMI got close to finding the right person, but it was never going to be easy persuading talented top people to leave their well-paid jobs and join what was seen as a troubled ship.

"Munns' problem in recruiting major executives in America was one that in the company's circumstances was impossible to solve," is how analyst Helen Snell sums up the situation, while Munns himself admits to being under constant pressure. "Always having to hit your numbers and producing figures for immediate scrutiny was like a monkey on your back."

For journalist Phil Hardy the fact that EMI could not get the right top-class person to run America was part of the sense of malaise in the company at the time. "When you are always going to be bought or sold then nobody is going to come and work for you, and on top of that they [Levy and Munns] weren't people who knew or understood America well enough," is how he sums it up, although former EMI Music president Jim Fifield sympathises with EMI's predicament. "I think the comments about the difficulties of recruiting executives or signing artists to a company that everyone knew was 'in play' is fair comment," he says. He compares it with the days when he ran the company and EMI was seen as the aggressor. "People would call us first and last, they wanted to do business with us."

Bhaskar Menon, the man who ran EMI Music immediately prior to Fifield, seems to place less emphasis on the speculation about EMI's ownership as the reason for the company's failings in America. "Poor judgement in selecting the succession of local leadership in the US, often chosen with little or no understanding of the market and the internal organisational problems in the company," is his assessment of EMI's long-term decline in the world's biggest market.

Internally the people at the very top of the EMI tree took pride in what they achieved while acknowledging the problem they faced. "We were breaking UK acts in America better than any company in this decade with Kylie, Coldplay, Gorillaz," says one top executive, "but the problem was still finding US acts."

"A great record company for me is characterised by having great music and EMI has had some great periods," is how *Telegraph* music writer Neil McCormick analyses the British major. Sensing that EMI's best years are behind it, he goes on to explain, "Even during its decline it's been a good company for British acts to sign to and then break America, although its roster has had far too many average bands stripping away at its profits."

Despite the problems affecting EMI in America, the UK company –

home to a long list of contemporary acts plus newcomers such as Joss Stone and KT Tunstall – was also able to complete a deal in 2005 with Buena Vista Music Group giving it the European rights to the series of hugely successful Disney *High School Musical* albums. Described by former industry journalist Talbot as "one of the most successful deals in the last 10 years for EMI", it brought the company sales of well over a million and a series of chart-topping titles from the hugely popular series of films.

EMI's assertion that it was both a major music company and, as it had no ties to a larger parent company, also an independent was confirmed when it became an associate member of the American Association of Independent Music. This was despite having no link to the UK-based AIM organisation, which, as part of the European IMPALA body, had objected to all EMI's attempts to merge. According to the company it was now "the world's largest independent and it's a natural affiliation", although it later left the US indies association.

EMI's figures for the first half of 2005 saw it outperform the world recorded-music market and report a 5.8% increase in turnover to £924.6 million with an operating profit of £86.7 million, up 12.6% on the previous year. It also claimed that revenues grew in all regions of the world, except Asia Pacific and North America, through major-selling new releases from The Rolling Stones, Paul McCartney and Keith Urban, which boosted recorded-music operating profits by 35% to £38.3 million.

Thanks to new songwriters such as James Blunt, Rob Thomas and Kelly Clarkson alongside earnings from the successful musicals *We Will Rock You*, *Mamma Mia!* and *Jersey Boys*, the music-publishing division also reported sales up 6.8% to £203.9 million.

The official industry figures put digital music sales in 2005 at just over 5% of the global recorded-music market and EMI estimated its own digital share, up to September 2005, at around the same level with sales of £35.9 million out of the EMI Group's digital revenues of £44.6 million, a rise of 142% from September 2004.

While it forecast new albums from Kate Bush, Depeche Mode, Massive Attack, Beastie Boys, Ben Harper and KoRn, EMI saw the end of 2005 approaching with an official global market-share equal to the previous year's 13.4%. According to official BPI figures its share of the UK market had grown by 0.8% to 20%, but the Nielsen SoundScan US calculations showed a 0.4% drop to 9.5% for EMI in America.

All this occurred at a time when the global recorded-music market for 2005 was valued at $33.4 billion, down fractionally on 2004's

$33.6 billion; global piracy had dropped to 1.2 billion units worth $4.5 billion (compared to 1.5 billion units worth $6.4 billion in 2004); and the US, UK and the world music markets all reported a 3% drop in value.

At the same time as the rapidly expanding market for digital music saw EMI become the first record company to link with T-Mobile in the UK and Europe and make full-track downloads available on the company's mobile telephone network, new talks were taking place at Apple regarding the price of downloading singles.

It seemed that EMI and some of its rival companies wanted to introduce a two-tier system whereby singles by major artists were charged at a higher rate than those from up-and-coming acts. According to Alain Levy, Apple boss Steve Jobs had indicated in "intensive discussions" that he would consider dropping the iTunes flat-rate model where singles were priced at 79p in the UK, 79c in the US and €0.79 in Europe.

With 85% of the world's legal downloads market, Apple was the big player with sales of over 1.8 million songs per day, but in late 2005 it refused to comment on EMI's expectations and Levy's assertion that, "We would like to reduce pricing on new and developing artists and charge a premium for our superstars."

One of the strong points in EMI's armoury was the boss of its successful UK operation, Tony Wadsworth, whose period as head of Parlophone and later EMI UK stretched back to 1993. During that time he had built up a reputation as a man committed to both his staff and the artists under his control and he was seen by commentator Phil Hardy as "the exception within EMI's short-term thinking".

But, despite the success in America of UK-signed acts such as Radiohead, Blur, Coldplay, Gorillaz and Kylie Minogue, there were still those who believed that he didn't have enough authority to persuade acts and managers that EMI was the company to be with in the US.

"He was driving it in from an A&R point of view in the UK but didn't have the international clout," says manager Pete Jenner. "He wasn't able to sign hot new acts and guarantee them they would get their records out and promoted in America, and many managers quickly realised that you shouldn't sign your band to an EMI deal that included America."

For manager Chris Morrison and Damon Albarn, leader of the million-selling band Blur, the EMI executive was an important part of the mix between record company and recording artist at a time when Blur actually "cared who was there at EMI but probably didn't care who owned it," explains the manager.

"Damon and I always felt secure when Tony Wadsworth was there, either as head of Parlophone or EMI UK," adds Morrison. "He was always part of our conversations and was someone you could always get to talk to."

In March 2005 both Wadsworth and EMI Music UK received some reward and public recognition of their achievements and performance when the company was voted fourth-best media company in the UK in a *Sunday Times* "best companies" poll, which questioned people about where they worked. Finishing 39th overall in the list of UK companies, EMI UK was placed in the top 10 in categories covering "stimulated by the job", "proud to work here" and "would miss this place", while Wadsworth was voted 10th in the "most highly rated boss" category.

Early in 2006, EMI chairman Eric Nicoli was at Midem, the annual music industry get-together held in Cannes each January, where he held court with *The Guardian* newspaper. Admitting to being the man behind the Yorkie Bar and the Lion Bar during his time at United Biscuits, Nicoli also owned up to a major interest in "consumer focus" and "industrial logic", while acknowledging that the 20% drop in the global recorded-music business over the past six years was not what he had planned for. "In all honesty I didn't realise, along with everybody else, just how badly the market would take a turn for the worse."

Explaining that what he brought to the music business was a "sharp consumer focus, which is not something the industry was famous for historically", Nicoli was not unexpectedly quizzed about his company's failed mergers and the suggestions from the money men that EMI's position was made harder by a desire to be the dominant partner in any deal. "Look at Morrisons and Safeway," said the music executive, bringing two of the UK's leading supermarkets into the equation. "Those companies struggled massively to execute a no-brainer combination. What I'm saying is, however compelling the theory, in practice there are many other things to consider."

Asked about his feelings if he left EMI without securing a major deal Nicoli said, perhaps somewhat surprisingly, "I won't be disappointed. We have transformed the company anyway," before going on to admit, "There is a mild frustration of course that there is a lot of discussion of a deal that hasn't happened and may never happen. It tends to deflect attention away from the good things we have done."

However, four months later the EMI/Warner merger was back in the headlines for a third time with *The Daily Telegraph* setting off the media coverage. It surmised that while EMI had been defeated in the past by "a combination of management differences, regulatory interference and simply being outbid", the time might be right for a new effort to combine EMI and Warner. "If egos can be swallowed then the regulators will find it hard to argue that an EMI/Warner tie is a threat to consumers," it said before signing off with another obvious punchline ". . . this time it could be music to Nicoli's ears."

This time, however, the analysts seemed underwhelmed by the new merger reports and dismissed them as "noise", despite the EMI share price jumping to a 52-week high of 294p amid general agreement that the regulatory climate had changed considerably since the company's initial attempt to link with Warner in 2000.

Within a week of the first reports of renewed interest on the part of EMI and Warner to attempt a third 'coming together', there was, on May 1, 2006, a rock-solid bid on the table from EMI to buy Warner for £4.23 billion. Offering $28.50 per Warner share, EMI confirmed its position in a statement that stated, "The board of EMI continues to believe that an acquisition of Warner Music would be very attractive to both sets of shareholders."

Warner Music chief executive Edgar Bronfman, however, was seemingly less than impressed with the bid and rejected EMI's offer within a day, adding, "Regarding EMI, we will have nothing further to say, other than the proposal was rejected by the board as not being in the best interest of shareholders."

At the same time the analysts, commentators and industry experts took the view that had EMI offered $30 a share it would have been accepted, and they were all convinced that the British major would return with an improved offer. In the midst of all this takeover activity Warner issued its figures for the first three months of 2006 and, despite increased sales thanks to the likes of James Blunt, Madonna and Sean Paul, it reported a loss of £3.8 million compared with the previous year's £2.2 million profit.

Assessing the Warner position – at a time when its share price stood at $26.50 just days ahead of the EMI bid – analysts took the view that it was "playing hardball – the issue is down to price and this is their strategy".

The ultimate success of the delayed Coldplay album and a doubling of revenues from digital music sales helped EMI achieve increased sales (up 4% to £2,079 million) and operating profit (up 11% to £250.5 million) for the year 2005–2006. While the total income from digital sales was up from £65.2 million to £112.1 million, recorded-music operating profits were up over 15% to £145 million at the same time as music publishing reported a 6% increase in profits of £105.4 million.

While his chairman's statement had undoubtedly gone to press before the latest round of talks with Warner took place, Nicoli took the opportunity, when he presented the end-of-year figures, to promote the major releases set for the coming year – including Janet Jackson, Robbie Williams, Norah Jones and The Beatles – as a positive in EMI's quest for Warner.

"It's always better to negotiate from a position of strength," he said, before adding that he was in no doubt that any future offer for Warner would see EMI's management running the new company. "I don't think you'll find many people who believe that a merger of equals is a good way to proceed."

In early June 2006, amid the financial gossip and acquisition reports, Warner's share price dropped to $27, its lowest figure since EMI's initial May offer, while EMI stock rose to 263p.

EMI's renewed interest in Warner Music came from a feeling that, with the share price hovering just above the $25 mark, the Warner shareholders and private equity investors might be getting impatient for a better return after three years of investment.

Having had its initial bid of $28.50 rejected by Warner, EMI found itself facing a counter-bid from Edgar Bronfman's US company, which was prepared to make an offer of 315p a share for EMI. At the same time as it turned down this offer, EMI made a second bid for Warner of $31 a share, which was still seen to undervalue the company and was in turn rejected by the American operation.

The next throw of the dice came from Warner with an offer of 320p per EMI share but this was once again refused by EMI, which also saw it as an offer that undervalued its company. There was some speculation within EMI that each time Warner came back with an increased offer it was in fact offering virtually the same amount that had simply been enhanced by fluctuating currency exchange rates.

True or not, it was apparent that neither side was close to the accepted 15% premium above the share price that the financiers and analysts considered to be the minimum in such negotiations. Assessing that neither side was being particularly generous, one analyst was moved to say, "In fact Warner is being cheeky in terms of price."

Speculation suggested that the venture capitalists behind Warner Music wanted an exit strategy but they also wanted the best possible return on their investment, while EMI was considered to be approaching the stage where, according to one City analyst it "must be thinking enough is enough".

This latest round of bidding and counter-bidding between EMI and Warner had taken up the whole of May and June 2006, and there was still no sign of progress when a European court announced a surprise decision regarding the Sony/BMG deal, which had been given the go-ahead by the European Commission in 2004.

The Court of First Instance in Luxembourg upheld an appeal brought by the European independent record companies' body, IMPALA, in a lawsuit against the EC over its ruling to allow the Japanese and German-owned music companies to merge.

While the Bertelsmann and Sony corporations were left with the prospect of resubmitting their applications to the EC, EMI and Warner were forced to assess the implications the decision might have on their ongoing negotiations.

Numis Securities media analyst Richard Hitchcock, who considered the decision to be "very significant", believed that it left the whole music industry in a state of flux. "With this decision the authorities are announcing a tightening up of any consolidation."

For EMI's Eric Nicoli, who now stood on the edge of losing out on his third attempt to complete a deal for Warner Music, the decision was "unprecedented" but he added, "I'm never shocked by anything that happens in this industry."

While he may not have been shocked by the court's decision, Nicoli was undoubtedly affected by it and it was, according to one EMI executive, a case of "all bets are off" until the Sony BMG situation was resolved.

In the last week of July EMI decided to shelve – albeit apparently temporarily – its attempt to acquire Warner Music. It had always been EMI's position that it would only propose to its shareholders a deal that would be approved by the regulators and, as that was no longer a certainty, the company announced that it was putting everything on hold "for the time being".

American investment analyst David Londoner became a non-executive member of the EMI board in 2003 and saw the bid for Warner as both a good and a bad move. "The effort to buy Warner Music made operational sense because of the very considerable cost-saving opportunities, but paying all cash for it would have been misguided. The financial leverage would have been excessive," he says. "Fortunately Warner rejected it, preferring to make its own bid for EMI and become the survivor."

The postponement of talks with Warner saw EMI's shares drop 17p to 244p, just a few weeks after they had reached a high of more than 300p while Warner's shares fell to $23.50 on the news that a deal with EMI was now on hold.

For one media analyst the whole EMI/Warner episode had gone on far too long by the time the 2006 scenario panned out. "At that point everyone had just got bored with the whole thing – it became almost an irrelevance," is how Mike Hilton describes the companies' final efforts to do a deal. "There was no premium involved, EMI had already taken a massive amount of costs out of its business and Warner had done the same. First time around in 2000 it had major benefits but by 2006 the savings were low and the probability of a deal was so low people just stopped caring."

That said there were still those inside the music business who saw EMI Warner as the perfect answer to an ongoing problem. "It was still the marriage made in heaven but you had to get over the ego problems," is how ex-Sony Europe boss Paul Russell, who still believes it is the ideal partnership, Paul sums up what went on in 2006. "It could have been done by share swaps – there were ways round the problems of not having any money as long as you've got the assets."

Similarly, for US-based music executive Bob Mercer, a deal between the British EMI and America's Warner had great merit then and still makes sense today. "It would have saved both companies at the time and in my view it is still the only option that is open to either of them. The business cannot sustain a large overhead, small label."

Taking the view that when he joined the company, Nicoli wanted to do a deal with Warner and in time that became "a need to do a deal", media editor Dan Sabbagh looks at the 2006 goings-on as an "extraordinary tit-for-tat summer". "What started out as a desire ended up as a need and people gradually accepted that Warner and EMI was something that was likely to happen," he explains, adding that it became the "the only game in town" after the Sony/BMG deal was initially approved and he believes it remains that way today.

"I don't think either company – whatever they might say in public – is ever far away from thinking about the price and the timing, who comes out on top, who exits and all that goes with a deal."

Sabbagh's concerns were also with the people who worked in both businesses and how they dealt with the constant speculation about the future of their companies. "The real impact was on the people who were on the inside – artists and managers were less bothered. The A&R

machines of both companies, particularly in the UK and EMI in the US – in as much as they had a machine – just fell to bits and the result was very poor rosters."

Covering the situation in its August 2, 2006 edition, *Music & Copyright* offered a scenario where even the potential to save £200 million through a deal with Warner did not please the EMI shareholders, as the company intended to fund the acquisition through a new rights issue. Suggesting that EMI should radically reassess its future as a stand-alone music company, *M&C* came to the rather surprising conclusion that, despite continued misgivings as to its long-term future, it could face the short term "with some confidence".

This upbeat thinking was based on the company reporting its best results for many years and also predicting further increases in profits in the financial year up to March 2007, but sadly all the enthusiasm and high expectations were dashed in October 2006 when EMI issued a less than positive trading update.

Looking ahead to the figures for the first six months up to September 2006, EMI warned that revenues would fall by 3%, compared with a 5% growth in the same period in 2005, and that pre-tax profits would fall by over £5 million.

While EMI complained of delayed albums from Robbie Williams and Norah Jones – who were scheduled to join the likes of Keith Urban, Joss Stone, Tina Turner, Moby, Depeche Mode and The Beatles for release during the second half of the financial year – they did boast of best sellers from Janet Jackson, Bob Seger, Chingy, Trace Adkins and Hikaru Utada alongside new releases from Corinne Bailey Rae, Lily Allen and The Kooks.

Even so, the Nielsen SoundScan report for the first nine months of 2006 in America made grim reading for EMI as its US market share dropped to 10% and unit sales fell from 44.3 million to 39.3 million. The news was made worse by the fact that Warner Music was the only one of the four majors to show any increase in market share (up 2% to 19.2%) and unit sales (up to 75.6 million from 70.9 million). And even the predicted increase in EMI's global digital sales for the six months to September 2006, from 4.9% to 9% of recorded music sales, fell below the industry's worldwide figure of 11% of total music sales.

EMI's trading update came on the back of another round of rumours, this time involving the successful head of the company's music-publishing division and, surprise surprise, Warner Music.

It seemed that Warner chief Edgar Bronfman, in the wake of the failed acquisition bids by both his company and EMI, met with selected EMI shareholders and confirmed to them that he believed the Sony/BMG merger would ultimately be approved by the EC and it would also approve a merger of EMI and Warner – when and if it was presented to them.

On the back of this news there was also speculation that EMI's publishing CEO, Martin Bandier, was pondering an early departure ahead of his planned 2008 retirement, to take up the role as head of Warner Music's publishing arm, Warner Chappell. The first reports regarding Bandier appeared in early October 2006 and suggested some sort of a link between Bronfman and Bandier involving Warner Chappell. They also put forward the idea of him actually buying EMI Music Publishing, the company he had built up over 18 years, with the backing of private equity investors.

In November came the news that Bandier would indeed be leaving EMI in April 2007, although it was still unclear where he would be going. While the smart money was on him taking over Warner Chappell or forming some new partnership with Bronfman, there was also the possibility of him attempting to acquire the company he had established as the world's biggest music publisher.

However, Bandier, famous as the man who regularly took out gatefold adverts in *Billboard* – which usually featured him, his cigar and his staff – to celebrate his company's achievements, explained that a new link with EMI was not out of the question either. "It's one of the alternatives. We talked about a potential sort of joint venture to make acquisitions in the music-publishing arena but these things take time to flesh out."

Tributes to Bandier's ability and track record – the latest round of figures for EMI music publishing in the first half of 2006 showed profits up over 5% to £51 million – came from industry legends such as Berry Gordy, Jon Landau and John Eastman.

Gordy, the man who sold his Jobete publishing operation to EMI, said, "Marty was more interested in developing the people than making initial money . . . it's about getting the product right and working with creative people." According to Landau, manager of Bruce Springsteen, "EMI is very proactive. They help to stimulate songwriting. Marty is just a great manager," while Eastman, lawyer to Paul McCartney and Billy Joel, added, "Marty is an old-fashioned creative publisher and he brought an activist culture to EMI."

In the light of these and other testimonies, music writer Phil Hardy holds the view that losing Bandier was a major blow to EMI. "The madness of EMI allowing Marty to leave was extraordinary. Here was somebody who was actually doing well and they let him go. You were never again going to see an EMI Music publishing advert in *Billboard* that you have to fold out because of the length of Marty's cigar!"

At the same time Hardy also understands why Bandier was forced to leave EMI. "What Marty wanted was the one thing EMI couldn't give him – a bit of it, a share in the company."

When EMI finally came to report its interim figures for the first half year of 2006, having predicted a drop of 3% in an earlier trading report, they in fact showed a 6% fall in revenues to £867.9 million while operating profits were down from £86.7 million to £62.7 million.

While the company's performance was affected by the anticipated late delivery of albums, it was made worse by the discovery of major fraud in its Brazilian affiliate that cost EMI £9 million, although it claimed it was on track to deliver £10 million in savings by the end of the financial year plus a further £30 million by the end of 2007–2008.

And, despite the loss of Bandier, EMI music publishing still boasted a prestigious line-up of writers including the newly signed Beyoncé alongside Natasha Bedingfield, The Scissor Sisters, Snoop Dogg, Sting, Pink, Christina Aguilera, Jay-Z and Amy Winehouse.

However, the acquisition of BMG Music Publishing by Vivendi in late 2006 provided Universal's parent company with the opportunity to create the world's largest music publisher through a merger with its own Universal Music Publishing Group.

But for Nicoli the music-publishing side of EMI was one that had been "exceptionally well run" throughout his time in charge. "It had been nurtured by Marty Bandier and latterly by Roger Faxon and has fantastic assets, which have been added to over the years," says the man who oversaw, and perhaps instigated, a dramatic change at the top of the business. "Roger Faxon has put together a world-class team and changed the way it is run, which I thought was important when Marty's reign came to an end."

In November 2006 the head of EMI Music rather surprisingly agreed to give the keynote address at the London Media Summit, and Levy focused on the impact of technology on the music business in the previous 10 years. "The music industry was the first entertainment industry that digital disruption hit squarely between the eyes," he stated before adding, "now only a few years later digital is no longer a disruption but our industry's bright future."

Noting that more than 10% of music revenues worldwide came from the digital arena, he predicted that by 2010, 25% of EMI's revenues would come from digital. This impact on physical sales was highlighted by the fact that between 2001 and 2006 only five albums topped the global 10 million sales mark, while IFPI Platinum Europe Awards for million-sellers hit an all-time low in 2005 with just 46 awards – down from 77 in 2004.

Two of those 10 million sellers were EMI's Norah Jones and Coldplay, and for EMI chairman Nicoli the success of these two acts represents a major achievement. "I still take most pleasure from the huge creative successes . . . and most notably Coldplay and Norah Jones," he explains. "When I started they were unheard of and the two of them have grown to be the biggest-selling artists in the world in a very competitive market and at a time when the market was under a huge amount of pressure."

Among the new platinum-award winners in 2006 were new EMI signings Corinne Bailey Rae and The Kooks, whose million-selling debut albums ranked alongside The Beatles' *Love* album, which segued remixed and remastered Beatles tracks into a strange but attractively sequenced medley of their music, as used in the soundtrack to a Beatles-endorsed Cirque du Soleil show in Las Vegas. The CD sold over two million in just two months . . . and possibly had more to come.

EMI UK boss Tony Wadsworth was confident that The Beatles' album could ultimately pass the same sales mark as Coldplay's *Rush Of Blood To The Head* and *X&Y*. "I think there's no reason why this [*Love*] shouldn't break the 10 million barrier. We are talking about something that could sell substantially."

One victim of the falling sales phenomenon was Virgin star Janet Jackson, whose final album for the label peaked at number two in America but failed to make the UK Top 30. Released in October 2006, *20 Y.O.* racked up US sales of less than 650,000 in the aftermath of a six-million selling debut release for the label, two three-million sellers and 990,000 for the 2004 hit *Damita Jo*, which the singer talked about in an interview with *Billboard*.

"Not to badmouth Virgin 'cause it was my family for a very long time but they kind of just lost touch," she told the US music industry magazine. Comparing the Virgin performance with things at her new Island Records home, she added, "It's teamwork and that's what Virgin lost."

If the previous seven years – since EMI first began searching for a partner in 2000 – had been dominated by talk and reports of a deal with

Warner Music, alongside a brief nod towards BMG in 2001, there came news of a new interested party as 2006 swung to a close.

EMI confirmed on November 28 that it had "received a preliminary approach for the company, which may or may not lead to an offer being made for the company." While it declined to name the interested party, reports at the time decided that the bid had come from UK-based private equity company Permira, while US companies Kohlberg Kravis Roberts & Co, Goldman Sachs Group and Apollo Management were all also listed as potential interested parties.

Permira, the company thought to be the front-runner in a new scramble for EMI, came with claims to have 19 funds totalling £22 billion and with investments in businesses covering 15 countries. Operating since 1985, its interests covered the chemical, media, IT and consumer markets with household names such as Birds Eye, Homebase and the AA listed among its investments.

The idea of a private equity company buying EMI also led to further speculation that, if successful, it could invite Bandier to stay on and run the EMI music-publishing arm while selling recorded music to Warner Music. While both EMI and Permira refused to confirm or comment, and analysts stuck with the idea of EMI and Warner as the "most sensible deal", the UK company's share price received a 30p boost to take its shares up to 290p, which valued it at close to £2.3 billion.

Interest in EMI from a private equity company should not have surprised anybody who had kept an eye on the various multi-million dollar music industry deals that had gone down during the two previous years.

Edgar Bronfman was supported by private equity when he successfully acquired Warner Music for £1.34 billion in 2004, and in 2006 Thomas H Lee and Bain Capital had acquired a major stake in radio giant Clear Channel for $18.7 billion – beating off at least three rivals – while Vivendi's $2 billion purchase of BMG Music Publishing was pushed along from an initial estimate of $1 billion by competition from a host of private equity operations.

The view, according to one analyst, was that private equity was "holding prices up and in some cases pushing them higher", and Permira's reported offer for EMI was in the region of £2.5 billion plus a further £1 billion in debt – but that it seems was not high enough.

On December 14 EMI announced that discussions with the company everybody assumed to be Permira had come to an end, adding that it had "not received an offer that fully reflects the prospects for and value of the company and which it could recommend to shareholders".

While the company spokeswoman assured everyone that it was "business as normal", it transpired that EMI had given an unnamed private equity company access to financial information in advance of an expected bid. However, it seems that reports of the EMI board rejecting a firm bid for the company were way off the mark as, according to one well-placed insider, "The board may well have approved an offer but it never materialised."

These new failed talks coincided with a major move in Japan where EMI took over control of the Toshiba-EMI (TOEMI) joint venture, which dated back to 1961. Paying £93 million, EMI gained control of the 45% share of the company owned by the Japanese corporation in what was seen as a move to "tidy up the portfolio", perhaps in advance of a new approach, and confirmed its name change to EMI Music Japan.

Described as a confirmation of its commitment to the Japanese music market, TOEMI's gross assets were reckoned to be around £141 million while reported pre-tax profits – from sales of major acts such as Hikaru Utada, GLAY and Kyosuke Himuro – were £3.4 million, up to March 2006.

Meanwhile back in the UK, there were signs of further unrest with senior executives seemingly unhappy about the performance of the flagship EMI UK company despite Tony Wadsworth's assertion that, thanks to the success in America during the past decade of UK acts Coldplay, Kylie Minogue, Corinne Bailey Rae, KT Tunstall, Radiohead and Gorillaz, his company stood apart from its rivals. "It's a long list and nobody had the consistency with their UK acts in America that we did."

Journalist turned charts company executive Martin Talbot backs up Wadsworth's view that EMI UK was the best in the game at breaking its acts in the US and he asks the question, "You might wonder how much bigger those acts could have been if they had been going through a record company which was really firing on all cylinders in the US."

Even though there was no concern over the quality of the acts being signed, there was a worry about the rate at which they were being discovered and launched. The in-house talk was of "cracks that were beginning to appear in the UK operation" at a time when its UK market share fell to 17.9% – its lowest figure for five years.

These figures, according to *Times* media editor Dan Sabbagh, confirmed his belief about the man who had run EMI UK for close on 10 years. "I think Tony Wadsworth lost his touch over the last couple of years and he has never been big on pop. However, the creative community loved him . . . he supported bands for a long time."

While the company's acts were nominated for nine 2006 BRIT Awards – one down on the 2005 figure when they won three awards – EMI had to make do with only Coldplay emerging as a winner. But more disturbing was the UK Top 100 album round-up, which featured just five EMI albums, with newcomer Lily Allen the highest placed at number 26.

This compared with Universal taking five of the top 10 places and Sony BMG claiming two, which gave EMI just 15.4% of the chart, a drop of 2.5% on the previous year when Coldplay, Robbie Williams and Gorillaz were all top 10 listings.

As if to emphasise EMI's current disappointing position, in 2006 the BPI produced a list of the best-selling UK albums of all time and Queen's *Hits* (1981), The Beatles' *Sgt Pepper's Lonely Hearts Club Band* (1967) and *Dark Side Of The Moon* (1973) by Pink Floyd were ranked one, two and six respectively.

However on the upside three of EMI's British-signed acts featured in the list of the UK's top global sellers for 2006, which was topped by rival Atlantic Records' James Blunt on 4.3 million sales. The Beatles' *Love* album took second spot with worldwide sales of 4.2 million, followed by Robbie Williams' *Rude Box* (in joint fifth place on 2.2 million) and Corinne Bailey Rae (equal eighth on 1.8 million), with KT Tunstall's *Eye To The Telescope* just outside the top 10 on 1.6 million.

While media analyst Helen Snell holds the view that, "The best thing EMI did in the previous 10 years was probably bringing Alain [Levy] and David [Munns] into the company," she also holds up a glass to EMI UK. "You have to toast the UK company, which was an absolute powerhouse over those 10 years – without the UK, the problems would have been unimaginable."

However there were those close to EMI's successful UK operation who noticed that things were not running as smoothly as in earlier years. Radiohead manager Chris Hufford, who describes Munns as "a hoot but a bit of a thug", observed some of Tony Wadsworth's discontent. "It was obviously massively frustrating for him to have deal with Munns' and Levy's crap all the time."

Part of that "crap" centred round the duo of Levy and Munns running the company and the complications caused by them discussing and deciding issues without much input from other interested parties. As one company executive commented, "It was very hard to overturn what they wanted to do . . . there was no way to divide and rule with those two."

The two executives certainly spent a lot of time in each other's company even though they were 3,000 miles apart, with Levy spending a week a month in New York with Munns who, in turn, spent a week a month in Europe. While Levy focused on dealings with the chairman and the EMI board, Munns got on with running the day-to-day business of a record company. But they always came together when it came to making decisions. Their mantra was quite simple – if they didn't agree then they wouldn't do it.

But even with an impressive track record that stretched back through both Parlophone and EMI UK, Wadsworth was not immune to pressure and the rumour going around the music business in late 2006 was that the men who ran EMI Music were considering making a change at the very top of their successful UK operation . . . and the man in the hot seat knew it.

"For me the last 18 months were hard," says Wadsworth. "I was pretty sure Alain and David were getting ready to get rid of me. I knew that was the case and yet I was sitting there thinking 'how unfair is that', at a time when I'm doing my numbers and I've got three or four debut artists selling millions around the world."

CHAPTER 8

Can't Buy Me Love

(The Beatles, Parlophone 1964)

2007 began on a bad note for EMI with the company finally being relegated to bottom place in the league of major music companies. For the first time in eight years of global market-share calculations, the figures for 2006 showed that the British company had fallen behind all its rivals – Universal, Sony BMG and Warner – with just 12.8%, its lowest figure since 1999's 11.4%.

The figures, calculated by the IFPI between 1999 and 2005 and then by *Music & Copyright* magazine, showed that its arch rival and long-time potential partner Warner Music had overtaken it for the first time with a world market share of 13.8%.

EMI's poor performance in the US, where it racked up a market share of just 10.2%, plus its below-par share of the world digital music market (EMI registered just 10.5% compared with Warner's 16%) were considered to be the main reasons behind its drop down the recorded music market table.

Then, within two weeks of the beginning of the new year, things went from bad to worse when Eric Nicoli stepped up to announce a new profit warning and, more importantly and dramatically, fire the two men he had hired just six years earlier to save the company. EMI music chairman and CEO Alain Levy and his vice chairman David Munns were both fired late on Thursday, January 11, 2007, leaving the company immediately in the wake of a predicted 6% to 10% decline in full-year revenues.

The decision to remove the two senior music executives, and for Nicoli to take over the reins as CEO of EMI Music and relinquish his role as chairman of the board of EMI Group, followed a review of the company's performance in the last quarter of 2006. By its own admission it was "below prior expectations" and in an official statement EMI attributed the problems to "weak market conditions, particularly over the Christmas period, and lower than expected sales from EMI Music's portfolio of second-half-year releases to date".

In the midst of this financial underperformance, coupled with the ongoing problems in America and well-reported rumours of low morale among the company's senior management, Nicoli believes he had no alternative but to remove his two most senior officers. "Alain and David were absolutely the right appointment in 2001. They did a stunning job for three years, then the nature of the job changed and they were struggling by year five to the point where I took the view that it wasn't sortable. Therefore I felt that I had to make the change."

With Levy and Munns at the helm, Nicoli oversaw and authorised a whole series of changes and generally supported the duo he had placed in charge, but as things got tougher so the pressure on EMI's chairman grew. "The whole environment was very difficult and Eric underestimated how tough it was," is how Munns sums up the situation.

For Nicoli steering the company through the period from early 2002 to early 2007, when the cumulative decline in the music market was close to 40%, required him to approve a series of cost-cutting exercises and redundancies in order to maintain the support of investors. "It is business and the objective of business is to deliver a return to investors whether they are private or public," he says. "And if you fail to do that then you have to change things."

Acknowledging that his own position was under pressure when he opted to sack Levy ands Munns, Nicoli admits, "It was always our share-holders' and the board's prerogative to change me. They chose not to do that and it was my job to put in place the management team and structure to do the best job possible."

Even though it was later reported that both Levy and Munns were handsomely compensated for the loss of their jobs – Levy's package was confirmed as being worth £4.6 million, including compensation, salary and "incentive remuneration" – it did not take away the shock that swept through the industry at their dismissal.

Among the managers of acts with EMI who were contacted at the time for their reaction to the news was Chris Hufford, who thought it was "certainly interesting" and confirmed that, looking back, there had been some "possible indicators" that changes were being planned. Kooks manager Rob Swerdlow took the view that, "These things tend to have no effect on artists as long as you keep your head down, make great records and remain vital," although he saw the departure of Munns as a particular loss. "David Munns was a music guy who galvanised projects when they got to a certain level. The only problem was that on an A&R level there were not enough Coldplays being put through to him, for him to put the ball in the back of the net," he said.

Meanwhile Bob Miller, manager of new best-seller Corinne Bailey Rae, was, he said, ambivalent about it. "It was inevitable that some changes had to take place given what they were trying to do with the company and when that happens there are always going to be casualties. They put this team in to do a certain job and it hasn't quite worked."

Norah Jones' manager, Sam Feldman, on the other hand, was less than happy about the moves, particularly the departure of Munns who had been closely linked with Jones' success on Blue Note. "I think David Munns is one of the hardest-working and [most] knowledgeable record executives ever," he said. "He is one of the few individuals who will give the straight goods and for that reason I was sad to see him go."

While the industry buzzed about a new cost-cutting programme taking in up to 20% of the company's total overhead and talked of the changes that removed a layer of senior global management, EMI's official statement explained that the moves would, "align EMI's business more closely to its operating environment".

Whether Levy and Munns saw what was coming their way when they flew into London from New York at Nicoli's behest remains unclear. There have been stories that Levy – being closer to the board and Nicoli than Munns – had an inkling and was not totally surprised by the move, while others have reported that Munns was completely unaware of the plan and assumed he was coming to London because of the profit-warning announcement.

Either way Nicoli is adamant that the move he made was not linked to his own survival. "The suggestion that I may have stabbed Levy and Munns in the back to protect my own position was ludicrous," he said. "I had a job to do as head of a public company and, while I very much wanted to support them, when we got to January 2007 it was painfully obvious that we were underperforming and, in particular, the US business was spiralling downwards.

"The board had no option but to issue a profits warning and I felt that we should announce the necessary major restructuring initiative at the same time," he explained in 2008. "This involved the elimination of a number of senior management roles including Alain's and David's."

It was a decision that, seemingly, both the board and shareholders understood and backed while insiders at EMI had seen it coming. "The tension between Eric and Alain and David was palpable and therefore there was only one conclusion to that – and Eric was the boss. Right or wrong doesn't come in to it at that point," was one long-time employee's take on proceedings.

Meanwhile, opinion in the media and the City over Nicoli's action was split. Writing in his editor's column in *Music Week* in January 2007, Martin Talbot took the view that the decision represented a move by the chairman to be more hands-on but warned, "It is a shame that the decisive action taken last week will be viewed as the latest panic measures of a music industry in crisis."

And while an unnamed analyst felt that sacking Levy and Munns "was pure desperation on Eric's part", it left a scenario with which long-time EMI watcher Helen Snell was less than impressed. "It then became the situation where you had Eric without Alain and Eric couldn't run the record company."

Acknowledging that during his time in charge of EMI he had removed two management regimes – that of Ken Berry, which he had inherited, and Levy and Munns, whom he had hired and fired – Nicoli explains, "I had to sort it out but not many people survive eight or nine years to have to live with the consequences of their own decisions – that was the reality."

One observer who was impressed by what Nicoli did to try and rescue his ailing company was Mike Hilton, who believes that the EMI chairman had no alternative. "He acknowledged the problems and reacted to them and was very decisive. He got rid of Levy and Munns and it takes a special person to say, 'I appointed these people, they've failed so I'm going to get rid of them.' But he is a survivor."

Former EMI Music chairman Bhaskar Menon knew both Levy, who had been a competitor when he ran Polygram, and Munns, who had been at EMI in the 1970s and 1980s, and saw their period in charge of EMI Music as "a time of probably irreversible crisis" and was equally dismayed by their departure.

"The absence of knowledgeable management supervision or answerability defied rational explanation and predictably precipitated a situation best illustrated by the bizarre manner of (and the grounds advanced for) the duo's sudden termination," says the Los Angeles-based former EMI main board director before adding, "This brought the final end of EMI as we knew it, and all that followed soon thereafter."

So those left standing alongside Nicoli in the new EMI set-up were music publishing chief Roger Faxon, chief financial officer Martin Stewart and, as the new non-executive chairman, John Gildersleeve, who had served as non-executive deputy chairman since 2004. They were joined within weeks by Ian Hanson, as the new chief operating officer, and former head of EMI Continental Europe Jean Francois Cecillon, who moved up to take over as chairman of EMI Music International, excluding the UK and North America, which left Tony Wadsworth as head of the UK company.

America on the other hand needed more surgery and before the dust had settled on Levy and Munns leaving, Nicoli announced plans to merge the Capitol and Virgin operations into one company under the banner Capitol Music Group. This meant that while the two labels would remain, the company could unite and streamline many of its operations in order to bring the US business back into profit and also improve its US market share.

Named as the head of the new combined Capitol Music Group was Jason Flom, who moved up from chairman of Virgin, while Capitol boss Andy Slater left after six years in the job with, if the rumours were to be believed, a combined compensation and pension package worth around $15 million.

The changes in EMI's operations in America coincided with a major push by the UK-based labels to break new acts in the biggest music market in the world. On the back of US platinum awards for KT Tunstall and Corinne Bailey Rae, EMI now put its resources behind Lily Allen in the hope that she would emulate Bailey Rae's achievement in delivering the highest-placed debut album by a UK artist on the Capitol label since The Beatles in 1964.

As EMI entered 2007 with an eventful first month, there was a crumb of good news concerning the share price. Apparently during 2006 EMI's shares improved 9.3% over the year – to finish on 265p – and was registered as the only British music and media stock (alongside Sanctuary, Chrysalis, HMV, EMAP and GCap Media) to improve on its position at the start of the year.

This tenuous success was short-lived, however. On February 14, 2007, the company announced its second profit warning in two months and immediately saw the share price tumble by over 12% to 210p.

Predicting a drop in revenues of around 15% for the year ending March 2007 – worse than the 6%–10% forecast a month earlier – EMI explained that the revision came as "a result of the continued and accelerating deterioration in market conditions in North America where, in the calendar year to date, the physical music market as measured by SoundScan has declined by 20%".

EMI also referred to an exceptionally high level of product returns affecting the sell-through of both new releases and catalogue, resulting in a higher than usual negative impact on gross margin. At the same time it forecast that music publishing was performing "in line with expectations".

To be fair to EMI the value of the global recorded music market dropped nearly $2 billion in 2006 from $33,456 to $31,813 million, while the retail value of the US market – including physical and digital sales – fell from $12,269 million in 2005 to $11,500 million in 2006. At the same time the UK market's retail value dropped in 2006 to £1,756 million from £1,895 the previous year.

On the upside, the value of the world's digital music market – stated at $1.1 billion in 2005 – nearly doubled to $2 billion in 2006. At the same time predictions forecast that the mobile music market would be worth $9 billion in 2007 and rise to over $30 billion by 2010, although Warner Music boss Edgar Bronfman was concerned that less than 9% of people with music-enabled phones were bothering to download tracks.

This statistic came as Apple boss Steve Jobs called on the four major music companies – Universal, Sony BMG, Warner and EMI – to abandon their policy of insisting on downloads being packaged with digital rights management (DRM) in order to control the range of playback devices.

In the midst of these dramatically changing times former Virgin executive and current CEO of the Music Managers Forum, Jon Webster, was one of many who sat on the sidelines as EMI lurched from crisis to crisis. "I watched it all with fascination . . . the value of the company fell against a background of falling sales at a time when they seemed to be doing the right things in terms of digital strategy. They did lots of deals with lots of companies that had finance, needed content and were ready to pay for it," he says.

Now that he was in direct control of EMI's music operations, Nicoli was faced with the dual challenge of running the record and publishing businesses while also dealing with the City and the financial community. This in turn put him in the firing line of investors and analysts who were quick to share their opinions with a media that, as ever, was more than happy to focus on the latest EMI story.

While he considers Nicoli to be "a very tough guy who is very bullish", media analyst Mark Beilby was left wondering about the reaction of EMI's largest financial backers. "It's puzzling why the big EMI investors like Fidelity and Schroder did nothing, but he [Nicoli] did have the support of both Warburg and Deutsche Bank, which was important."

In America *The New York Times* reported SG Securities analyst Anthony de Larrinaga's dire assessment of the latest EMI profit warning. "This will put them in a potentially perilous financial predicament and they'll need very understanding bankers," while Iain Daly from UK brokers Bridgewell told *The Guardian* that there was only one solution to EMI's dilemma. "Our view is that private equity is the only realistic buyer, given the immediate regulatory issues surrounding other potential trade buyers."

Those people with money invested in EMI were not inclined to be any more forgiving or understanding of the position it found itself in with both EMI's value and share price falling. Tim Rees from Insight, the biggest EMI shareholder, told *The Times*, "The management has to deliver on promises to cut costs."

Reporting in *The Financial Times* on the same day – February 15, 2007 – when the profit warning commanded acres of newsprint, an unnamed top 20 shareholder complained, "The guidance has been atrocious. It is only a month since the last statement," while a fellow investor described the announcement as "astounding and a disgrace".

While the recently departed Levy and Munns were generally blamed for most of the problems, there were shareholders who held a different view. One investor told the *FT* that "the buck shouldn't stop there" and the *Telegraph* reported that one major investor was urgently seeking a meeting with chairman Gildersleeve to discuss Nicoli's future.

"I think he's a dead duck," said the shareholder. "I think this company is now very vulnerable to a bid and Nicoli is not in a position to defend anything." And he didn't stop there. "I think the finance director [Martin Stewart] has also been tainted because it suggests that they did not get to the bottom of the numbers," he added.

Extraordinarily, on the same day as EMI received this mauling from the media the share price rose nearly 4% to finish at 219p, but this was undoubtedly due to further high expectations of a renewed bid on the back of the predicted poor performance.

Writing in his February 17 Record of the Day article, former *Music & Media* and *Billboard* editor Emmanuel Legrand suggested the New Year upheaval at EMI, "could be seen as either a way for chairman Eric Nicoli to save his seat or a much necessary change in governance to adapt the company to the market", before adding, "and actually it may be both".

He, like many other commentators and analysts, was also busy mulling over what would be the next best move for EMI. Would it be Bronfman riding in again with another bigger bid to add EMI to Warner Music, or would a private equity company return with a better bid than the one rumoured to have come from Permira? Or was there, Legrand wondered, a chance of "a white knight buying both Warner and EMI and combining the two"?

For his part Nicoli always understood that the music business was both unpredictable and volatile and that there would be peaks and troughs along the way. He also knew that while you could to some extent manage share-holders' expectations and disappointments, you could not expect to get any credit when you got it right with a best-selling artist such as Norah Jones or Coldplay. He also knew that in a declining market there was always a need for constant rationalisation and restructuring in order to survive, but it was hard to do these things in the full glare of the City and the media.

"In my last five years we had four big restructuring exercises. We had to run like hell to stand still," is how he described it in 2008. "The math is simple and devastating. If you maintain your market share – and we did better than that – and the market halves in size – which it did – then your sales halve. If your sales halve and you do nothing about your costs you go out of business.

"Some people say you can't cut costs in a creative business – not to do so is to choose to go out of business," he added.

The fact that the 2007 BRIT Awards ceremony came on the same day as the company's profit-warning announcement served to highlight EMI's dilemma. Its return of no wins from eight nominations was a major disappointment and by now the situation was even getting through to the company's creative community, according to former EMI UK boss Wadsworth. "These are artists, who are ambitious and bright people, who were concerned at that point about the perceived instability."

Paul McCartney, one of EMI's biggest and longest-serving artists, was among the first to comment publicly on the company as he signed a new deal with Hear Music, a joint venture between Concord Records and the Starbucks coffee company, and confirmed, "I have left the family home, but it doesn't feel bad."

Moving on from EMI outside North America after nigh-on 45 years, McCartney said he wasn't particularly saddened about leaving the record company he first signed to as a Beatle in 1962 and explained, "The people at EMI sort of understood. The major record companies are having major problems. They're a little puzzled as to what's happening and I sympathise with them."

Reviewing McCartney's *Memory Almost Full* album, which became the first music by a member of The Beatles to be available as a digital download, *Daily Telegraph* rock critic Neil McCormick pointed out that McCartney "has jumped ship from the ailing EMI into business with a coffee chain".

Radiohead manager Chris Hufford was harsher in his criticism of the company he had been associated with as an artist and manager for over 20 years. "EMI's decline has been faster than [that of] anybody else because they were the first company to have to stand on their own outside of any corporate structure and still be a plc," he says, suggesting it was then that it all started to go wrong. "After that everything got speeded up because there were some serious executive cock-ups as regards who they got to run things."

As speculation grew about EMI's future there came a suggestion that the company could raise anything up to £1 billion by borrowing against its successful and richly laden music-publishing catalogue in order to repay its debt, which was rated as being close to £1 billion, and possibly hold off any interested parties.

Once again the names of Warner Music and Martin Bandier plus a variety of private equity groups were being put in the frame, and even the debate over the future of the Sony BMG tie-up was ongoing and a cause for concern.

However, Warner Music was seemingly undaunted by the EC's concerns over the merger of two of its rivals as, on February 20, 2007, it launched a fresh attack on EMI. Although it did not constitute a formal bid, Warner's approach was based on what it described as "compelling, strategic, commercial and financial logic".

For its part EMI responded by confirming the approach and saying that it would be "considered with a particular focus on conditionality, the regulatory and operation risk profile and on valuation in relation to the company's stand-alone value and the creative value available from a combination." All of which meant that management would think about it, see who objected to what and work out how much it might all be worth to them.

The timing of Warner's approach centred on an effort to try and complete a deal before the private equity companies made a move for

EMI, and also in the light of a controversial agreement with the European independent labels body, IMPALA.

In return for the Brussels-based indies' organisation supporting Warner's acquisition of EMI, Warner would, apparently, help fund Merlin, the independent sector's global digital-rights licensing platform, and also divest "certain recorded assets" to independent labels.

While a Warner executive claimed that Edgar Bronfman was trying to "inject a new spirit of entrepreneurship" and reflect a "different corporate culture", two UK independent labels, Ministry of Sound and Gut, both resigned from AIM, the UK independents' association and members of Impala.

Martin Mills, founder of the biggest UK indie, Beggars Banquet, and also chairman of IMPALA, described the arrangement as "pragmatic" and stated, "We're not in bed with WMI." At the same time *Music Week* editor Martin Talbot saw the sense of the American company's move. "It looks like really smart political manoeuvring by Warner to remove what was the main obstacle to a deal."

For AIM's Alison Wenham the proposed merger between EMI and Warner in 2007 was significantly different from the approaches made in 2000, 2003 and 2006 and reflected the importance to the independents of "building market capacity in the digital supply chain". She suggests that up to this point the major operators in the digital business "very much ignored the independents".

Warner was keen to see if an agreed package of "remedies" could be achieved with IMPALA, which, if the US major was to make a bid for EMI, it could take to the EC and show that it acknowledged the important role the independents played in the music industry as, in Wenham's words, "the A&R seedbed, the entrepreneurs and risk takers".

While she never doubted that Warner's end game was always to find a way of merging with EMI, Wenham gives the American company credit for "the first intelligent pre-planning move made by any of the majors" and adds, "They were smart enough to realise that our arguments had strengths and therefore our position should be acknowledged."

On the back of these discussions with the indies, rumours of a likely firm bid for EMI by Warner were hotting up and on March 1, 2007 there came reports of it offering £2 billion for EMI and paying 260p a share . . . on a day when they were trading at 240p.

In America there was an unenthusiastic reaction to the possibility of Warner buying EMI as analysts assessed the less than impressive financial performance of both companies. Rich Greenfield from Pali Capital told investors in mid-February, "We simply do not believe that a combined WMG/EMI would be an attractive stock," while other analysts set the debt of a combined Warner/ EMI at somewhere between $4.5 billion and $8.5 billion.

By March 3, when EMI's shares finished up at 246p, EMI had rejected the £2 billion approach by Warner, having concluded that it was not in the best interests of EMI shareholders and "inadequate". The speed with which EMI spurned the offer apparently surprised the US company, but there was one piece of the jigsaw that perhaps the Americans had failed to put in place.

While the second profits warning resulted in an anticipated level of interest from various parties, EMI's stance was not to entertain any bidders during the last quarter of its financial year. Having announced a major restructuring and, with a fiscal year to see through to the end of March 2007, it chose to focus on delivering the best numbers it could manage.

Consequently all bets were off until April 1, 2007, the start of EMI's new financial year, by which time the company would have more definitive figures and be prepared to have what one executive called "sensible conversations about the value of the company and where it might be headed".

To one observer EMI's problems stemmed from a seeming lack of proper financial controls coupled with reduced investment in new talent. "The financial aspects of the company were chaotic," says media editor Dan Sabbagh, who believes that Nicoli failed to spot the problem and also missed out on another important aspect. "They didn't put enough effort behind A&R. Being a purely public company, which is a tough place for a music company to be, they focused on a steady stream of profit so they put a lot of energy into music publishing. They put some effort into catalogue but in recent years they lost it with new repertoire."

In the first week of its fiscal year, EMI broke ranks with its rivals – and put any deal with Warner firmly in the shadows – by aligning itself with Apple and offering its entire download catalogue without DRM through iTunes. The deal saw traditional copy-protected tracks being sold for 79p while consumers could get higher-quality tracks without protection, which they could download on iPods and mobile phones, for an extra 20p. All this was being done in an effort to ensure that 25% of EMI's total revenues came from digital sales.

Described variously by some analysts as "ground-breaking" and presenting "a revenue opportunity", the deal was seen by others as "a big gamble" with the risk that Nicoli might be "selling short the crown jewels of the music portfolio".

While a host of acts from EMI's star-studded roster were part of the new deal with Apple, the company's – and the world's – biggest-selling act did not feature even though The Beatles and EMI had settled an outstanding two-year-old £30 million royalty dispute in February 2007.

But hopes were high that EMI and the band's company, Apple, could thrash out the details of a royalty to cover sales of downloads of The Beatles' catalogue, which remained the biggest earner for the company. The fact that Jobs and his Apple company had, in a February 2007 settlement, won ownership of The Beatles' Apple name and famous 'Granny Smith' logo – then licensed it back to the group – was seen as an indication that The Beatles' music would be available to download through Apple in the near future.

Within two weeks of the new EMI year opening, a major Warner Music shareholder broke ranks to express his concerns over the value of EMI and what the US major should pay to acquire its British rival.

Scott Sperling, co-president of Thomas H Lee Partners, owners of 32% of Warner Music, told a New York private equity summit that EMI's sliding profits and poor growth made any potential offer "increasingly problematic". Referring to the 320p per share offer made by Warner in 2006, Sperling added, "Clearly that's not anywhere near what you'd want to pay today."

With talks between the two companies affected by EMI's decision to link with Apple and issue tracks without DRM, the US private equity investor and shareholder warned, "EMI has announced a series of disappointing results and we don't see it turning around."

Ironically, as the likelihood of an EMI Warner deal receded, Nicoli took the opportunity to add to his executive team the man he had talked to seven years earlier when the companies first considered a merger. Roger Ames, who left his job as chairman of Warner Music in 2004, had been acting as a consultant to Nicoli and EMI since 2005, and was now appointed chairman of the company's North American record operations.

As David Munns had returned to EMI in 2001 after leaving in 1987, so Ames returned to the company he left in 1979 – to pursue careers with Polygram, where he created the modern-day London Records, and Warner Music – to oversee the ailing US operations. And just as Bob Mercer, a former boss of both Munns and Ames during their EMI days, asserted that the British company held a special attraction for Munns, he saw the same situation with Ames whose reaction, when offered the chance to return to the fold, was to say to him, "It's EMI. We all feel differently about EMI, it's where we all got our start."

While the new front-line team was taking its seat on the EMI roller coaster, the company's figures for the year 2006–2007 showed that turnover was down to £1,751.5 million from the previous year's £2,079.9 million and operating profits slumped to £150.5 million, a massive fall of £100 million from the 2005–2006 figure.

Within this performance, music publishing once again delivered increased operating profits of £105.6 million despite a small drop in revenues, while the recorded music division came in with a huge 68% decline in operating profits, down to £44.9 million, after worldwide sales dropped by 15% with North America, the UK and Latin America the major problem areas for EMI.

On the upside the company's earnings from digital music sales rose from £112 million to over £164 million (an increase of over 46%) and accounted for 9.4% of the group's total revenue. Delivering the annual report for the first time as chief executive officer rather than chairman, Nicoli acknowledged the year had been both "challenging" and "difficult", but stressed that his company was "fundamentally redesigning our business to make it fit for the future".

However, with the latest set of predicted disappointing EMI figures out in the open, the company's future was anything but assured. During a period running from May to August 2007, there were newspaper and music magazine stories on an almost daily basis about bids, counter-bids and interested parties seeking to acquire the last great British music company in its 110th year as a major music maker.

May 4: US private equity company One Equity reported to be behind a £3 billion bid for EMI.

May 13: American hedge funds Fortress and Cerberus said to be planning to join forces and offer 260p a share to gain control of the company.

The general consensus is that the hedge funds are interested in acquiring EMI's back catalogue and possibly selling on the current record business.

May 18: EMI opens its books and sets aside a data room for potential suitors who are named as Cerberus, Fortress and One Equity.

May 21: Warner Music offers EMI a break-up fee of something between £50 and £100 million if its planned takeover is blocked by the EC.

May 22: UK private equity company Terra Firma's £2.4 billion (£3.2 including debt) bid recommended to investors by the EMI board.

EMI confirms that, "Terra Firma's offer is the most attractive proposal received and delivers cash flow without regulatory uncertainty and with the minimum operational risk to the company", although there is speculation that if Terra Firma wins control there will be heavy job losses. Contemplating a major bidding war, one analyst says, "This is the beginning of the end for EMI."

May 23: Warner Music said to be considering a new bid trumping the Terra Firma offer.

UBS analysts express surprise at the size of Terra Firma's bid but argue that "it is likely Warner will return with another bid".

May 24: Geneva-based investment company Corvus Capital drops out of the race for EMI.

Corvus chief, Andrew Regan, confirms that while he has the "necessary funding" to mount a bid for EMI, he has no intention of doing so in light of Terra Firma's recommended offer.

May 25: Former EMI Music president Jim Fifield confirmed as a potential new bidder for EMI in partnership with ex-colleague Charles Koppelman and with backing from Corvus and Qatari royal family.

Fifield says that despite Corvus' announcement he "remains interested in potentially making an offer for EMI" and Barclays strategist Henk Potts says by agreeing to Terra Firman's offer, EMI was putting "a price on the table that they are prepared to sell at."

May 26: Warner Music linked with Cerberus in a new joint bid for EMI.

May 31: EMI said to be prepared to reject any Warner Music bid if it falls below 300p a share.

Terra Firma confirms that it has had no discussions with EMI management about future roles in the company and adds, "The offer is not conditional on senior management participation", while one US banker suggests, "It will be difficult for Warner and private equity to go higher than Terra Firma."

June 2: Music industry media suggests that the attraction of Terra Firma bid to EMI is based on a good price without conditions and immediate delivery, and that Nicoli is "certainly more likely" to retain a role under new owners than he would if Warner bought EMI.

June 6: US private equity companies said to be prepared to sell EMI's recorded music division to Warner if any of them succeed in beating Terra Firma offer.

June 11: Warner Music confirms its continuing interest in acquiring EMI.
In an official statement the US music major says that it "continues actively to consider an offer for EMI Group".

June 23: Bronfman's Warner Music reported to be considering a counter-offer and also to be in talks with Terra Firma about a possible deal after EMI has been acquired.

June 26: City brokers forecast that a new Warner bid will be in the region of 290p to 300p a share.

June 27: Terra Firma's £2.4 billion offer rejected by EMI shareholders as first deadline for acceptance passes and is extended.

July 5: Second deadline reached and a further extension granted as shareholders with only 3.6% of the stock vote in favour of Terra Firma's offer.
Analyst Alex DeGroote from Panmure Gordon suggests, "If you were a shareholder you would possibly be sitting on your shares until the last possible moment in case Warner comes up with a higher bid."

July 11: Warner Music said to be in further talks with US bankers in the run-up to the deadline for acceptance of Terra Firma bid.

July 14: Warner still considering a bid as deadline for EMI shareholders is further extended.

July 18: Warner Music finally announces that it is not going to make a counter-bid for EMI on the eve of the July 19 deadline.

July 19: Jim Fifield reported to have also withdrawn from the bidding and Terra Firma further extends the deadline for EMI shareholder acceptance to July 29.

July 21: European Commission approves Terra Firma's proposed acquisition of EMI.

July 26: Terra Firma reported to face potential problems in securing the backing for its bid for EMI as Citigroup is said to be seeking new terms.

July 28: Terra Firma confirmed as having a clear run at EMI and company spokesman says they are relieved and states, "We want to own the company."

July 30: Takeover Panel agrees to extend the Terra Firma deadline until August 2 in order for it to gain acceptance from a further 5% of the owners of 90% of EMI shares.

The view among analysts and bankers is that EMI's investors would be "stupid not to accept now and take the money otherwise the EMI shares will go under 200p".

Aug 2: Terra Firma confirmed as new owner of EMI when 90% of EMI shareholders agree to accept the offer of 265p per share.

The view is that Terra Firma chief, Guy Hands, will have to put some cash into EMI in order to attract big-selling artist to the company. "Being able to offer decent advances is one way of achieving this," says Bridgewell Securities analyst Patrick Yau, who adds that he also expects Hands to "weed out underperformers" on the company's roster of acts.

So a deal had finally been done for EMI and it was the private equity firm Terra Firma run by entrepreneur Guy Hands, reckoned to be the owner of Britain's largest collection of karaoke songs, who triumphed over Warner and a host of rival private equity businesses.

With a career background as a bond trader with Goldman Sachs in London and a principal investor with Japanese bank Nomura, Hands was supported by Nomura when he launched Terra Firma in 2002. Since then it has owned a wide range of companies including the UCI cinema chain, William Hill betting shops, Inntrepreneur pub group, Threshers off-licence chain and WRG, the UK's largest landfill operator.

In 2007, before bidding for EMI, Hands was defeated in an £11 billion race for the Alliance Boots chain of chemists, which was seen by some as a typically ambitious move by the Oxford-educated entrepreneur. "Guy is like those people you always see at charity dinners who insist on bidding first, they just want everyone to see they are involved," was how one City insider viewed his quest for Boots.

As another analyst observed, had Hands succeeded in buying Boots he almost certainly would not have gone after EMI but, having raised the money to support his bid for Boots, he was not about to let it go to waste. So when EMI came into his sights it became a viable target.

While the battle for EMI was going on during the summer months of 2007, the music industry continued to do business with, according to *Music Week*, Universal "looking to consolidate its position as the market leader in music worldwide". On the back of its acquisition of BMG Music, the number one company made a June offer valued at £104 million for the UK-based Sanctuary Group, which boasted artist management, agency and merchandising divisions.

This move came just a month after Warner Music, despite still bidding for EMI, announced plans to cut 400 staff around the world and at the same time as Universal also let 40 people go from its Island Def Jam division. However, the Nielsen SoundScan figures for the first half of 2007 still showed Universal ahead with 31.6% of the US market followed by Sony BMG on 25.2% and Warner on 20%, while EMI lagged behind on just 10.3%.

These figures also showed that physical sales dropped by over 15% while digital sales increased 48.5%. The total number of single track downloads was 417 million compared with 281 million in the first half of 2006. Despite these increases, a digital survey by Entertainment Media Research suggested that illegal downloading was also on the increase. Of the 1,700 people surveyed, the report found that 43% of them were downloading tracks illegally, an increase from 36% in the previous year.

After being beaten in the race for EMI, the company's former music president Jim Fifield reflected on the situation he found himself facing in the summer of 2007. "I was definitely interested in EMI. We developed a good business plan with significant upside opportunity but the price became too rich and the credit market too tight," he says. "It's not easy getting people to invest in a company losing market share in a declining market."

Looking at the new owner of the company he had presided over for nearly ten years Fifield observes, "Now Terra Firma – under Guy Hands – owns the company and Guy is trying to change it overnight. The jury is out, but one thing I do know is that it's the music that counts.

"If you have a lousy organisation but produce good music you may be successful. On the other hand," he warns, "if you have a great organisation and no music you are going to fail. Music development will take time. I doubt if they will have the patience."

It also became clear that Fifield wasn't the only ex-music company executive interested in buying EMI. Former chairman of Sony Music Label Group Don Ienner confirmed that he was a partner in the One Equity bid and told *Billboard* in 2008, "I was involved in the bid that made the second best bid for EMI."

The one-time president of Columbia Records added, "I was going to run it because I believe in that catalogue; I believe that for the price that we were going to get it, it was going to be a very profitable company."

Reflecting on the failure of EMI and Warner to come together in some shape or another after a courtship that lasted over seven years, Andy Heath rejects the notion that a merger was something of a fanciful notion. "I don't think they were follies and I think it was a sensible thing to try to do," he says before suggesting why it all ended in failure. "Not to put too fine a point on it I think Eric [Nicoli] found himself in a pissing competition with Dick Parsons and Roger Ames and then after that got into another with Edgar Bronfman. They all wanted to win and it didn't appear to be adult commercial behaviour."

For Nicoli selling EMI to Terra Firma and getting 265p a share represented good business. "My job was to maximise value for EMI's shareholders and at 265p a share in August 2007 I sincerely believe we did that." He also holds the view that "a period in private ownership would benefit the business".

Reflecting on a sale that required all offers to be fully funded with letters from banks alongside formal undertakings and on the understanding that if 90% of the shareholders approved an offer then the bidders could not withdraw, Nicoli goes further on the 265p price per share. "It's now clear that it wasn't just a good deal but a fantastic deal for EMI shareholders."

While he accepts that some commentators wanted to focus on what might have been and the various failed mergers with Warner and BMG, which were subject to approval by the EC, Nicoli looks at what would have happened had EMI not been sold into private ownership. "Had EMI remained public and tracked Warner Music – the only other stand-alone publicly quoted music company – we would have been trading at about 50p a share by October 2008."

Assuming Nicoli had concluded that he would not have a role in the future running of EMI, analyst Mike Hilton believes that the deal he did made perfect sense. "He'd resigned himself to not being there and at that point in time it's the shareholders that matter and 265p is absolutely not bad if you were a shareholder. His 2008 estimate of 80p a share is generous, if it had the same level of debt today that it had then, you could be looking at 30p or 40p a share."

Even though he accepts that the offer price of 265p a share was "a good price" in 2007, the chair of UK Music reflects on what might have been. "Everybody agrees that it was a good price then, except that it was far less than what it was two years before," says Andy Heath, head of the umbrella organisation representing the interests of the UK's commercial music industry. "He picked a good moment to do a deal but clearly not the optimum moment."

As the man who brought Nicoli into EMI and watched as the company drifted downwards, Colin Southgate also believes the final price wasn't too bad. "I think it was probably an all-right price although you could argue that Hands paid too much for EMI," he says before admitting that he doesn't know if Nicoli had any alternative but to deal with private equity. "I am quite surprised they didn't follow up the deal with Warner. The EC crumbled over Sony BMG and I think they would have eventually crumpled under pressure to merge EMI and Warner."

Music journalist Legrand, however, has a slightly different view of the EMI sale. "Eventually the company ends up in such bad shape that they made a not so good deal with Guy Hands, who ends up with something that is probably in a worse shape than he thought it would be."

But even as Hands was putting the finishing touches to his acquisition of EMI, there was speculation that falls on the world's major stock markets in early August 2007 might affect the funding of his £2.4 billion takeover as backer Citigroup faced increased interest rates. While one City analyst described the EMI deal as "touch and go", another said it was unlikely that Citigroup would "throw a spanner in the works".

For Warner Music the failure to do a deal with EMI was proving to be costly as it announced a $17 million net loss for the quarter up to June 2007. This figure included $8 million the US company had spent in connection with its bid for EMI and prompted chief executive Bronfman to explain, "EMI created market expectations for a price from us we couldn't justify."

As Terra Firma announced that it would probably "take the keys to EMI at the start of September", the music industry buzzed with comment and speculation about the future of the company and its existing executives, including the former chairman. "Nicoli is exposed because he's sacked all the people who know something about music and his track record outside music hasn't been particularly good," was the view of analyst Patrick Yau.

Talking to *Music Week* in the week after the deal was approved, managers of a host of EMI acts gave the thumbs-up to the takeover. Simon Banks, manager of KT Tunstall, reckoned that the move was a breath of fresh air for the music business and added, "We need someone to mix it up a little bit."

Corinne Bailey Rae's manager, Bob Miller, believed that, while the music business had to change, the music still had to come first. "Terra Firma not being a creative company is no big issue," he said. On the other hand Neale Easterby, whose company looked after Lily Allen, predicted a "blood bath" with major staff cuts.

Even though there was undoubtedly talk of Nicoli staying with EMI under the new regime – it's even rumoured that a job offer was on the table at one stage – it came as no real surprise when it was announced at the end of August 2007 that the man who had led EMI through the most traumatic period in its long history was leaving.

While an unnamed analyst said bluntly, "He did a terrible job. I thought he was awful," Hands paid tribute to Nicoli. "Eric steered EMI through a period when the industry has faced extreme change and we thank him for providing a smooth transition into our ownership."

As Nicoli left with a pay-off reportedly worth around £3 million, he was followed out of the door by finance director Martin Stewart. Hands duly appointed Chris Roling, a former vice president with chemical group ICI, as chief operating/finance officer, and Ashley Unwin, from Deloitte Consulting, as director of business transformation.

In an editorial item dated August 30, 2007, *The Financial Times* set the scene for all those associated with the new EMI, stating, "Nobody really expected the new bosses to appoint a board consisting of Robbie Williams, Sir Simon Rattle and The Spice Girls, but still the record company's new executives – a former ICI senior vice president of finance, a management consultant and a lawyer – could hardly be greyer. In case the message that change is in the air is lost on employees, one of the trio has taken the ominous new title 'director of business transformation'."

Over a year after leaving his EMI office just off London's fashionable Kensington High Street, Nicoli suggests, "Time will tell if the Terra Firma approach has merit for this kind of business," and reflects on the scenario that had unfolded during the summer of 2007. "Public criticism of me and my senior team – and indeed the removal of us all – was not a surprise. I'm sure our successors can see opportunities to create value – just as we could – but they're beginning to understand how tough it is to deliver in such unhelpful conditions. "I wish them well," he added.

US-based investment adviser David Londoner ended his time as a non-executive director of EMI as Terra Firma completed its takeover and he holds the view that Nicoli "did a good job in the circumstances".

As a member of the EMI board for four years he was close to the action as the company and its chairman dealt with the problems. "He [Eric] took three large-scale cost reductions, painful but necessary stopgap measures. However the upfront costs of these – mostly severance – necessarily stretched the capitalisation beyond what some felt was prudent. I'm not sure anyone could have put the company back in good shape once the market for recorded music began to spiral down."

Even though it brought to an end his association with EMI, Londoner welcomed the interest from Hands who, even though he never actually met with the full EMI board to make his 265p offer, had it accepted unanimously. "The Terra Firma purchase was a gift from heaven. Without it the shares would today be selling for 70p or less."

As befits a company of the stature of EMI, the interest in its future brought forth a variety of opinions from managers, analysts, commentators and former executives, who in turn either applauded, criticised or simply understood the decision to sell out to a private equity company with no history or experience in the music industry.

> *"The sale to a private equity company was inevitable. It is possible that Guy Hands will apply a fresh business model that will give EMI a chance to succeed. There will have to be massive write-downs and staff restructuring first . . . there will also have to be in place a layer of artist-savvy executives if they have any intention of growing the business from there."*
>
> – Sam Feldman, manager of Norah Jones.

> *"It made me very nervous when it was bought by a non-traditional music entity. Does Hands understand what he has acquired; coming at things from*

a different perspective is not always sensible. It may all turn out for the best and EMI needed something drastic to happen but whether this is the right thing I don't know."

– Ed Bicknell, former manager of Dire Straits and Bryan Ferry and former William Morris executive.

"Assuming a merger wasn't going to happen it was the only deal left to EMI. Staying public was never going to work – music companies have too many ups and downs to ever be stand-alone quoted companies. In retrospect it was wrong in 1996 to go it alone and remain a public company"

– Andy Taylor, manager of Iron Maiden and former Sanctuary Group executive.

"I have no idea what was behind Hands buying EMI. I think he was very surprised by what he's bought; it's not anything like he possibly thought it would be."

– Chris Morrison, manager of Blur and Gorillaz.

"Logically what Hands has done in making EMI a privately owned company should theoretically give it a chance of doing a bit better."

– Bryce Edge, co-manager of Radiohead and Supergrass.

"He's a bright man but has absolutely no idea about the music business. If you thought Eric [Nicoli] had no idea about it, then he's an expert compared to Guy Hands."

– Chris Hufford, co-manager of Radiohead and Supergrass.

"They [EMI] are very worried and what I would be worried about is that you are dealing with people purely interested in making money, and someone might just tell Guy Hands that if he goes into liquidation and sells off the catalogue in the right way and to the right people, he would suddenly find that he didn't have to pay any more royalties. That I think is the really scary thing knocking around – that they could take the record company into liquidation."

– Pete Jenner, manager of Billy Bragg and former Pink Floyd and Syd Barrett manager.

"The big attraction to private equity was the publishing revenues. They were doing reverse financial engineering – saying if recorded music is actually worth nothing, what is publishing worth and what can we do with it. Guy Hands is

213

a real out-of-the-box thinker. I don't think he has any interest in the music business at all but he looked at a business in which he could see abuses and bad practices that you could eliminate."

– Mark Beilby, former media analyst with Deutsche Bank and
Dresdner Kleinwort.

"It's the first time that he [Hands] or a private equity company has taken on a talent business. There's always an intangible reason, but with Hands he would have looked at the publishing business and seen it as almost an annuity while the recorded music he probably saw as a punt, and if the worst came to the worst he could always sell it on."

– Mike Hilton, media analyst with ABN-AMRO and UBS and
partner in PMM.

"He probably overpaid for EMI but Guy Hands looked at [it] and said, 'It's a mess', and it was a mess. There were far too many people on inflated salaries just shoring up their position and A&R was suffering – there was a lack of creativity and they had to find a new way of doing business. He undoubtedly recognised that EMI was in a parlous state and he recognised that it was right for the taking, but what he hasn't recognised is what the nature of the business is."

– Neil McCormick, *Daily Telegraph* music editor.

"If Hands had bought Boots he wouldn't have bought EMI and on balance him buying EMI has so far been a good thing. They had a view that they could really restructure it and turn it round and Terra Firma is unusual for venture capitalists. Most of them supply the money and then a bloke to run it, but what Terra Firma does is find the money, bring in a team of people and they'll try to bring in some method."

– Dan Sabbagh, *The Times* media editor.

"The big problem for EMI is to be profitable at a decent level for Terra Firma and in order to do that it has to outperform the industry, and EMI has never outperformed the industry except in music publishing, which is a pond compared to the sea that is music revenue."

– Phil Hardy, *Music & Copyright* editor.

"It is extraordinary that EMI is in private hands but it is symptomatic of the way in which the City always views companies like EMI – they don't under-stand the way the business works. I don't look at the future of EMI with

optimism. I don't think Guy Hands has a clue what he is doing. He might be a great saviour but he doesn't seem to be that right now."

– Jon Webster, former Virgin executive and CEO Music
Managers Forum.

"He [Hands] is now trying to control what the music business should have controlled years earlier – lavish executive compensation, high-risk artist contracts and ego-driven promotion costs. His big risk is artists vacating EMI for competing companies whose executives still pour traditional perks on them."

– David Londoner, former non-executive director of EMI.

"Emotionally the deal with Terra Firma is absolutely awful for EMI. This is a 110-year-old company – a proud British company – that should not disappear but sadly I think it is going to. Other majors merged to make themselves stronger while EMI sat there, alone and in the weakest position of all the majors. The demise of EMI cannot be denied whatever its future might be."

– David Hughes, former marketing & PR director,
EMI Records UK.

"I had no knowledge of where Terra Firma came from nor on what basis their due diligence established the value of what they bought. It has subsequently seemed clear that they did not really know what they were buying, nor possibly why they were buying it at the price they paid. They seemed to have little idea of how to go about managing the ferocious tiger whose tail they had caught impetuously."

– Bhaskar Menon, former chairman EMI Music.

"I have no idea why he [Hands] bought it – I think he probably needed to do a big deal. It is not a business to put your own money in and it's certainly not a business that you should treat as though the people in it are dumb, even though it is a business that needs a great deal of rethinking."

– Colin Southgate, ex-chairman Thorn EMI & EMI Group.

A former top EMI executive who was there when Hands bought the company but who prefers to remain anonymous says that Terra Firma was pushing at an already "open door" when it arrived. "Everybody knew something had to happen, that the future of EMI needed to be secured in some way and there was a real positive to being taken off the stock market."

In fact the man who was now in charge of EMI had actually considered making an offer way back in 1996 when the company demerged from

Thorn. Prompted by friends who believed that EMI had been a great company with a great history and a great catalogue but was being run by people who didn't have the right creative feel, Hands saw an opportunity, even before the days of Terra Firma, to acquire what was seen as a badly run company.

But a combination of a high price and difficulty in raising the finance for a multi-million pound venture meant EMI remained a public company for a further 11 years until May 2007, when a falling price and increased debt availability meant Hands was finally able to move in.

While it's no secret that Hands has never been impressed by the quality of the management in the music industry, he nevertheless understood what was on offer at EMI, where the valuable catalogue and publishing arms could be securitised even though the creative side of the company was in need of some improvement.

Speaking on the BBC Radio 4 documentary *The EMI Story* in December 2008, Hands confirmed that it was not his job to be loved. "My job is to change businesses and to make businesses function better and to do that you have to break eggs. The reality was that the EMI we purchased was not working and it needed change."

Fairly early on in his career as owner of EMI, Hands took the reins as chairman of the newly created supervisory board to oversee the workings of the music company and this meant he had to get involved in negotiations with artists and managers.

Iron Maiden's contract with EMI ran out in 2007, and while negotiations had begun under Nicoli they were delayed while the company was being sold. "EMI was prepared to look at a wider involvement in other areas involving Maiden and this was important because our catalogue is with them," says Andy Taylor. "The deal did go over the acquisition period and it was put on hold for a while and then had to be approved by Guy Hands. There weren't any hiccups from Hands or his team over the deal."

However, a more difficult prize to capture was always going to be the signature of Radiohead, which proved to be among the earliest of Hands' encounters with artist management. The Oxford-based band's contract had expired in 2003 and for four years the group and their managers, Edge and Hufford, considered their future, observing how the company and the industry changed before deciding what to do with the group's next album.

"We talked to everybody about a deal including Warners and EMI," says Edge, before band and managers decided to go their own way and launch the album as a download, inviting fans to pay as little or as much as they wanted. "When we finally announced our plan to do things ourselves it did seriously piss off EMI and Warners," recalls Hufford.

According to Edge, Hands was involved in the discussions between Radiohead and EMI but failed to impress the former. "Guy Hands' first serious attempt at negotiating with a band was with us and the one card he had was the catalogue," says Edge, who points out that the new boss of EMI failed to understand the importance to artists of their collected works. "If he had been prepared to negotiate in a sensible way on those six albums in the catalogue we would probably have released a record on EMI . . . and regretted it. But he would not entertain negotiating on any level on the catalogue so that made our minds up and we pushed the button on our own plan."

On Friday, September 14, 2007, Hands spoke in Cambridge at the Royal Television Society convention, and bizarrely chose this event to inform the assembled audience and the media about his plans for EMI's recorded music division and his reasons for buying the company. "We are determined to keep that part of the business and we are determined to make it viable," he announced before explaining "We look at the worst business we can find in the most challenged sector and we get really happy if it's really bad. EMI, our most recent investment, is a classic example. We're just hoping EMI is as bad as we think it is."

On the following Monday, in the aftermath of those remarks, Hands felt the need to send an internal note to EMI employees explaining that his comments about EMI also applied to the entire music industry. He explained that at EMI specifically, "There has been too much management focus over the last seven years on a potential merger with Warner and on a continuous cost-cutting program, which has failed to deliver a new business model and sadly has led to the loss of many talented people from the business."

He then added, "Put simply, focusing on the production of multi-million selling albums cannot produce a sustainable business model."

While some have claimed that the way Hands explained his thoughts about EMI to the audience in Cambridge and the manner in which it was headlined in the newspapers point to an unfair representation, the man himself accepts he could have done better. "What happened was that I said some things which maybe could have been expressed a little bit better," he told Radio 4 before adding, "But it's not a popularity game, it's about trying to do the best I can for the business and all I can say to them is that I am passionate about EMI succeeding."

The next step for the new EMI was to be delisted from the London Stock Exchange after more than 70 years as a major public company, and the date for this landmark event was set for September 18, 2007. A week later the CEO of Terra Firma assembled EMI's UK-based staff in one of his own cinemas for a behind-closed-doors meeting.

Although the press were not invited, staffers leaked news of the get-together and what came out of it all was that Hands was committed to turning EMI around, that selling recorded music to Warner was not on the agenda and that Terra Firma would remain in control of EMI for at least eight years.

Insiders told reporters that in the main this was reassuring news and that Hands had impressed most people in the room. "He was able to clarify a lot of the wilder rumours that have been going round, people were pretty impressed with him and they thought he was very open," said one anonymous EMI staffer before adding, "He made a big point of saying that he wants to engage with the staff and that went down very well."

If he had managed to bring some comfort to his staff, Hands still faced a potential problem with his artists and, more importantly, their managers, who were the ones in regular contact with the record company. "Managers are terribly important people and I don't think Hands really understands this," is how music writer Phil Hardy sees the situation. "He thinks of them as things to throw against the wall."

Even if that was so, Hands did recognise that appeasing the management community was important and he spent much of his time meeting them. But the concern was that while his message about trying to change EMI and getting the people within the company to think more about artists, managers and fans was generally welcomed, there was another part of the message that caused unrest.

His worry was that EMI could not afford to keep artists who made no money – and with a roster close to 2,800 acts it was likely that the majority did not make a profit. The idea that launching perhaps just 50 acts in a year would be a more sensible approach made sense to the managers until it dawned on them that there was a chance their acts might not be on the list of the chosen 50.

With an average launch cost of close to £500,000 per release, without factoring in the high wages of EMI's executives, Hands clearly faced a financial dilemma about signing and releasing new acts.

One manager who was less than impressed after his first meeting with Hands was CMO chief Chris Morrison, who recalls what was said with embarrassment. "He said to me – and he said it in front of Tony Wadsworth, which was embarrassing and inappropriate – 'In my view the level of salary is not matched with the level of expertise within the record industry'. He said he wanted to run a low-cost, high-profit organisation and my comment was, 'Why don't you get rid of the very expensive Wrights Lane [Kensington] headquarters?'"

In fact, rather than disposing of its corporate headquarters in Kensington, in 2009 the company chose to move EMI Records UK out of its home for the past 14 years in Brook Green, Hammersmith and put it in with the rest of EMI's music operations in Wrights Lane. Also making the move to Kensington was the famous 'Beatles balcony' featured on their album covers and described by EMI as "a very important part of Beatles' history and EMI history".

Interestingly, media analyst Mike Hilton shared Morrison's view about the company's location and its cost. "If you really are running this for cash you are in Croydon not Kensington or Hammersmith, but the industry is still acting like it's a global, highly profitable and massively important industry . . . which it isn't."

His advice to Hands on how to survive is to "continue to take your cost base down ahead of declining sales", and he also had a thought as to why the world's biggest media companies had shied away from the music business. "If you spoke to people at News Corp or Microsoft and asked them why they were not in recorded music, they will say it's an ex-growth business that we don't need to be in – it's volatile, it's talent-led and it's very fickle."

Meanwhile Morrison also recalls that Hands, at a dinner with a number of other managers, told him that he would be interested in knowing what the artists felt about the future of the record industry. "My thought was that Damon Albarn doesn't give a fuck about the future of the record industry, he cares about the music.

"He [Hands] needed to understand that artists hate the major record companies because they are paid less than they should be, they are dictated to and the executives are usually paid more than they should be."

Hands caused further unrest with what was meant as an amusing comparison between his own working hours – he's an early-morning starter – and those of record company A&R people, who tend to drift in around noon after a late night. Not only was this interpreted as a suggestion of laziness on the part of the talent scouts, but it implied he had no real knowledge of what A&R people were required to do in the course of their job.

For *Telegraph* music writer Neil McCormick his remarks indicated a major PR failure on the part of EMI's new owner. "His PR has been absolutely appalling. His denigrating remarks about A&R were terrible for people at EMI. He was talking to a different audience and playing the crowd but it was a major PR mistake."

While journalist Emmanuel Legrand had some sympathy with what EMI's new boss said, he could also see why it caused unrest. "He was not totally wrong in what he has said about artists and A&R but it's not the right message to send out. The structure – A&R on one side, service on another plus back office – is a very complex one to make work and the relationship between artists and record companies is about trust and understanding."

The experienced music reporter goes further. "What is surprising is that Guy Hands comes in and says it's a fucked-up business and I'm going to bring in the wisdom of the outsider and I know better. But it will be a structure that comes from people with no understanding that what you are dealing with is not a piece of plastic, but people and creativity."

Again speaking on radio, Hands admitted that he had learnt an enormous amount since taking over EMI. "I've probably learnt more in the last year than I learnt in the previous five years," he said while also accepting that he would always be open to criticism. "I thought it appropriate to put myself in the firing line and I've got some brickbats and it's been very painful, but frankly that's what good businessmen do – they shouldn't go and hide."

By early October, 2007, Hands was once again writing to his staff to tell them that the record industry had been too slow to embrace the digital world and the new opportunities for promotion and distribution through multiple channels and "has stuck its head in the sand".

This confidential but widely leaked missive came on the back of Radiohead's decision to spurn EMI and release their new album as a digital download. "In a digital world it was inevitable that a band with the necessary financial resources and consumer recognition to be able to distribute their music directly to their fans would do so," he wrote on October 5, 2007.

In yet another of his supposedly confidential internal e-mails, Hands told staff on October 31, 2007 that, even after just a few weeks in the company, "I do see a need for fundamental change in how we approach the music business and how we deliver the interconnected triangle of the consumer, EMI and the artist."

He went on to clarify the situation with regard to artists and their future dealings with EMI. "While many spend huge amounts of time working with their label to promote, perfect and endorse their music, some unfortunately simply focus on negotiating for the maximum advance . . . advances which are often never repaid."

The non-stop leaking of Hands' internal notes to a wider audience along with the industry's incessant gossiping about EMI was the subject of a conversation between ex-Sony man Paul Russell and Hands when they met in 2007. "I have some sympathy for him because the problem is that if you put something in an e-mail and send it to people in your company, within minutes it will be public knowledge and I think that came as something of a shock to him.

"I said to him that the primary reason the music industry exists is for the rumours and the music comes second. The industry leaks like a sieve and everything the poor guy said or did, everybody in the world knew in about 15 seconds."

But leaked e-mails wasn't the only subject that Russell and Hands – who was rapidly coming to the conclusion that most of what the press wrote about him and his companies was simply made up – spoke about. "He's very interested in the music business and he's very interested in EMI. I don't think he's there for the short term or just as an asset-stripper. I think he wants to be in the music business for some time."

As both an experienced record and music-publishing executive Russell was also able to pass on some advice to EMI's new owner about where to locate his music business. "I told him trying to run EMI out of the UK is like trying to kill an alligator by the tail – you're at the wrong end, you've got to be at the head. I don't think EMI has ever had one true music person sitting in New York with worldwide control over both records and publishing, and that was what it needed then and what it needs now."

And unless the structure and the location of EMI's music operations are altered Russell sees only one outcome. "They are in fifth place now behind the combined indies and unless they change they may be destined to stay in fifth place."

While Terra Firma continued with its "strategic review" of the EMI business there were reports of major job cuts and also of talks with private equity firms and hedge funds to offer stakes in the music operation. If successful these would enable Terra Firma to recoup some of its £1.5 billion equity invested in EMI.

And even if that wasn't the plan in late October 2007, Hands certainly confirmed on Radio 4 in December 2008 that was how it was supposed to work. "Normally what we would have done is to take that £1.5 billion and sell roughly two thirds, so Terra Firma would have ended up with £500 million and about a billion would have been sold to investors all over the world who invest in private equity."

With the world in the midst of a major credit crunch, Hands accepted that was unlikely to happen at any time soon. "Obviously that sell-down didn't take place, which is obviously a big difference," he admitted before going on to discuss the question of how much he paid for EMI. "Only time will tell, in absolute terms, whether we paid too much. In relative terms at the time we looked at the value of publishing [about £2.4 billion] and the catalogue was valued at about £1.4 billion, which gets you to about £3.8 billion. Then on top of that you have new music, classics, Blue Note, country, which must be worth £1.2 billion, so on a break-up basis, we clearly didn't."

However the multi-millionaire investment entrepreneur also admits, "The reality is that anyone who bought anything in 2007 – pretty well anything – clearly as of today one has to look back and say one paid too much whatever one bought in 2007."

One man with a particularly strong view on the value of EMI and the deal Hands did to get hold of the music company is experienced media analyst Mike Hilton. "EMI has no value," he says. "The debt is bigger than the value of the equity, the price he paid could only be justified because he could borrow money so cheaply and the performance level of the company has deteriorated as well."

Certainly the credit crunch put paid to a lot of the new EMI's plans, which involved buying up and consolidating with a number of independent music companies in an effort to create a platform and establish EMI as the largest independent with a much more aggressive and creative culture. It has been left to focus on simply making changes to disciplines and structures, while at the same time ensuring the business survives and is able to meet the interest payments on its debt – and that means not being able to invest in genres such as India's Bollywood music, which, perhaps surprisingly, was something that was high on its agenda.

As the media continued to speculate about EMI's finances – there were reports in late November 2007 that Terra Firma had sold on, depending on which paper you read, either £100 million or £250 million of its equity investment and that Citigroup had been unable to sell on any of its £2.5 billion loan – Hands announced the arrival of some unlikely new faces to oversee the revival of EMI.

Lord Birt, former BBC director general and for four years Tony Blair's much-feted "blue skies" strategic thinker, joined the supervisory board and was given the role of reviewing EMI's creative talent, alongside former Northern Foods executive Pat O'Driscoll, who was added to the investor board assessing EMI.

Meanwhile, savings became a vital part of the management of EMI as CD sales continued to fall and the company's own selection of releases failed to make a major impression in 2007. In the all-important run-up to Christmas, the company could boast only six albums in the UK chart – current acts Kylie Minogue and KT Tunstall alongside the likes of The Spice Girls, Cliff Richard, Phil Collins and Genesis – and only Kylie was in the Top 10.

According to *Music Week* editor Paul Williams, sales in the final quarter of the year were usually dominated by superstar acts, greatest hits titles and all-year-long big sellers and, as he explained, "EMI is struggling in all three categories."

The company's performance in the UK over the year was also disappointing with EMI hitting a six-year low on its 15.7% share of the vital album market, down from 17.9% the previous year and a 2002 high of 21%. Its two closest rivals, Sony BMG (19%) and Warner (10.4%), also reported lower album sales, while market leader Universal increased 2.7% to a 10-year high of 32.7%. EMI's only entry in the top 10 best-selling albums of 2007 was Corinne Bailey Rae with the same album that had been listed a year earlier.

On a global scale EMI's share of the world market in 2007 dropped from 12.8% to 10.9%, according to *Music & Copyright*, while in the US it dipped below the magic 10% number to just 9.4% with only Norah Jones' *Never Too Late* album appearing among the list of US 2007 best sellers. The number of units sold by EMI in America in 2007 also dropped substantially – from 60 million albums in 2006 to 46.9 million.

Also disappointing were the figures for EMI's digital business in 2007. With not a single title in the *Billboard* year end top 10 lists of best-selling digital artists or albums, the company's US digital market share, according to Nielsen SoundScan, shrank from 7.9% in 2006 to 7.7% and the speculation was that its share would have been even smaller had it not linked with Apple's MP3 strategy.

In Europe only Norah Jones featured on the year-end list of best sellers – with Universal taking the top three places – and the company was at fourth place with a 12.9% share of the European album chart. This was down nearly six points from 18.3% in 2006 and just under 30 percentage points behind leader Universal's 42.8% share.

On the other hand EMI Music Publishing completed 13 years in a row as top UK publisher, even though its crown as top world publisher was taken by Universal following its acquisition of BMG Music.

In light of these figures – and on top of some ill-judged remarks from the new management about how much the company had supposedly spent half a decade earlier on candles, fruit, flowers and apartments in LA and London – the reports of no bonuses for EMI executives until new levels of earnings were met, a freeze on new hirings and a 10% cut in marketing costs came as no real surprise.

One thing that did possibly surprise Hands, however, was the reaction of his acts and managers to his previous comments about artists and their advances. He was forced to write to artists signed to EMI reassuring them that they were "at the epicentre" of his plans and telling them the quotes taken from his earlier note were "highly selective".

Jazz Summers, manager of The Verve and a founder member of the infamous group of EMI artist managers who regularly gathered together under the banner of the Black Hand Gang, met Hands in the midst of the company's review. "I have found him bright and willing but, since reading his statements, Terra Firma need a lesson in artist management," was his reported comment and he went on to compare some of Hands' other business ventures with his role at EMI. "He's not dealing with motorway cafes in Germany or pubs. I don't think he really understands the artistic process."

At the same time, Iron Maiden's long-time manager Andy Taylor thinks that much of what Hands has in mind for EMI is right. "I think Guy Hands is a shrewd businessman and I think the model he is endeavouring to create for EMI is right. I also think he realises now that he was over-confident in what he believed he could do."

While suggesting that given a shift in time Hands wouldn't choose to buy again, Taylor emphasises the things he has to do to make it work. "He's got to streamline it, focus on high-earning acts and try and earn more with them, try and clean out your loss-making acts, reduce your overheads and focus people on revenue streams."

Reflecting on what he found when he acquired EMI, Hands told the BBC that his first impression was mixed. "Publishing was exactly what we expected – absolutely world-class business run very well indeed. The catalogue was actually better than we expected; there was an awful lot of catalogue which was not being exploited," he said.

But where did that leave the current music business? "Where we were disappointed was where we were with new music, where the results were actually quite a lot worse than we were expecting."

The business of how Hands presents himself and the company he bought is something that journalist Neil McCormick feels strongly about and his concerns go back to the time before Terra Firma bought EMI. "EMI's name has been trashed by the bad PR that Eric [Nicoli] was getting and then the worse PR that Hands has got so, ultimately, the future of the company is going to be based on the music it releases.

"All of the superstar acts have lost confidence although maybe Coldplay's success will restore some of that, but it is a confidence game and why would anybody want to sign to EMI?"

The bad PR was something that also caused concern for manager Jonathan Shalit who believes that Hands underestimated the "sexiness" of the music business. "If you make the smallest comment it becomes a headline. The amount of press coverage EMI got in 2008 far exceeds the actual size of the business, but because it's sexy the media love it."

Over at *The Times*, media editor Dan Sabbagh also reflects on the coverage of EMI in the months following Hands' deal. "Every cough and spit at EMI is a headline, you only have to fall out with one artist and it's all over the paper. It is a jewel and within six or eight weeks they [Terra Firma] realised that, but they didn't get it at first."

The journalist also has a theory about the attraction of the music business to people on the outside. He cites a banker who once told him he had never seen so many people waste so much time on an industry as they do in music but, that said, Sabbagh still understands its appeal. "People love chasing music, following music deals, there is something sort of uniquely exciting and wonderful about it, and I think Guy would have been attracted to the romance of the music."

But there wasn't much romance on offer as 2007 came to an end and Hands completed his first few months in charge of a music company. All the warnings about a fallout and artists making headline news came true when first Radiohead, then Paul McCartney and finally Robbie Williams decided to voice their disappointment and concern about life at EMI.

Reflecting on their refusal to sign with EMI, Radiohead's Ed O'Brien said that while it was "really sad" to leave the label they had signed to in 1993, "EMI is in a state of flux. It's been taken over by somebody who's never owned a record company before, Guy Hands and Terra Firma, and they don't realise what they are dealing with."

In guitarist O'Brien's opinion Hands and EMI, "wouldn't give us what we wanted, he didn't know what to offer us", and while the company wouldn't confirm offering a reported £3 million advance, it claimed that Radiohead were "demanding an extraordinary amount of money".

Lead singer Thom Yorke was more specific in his criticism when he told *Wire* magazine why the band had gone their own way with the album *In Rainbows*. "It's partly due to the fact that EMI wasn't giving us any money for the digital sales. All the contracts signed in a certain era have none of that stuff."

While the band chose to finally release the physical version of the album on XL Recordings outside Japan and North America – where they would conclude separate deals – manager Bryce Edge went on record to reiterate his point that the band's catalogue was the major sticking point. "We sold 25 million records and we have the moral rights over those six albums and we wanted a say in how they are exploited in the future."

He also denied the reports about seeking huge advances and guaranteed marketing spends by explaining, "Discussions never got that far."

Next up was Paul McCartney, whom many might view as EMI's most prestigious artist and who had ended his illustrious 45-year association with EMI in the summer of 2007. Speaking to *The Times*, he complained that the company was "unimaginative" and said he "dreaded going to see them". He also voiced his displeasure about the marketing treadmill that he was expected to be part of. "You go somewhere, speak to a million journalists for one day and you get all the same questions. It's mind-numbing. So I started to say, 'God, we've got to do something else.'"

Finally he announced that everybody at EMI had become part of the furniture. "I'd be a couch, Coldplay are an armchair. And Robbie Williams, I dread to think what he was. But the most important thing was I felt [the people at EMI] had become really boring."

While McCartney was no longer the guaranteed multi-million seller he once was, criticising the company after his long association was not good for EMI as, in the words of Neil McCormick, "Ultimately a music company has to be about its music and if you've got people like The

Beatles and Pink Floyd in a good relationship with the company then that's your PR."

The *Telegraph*'s chief music writer, while acknowledging that the confidence had gone out of EMI even before Hands bought it and that this was not the first time that McCartney had complained about the company's rigidity, reckons McCartney has probably sold no more records at Starbucks, "but he's having more fun than he was at EMI", he adds.

And last, but not least, up popped Robbie Williams' manager Tim Clark to tell the *Daily Telegraph* that he would be "very wary about him signing to any major at all". Arguing that the internet offered artists more opportunities to reach their fans without the need for a major record label, Clark said, "What concerns us with the old ways is that we take overpriced and shoddy services, particularly now when we have a fantastic opportunity of getting to a fan base direct.

"What we really don't want is the dead hand of the multinationals throttling those brilliant opportunities."

One of the concerns voiced by the new EMI management was aimed directly at the manner in which staffers dealt with the creative community. Apparently they were concerned about an ongoing tendency to agree, at all times, with the artists and managers.

It seemed to the team who had taken over that in face-to-face meetings, managers and artists were told how wonderful they were by their EMI contacts before later being stabbed in the back. The new maxim the management wanted to put in place was for their people to tell the creative community to their faces if they thought a record, a campaign or an album cover was crap.

Music & Copyright editor Phil Hardy was one of the many who were perplexed by the notes Hands sent out to his staff. "I was bemused by his e-mails, which were great speeches to exhort the troops to do something then, halfway through them, he basically says you're shits – it was very odd. But what does a new broom do? He doesn't go round just daintily clearing up."

CHAPTER 9

The End Is The Beginning Is The End

(Smashing Pumpkins, Virgin 1997)

HAVING bought himself the world's least successful major record business but the UK's only surviving member of the big four, the dilemma facing Guy Hands in 2008 was how to turn EMI into an efficient, competitive and above all attractive proposition.

Former Virgin man Jon Webster's assessment of the situation, after listening to the influential people he dealt with through his role with the Music Managers Forum, was not encouraging. "The overall feeling I get is one of astonishment about Hands and EMI, and there is absolutely no question that EMI is the last record company you would ever sign an act to," he says.

One executive who didn't wait long to decide that life at EMI under the new owners was not for him was one of the most important and successful members of the senior team assembled by Eric Nicoli. Chairman of EMI UK Tony Wadsworth brought to an end his 26-year career with the company by quitting in January 2008. The move sparked rumours of further job cuts that Hands refused to confirm, although he was quoted as saying about the departure of his UK boss, "This is part of the ongoing restructuring of EMI Music."

While it was no secret that former EMI chiefs Alain Levy and David Munns had considered removing Wadsworth from his role before they themselves were fired, the UK chief's departure was still high-profile news even though it followed close on the heels of the departure of EMI's chief operating officer, Ian Hanson. His responsibilities passed to former BAA chief executive Mike Clasper, who joined the other Terra Firma-appointed executives who had no experience of the music business but were running the rule over EMI.

All this was in keeping with Terra Firma's established modus operandi of installing its own people into a company that requires serious surgery and letting them take the blame and the brickbats for any wholesale job cuts.

By allowing these short-term executives to take what one person describes as "a good beating and a good whacking" for doing the bad stuff, Hands and his team could then install a new team that arrives, in the words of a close observer, as "the nice guys with a clean plate".

In the immediate aftermath of Wadsworth's departure, a colleague of his told the media, "This is just the start. There is going to be blood all over the carpets, swathes of people are going to be got rid of."

One man who was not going anywhere for the time being was US chief Roger Ames, who immediately took over responsibility for all UK A&R activities, and he did so in the midst of a host of tributes to Wadsworth.

"He was a real music fan and his support for the artists he signed to EMI was whole-hearted," said Tim Clark, manager of Robbie Williams. Coldplay's manager, David Holmes, also paid tribute saying, "Tony was the reason a lot of bands signed to EMI. Artists want to work with music people not finance guys," before warning the new owners, "Why would you want to release an album with a record company in the midst of massive lay-offs? Coldplay have a lots of options, they are in no hurry to deliver their new album."

Somewhat surprisingly *Independent* columnist Janet Street-Porter, a close friend of the Pet Shop Boys' Neil Tennant, also joined in and wrote in her column that "shedding popular UK chief executive Tony Wadsworth was a PR disaster", while adding that John Birt – once called a "dalek" by dramatist Dennis Potter – was "not known for his people skills".

Adding further fuel to the fire was Paul McCartney, who dubbed Wadsworth "a mate" and revealed that he had sent the former EMI executive a personal note following his departure. "It's not the most comfortable thing to be working in a company when people you know are losing their jobs," said the former Beatle, who moved from EMI after over 45 years but whose group and solo catalogues remain with the company. "So you might as well just look around for something kind of better."

There was less sympathy for Wadsworth from Jonathan Shalit, who suggested that being "too nice" was Wadsworth's biggest fault. "If in the time he was in power he'd fired more people and restructured the company it would have been better for EMI," says the man who looks after actor Christopher Biggins and newsreader Kate Silverton. "It wasn't the fault of incompetence, it wasn't the fault of not understanding the business but it was the fault of pursuing an ideology that was out of date about how a record company should be shaped and not firing people who should have gone."

But, if media reports were to be believed, Shalit would get his wish as, early in the new year, the financial columns were forecasting the loss of anywhere between 1,700 and 2,000 jobs around the world of EMI.

While *Billboard* magazine was predicting that 2008 would see Hands sell off part of his newly acquired EMI company, *The Sunday Times* chose to remind people that he was the man who ousted managers from his Odeon cinema chain because they jetted off to Hollywood for film premieres. "They thought they were in the movie business but actually they were in the popcorn business," was a quote the paper attributed to the executive chairman of EMI.

The article also suggested that Hands was unmoved by criticism in his quest to find a new business model for the music company. "He is not perturbed by controversy," said a source close to the man. "Quite the reverse. If he's not making waves he's not doing his job."

One person who, however, did seem to upset the man at the top of EMI was Williams' manager Clark. In the midst of stories about Coldplay quitting the label after the anticipated delivery of their final album in 2009 and The Rolling Stones signing with rival Universal, he made some remarks that brought him an unexpected response.

While busy denying reports that his artist was going on strike, he confirmed in mid-2008 that the multi-million-selling singer was not entirely happy with EMI. "Neither he nor we are on strike. What I actually said was why would Robbie Williams deliver an album and why would we advise him to deliver an album when we had no idea whether the record company was going to be able to do a good job for him?

"That was interpreted as Robbie being on strike but Robbie never said anything, he made no comment," confirms Clark. "It was our comment and we still hold to it."

However, it was another comment attributed to Clark that upset Hands and brought the two of them to the brink of a lawsuit. Williams' manager was reported as saying that Hands had bought EMI as "a vanity purchase" and that the executive chairman was behaving like "a plantation owner", but he is adamant that for the second time in a matter of days he had been misquoted.

"I didn't actually say he was like a plantation owner. I said that if he behaved like the old American record executives then to all intents and purposes he would become a plantation owner." Although there was no official on-the-record response from EMI over the remarks, they did, according to Clark, bring an interesting reaction from Hands.

"He reacted by sending a string of letters from his solicitors saying that they were considering suing for libel, and they also thought there were grounds for some sort of racist action over the phrase 'plantation owner'. Our solicitor wrote a brilliant riposte pointing out there were plantation owners all over the world who employ all sorts of people and there are no longer any slaves."

There was no denying that Clark was not impressed from the earliest days with the man who now owned EMI. "I knew of Terra Firma and Guy Hands and his reputation as a money man, as an asset stripper who in many ways did a job that worked and had saved companies," but he had reservations about Hands' decision to buy EMI. "It was widely reported that I said it was a vanity purchase and I felt that he didn't really know what he was buying and I'm not sure that hasn't already been proved."

All this coincided with huge unrest within the EMI camp as staff awaited their fate. Hands set January 15, in an Odeon cinema in Kensington, as the date and venue for the long-awaited unveiling of his plans for the future of EMI. He was also due to meet artists and managers on the same day.

In advance of that meeting Jazz Summers, manager of The Verve, made his feelings known when he said, "Why would we deliver a record when EMI is cutting back on the marketing and is in financial difficulty? I am going to tell Guy Hands I want assurances. Nobody is going to go in there and sign to them. This business is all about confidence and the new boss has lost confidence in his own staff."

At the meeting on January 15 Hands arrived flanked by a wall of body-guards – which was criticised by some as being a bit too much like a rock star arriving at a gig. The EMI boss told his assembled audience, which included both managers and artists alongside 500 UK staff, that up to 200 jobs would go in 2008, the roster of 14,000 acts would be slashed, and the company would be restructured into three divisions – record labels with A&R handling talent; music services looking after manufacturing, sales and distribution; and support services including marketing.

While the meeting was held behind closed doors it became clear in comments made later by Hands that "there is a job to be done restructur-ing this company". His intention was to make EMI "the world's most innovative, artist-friendly and consumer-focused music company" at the same time as dismissing both the industry's and EMI's tried and tested business methods. "In the past we have followed the industry model of signing as many artists as possible while taking huge bets on a few. This is not sustainable. We cannot provide meaningful support for that number and everyone suffers as a result."

From those managers who attended the meeting, there finally came some encouraging remarks about Hands, his plans and style of doing business. The previously critical Summers – who had once described Hands as being "very full of himself" – now said, "He came over as quite humble. He emphasised the importance of artists and made assurances that he had enough money to run the company until 2011. He is showing signs of beginning to understand the industry."

With Jonathan Shalit claiming that "the majority of managers left the meeting encouraged and pleased", Corinne Bailey Rae's manager, Bob Miller, reckoned that Hands came across as "a very genuine man who has quickly got to grips with the amount of deep surgery required" and declared himself "optimistic for the future".

The major broadcast media carried news of the meeting and the BBC described what was about to happen as the "biggest shake-up at EMI in decades" and even suggested that "some worry that the iconic company has lost its way". On the other side ITV managed to get it wrong and announced that Coldplay had already left the company before suggesting that, "The Verve say they may join the protest by refusing to deliver their first album in 10 years."

Among those interviewed after the staff meeting was the MMF's Jon Webster, who said EMI was hoping the shake-up would usher in a new golden era before adding, "If it works it could become a blueprint for the rest of the record industry."

Quoted in the *Telegraph* a few days later, experienced artist manager Ed Bicknell repeated a previously voiced and highly contentious theory on how to make EMI work.

"If Terra Firma was just thinking about making a profit, they should dump all new releases, reduce overheads to a minimum and just resell back catalogue. It wouldn't be exciting but it would be much more profitable."

This sort of move also makes sense to manager Pete Jenner, who is not sure that Hands has "done his homework" when it comes to assessing EMI's income sources. "If he looked at what's in there he'd see that 40% to 50% of income comes from the back catalogue. Now that should tell him something," he points out, adding, "He should do an analysis to see what EMI's signing policy has generated and ask, 'How can we become involved in the back catalogue of the future?'"

On the back of talking to his staff, artists and managers, Hands decided that it was time to address the wider music community through interviews with UK-based *Music Week* and the US industry's principal trade publication, *Billboard*.

While *Music Week* chose to mention his dress sense – "more City than street" – *Billboard* was fascinated that by the fact that for a man keen on making savings he turned up for the interview "flanked by no fewer than five publicists".

Between them the two magazines focused on most of the salient issues facing the music industry in general and EMI and Hands in particular, including subjects such as his own presentations, artists and managers, consumers, digital, sponsorship, staff cuts and advances.

Of his January 15 presentation he said: "No one had to applaud so the fact that they applauded was very kind. A number of them said to me afterwards that this [cost cuttings and savings] is something that should have been done in the recorded music industry years ago."

Artists & managers: "They're a tough crowd but a demanding, intelligent, dedicated crowd and it's their livelihoods – when you talk to anyone about their livelihoods they tend to have strong feelings. My job is to take the bullets and the shouting and the screaming. It is something you have to live through. Would I rather it didn't happen? Absolutely."

Consumers: "The consumer is very important – you can't push things to them any more. You need pull. And to get pull you need a different approach to how you market, how you sell, how you use digital."

Digital: "One of the ways we want to use it [digital] is to form a connection with the consumer where the consumer effectively gives us a better insight into the music they would like to buy, how they would like to buy it and how they would like it to be delivered. Radiohead came up with what was a great way to promote their music that should have been done by one of the labels not by Radiohead."

Sponsorship: "Yes we have to get involved in that. Think how much the banks spend trying to get particular demographics to join them . . . music should be in that situation. I love the idea of The Sex Pistols being sponsored by Lloyds Bank."

Staff & roster cuts: "This isn't about cuts for cuts' sake, it's about creating efficiency. We have artists that haven't frankly sold an album in years. Most of the artists I see work their guts out, as do most of the people at EMI."

Advances: "I think advances are totally appropriate but the advances need to be calculated on a rational economic basis, and in reality advances over the last few years have been calculated with frankly fun economics."

Music Week editor Paul Williams' take on all this was to suggest that Hands had made a tough job even tougher by "earlier unnecessary and unwise comments" and that he was left with the vital task of "proving to EMI's artists and their managers that his vision is right if he truly wants to make the major successful again".

One man who has yet to be convinced that Hands is the right man for the job is Neil McCormick. "Hands has his work cut out and he is unquestionably the wrong man for the job and follows in a long line of wrong men for the job," says the *Telegraph* music writer.

While he believes that EMI is a label that few new artists would ever sign to in the current circumstances, he also finds Hands "a fairly reprehensible individual" and is unimpressed with either his haircut or his dress sense. "He is obviously fairly intelligent but I don't understand how a guy can have that much money and look that bad, and how a guy can be in the music business and he can't even get a decent haircut. Hands' haircut tells me that he does not trust creative people because if he can't even trust his hairdresser – who is about the least creative person he's ever going to meet – how can he trust some 20-year-old artist?"

And McCormick has one final word on Hands' appearance: "But maybe he wants to send out a message that these things are not important to him – it's only the money that's important."

In his quest to get to know, understand and convince the managers, Hands invited the men who represent the acts signed to his various labels to a variety of dinners. Tim Clark recalls that the next thing that happened after his tangle with Hands' lawyer over his 'plantation owner' remarks was that he got a call inviting him and his business partner to dinner. "We had a very pleasant dinner and a wide-ranging discussion during which I said to him that I didn't know who at EMI to discuss any business issues with any more."

Acknowledging that Hands was sympathetic to his concern, the manager of Robbie Williams still has reservations. "I am still not absolutely convinced at all about him being good for EMI. He is a money man and what he deals with is figures, and if the figures ain't working he'll get out."

Nor is Alison Wenham, the head of the UK's independent music organisation, entirely convinced that Hands will not just follow a route trodden by a host of other 'outside' executives who tried their hand at the music business. "Any number of individuals have come from very successful careers in other industries, walked into our industry and felt that they are the solution, God's gift to all our woes and ills, our apparently misguided practices and our lack of vision," she says. She believes that most of them failed to understand that the music business is "a people industry, a very sophisticated industry, complex, anachronistic, creative, successful and blessed with a natural arrogance born out of creativity".

And while she hopes that Guy Hands is the man to break that mould she cautions, "somehow I doubt it", while adding that her colleagues in the independent sector were "somewhat underwhelmed" by Terra Firma's acquisition of EMI. "They were also somewhat perplexed that EMI would see this as the most fitting partnership."

While the talk of massive cuts at EMI wasn't entirely unexpected, there was still surprise that nothing actually happened in the immediate aftermath of Hands' announcements. Former Virgin man Ray Cooper explains: "It all seems a bit weird. For someone to say that there's going to have to be cuts and then put everybody on a knife edge for several months seems to be odd."

But still the ex-head of Virgin US believes that the cuts were necessary and in fact his own answer to the problem is even more drastic. "You could run EMI with 75 people and back-room everything else. Just have a back-catalogue department, some savvy promo guys and a good A&R person and be like the independent labels used to be."

Manager Pete Jenner takes a similar view but would go even further by combining recorded music and publishing. "I would fire everybody in EMI apart from two or three people with ears and the people who know the contracts and the catalogue, and have one or two people in every country. Then perhaps merge the record company into the publishing company, build up publishing and do deals through publishing."

The man who looks after Billy Bragg also suggests going a step further by finding the best managers of the future and backing them and their artists. "Give them money for that band, let EMI put themselves in the position of being bankers, and do great licensing deals for distribution, for Europe, for online etc."

But whatever Hands had planned for EMI it was clear that it would not succeed unless he had the support of the entire music industry. Even a man as experienced and determined as Hands could not come up with a change to the established music industry model and force it through, so it just affected his own company.

"If Hands does all this alone, without the other companies, he could destroy EMI's business as artists leave and new ones won't sign on," says US-based investor and former EMI board member David Londoner. Even Hands himself admitted as much when he reportedly observed, "For everyone who runs a major label, making changes is a big personal risk. If you keep things quiet you can continue to earn some pretty massive salaries for a few more years until the whole thing comes to an end."

Londoner adds that he believes that if the whole music business adopts Hands' policies then the industry can right itself. "If not, profits will continue to decline. My guess is that the business ways are too ingrained to be changed and that is not good news for Hands."

Nick Stewart, who is credited with signing U2 to Island Records in 1980, takes the view that businesses are best transformed by vision and new products. "They are not transformed by new financial models and I've seen nothing from Guy Hands and his cohorts to suggest to me that they've come up with anything new," says the man who during a 30-year career worked with Polygram, Sony BMG and Warner.

Among the important people looking in at EMI from their position as managers was Coldplay's David Holmes, who seemed to give Hands a nod of approval when he said, ". . . anyone who bought this company would have made the kinds of changes that are probably in the works", and Norah Jones' representative Sam Feldman, who was concerned that the company found the right people to ensure success, explains, "Our business is dependent on relationships and people. It's like a Moroccan bazaar – 'Who's selling the real carpet?' And if you don't know, you're kind of in trouble."

By February 2008, Hands was seemingly feeling the strain of trying to solve all EMI's problems. He told a venture-capital conference in Munich that rebuilding EMI had been "emotionally and physically" harder than he imagined.

But even as he got a hint of good news that best-sellers Coldplay would deliver a new album in the coming months and that Robbie Williams might be returning to the studio after a break, the man who had earlier upset his own A&R men by inadvertently suggesting they were lazy seemed to have another go at his company's creative ambassadors.

"What we are doing is taking the power away from the A&R guys and putting it with the suits – the men who have to work out how to sell music," he said. And as if to explain his actions he went on to tell the money men gathered in Germany: "We had labels at EMI that were spending five times as much on marketing as their gross revenues. We told them you could stick a £50 note on the cover of a CD and have the same effect and we also wouldn't have to pay them."

He seemed to grasp the impact his remarks might have when he added, "Those sort of comments don't go down too well", although he appeared to have an ally in *Daily Telegraph* head of business Damian Reece, who described the old EMI model as an "expensive, scattergun approach" that Hands was busy ripping up. "It needs fewer, better-resourced investments – and fewer better-resourced A&R men," was the journalist's view.

But once again Hands' tendency to say that upset the people who worked for him and the industry as a whole brought a reaction from observers and commentators. "The real damaging comments he made about A&R people really showed contempt for everything the business stood for and a total misunderstanding of what the priorities are," says Emmanuel Legrand, who wonders why the man at the head of Terra Firma chose to speak at all.

"For years EMI was crippled by having to justify every single move it made and then there is Guy Hands who could be as free as a bird to do what he wants. And what he does is go and do exactly the same thing, which is damaging not only to the company but also to the rest of the music business."

While the music writer suggests it is all down to "a spot of bravado", analyst Mark Beilby has another view. "Maybe he thought he had to stamp his authority on cliques or surly people who thought they didn't have to toe the line, and he decided to do it publicly as part of a plan. Guy Hands is not an idiot and nobody should be fooled into thinking he is."

As half of the management team that decided Radiohead would not re-sign to EMI, Bryce Edge continued to follow what was going on at the company, not only because the band's catalogue remained in EMI's hands but also because he was also involved with Supergrass, who were still an EMI act. He was disappointed at what he saw. "He [Hands] did manage to completely demoralise the staff with some of the things he said at the start of 2008, which, as he had no shareholders, he had no need to say."

So why did he do it? According to Edge the reason could have been two-fold. "He was either trying to impress his mates in the City or get a message across to the people who loaned him the money to buy EMI."

Despite the man's very public comments about the company he bought and the industry he was now part of – which apparently caused one senior executive at a rival music company to say about Hands "this guy has to be stopped, he's got to be shut up" – he found an unlikely ally in Blur manager Chris Morrison.

While he was unhappy at the lack of information coming from his record company – "despite having one of their biggest acts, nobody called, nobody got in contact and I was reading what was going on at EMI in *Music Week*" – Morrison didn't understand what he called the "ground-swell of criticism" levelled at the chief executive.

Confirming that none of his acts were likely to withdraw their labour, he said, "All those threats about artists going on strike was bollocks. I didn't get why managers were hammering this geezer [Hands] before any of us had had a run out to see whether his new company works or not."

Although signed to Universal for recording, Amy Winehouse is an EMI act for her music publishing and the company was able to enjoy some success as the British singer-songwriter picked up an impressive five Grammies, alongside EMI act The Chemical Brothers picking up their fourth US award and The Beatles' *Love* album collecting two awards at the 2008 ceremony.

When the year's first-quarter figures for the US business came to light in April, they showed EMI's album-market share down to 8.7% (from the previous year's 11.6%) and Nielsen SoundScan's calculations gave EMI total sales of 9.1 million, down on the 2007 figure of 13.6 million. It wasn't a good start and it wasn't helped by news that The Rolling Stones decided against signing a new deal with EMI, which they had first joined in 1977.

And as news came in that Apple's iTunes was the biggest retailer of music in America – eclipsing the supermarket giant Wal-Mart – thanks to over 50 million customers buying four billion songs, it was followed by an announcement that the social networking group MySpace was entering the music business.

With over 30 million users per month, MySpace, owned by News Corporation, launched a music downloading service in early 2008 to rival iTunes, but it did not include EMI. While Universal, Sony BMG and Warner were all in bed with the new service, the British major was conspicuous by its absence until September when it eventually joined its rivals in a MySpace joint venture.

Perhaps the company had other things on its mind such as the consultation period on the planned redundancies, which began in March and was expected to run for 90 days. The company told interested parties that the new management was leading a "radical reorganization", which was designed to "drive out bureaucracy and improve the service that EMI supplies to its artists and consumers".

It was also rumoured to be in talks to buy the Chrysalis music-publishing business, including songs by Blondie, David Bowie and Gnarls Barkley, but its £104 million offer was apparently rejected by Chris Wright, who had sold Chrysalis Records to EMI 20 years earlier. This time he deemed that the offer from Hands and his team "significantly undervalued" his company.

And while EMI was also busy denying newspaper reports that it was to shed a further 1,000 jobs on top of the 1,500 to 2,000 announced in January, there came news that Citigroup, which financed Terra Firma's acquisition, had decided against selling-on £2.5 billion of the loans it provided.

Apparently the loans were considered not marketable in April 2008 in light of investor anxiety about EMI's future, but by May it seemed that Hands was fighting to meet the financial targets set by the bank. Having gained a three-month extension on some of the terms, EMI had to achieve earnings of £180 million by September 2008. However, City sources reckoned the company would be stretched to make £133 m, which in turn would impact on executive bonuses.

According to *Times* writer Dan Sabbagh, by acquiring EMI Hands bought the company time in which to restructure and rebuild and, he says, they can also "miss some quarterly numbers", which were a prerequisite of a public company.

As a man who says he caught sight of one of the company's early business plans – "It assumed they would make some progress from day one, but there's no deal that's ever been done that works like that" – Sabbagh believes Hands has to be patient. "He and Terra Firma need to run music for a bit and see what they think they can do with it."

He is also comfortable with the level of debt that Hands ran up in order to acquire EMI. "Guy's debt is on easy terms and he's got it for eight years so he has time. He has never been involved so closely in one of his businesses as he is with EMI and it's better that he is the boss right now, that people report to him and he's available to meet top acts," says the media editor. "That's the right structure for EMI right now."

Over the river from the *Times'* Wapping headquarters, the *Telegraph*'s Neil McCormick is less than impressed by what he sees and hears about EMI. "I'm going around places and the word about EMI is not good. I don't hear anybody saying a good word about Guy Hands or EMI," says the music critic, who goes on to give his own impression of EMI's top man. "He doesn't understand and he's almost proudly philistine when it comes to culture and he doesn't understand the impression that can make. He doesn't care and he says this is like any other business and it's not. You cannot road-test an artist and then tinker with and change things around a bit, adjust this or that; you can't treat it like another business."

Music industry journalist Phil Hardy is similarly concerned about Hands' understanding of the business he bought into. "He doesn't believe that the music industry is any different from any other industry, while everybody who works in it thinks it is very different . . . and obviously both sides are right."

With Hands urging his company to grasp the new digital age with considerably more enthusiasm than he believed had been the case in the past, new-media consultant and ex-Warner executive Pete Downton offers a word of warning. "The feeling is that the cuts at EMI were entirely necessary but there is absolutely no sense of any go-forward plan and that's coming from both the artistic community and the digital community."

Perhaps in an effort to rectify that situation, in April 2008 EMI recruited a senior US executive from Google to take over as president of the company's digital business. Describing himself as an "experimenter" and agreeing with his boss that "the future of music is digital", Douglas Merrill surprised everyone even before he had started with his stance on file sharing.

"Everybody thinks file sharing is bad. However there is some data that shows file sharing is a good thing for some artists and not necessarily bad. We should do a bunch of experiments to find out what the business model is," explained Google's former chief information officer who added that some of the people the music industry thought were not buying music, actually were. "They're just not buying it in formats that we can measure." However, less than a year later Merrill was out of a job as EMI abandoned its stand-alone digital division.

Hard on the heels of EMI getting a new digital leader, there came news of an important A&R appointment. Nick Gatfield, ex-member of Dexy's Midnight Runners and an EMI A&R man in the 1980s, returned as president of A&R for North America and the UK.

He returned to EMI from his role as president of Island Records – where he oversaw the success of Amy Winehouse and Mika – and quickly stepped up to defend his new boss. "Whatever you read in the press and certainly the emotional reporting about EMI, the impression you are given is wrong," said Gatfield. "Guy is a winner. He believes that quality music is absolutely the key. He just believes that fundamental mistakes have been made in the business."

As Gatfield arrived at EMI so Roger Ames departed for a second time, although the news was that the head of the company's US operations would continue to act in an advisory capacity, which meant he was given a place (as acquisition adviser) on Hands' new 16-strong Chairman's Board. This was to operate alongside a four person Restructuring Board and an Operating Board with 14 members.

However, for US-based Bob Mercer the management structure being established by Hands was "unworkable". He saw it as matrix management with major units such as A&R, marketing, catalogue, studio, finance and distribution all coming under a global chief who then had a series of territorial heads. "For instance the head of North America doesn't have control over A&R, marketing or sales and I don't see how that works." And when the Terra Firma people explained to him how it worked, the marketing executive says he told them, "That has my bullshit buzzer going overtime."

He also suggests that maybe it was a justification for getting rid of 2,000 people and that the dotted management lines are not a solution to the problem. But, as he says, "They paid the money – although it was perhaps a billion too much – so it's their call."

On the other hand Iron Maiden manager Andy Taylor senses that Hands' matrix system might just have a place in the music business. "He is trying to structure it so that everything is looked at on a global basis, which is a much more logical thing to do, but by default it changes the whole perspective of a local record company."

And the accountant-cum-rock manager adds, "The fact that the music business has never been run that way doesn't mean it's wrong although there is a tendency in the music industry to say, 'That's not the way it was done in the past, it can't be the right way.'"

Meanwhile, in the midst of the arguments about the merits of matrix management, there are comforting words for Hands on his choice of Gatfield as his new top A&R man. "Nick Gatfield is the best move he has made and he has moved it back a bit in the right direction," declares Chris Morrison while Dan Sabbagh adds, "I think at least bringing in Gatfield means he has brought in a record man so that he has provided some reassurance. I feel they have turned a bit of a corner."

Jonathan Shalit too is impressed with the move. "Putting Nick Gatfield in place is a fantastically intelligent decision and from what I understand EMI will now get stronger in America."

At the end of April 2008, in its annual Rich List, the *Sunday Times* highlighted the wealth of EMI's new owner when it ranked Guy and wife Julia Hands at number 325 with a combined amount of £250 million.

In its brief entry for the couple, whose wealth was listed as coming from finance and hotels, the paper suggested that after buying EMI, Guy Hands "told its highly paid stars that they would have to work harder or risk being axed", and it cited Sir Mick Jagger as among those "reported to be disgruntled".

While the Hands were up from 351 and just £200 million in 2007, ex-EMI US chief Ames found himself on the slide, dropping from 438 and £160 million in 2007, to 724 and £110 million in 2008.

One release that would hopefully make EMI richer and more successful in 2008 was the fourth album from Coldplay, and their leader Chris Martin seemed keen to explain the details of his relationship with the new EMI. Talking to *Billboard* in advance of the June 2008 release of *Viva La Vida* – described by Hands as being "the most anticipated album of the year" – Martin confirmed that he had been reassured by his record company. "Guy and I have been talking about this record since he took over the company and we've made sure that both of us feel confident that the label can handle it amidst all the change."

Even so, the man charged with delivering the all-important follow-up to the 10 million-selling *X&Y* album was still unconvinced about the merits of being signed to a major record label such as EMI, likening it to living in your grandparent's house. "Everyone knows they need to move out, and they will eventually, but we kind of like our grandmother. It's obviously an antiquated model because of the internet."

Having sold a total of over 11 million records in America since their 2000 debut, Coldplay were among the major acts rumoured to be so concerned about the takeover of the company that they were on the brink of leaving. Martin, who was never actually quoted as saying anything negative, explained in his interview with the US music industry magazine, "We were just, 'Watch and see.' Things got a little blown out of proportion in the press. There was talk about [artists] going on strike, we should never have been lumped into that."

For two managers, the changes at EMI were, however, too much to bear. "For very specific reasons I put the Monkeys project with XL Recordings because I could. We went where we were wooed," says Chris Morrison of Damon Albarn's creation, which does not feature him as an artist and therefore does not come under his EMI contract.

The final experience with Supergrass and EMI was almost too painful for Chris Hufford. "Doing the last record with EMI was a really dull and uninteresting experience. It came out, there was no budget, no nothing and it failed – isn't that a surprise. The band were so proud of the record and then nothing happened – they were demoralised and it was so sad watching it all go on."

Nevertheless, Coldplay's album was one that EMI could under no circumstances allow to fail. By July 2008, a month after its release, *Viva La Vida* was number one in 36 countries and heralded for setting the highest first-week worldwide album sales on iTunes. The title track also made Coldplay the first British group for over 10 years to top the *Billboard* Hot 100 singles chart.

Destined to reach number one in America – where sales have passed two million – and the UK, with over one million sales, the album signalled a first major global success for the 'new' EMI. By July 2008, the company could claim a total of nine albums in the UK top 75, although Coldplay were the only act in the top 25, which gave them third place with a 14.2 % share of the chart.

The success of Coldplay, and the marketing campaign that was rolled out in support of the album, caused some within the industry to question whether new precedents were being set. There were those who believed that their manager, David Holmes, realizing the importance to EMI of his act's new release, had shrewdly done a deal with Hands that gave him control over the campaign and – more importantly – the marketing spend.

Dan Sabbagh says simply, "The Coldplay success showed that it could be done although it seems to have been done as sort of a bilateral agreement between David Holmes and Guy Hands, where Guy said, 'You pick the people you need and just do it.' "

Either way it worked and the journalist believes that for EMI it was the only result that mattered. "It had to be a hit. If that had failed I think that was probably it for EMI's recorded music business. But it showed executives from other labels that there was still life in EMI."

EMI artist manager Jonathan Shalit was another who saw the Coldplay album as a true test of the company's intentions and ability and whether they had become so thin that they couldn't deliver. "The answer is no," he says emphatically. "The marketing of Coldplay was a very clear statement that EMI has the infrastructure in place to get global number ones, which is very encouraging to all artists."

While the success of Coldplay's new album – it sold over 300,000 in the first three days after release – brought some comfort, EMI set about restructuring its operations around the world. As America was on the verge of losing Jason Flom from his role as head of the Capitol Music Group, in the UK a senior international vice president, a UK managing director, an international marketing senior vice president and senior commercial vice president all left within a matter of days.

At the same time, EMI France made 21 positions redundant following nearly 30 jobs cuts in EMI Italy, alongside the departures of the head of EMI Germany/Austria/Switzerland, the president of EMI Japan and the managing director of EMI New Zealand, where nine jobs were also lost.

The fact that the moves came about some six months after Hands had warned his staff that cuts were on the way was a worry to Shalit, who believes that the delay did cause "some animosity" towards Hands. "He announced he was going to make changes but it took six months to get to that point and it meant there was a six-month gap in the life of EMI where some internal damage was being done."

The moves, however long they took to implement, were not making Hands any more popular with the artists signed to the company according to hedge-fund investor and former EMI shareholder Hugh Hendry. "They hate him," he was quoted as saying. "He's rude. He's abrasive. He wants to make money. He's the first to say to artists, 'We are not going to pay you too much money. Now get out of my office.' "

An analysis from McKinsey and KPMG revealed that rather than making any money EMI had in fact lost £750 million from selling new music over the past five years. Hands' first response was to point out that, while the company was losing large amounts of money in new music, the good news was that it was "making a fortune in catalogue". A rival music executive also questioned the huge loss. "It's hard to make sense of a number like that – is it every unrecouped advance, every video ever made? And how do you define new music and catalogue?"

In the light of this figure, details of a confidential business plan shown to investors in 2007 revealed that EMI's projected pre-tax earnings would grow from £167 million in 2007 to £580 million by 2010. This was despite almost every analyst predicting a fall in industry sales and earnings and one report forecasting Warner Music's pre-tax earnings over the same period would drop from $461 million to $444 million.

As The Rolling Stones finally made their move from EMI to Universal permanent in July 2008, taking their catalogue with them in a £7 million deal, they were quoted as taking a swipe at their former label by saying, "Universal are forward-thinking, creative and hands-on music people." At around the same time the boss of the band's new label went on the record about EMI – albeit briefly.

Chairman and chief executive of Universal Music Group, Lucian Grainge, said of Hands, "I think he's a very clever person and has some interesting ideas," while one-time EMI staff producer and long-time Beatles producer Sir George Martin was more expansive when asked about the goings-on at EMI. "It's very sad. EMI was a fantastic company. It's gone through so many changes and now it's been bought by a venture capital company," Martin told *Billboard* in 2008. "They're trying to make something of it but it's a bad time for the record business generally. I've met Guy Hands . . . and he knows the problems and he's trying to tackle them. He has my support because it's too valuable a business to lose."

As a man who worked closely alongside Martin for many years at EMI, Bhaskar Menon retains a similar affection and interest for the great British company but is not convinced about the people who took over in 2007. "Terra Firma's early ownership actions to revive EMI Music after their purchase will in time I think be regarded as utterly bewildering. Most of their recovery measures were dominated by damaging and uninspired experimentation."

Seemingly undaunted by the criticism of him personally, Hands was able to issue what he described as "a dramatic improvement" in EMI's financial performance for the company's first fiscal quarter from April to June 2008. In another e-mail to staff the company chairman announced ebitda (earnings before interest, tax, depreciation and amortization) of

£59.2 million compared with a loss of £45.1 million in the first quarter of 2007. Total revenues were also up 61% to £228 million.

Warning that it was still "early days" and that the music business is "extremely volatile", Hands reckoned the performance showed, "We now have in place a reshaped organizational structure with clearer accountability for profit and loss." What he didn't say was whether the second-quarter performance would be good enough to take the £59 million earnings up to the £180 million target set by Citigroup as part of its three-month extension to loan repayments by EMI.

While the figures did not reveal any breakdown of the performance of recorded music or music publishing, the fact that the bulk of sales of Coldplay's *Viva La Vida* were not in the first quarter and that EMI Music Publishing was top in both the UK and US in the first three months of 2008 suggested the target might be met.

Coldplay's global success was matched by American singer Katy Perry, Japan's Hiraku Utaka, Amaral from Spain and German act Helene Fischer all hitting number one in their respective charts, although EMI still saw a drop in its all-important share of US album sales in the first half of 2008.

The Nielsen SoundScan figures calculated, despite Coldplay's number one album and Katy Perry's Top 10 album *One Of The Boys*, a figure of 9.4%, a fall of 1% on the previous year. The total number of albums sold by the company in the US in the same period was 19.2 million compared with 23.9 million in 2007.

Although it had little or no direct impact on EMI, in August 2008 Sony took the German media giant Bertelsmann out of the music business by buying the Bertelsmann Music Group (BMG) for $1 billion, consolidating the previously combined Sony BMG operation under one banner and claiming a 24.8% joint half-year 2008 US album market share for the Sony Corporation of America, although it still trailed Universal's 31.2% share.

More relevant to the British music company was the decision by award-winning songwriter and producer Mark Ronson to extend his worldwide deal with EMI's publishing division and Depeche Mode's new global deal, which, for the first time, included EMI in America. But the edge was taken off the news by the fact that one of the acts Ronson worked with was seemingly less than happy.

Lily Allen's debut album, *Alright Still*, notched up sales of 2.5 million and earned the British singer Grammy and BRIT Award nominations, but in 2008 she reacted to what she saw as an unnecessary delay in the release of her follow-up album. "The album has been finished for a while now. I don't really know what's going on with it," she complained on her MySpace blog before explaining, "The record industry is a very political place and I am on EMI Records. Lots of people have been fired or have taken redundancy recently as the company was taken over by a private equity firm called Terra Firma."

She went on to suggest that this was the main reason behind the delay in the release of her new album. "Many of these people were people assigned to my projects and now I don't quite know what's going on." EMI, by now getting used to answering questions about disgruntled artists, said, "We are really excited by what we've heard and we are all now discussing a release date for the album."

The album, *It's Not Me, It's You*, was finally released in February 2009 and even then Allen, one of the last acts to be signed to EMI prior to its takeover by Terra Firma, still had concerns over the label that is due to receive from her what she describes as "loads more albums".

Talking to *Billboard* in January 2009 she suggested that she would probably not sign to a major label if she was starting out today although she seemed happy with the long delay in the release of her album. "People were still getting laid off and I didn't want my album worked on in an environment where people weren't happy," she said while expressing some displeasure with EMI's cost cutting. "When you've gone from nothing to selling 2.5 million albums you want to be staying at nicer hotels and going out for nicer dinners . . . that's not happening."

However, just as her new album hit the shops, she was back in the papers, telling everyone, "I hate Terra Firma. They're wankers and they don't know what they're doing."

Seemingly happier with his situation was Depeche Mode's manager, Jonathan Kessler, who agreed to be part of BBC Radio 4's 2008 documentary about EMI and, while he was not entirely impressed with the new management's PR style, he explained why he was not put off signing a new deal. "I was impressed with the acute level of sensitivity they did have to what was going on in the music business," said the man whose act came to EMI when it bought Mute. "We did manage to secure certain things from Terra Firma: we were very careful in securing marketing budgets, marketing amounts and having a lot of control of those as well – so far so good."

One of the most important and, in turn, arguably one of the most controversial appointments made by Hands in 2008 was naming Elio Leoni-Sceti as the new chief executive of EMI's recorded music division.

The Italian-born executive arrived at EMI from Reckitt Benckiser, where he was executive vice president Europe and oversaw products such as Airwick, Nurofen, Calgon and Cillit Bang, just as JF Cecillon, European president and international A&R chief, departed.

Variously dubbed "Nurofen man" and "dishwasher tablets star", Leoni-Sceti's arrival allowed Hands to stand down and become non-executive chairman, and seemingly completed what the outgoing chairman described in an internal e-mail as "the difficult but necessary organizational restructuring of EMI".

Admitting that he would not be running A&R – "It's not my area of competence" – Leoni-Sceti said he came from a branded goods industry and added, as an indication of how things would work in the future at EMI, "What the music industry needs is an equal understanding of how to build branding around artists."

With a career in consumer brands, the new chief executive's background was compared with that of two former EMI high flyers – Jim Fifield and Eric Nicoli – who arrived from General Mills and United Biscuits respectively.

Asked about the differences facing Leoni-Sceti as he moved from packaged goods to music, Fifield said, "In the music industry you have to remember the artist has an opinion. If you propose a promotion, it is the artist's career and their persona that we are helping to manage and if the artist says no, then that is the end of the meeting. If you can manage that transition you can do well and if you don't handle that, then you will fail."

Opinion on the new man's arrival was divided with a former US label chief suggesting, "It's a brilliant choice to have someone on the front line of the consumer brand relationship move," while a rival executive commented, "He has a strong pedigree but this is a very different business – unlike artists, dishwasher tablets don't answer back."

At the same time Gartner media analyst Adam Daum explained, "Bringing in someone unconnected with the music industry but who understands branding and marketing could be better because they are more likely to have lots of examples of ways to make money."

Meanwhile *Music Week* editor Paul Williams simply stated, "Depending on how events turn out, Guy Hands' decision to put a man in charge of EMI recorded music with absolutely no music experience could ultimately be judged as either a stroke of genius or one gamble too far." He went on to say, "It changed the rules of the game of the industry forever."

Leoni-Sceti has restructured the company into three business units –

new music, catalogue and music services – and also launched EMI.com, which has been described as a "learning lab" and was established, in the words of the new EMI chief executive, to "enable us to interface with consumers on a constant basis".

One of the issues concerning the industry and some people inside EMI was the continuing absence of a 'music man' at the top of the restructured company. It's no secret that the only person the new owners thought would be good enough for the job was Universal boss Grainge, but they also accepted early on that he was not available. In the words of someone close to the hiring process, there was nobody else out there "who really lit our fire".

This was a situation that worried *Telegraph* writer, Neil McCormick, who reflects that when Hands bought EMI he did not seem to have a music man among his advisers. "People who buy football clubs always have an ex-player or former manager at their side to advise, but Guy Hands just went in and said this company isn't working and it's underpriced – when it was actually overpriced – and I can get it and make it work.

"He didn't talk to managers or artists before he bought it," says the journalist, who remains unconvinced about EMI's future as an attractive record label. "The greatest way to future profits is through the smallest part of the company – the artists' roster – but it is the hardest thing to build, and Guy doesn't like A&R men and right now there are very few acts who would want to sign to EMI."

With deposed Capitol Music chief Jason Flom said to be in discussions about starting a new label under the Universal banner, it was time for the head of this, the biggest music company in the world, to express an opinion on his British rival. In a *Billboard* magazine Q&A Doug Morris was asked his opinion of Hands' dealings at EMI. "Cost cutting is not a bad thing," he answered and added, "Did he make a good deal or a bad deal? Time will tell."

As financial analysts were suggesting that EMI could well produce figures that would enable it to meet its September 2008 debt obligations to Citigroup, the company put out an annual review of its performance up to March 2008. It was issued by Maltby Capital, reflecting the vehicle through which Hands and Terra Firma own EMI, and signed off by Maltby chairman, Lord Birt.

While announcing what was reported in one case as "eye-watering" formal losses of £757 million after tax, compared with £287 million in the previous year, and revenues down 17% to £1.45 billion, Maltby pointed out that its ebitda of £164 million had been wiped out by a variety of charges including £192 million arising from revaluation of its balance sheet; £123 million restructuring costs; £109 million depreciation and £520 million of net financing costs.

At the outset Lord Birt made it clear that this was "not a typical company report" and he suggested that people may be struck by the "forthright presentation of problems and absence of rosy assurances about the future". He went on to highlight the fact that EMI Music had a culture "where high expenditure at odds with the challenges it faced was widely accepted".

A calculation showed that the company's loss amounted to £166,000 for every employee and Lord Birt added that his involvement with the company over the previous year had "exposed how internal factors within EMI Music had significantly eroded the group's profitability".

Covered in the media under banner headings declaring "Lord Birt sounds a harsh note at EMI" and "Terra Firma brought down to earth by EMI's woes", the company review showed that up to March 2008 EMI had spent over £700,000 on London taxis and was the fourth-largest account with a major cab firm; that 88% of all its artists made no money; a total of £125 million had been lost on new music; some executive salaries were double the market rate; CD returns reached 50% in April and May 2007; and EMI had over 10,000 suppliers in the UK alone.

While Lord Birt suggested that costs were now under control and the company "expects first-half results to demonstrate that EMI Music has begun its journey to recovery", the report reflected badly on EMI's outgoing management and also suggested to some that Hands' decision to buy EMI in the first place was questionable.

Without doubt the figures made it clear that the company was not in a position to pursue any of the acquisitions it had planned early on and while the claim was that the business plan hadn't changed, it was accepted inside the company that "what's changed is the risk exposure".

An unnamed industry consultant reacted to the figures by saying, "These numbers are truly awful and show what a complete disaster of an investment EMI was," while commentator Phil Hardy observes, "Guy Hands wasn't the lucky bunny to buy it ahead of the current financial problems but I don't think EMI is a plaything for him."

According to Neil McCormick the circumstances were likely to force Hands to keep hold of EMI for the long term despite some earlier rumours to the contrary. "He definitely overpaid for it and what I heard was that after about six months he had lost his appetite for it and realised it was a bigger and more unwieldy monster than he thought."

Suggestions that the company might be in some way strapped for cash to continue to fund both its debt and its operations were dismissed out of hand by an EMI spokesman when he said, "Any suggestion of any difficulty in the [EMI] debt structure is schoolboy silliness and is not worthy of sensible comment."

By the end of 2007 the value of the worldwide recorded music market had fallen from close to $32 billion to just under $30 billion. Overall business around the world dropped by 8% with the US recording a 9% drop in trade values and the UK a worrying 13% fall.

However, in the same year, the digital business, to which Hands was committing his company for its future success, was up by 4% to 15% around the world with the US's digital business increasing from 17% in 2006 to 25% and the UK's up just two points to 8%.

Twelve months on – by the end of 2008 – sales of digital albums in the US stood at over 65 million, up from 50 million in 2007, according to Nielsen SoundScan, and EMI's performance was lifted by the fact that Coldplay's album was the biggest-selling digital album in America with over 540,000 units sold in the first nine months of the year.

These figures compared with total US CD sales falling from 449 million in 2007 to 360 million in 2008. At the same time in the UK, according to the BPI, album sales fell by 3.2% to 133.6 million while digital album sales rose 65% to 10 million, although the IFPI reported that in 2008 just 5% of all music downloads were legal, even though the international digital music business grew in value for the sixth consecutive year to $3.7 billion.

Figures confirming the problems of continuing illegal downloading inspired EMI's new CEO, in a speech at Ofcom's Next Generation-Net Generation conference in late 2008, to point out that "for every legitimate paid download there are more than 19 that aren't paid for". Leoni-Sceti further warned, "Paying for music seems to have become almost voluntary and its illegal consumption at times is considered acceptable – that's a disturbing development in our society."

And in the light of the increase in digital trade, it came as no help to EMI to hear Paul McCartney warning that The Beatles' music was not likely to be available on iTunes any time in the near future. Launching his second album away from the major, McCartney said EMI and The Beatles' own Apple Corps had still not yet agreed on terms for the release of The Beatles' catalogue as downloads. "We are very for it," he said before adding, "But there are a couple of sticking points."

As the end of 2008 came into view so a couple of the men installed by Hands and charged with recharging EMI's batteries found themselves out of a job. EMI Group COO Chris Roling and UK and North America COO Ashley Unwin left in the aftermath of Terra Firma reportedly injecting up to £75 million into EMI to avoid a potential default on the loan from Citgroup, which in turn was being underwritten by the US government.

At the same time there was confidence in the City over the company's ability to avoid defaulting on the March 2009 deadline. "EMI had a solid first half and if its performance continues in the same way then there is no reason why it should run into any problems," was one source's assessment.

One of the essential ingredients in any recipe for future success at EMI is its artists and the company can – and does – put forward three reasons why it believes acts should sign on the dotted line. Firstly the fact that any new-comers are going to be more important to EMI than to its rivals simply because EMI has fewer acts; secondly that being linked with EMI will bring them automatic press coverage; and thirdly the company has done pretty well with the likes of Coldplay and Katy Perry.

There are also those within the company who believe that Radiohead would have been more successful had they stayed with EMI rather than plotting their own course. Whether managers Chris Morrison and Jonathan Shalit agree is another question but they are not, it seems, put off the idea of approaching EMI for a deal. "I am a 100% optimist about EMI and I would have no concerns about signing any act to EMI; in fact now is a perfect time to sign to EMI," says Shalit.

At the same time Morrison admits he would have to "think very deeply about it". The man who had three of his acts dropped by EMI in one phone call – he names them as Graham Coxon, Turin Brakes and Siobhan Donaghy – says he wouldn't discard the idea of signing with EMI. "EMI would be considered equally alongside any other offers but they have a lot of ground to make up. They have to be exciting and they have to promote their success; they have to do things now after over a year of uncertainty."

For manager Pete Jenner there is only way in which EMI can attract any new acts – and that's through money. "They have to say, 'Come in, we will work with you as far as you want to work with us, we will make available to you £100,000 for your act for recording, promotion, market-ing and if you want to use our facilities you can, otherwise you can hire people in'," he says, arguing that it would give artists and managers the freedom they would want in order to link with today's EMI.

At the same time he doubts that any of this is likely to happen because – as he puts it – "There is no indication that Hands has that foresight." Whether Jenner's business plan fits in with new A&R chief Gatfield's way of thinking is also up for debate as the latter explains, "We are looking to spend more wisely in A&R, advances need to be realistic, it needs to match what we believe the market potential is for the artist." He also concedes that there is more pressure now than ever before to spend money smarter, be more prudent and be more strategic.

One act managed by Morrison who has not been dropped by EMI but has taken one project away from them is Damon Albarn, and he made his feelings about the company clear in a January 2009 interview with *Word* magazine. In fact I met him in the summer of 2008, when I was interviewing the former head of his US record label for this book. Mentioning that I was writing the recent history of EMI, Albarn simply said he hadn't been there for over two years and saw no reason why he should go there again in the near future.

A few months later he told *Word*, "For me EMI doesn't exist anymore, they should rename it. It isn't the company that it was – not in any way," said the million-selling leader of Blur and Gorillaz, who still views the departure of EMI UK boss Tony Wadsworth as the end of an era. "It was bought by venture capitalists. They got a guy in who previously sold bleach. I'm not prejudiced against people who sell bleach, but I've never felt that the people who took over EMI gave a shit about music or the musicians on the label."

And if, as he told me, he had no intention of visiting EMI, it seemed the company had not made much of an effort to contact him either. "Not one single person from the company that bought EMI has ever come to see me or talk to me."

Speaking in the midst of the success of his *Monkey: Journey To The West* stage project, Albarn finally confirmed, ". . . I'm not sure the people who own it now are interested in that [music]. I think they love money. Money and music are not necessarily a good mix. EMI has lost some of its humanity."

While the likes of Paul McCartney, Lily Allen and Damon Albarn all went on the record to voice their criticism of the 'new' EMI, Andy Heath, who was honoured in the December 2008 New Years Honours List with an MBE for services to music publishing, argues that acts, like financiers, have a somewhat distorted view of things.

"I don't care about the City's opinion of record companies and artists' opinions of record companies are hardly objective. Artists have always disagreed with their record companies," he explains. "And now they see EMI as a wounded dog they're going to declare how right the artist was all along when, in fact, success is always greatest when the artists and the business people understand and respect each other."

It seems that the new EMI's alleged obsession with money also got under the skin of the manager of one of its most successful acts during negotiations over a new contract. As a female Terra Firma legal executive attempted to significantly reduce the cost of the deal to the company, the manager told her, "Listen you're not selling fucking chips down the Odeon now, luv," at which point she hung up the phone.

Even as 2009 began there was still ongoing speculation about Hands' intentions towards EMI – would he stay or would he go? His reputation as a hard-nosed businessman who turned companies around before selling them on had preceded him, with a prominent former journalist-turned-music-executive suggesting in 2008, "I think they are destroying what there is left to destroy. I genuinely think that we could in two years' time be looking at the dismantling of the great British institution."

While his outlook for the future is less bleak, Jonathan Shalit still has his concerns. While he believes that with Hands in charge EMI will flourish, he sees a potential downside. "The question mark at the moment is the credit crunch and the people funding him and whether he will be able to keep hold of EMI long enough to resurrect it."

Although Beggars Group director Andy Heath doesn't see Terra Firma's acquisition of EMI as "a death knell" for the company, he does suggest that it will be the company's new owner who is in most danger. "The person who is going to take the hit is Guy Hands; there's every reason to think that when he sells it – and he will sell it eventually – he will almost certainly have lost a significant amount of money.

"And it's not inconceivable that someone could buy a really good business at a very good price."

That business would have been boosted by EMI's success at the 2009 US Grammy Awards when it took home 15 awards – its highest tally for five years – with Coldplay grabbing three prizes. On the other hand, the band with the biggest-selling album in the world in 2008 surprisingly missed out on four awards at the UK BRIT Awards while Capitol signing Katy Perry and veteran group Iron Maiden triumphed.

A new threat to the global music industry emerged in early 2009 when the world's number one concert promoter, Live Nation, began merger talks with the largest ticketing and artist management company, Ticketmaster.

The potential $700 million deal would see the new company tempting top artists away from major record companies – in the footsteps of Madonna, Jay-Z, Shakira and U2, who all have deals with Live Nation, and The Eagles, Neil Diamond, Fleetwood Mac and Christina Aguilera, all managed by Ticketmaster – into the world of all-encompassing 360° deals.

Even though there are a host of legal hurdles to be overcome before the merger can be ratified, the UK's leading promoter, Harvey Goldsmith, commented that the idea of these two music giants "becoming one group is certainly scary".

There is no doubt that Hands has always accepted that turning EMI into a highly successful and profitable company was going to be a long haul involving the securitisation of publishing and catalogue in order to get both Citigroup's and his own money back. It seems that the original plan was to grow the company for seven to 10 years and make acquisitions along the way.

Now, the essential change to that long-term plan is that neither Citigroup nor Terra Firma have got their money back and there is nothing left in the pot for expansion, but Hands, as he said publicly, is still confident. "I think EMI will end up being profitable – I passionately believe that."

He also knows it will take longer than he expected and cost more than he originally hoped but, he stresses, "We're totally determined all the way through to do the best for the company and it is our belief that we'll succeed."

In an ironic twist the man who took over as chairman of Citigroup in early 2009 – and who Hands will undoubtedly have to talk to about his huge long-term loan – is Dick Parsons, the former Time Warner chief executive who tried unsuccessfully to merge Warner Music with EMI in 2000. And already there are rumours that in his new role, Parsons might yet see the day when his former head of Warner Music, Roger Ames, gets to lead a buy-out of EMI as the financial pressures prove too much for Terra Firma.

One man who does not share Hands' optimism is Nick Stewart, who now heads up his own music consultancy. Speaking in early 2009 he offered up a particularly pessimistic view about EMI's future. "Financially they are in a certain amount of disarray and I've no doubt in my own mind that this is a train wreck waiting to happen."

While it's foolish to think that the results for the half year to September 2008 will have knocked Hands' determination, they still show how much work lies ahead. On increased net revenues of £737 million (up from £667 million), EMI reported a loss of £155 million, an improvement on the 2007 loss of £324 million.

The figures showed that EMI's front-line recorded music division generated ebitda of £59 million compared with the previous year's loss of £12 million, despite physical sales declining by 8% to £298 million while digital sales increased by 38% to £102 million.

However, in his statement Maltby chairman, Lord Birt, proposed that consumers who were turning away from recorded music were "experiencing recorded music in a variety of different ways".

Suggesting that the half-year report "gives grounds for qualified optimism about the progress EMI is making", he stressed that games such as *Guitar Hero* and Nokia's Comes With Music mobile phone, plus the launch of a game featuring The Beatles and Sainsbury's selling clothes with lyrics licensed from EMI Music Publishing were all positives. "Even toothbrushes can now come with music," he added.

It was also reported that out of a £250 million fund raised to cover the cost of restructuring EMI, £68 million had been injected into the company including a £16 million "equity cure" to ensure it was able to meet its banking covenants.

In its own annual report published in March 2009 and running up to December 2008, Terra Firma acknowledged that while EMI's ebitda in the last nine months of the year had more than doubled to £195 million – thanks in the main to Coldplay and Katy Perry – there was little chance of the company recovering its £2.4 billion investment in the music business as it wrote off more than 50% as part of an impairment charge of £1.2 billion.

The fact that Hands, who also handed back to investors a £40 million package of performance fees due to him, revealed a write-down of £1.2 billion effectively made EMI worth £1.1 billion in early 2009.

On the back of the Terra Firma boss' earlier comment that there was "no quick fix" for his music division, the company pointed out in its report that it would be "more selective" with its artist relationships and was on track to make savings of £200 million from EMI's cost base of £700 million, in part by reducing the head count by up to 2000.

If appointing Lord Birt to oversee EMI's activities shocked some people, Hands added to the sense of bewilderment when he named former ITV chief executive Charles Allen as the new non-executive chairman of EMI Music.

The man famously known for being thick-skinned and often referred to as "the beleaguered chairman of ITV" in light of takeover bids and a falling share price during his two-year period with the broadcaster, joined Lord Birt as an unlikely music business executive despite his involvement with Global Radio, TV production company Endemol and Virgin Media.

While Hands welcomed him aboard and announced, "Charles has vast experience of managing change in creative businesses", one analyst suggested that by joining EMI, Allen could now claim to be involved with two British companies that have seen their share price plummet dramatically in recent years.

In would seem, in light of the various new executive appointments and Hands' own words, that there is little or no likelihood of a sale anywhere on the horizon but still there are those who believe that one day the much-vaunted deal between EMI and Warner will eventually be completed.

It was certainly the general assumption in the aftermath of Hands' acquisition of EMI that some – maybe the recorded music division – if not all the company would be put on the block and sold off. Former chairman Eric Nicoli is one who believes the deal still has merit no matter what the protagonists say. "EMI and Warner is still a combination that will create a huge amount of value for the owners. There is still a big prize to be had – but nothing like as big as it was," he says.

Nicoli's predecessor as EMI chairman, Colin Southgate, also believes a deal with Warner Music is still a possibility but outlines another option for Hands. "If I could not do a deal with Warner I think I would hive off publishing and sell the other bits. I can't see what else can be done," he says, and also questions the new owner's long-term commitment to EMI.

"It's nonsense for Hands to suggest that he is in for an eight or nine-year period. He would be the first man in the private equity market who actually goes into a business for that long. It's usually three years or five at the most and while it might be what he is saying now, I doubt it's what he had in mind at the beginning."

Times media editor Dan Sabbagh is another who agrees that the deal that died at least four deaths between 2000 and 2007 is not completely dead. "I think the deal with Warners is the deal to be done but I'm less convinced by the sooner-rather-than-later argument. But it may be the case that Terra Firma need to run music for a bit and see what they think they can do with it," says the journalist before predicting, in 2008, that, "Warners is maybe a conversation to be had again in the next year or two".

However, speaking in March 2009, Warner Music chief Edgar Bronfman appeared to pour more cold water on any merger talks when he told a media conference in Palm Beach, Florida that the people who financed the acquisition of Warner Music had "voiced no concerns with [the company's] balance sheet and ability to meet its debt covenants" and then told the audience that there were no prospects of his company reviving discussions with EMI.

Interestingly, in its January 24, 2009 issue *Billboard* reflected on an article printed a year earlier that had predicted, "Guy Hands Sells Off Part of EMI Group". Acknowledging that it had got it wrong that time, the US magazine was now suggesting that "the prospect of divesting recorded-music assets might yet prove irresistible in 2009".

Alongside this prediction there are unconfirmed reports of Warner Music actually making an $800 million bid for EMI's recorded music business – without music publishing – in the latter part of 2008 but being turned down despite the very public concerns about EMI, including it being tagged "a huge loss maker for Hands".

Speaking at the start of 2009, former EMI Music senior marketing executive Mark Collen took the view that by the end of the year EMI "will no longer be considered a major player". Now a director of Mubito.com, he believes that Hands will make a move to "offload" the recorded music business and suggests that, "With a bit of luck a consortium led by Roger Ames will buy it, or more likely Warners. 'EMI 2.0' will go down as a very high-profile mistake."

In February 2009 Hands surprised the City by coming to the rescue of three cash-strapped investors in his Terra Firma business that were struggling to meet their financial commitments to the company. He bought their holding in his company for what was reported as "a nominal sum", while the media suggested the move underlined a "growing turmoil" in the world of private equity.

Within a month Hands had also decided that the time was right for him to step aside as chief executive of Terra Firma in order to focus on the company's investments, which now included 17 Australian cattle ranches bought from James Packer for around £200 million. As he came under pressure to make his purchase of EMI pay dividends, Hands handed over the day-to-day running of Terra Firma – with its 100 head-office employees and assets worth over £10 billion – to company lawyer Tim Pryce, although an insider was heard to comment, "If the day comes that EMI is to be sold then it will be Guy Hands who ultimately makes that decision."

At this stage there are no indications that Hands wants to sell or that Warner wants to buy and while he is confident EMI will survive, he wants it to be known that, "I didn't go into the business expecting to make money out of it quickly."

And hopefully he didn't buy into EMI and the music business expecting to make friends and influence people. His antics moved one experienced industry observer to suggest that while he is undoubtedly successful, Hands is also "the stupidest person I have ever come across".

At the same time one of the company's longest-standing artists, with over 30 hits in a career spanning more than 20 years, has not been won over by the EMI boss's PR campaign either. When he received his 2008 Christmas card from the great man it was signed simply Guy. Unimpressed by the gesture, the million-selling artist asked, "Guy who? Could have been from Guy fucking Fawkes for all I know."

It also seems that Blur and Gorillaz star Damon Albarn was less than impressed with the gift he received from the new team in charge of his record label. "I've had some champagne. But I don't want their fucking champagne! I want to wander down to the office, have a cup of tea and talk about music."

Surely this isn't too much for any artist to expect from their record company – and maybe it's something which Hands and his cohorts should bear in mind as they play the music game?

CHAPTER 10

Broken

(Gorillaz, Parlophone 2010)

DECEMBER 2009 marked not just the traditional conclusion to the calendar year. It also signalled the end of the first decade of the new millennium and the act stealing the headlines for EMI was a group from Liverpool who had broken up close to forty year earlier

In the list of America's top album sellers of the decade EMI were saved from complete embarrassment by The Beatles who took second place with sales of 30.1 million – just behind Eminem's 32.2 million – and were the only EMI act in the top twenty.

The famous four-piece who last recorded together in 1969 also racked up the decade's best selling album with 11.5 million copies of their *1* collection, ahead of N'Sync and EMI stablemate Norah Jones whose *Come Away With Me* hit 10.5 million.

And EMI Music's overall performance between 2000 and 2009 – as new technologies threatened to thwart the music industry's best laid plans – highlighted the problems facing Britain's last music major. They finished bottom of the pile in the US market share listings compiled by Nielsen SoundScan with just 9.8%, behind Universal (26.8%), Sony (16.7%), BMG (16.3%), Warner (16.2% and the combined Independent labels (14.4%).

2009 itself was a year in which the number of albums selling more than one million copies in the US hit an all-time low of just 16 titles, down from the 2000 figure of 88, while Digital Album sales grew from 5.5 million units in 2004 to just under 70 million by the end of the decade. Over the same period legally downloaded Digital Tracks grew from 142 million in 2004 to a massive 1,056 million.

In the UK EMI performed significantly better with Robbie Williams named as Best Selling Artist of the Decade, according to Official Charts Company figures. He was followed by fellow-EMI acts Coldplay (number 3), The Beatles (number 7) and Queen (number 19).

Chris Martin's group also notched up the highest one week sales between 2000 and 2009 with a total of 464,000 in June 2005 and Coldplay then topped the list of Most Weeks on the Chart with 394 weeks, just ahead of the late Michael Jackson on 343 weeks.

This was in a period when UK album sales grew for four consecutive years from the 2000 figure of 134.6 million before declining over the next five years to a 2009 total of 128.9 million. At the same time EMI totalled 19 Top 100 UK albums, trailing behind Universal (35) and Sony BMG (27) but ahead of Warner (13).

At the same time, in terms of music publishing, EMI were listed as the UK's top publisher during the decade with a 19.6% share ahead of Sony ATV (17.4%) and Universal (14.9% including BMG from 2007) and Warner/Chappell (11.6%) while the British company ended the decade as *Billboard's* Top Publisher in the US.

However, during those same ten years EMI failed to conclude a deal with any of the potential partners, buyers or sellers who showed an interest in taking on the company's roster of recording and song writing artists. That was until Guy Hands turned up in 2007 and added EMI Music to the portfolio of companies within his private equity company Terra Firma.

In 2000 Roger Ames was head of Warner Music and had played an important role in the attempt to force through a merger with EMI Music which ultimately fell foul of the European Commission. Having left Warner in 2004, he acted as a consultant to EMI chairman Eric Nicoli from 2005 until he was hired as chairman of the UK company's North American business in 2007.

Looking back he recalls why he decided to return to the company he originally joined in the early 1970s. "I thought maybe I could promote some changes within EMI – not in an overbearing way but perhaps could be a different voice." Even then he knew that the idea of EMI merging with a rival or being acquired was more than a distant possibility.

"I thought at the time that eventually it would make sense for EMI to try again and do a deal but I wasn't worried about it," says Ames who continued to operate under the leadership of Guy Hands after Terra Firma's acquisition. "Somebody had to buy it (EMI) and he was a financial whiz."

Reflecting on Hands' reasoning in chasing and capturing EMI, Ames says, "At the beginning he appeared to like the business and I presume he thought he could make some money out of it. I was neutral about him coming in, I didn't know Guy Hands, had never met him before he bought it but he had a big reputation as a financier."

Nick Gatfield was one of the few people with a background in the music business to be hired by Hands and in 2011 he recalled what he faced when he joined in July 2008 as head of A&R for both North America and the UK. "I went in with a view that I could re-structure it from the inside into more of a shape that worked," he explains but what he faced was a dilemma. "There were some elements of what Terra Firma planned to do which were sensible and proven and pragmatic but from an emotional artist-centric understanding of the business they wouldn't necessarily work."

Gatfield also had to contend with EMI's long term problems in the biggest music market in the world. "Its reputation and image in America was terrible," he says and he made Hands aware of the situation that faced the company in the USA. "I spoke with Guy and told him that for EMI to succeed in the US you have to be prepared to lose money for five years – bringing the best creative talent on board and building a strong repertoire stream."

While Hands, according to Gatfield, took the view that it was all about taking costs out of the business, the global A&R chief argued, "In America it was arguably the reverse. There is no cheap route to the market in the US." And failure in the huge American market, he suggested, would hamper the growth of EMI in the rest of the world.

The former member of Dexy's Midnight Runners and ex-president of Universal's Island label also knew that being responsible for finding and signing talent in both North America and the UK was never going to be easy. "In my case it certainly didn't make sense to have a Brit based 6,000 miles away trying to run a creative operation in North America – it seemed absolutely ridiculous."

The concerns Gatfield had about Terra Firma plans fitting in with the creative community are echoed by Chris Morrison, manager of Blur and Gorillaz. "I don't think Guy Hands ever got any wiser about dealing with artists and managers. With EMI you are talking about reliance on people's creativity and building good solid relationships and you don't bully and you don't demand."

Head of business for the *Telegraph Media Group*, Damian Reece is another who reflects on the management skills of the man who bought EMI. "The Guy Hands/EMI scenario might reflect how good private equity is at managing people businesses such as pubs, transport and utilities but when it comes to dealing with people that sort of management science doesn't necessarily apply."

But the business journalist and broadcaster does believe that Hands' intervention in attempting to secure the future of EMI in 2007 was an absolute necessity. "It was the case in 2007 that EMI was a good example of a public company that was never going to given the open heart surgery that it needed while being quoted on the stock market.

"To be fair only private equity could supply the necessary electrodes," says Reece. "But the problem is that when you buy a company like EMI and radically restructure it that's fine but if you do it by loading it with debt then you've got a problem. The price he paid and the amount of debt he took on and attached to the company was fatal."

As a former highly placed executive and consultant to EMI and its senior management, Ames was in a unique position to see how Hands viewed the people who ran both EMI and its rival music companies. "I don't think he had a very high opinion of the ability of anybody in the music business to actually run a business," says the man who is now an international executive with the leading global ticket agency Ticketmaster which merged with Live Nation in 2010.

"He thought of people in the music business as individuals who had relationships with artists and didn't understand that there needed to be a new model for the business," adds Ames.

One of EMI's most senior former executives, who prefers to remain anonymous, is even more scathing about Hands' attitude to the business he bought. "He had no sense whatsoever of how to run a creative business and no respect for the important relationships that make the business work."

For the whole of 2008 and through to March 2009, EMI's financial performance – despite the success of artists such as Coldplay, Katy Perry and Lily Allen – had shown an operating loss of £258 million on reduced revenues of £1.4 billion.

At the same time the company's share of the global music market for 2008 was an estimated 9.7% compared with Universal's 28.7%, Sony' 21.2% and 14.9% for Warner – and this was for a year in which the worldwide music market was worth $18.4 billion and global album sales totalled 1.6 billion compared with 2000 totals of $37 billion and 3.2 billion albums.

Meanwhile Paul Williams, editor of British business magazine *Music Week*, reflected on Hands' approach to the music industry and the people who worked within it. "Part of his theme of 'we know better than the music industry how to run the music industry' was reflected by the number of people with no music business experience he brought in."

Confirming his belief that the only reason there is a music industry is because of the talent – songwriters and recording artists – Williams adds, "If you start treating it as 'we employ some cleaners and some artists – and one maybe slightly above the other' – then you have a problem."

And for manager Morrison the changes within EMI throughout 2008 and 2009 were never going to stabilise the company. While he reckons that Hands lacked knowledge of both the industry he was buying into and how that business operated, the head of CMO Management was also concerned about the intruders. "I didn't completely disagree with his thought process where he was bringing in other people from outside but he relied more on the people from outside than he did on the music knowledge he had on the inside."

According to reports Warner Music had again reared its head as a potential buyer for EMI Music during 2008 but talks between its chairman Edgar Bronfman Jnr. and Hands floundered over disagreements about the value of the two companies.

Having failed in an attempt to merge with EMI in 2000 and had subsequent take-over offers rebuffed, the independent American music company, which traditionally vied with its British counterpart for third and fourth places in market share listings, was still seen by many as 'the deal to be done'.

While EMI was weighed down under its $2.6 billion debt to its financing bank Citigroup – even though EMI's holding company Maltby Capital was given a cash injection of £28 million mid way through 2009 in order to keep it within the terms of its debt agreement with the US bank – Warner eased its own financial problems by raising $1.1 billion through a bond sale.

Described in June 2009 by *Daily Telegraph* writer Amanda Andrews as "one of the longest running, most inconclusive, takeovers in corporate history", the saga of EMI and Warner was, however, destined to run for a while longer.

Around the same time Hands took both himself and his business empire out of the UK and into the tax haven of the Channel Islands. Apparently unhappy at the Government's decision to increase the top rate of income tax to 50%, Hands sold his London house and moved to offices in Guernsey from where he operated as chairman of Terra Firma and EMI Music.

Hands next move in his efforts to deal with EMI's debt problem was to propose a major restructuring involving a huge cash injection. By putting between £250 million and £300 million into EMI, Hands was hoping

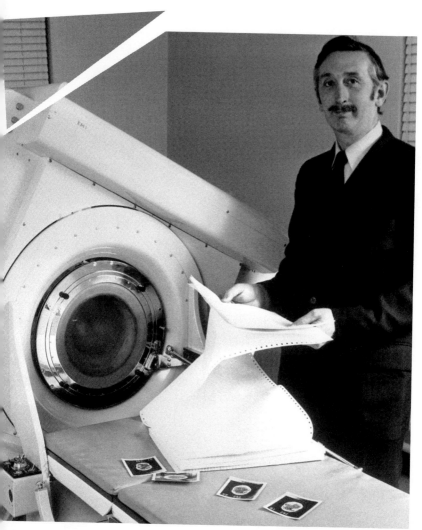

Godfrey Hounsfield in 1972, with his revolutionary CAT scanner which brought EMI to the brink of bankruptcy. (PA ARCHIVE/PA PHOTOS)

Manager Malcolm McLaren (left) with Sex Pistols Steve Jones, Johnny Rotten, Glen Matlock and Paul Cook after signing to EMI in 1976. (HULTON ARCHIVE/GETTY IMAGES)

Million selling singer Kate Bush brought success to EMI before the take over by Thorn. (BRIAN RASIC/REX FEATURES)

Virgin Group board members after the company went public in 1986 - from left to right -
Rob Devereux, Cob Stenham, Ken Berry, Sir Phil Harris, Trevor Abbott, Don Cruikshank,
Richard Branson and Simon Draper.

American Jim Fifield brought a new 'winning culture' to the British company when
he became president of EMI Music.

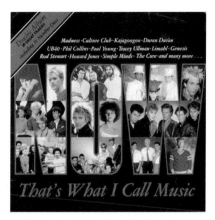

The first *Now That's What I Call Music* album was launched by EMI and Virgin in 1983.

EMI's famous home for 25 years was in London's Manchester Square

Posh, Sporty, Ginger, Scary and Baby - the Spice 'school' Girls - made EMI nearly £50 million in one year. (LFI)

Sir Colin Southgate - the man who served as chairman of both Thorn EMI and EMI.
(MATTHEW FEARNE/PA ARCHIVE/PA PHOTOS)

Eric Nicoli (right) and Consumer Affairs Minister Kim Howells pose with 'Nipper' after EMI received
a Centenary Trade Mark award for HMV in May 2000. (MICHAEL STEPHENS/PA ARCHIVE/PA PHOTOS)

Almost partners in Warner EMI — Roger Ames (left) and Ken Berry celebrate a bit too soon.
(FIONA HANSON/PA ARCHIVE/PA PHOTOS)

EMI UK chairman Tony Wadsworth (left) with his record signing Robbie Williams after the 2002 multi-million pound deal. (BRIAN RASIC/REX FEATURES)

Head of EMI America David Munns poses in New York with British singer Joss Stone, June 2004.
(PETER KRAMER/GETTY IMAGES)

Chris Martin of Coldplay, whose *Viva La Vida* album would bring EMI its biggest worldwide success in 2008. (FGO/LFI)

EMI Classic president Costa Pilavachi (left) with Paul McCartney (centre) and David Munns at the 2006 launch of Sir Paul's *Ecce Cor Meum* album. (BRIAN RASIC/REX FEATURES)

Eric Nicoli (left) and Blur/Gorrillaz leader Damon Albarn on the day EMI announced their iTunes catalogue deal with Apple in 2007. (AFP/GETTY IMAGES)

Guy Hands (centre) at the time he met EMI staff in 2008. (REX FEATURES)

that Citigroup would write off around £500 million of the debt. His argument was that if the company was better financed and on a sounder footing, then the US bank would have a better chance of syndicating the debt which EMI had to be pay back by 2015.

In November Hands went a step further and offered to inject £1 billion into the EMI Group in return for Citigroup agreeing to write off the same amount from their loan. The New York-based bank seemingly refused the deal, leading to speculation that Terra Firma and Citigroup would share ownership and control of EMI.

While The Beatles were the success story of 2009 for EMI – as their re-mastered catalogue sold over 600,000 copies in the first week of release in the US and *Abbey Road*, *Sgt Pepper's Lonely Hearts Club Band* and *The Beatles* (the 'White' album) took the top three spots on *Billboard*'s Pop Catalog Albums chart – the company still laboured in fourth place in the year end statistics.

Their 8.8% share of the US Album Market equalled their 2008 figure while their unit sales fell from 47 million to 43 million according to Nielsen SoundScan figures. At the same time Universal fell from 31.4% to 30.7% (unit sales dropped from 168m to 150m) and Warner dropped from 21.2% (113m) to 20.3% (99m) while Sony increased from 25.2% (135m) to 27.9% (136m).

This was all in a year when not one EMI artist appeared in the list of America's top ten list of Album Best Sellers and only Robbie Williams (*Reality Killed The Video Star* number 21) and Norah Jones (*The Fall* number 29) appeared in the Top 30 list of Global Best Sellers. Alongside these successes, Coldplay became the first act to sell a million downloads in the US and two million worldwide.

Meanwhile in the UK EMI claimed Lily Allen at number 10 in the list of UK Best Selling Albums with *It's Not Me It's You* alongside Robbie Williams at number 12. But despite these two artists selling 1.5 million albums between them, the company's UK album market share, according to the BPI (British Phonographic Industry), fell from 13.4 % in 2008 to 13%. And while market leaders Universal saw their share fall from 35.7% to 33.4%, rivals Sony increased their share from 19.1% to 22.6% and Warner added 1.9% and grew to 12.4%.

This was in a year when global recorded music revenues fell by 7.2% from $18.3m to $17.0m and sales of physical albums dropped from $13.6m to $11.9m while digital sales increased from $3.9m to $4.3m and accounted for 25% of global music revenues. The figure for global digital sales stood at just 5% in 2005 and 15% in 2007 while digital sales in 2009 in the US were up to 43% (up from 36% in 2008) and the digital share of the UK market in 2009 was 19% compared with 14% in 2008.

The company that was described by journalist Reece as "a dog" when Hands took it over, was now dependent on having a good Christmas to stabilise its finances and meet the terms of its loan from Citigroup which required the music company to meet regular profit-to-debt ratios.

However as the year's busiest sales season came to an end EMI found itself with just four albums appearing in the December UK album charts – Williams and Allen plus compilations from Queen and UB40. In America, the year ended for EMI with just three albums – from Norah Jones, Lady Antelbellum and Darius Rucker – in the Top 50 of the final US album chart of 2009 while Katy Perry was listed at number 12 in the list of US top artists for the year.

Meanwhile the company's strong performance in country music resulted in Capitol Nashville becoming the number one Country label thanks to the likes of Keith Urban, Darius Rucker, Lady Antelbellum, Dierks Bentley and Trace Adkins.

At the same time EMI's renowned music publishing arm once again took top spot in both the US and the UK in 2009 thanks to writers such as Alicia Keys, Beyonce, Gorillaz, Jay-Z, Train, Kanye West, Jamie Cullum, Kasabian, Simply Red, Starsailor, The Priests and Take That but the head-lines still focussed on the parent company's financial difficulties and the impact they were having on its long term prospects.

In *Billboard*'s review of 2009 'Terra Firma Fails To Restructure EMI Debt' was number two in the lost of Top Stories from the year and the magazine concluded that the outcome might be the British private equity company sharing ownership of EMI with Citigroup – "or perhaps be forced out altogether".

But before the year was out there was another extraordinary twist in the tale. In December Hands decided to go to war with Citigroup and file a $2 billion lawsuit alleging that the bank deceived Terra Firma at the time of the take over in 2007.

Citi banker David Wormsley was accused of misleading Hands about the presence of other potential buyers in the auction to buy EMI and the UK company also alleged that Citigroup were intent on driving EMI into bankruptcy in order to bring about a merger with rivals Warner Music. Citigroup denied the allegations and commented, "This suit is without merit."

The lawsuit, which appeared to result from Hands' unsuccessful attempts to persuade Citgroup to restructure the terms of the deal, was destined to push the relationship between the UK company and its US bankers to the very limit. And it seems that Hands was pushing the people who funded his purchase of EMI from the very beginning of the deal.

"My understanding is that Citigroup got the first request to re-negotiate in September 2007 – just a month after the deal was done," says experienced music industry analyst Claire Enders. "He immediately wanted to extend the loan and change the covenants but Citigroup said no straight away . . . and they said no again every three months after that."

Hands' attempts to change the terms of his deal with Citigroup were seen by music industry magazine editor Williams as evidence of the situation the British entrepreneur found himself in. "He tried to get better terms because he had to try something because the size of the debt is so massive he's not able to just carry on as things are. But I imagine Citigroup's message was 'why should we do you any favours'."

As far as Williams is concerned Hands got exactly what he signed up for. "They deal they had was one he accepted. He had business experience and is not some novice. He supposedly had this brilliant track record so you image he knew what he was doing and you presume he drove a hard bargain."

Nearly a year before Hands and Citigroup faced each other across a New York court room, *Billboard* offered their opinion on five major music events and deals that they were convinced would NOT happen in 2010. Taking into account the impending law suit, the likelihood of Terra Firma defaulting on its loan repayments and the unlikely event of a bank financing a merger between EMI and Warner and taking on the combine debt of $6 billion, the US music magazine suggested in January 2010 that it would be another 12 months before anything concrete happened.

Senior publishing/retail correspondent Ed Christman wrote, "Chances are that Hands' balancing act will be over before the end of 2010 but not soon enough for Citigroup to negotiate a sale of EMI to Warner – or anyone else, for that matter. For that stay tuned for 2011."

One man who was perhaps surprisingly cheered by the performance of EMI's operating team and the UK company in particular was Tim Clark, manager of one of the company's prime assets Robbie Williams. A critic of Guy Hands and the Terra Firma regime, Clark was quick to praise the company when Williams' *Reality Killed The Video Star* passed the 800,000 sales mark in the UK and topped the German charts for five weeks.

"We think that from an operational point of view they've really got to grips with things," he said before praising the President of EMI UK & Ireland Andria Vidler, who moved over from Bauer Media in April 2009 after a career in radio. "The current team in the UK, with other good people around the world, are really starting to get it right. From a financial point of view they're making money."

And the release in May 2010 of the company's figures for the financial year 2008–2009 showed what Clark was talking about as EMI's recorded music division declared an increased operating profit of £163 million, alongside music publishing's £133 million profit. However these were the only two bits of good news in the Maltby Capital financial report.

Overall the EMI Group reported a loss of £1.75 billion, including more than £1 billion in write-offs, restructuring costs and finance charges, even though revenues were up from £1.46 billion to £1.59 billion. All this came ahead of Terra Firma and its investors being asked to raise £120 million to satisfy the terms of the loan from Citigroup. Failure to repay this in June 2010 would allow Citigroup to assume control of EMI.

The figures prompted the *Financial Times'* influential *Lex* column to describe Terra Firma's position as "pretty bleak" and also urge the private equity company to "admit defeat and move on". Even the company's forecast that recorded music profits in 2010 would exceed £200 million failed to generate any enthusiasm in financial quarters as they would be instantly wiped out by interest and other financial charges.

Ironically all this was happening just as EMI was experiencing its best performance in the US for many years with four albums in the top ten including the country pop trio Lady Antebellum at number one while in the UK singer Corinne Bailey Rae (who was at number seven in America) and Hot Chip both debuted in the top 20.

At around the same time – during the music industry's awards season – EMI managed to collect just two UK BRIT Awards at the 2010 ceremony when Robbie Williams took home the Outstanding Contribution to Music prize and Lily Allen collected Best British Female. Things did not go much better at the US Grammy Awards where country stars Lady Antebellum (Best Country Group) and Keith Urban (Best Country Male Artist) were EMI's only major winners.

Meanwhile the BBC's influential Business Editor Robert Peston was producing some financial numbers which made worrying reading for followers of EMI. With EBITDA (earnings before interest, tax, depreciation and amortisation) of around £300 million being multiplied by the standard valuation multiple of six or seven, Peston reckoned it put the total value of EMI at £1.8 billion.

Switching to US dollars, the BBC journalist suggested that if Hands bought EMI for more than $8 billion in 2007 – his takeover being financed by $3 billion from Terra Firma and its backers plus a $5 billion loan from Citigroup with a further injection in 2009 of $500 million from Terra Firma – he was now in charge of a business worth about $2.8 billion (£1.8 billion).

"Which means that every single cent of Terra Firma's equity has been wiped out," he wrote on his BBC blog. "It also means that Citigroup is facing a loss of more than $2 billion on the loans it provided and the total loss for Terra Firma and Citi together would be something like $5.7 billion. Ouch." He further reckoned that if Terra Firma's backers were to come up with the necessary £120 million to keep control of EMI it would "provide their only chance of recouping some of their losses – on the assumption that EMI is over the worst and that the business will gradually recover."

In the midst of the concerns of both the financial community and the music industry, EMI's CEO Elio Leoni-Sceti revealed his plans for the future while declaring that he was not concentrating on the company's debt. "We are focussed on building opportunities and building value, creating the right environment for music to come out."

And reflecting on an increase in EMI's global sales of 2% between April and December 2009, when the market declined by 5%, he declared "That is much more interesting now than profit." The former Reckitt-Benckiser executive, who was talking two years on from his arrival at EMI, also acknowledged that digital music sales had become "normality" for many people. "To me the opportunity for the music industry and EMI is to create the conditions for digital music consumption to be monetised."

However, within weeks of these pronouncements about the company and business, Leoni-Sceti had left EMI and was replaced by non-executive chairman Charles Allen who took up a new position as EMI's executive chairman.

The departing Italian, who told surprised colleagues and rivals that his job was "now done" had earned himself a good deal of respect during his time at EMI. Bob Miller, manager of Corinne Bailey Rae believed that, "He did a very good job in very difficult circumstances" while EMI colleague Gatfield reckoned he was "an extremely nice guy and he got a bad press" and analyst Enders reckoned, "He did some good things, increased the market share and was very popular."

In the wake of his sudden departure there was speculation that an internal memo Leoni-Sceti had written in late 2009, and which was subsequently made public, had put him in an uncomfortable position at EMI. In his note he told his bosses, "Not only are artists and artist mangers raising concerns but morale within the company has reached a low point. In addition, the top management team are increasingly concerned about the future of EMI Music and seeking assurances about their personal positions."

He went on to explain, "We also have a number of global artists who are considering whether they should postpone their next albums until the future with respect to EMI is clear. I estimate that about £10 to £15 million of gross margin relating to new music from global artists could be at risk this year as a result of press speculation about EMI's future."

The media's continuing interest in EMI, even though it had ceased to be a public company in 2007, is something that music magazine editor Williams reflected on. "It was said at the time of Terra Firma's take over, that taking EMI into private hands would mean no focus on the share price and the City wouldn't be looking at EMI every day. The company would be able to quietly get on with things – how wrong they were!"

Fellow journalist Reece readily acknowledges that for the business pages of a national newspaper, the chance to feature Kylie Minogue or Coldplay or The Beatles is a welcome diversion from some of the more tedious aspects of financial reporting. "EMI is still a great story because of what it does – people are interested to read about rock artists and the recent corporate history over the past 10 or 20 years has been remarkably dramatic."

It was exactly that "dramatic" history which appealed to *Wall St Journal* writer Dana Cimilluca, when he spoke to BBC Radio 4 in June 2010. "It's got every element of great drama. It was a deal that was done at the height of the deal boom in 2007 that has really unravelled," he explained.

"It's got great personalities starting with Guys Hands, and it's a business – EMI – that isn't the biggest in the world but it's famous and it resonates on both sides of the Atlantic because everybody in America knows about The Beatles, Radiohead and the other acts that EMI made famous over the years."

And Ames, who began his EMI career way back in 1975, also understood why both the media and then public had a long standing affection for EMI. "EMI did have The Beatles and is the quintessential British record company and because it was an industry in which England excelled on a worldwide basis, it was important to England."

As one of EMI's senior executives Nick Gatfield had a close up view of how Hands reacted to the media's fascination with the company he bought. "He could not believe the level of interest there was in EMI. He had bought companies far bigger than EMI but he underestimated and didn't understand the power of the brand and people's interest in the company."

It was in this never-ending glare of the media spotlight that Allen chose to speak just a few weeks after his appointment and he immediately denied he had any thoughts of a merger with rivals Warner Music. Stressing that "it's not on my agenda at all", he went further and explained that it was "absolutely not the case" that he had been appointed to speed through a sale of EMI.

While that may well have been the case, he also inherited a situation which on the one hand had new UK artist Tinie Tempah celebrating a debut number one album and both Gorillaz and Lady Antebellum enjoying global chart success while on the other side established artists such as Pink Floyd, Queen and Paul McCartney were all considering the situation with regard to their EMI contracts.

At the same time *Telegraph* business writer Reece was one man who agreed that keeping the good ship EMI afloat had its merits . . . "improving financials make it a business worth keeping together and investing in rather than breaking up in a fire sale."

Allen's appointment brought a mixed response from two of EMI's most experienced managers. Managing director of IE Management Tim Clark described the new head of EMI's recorded music operation as "a safe pair of hands and he's helped turn EMI around" while Chris Morrison, the head of CMO Management, recalls his first meeting with the new music company boss. "The next person I met was Charles Allen who was affable and friendly and we sat down and had a chat . . . about nothing."

Before the end of March 2010 the newspapers were full of more rumours and this time a new company appeared on the horizon as a possible buyer for EMI. The company KKR (Kohlberg Kravis Roberts) – which describes itself as a "leading global alternative asset manager" – was apparently in talks with Warner Music about joining forces to make a bid for the beleaguered music company.

The unconfirmed plan was for Warner Music to take control of EMI's recorded music division as KKR took over the music publishing arm and while talks were understood to have taken place, there was no suggestion that any approach had been made to Terra Firma. EMI's on-going difficulties – it was now being described in the press as "the embattled record company" – were further confirmed when it was revealed that the company was seeking a deal with a rival record company to lease its important back catalogue rights for North America.

The suggestion was that in return for something like £400 million, EMI would allow either Universal, Sony or Warner the rights to sell its catalogue – including The Beatles and Queen – for a five year period but by April it was clear that if any of the British major's US rivals were interested in the deal they were not prepared to meet the asking price.

And as Allen ended the talks, the £120 million required to meet Citigroup's loan loomed large on the horizon which meant Terra Firma CEO Guy Hands had to seek the help of his investors. Having won the right to take Citigroup to court in New York over its role in the original 2007 take over, Hands was now looking to keep the bank from taking control of his company.

With Terra Firma having written down the value of its investment by 90% since 2007, the situation, according to Enders Analysis founder Claire Enders was drastic. "It's do or die. EMI is in a desperate situation," she said before adding, "In business terms this is the final scenario before administrators are appointed."

In the shadow of these dire predictions, EMI's performance in the US for the first quarter of 2010 brought some welcome relief. With Lady Antebellum's *Need You Now* the top selling album (1.6 million) – albeit the company's only album in the top ten – EMI increased its album sales from 10.6 million in 2009 to 11.9 million and reported an increased market share of 10.4%, up from 8.7%.

On the down side Paul McCartney, who left the label in 2007, also decided to take his catalogue of post-Beatles recordings away from EMI, severing his last link with the company he joined in 1962. The ex-Beatle also suggested that it was only EMI who were stopping the multi-million selling Beatles' recordings being made available on the digital iTunes system. "It's been business hassles, not with us or iTunes," he was reported as saying. "It's the people in the middle, the record label. There have been all sorts of reasons why they don't want to do it." EMI's response was to confirm that "discussions are ongoing".

Although name acts such as Radiohead, McCartney and The Rolling

Stones left EMI before he re-joined the company, Gatfield was still affected by the fall-out. "I wasn't there when they left but you did absolutely pick up the problem when it came to attracting artists." And the man who was head of the A&R team which signed the likes of Tinie Tempah, Eliza Doolitttle, Dead Mau5, Alice In Chains and Snoop Dogg, acknowledges the impact the departures had. "They were big acts and they made big headlines irrespective of how many records they might sell."

Journalist Williams agrees that the departure of major acts from EMI has a knock-on effect when it comes to signing new artists. "One of the reasons an act signs with a company or a label is the company it keeps; artists can be swayed by a label having their own favourite acts already signed. And if I was a manager I would be asking why are these acts leaving EMI."

Emphasising the impact of McCartney's decision to take his catalogue recordings away from the company, Williams adds, "They have now lost McCartney completely – one quarter of the reason EMI still exists. If it weren't for The Beatles, EMI would have gone years ago."

And there were others who also saw the departure of these stellar name acts as a negative for the great British record company. Former EMI executive Ames is one, as he explains, "People want to be on the label that has The Rolling Stones or Paul McCartney or Queen or Blur or Radiohead, artists want to be with acts that they have admired or been influenced by and hold in high regard."

The *Daily Telegraph*'s Reece is another. "Those major acts walking out on EMI created this impression that EMI's management didn't know what they are doing, allowing their assets to walk out of the door. It also showed a lack of foresight from the management of EMI in terms of managing the company's reputation – in terms of PR they could have done more to circumvent those problems."

Having sweated through the first quarter of 2009, while Terra Firma's investors decided whether to come up with the money to stave off US bankers Citigroup, Hands was relieved when more than three-quarters of them opted to help out and pump a further £105 million into the ailing record company.

The much needed funds meant that EMI was now secure until the next round of covenants covering its loan from Citigroup became due in March 2011. But music business analyst Claire Enders believed that Hands and EMI was just "treading water" and still faced difficult times ahead. "All Guy has managed to do is buy another year for the company. Nothing will secure the company's future unless it can develop a long term funding plan."

In the midst of this much needed rescue EMI suffered a further major blow when Queen decided to leave the company they signed to in the UK in 1972. The departure of the band which made the hit singles 'Bohemian Rhapsody', 'Radio Ga Ga', 'We Are The Champions' and 'Under Pressure' plus more than 20 UK top ten albums was, for one former EMI executive, a major turning point.

"For Queen to leave it takes a lot – when I heard they were leaving EMI, for me that was it," was his reaction while the industry revelled in another story that Queen's manager Jim Beach had made the decision to leave EMI and move to Universal not just because of the financial uncertainty surrounding the company but because he no longer knew anyone at the label.

This shock departure of the group whose album *Absolute Greatest* was number 20 in the UK's list of best selling albums in 2009 – and who appeared at number nine in the 2008 chart of Top UK Catalogue Downloads with the 1979 hit 'Don't Stop Me Now' – was followed by the news that EMI were considering selling a 49% stake in its profitable music publishing arm in an effort to raise some much-needed cash.

Alongside the headlines about Freddie Mercury's former band leaving, there were also stories going around that EMI's world famous Abbey Road studio was about to close or be sold off, possibly – it was rumoured – to be a property development company which might demolish the building and put up a block of flats on the site. Naturally, this provoked an outcry and a further slew of embarrassing bad publicity.

Opened in 1931, Abbey Road was apparently being losing money and proving a headache for the accountants. EMI had already closed their Olympic Studios complex in 2009 (and reportedly sold the site for £3.5 million) but in March 2010 Abbey Road, after which The Beatles named the final album they recorded there, was seemingly saved for the nation when English Heritage stepped in and gave the building a Grade II listing. A few months later the pedestrian crossing outside the studio was also granted the same Grade II listing by English Heritage even though it was not the original zebra crossing that John, Paul, George and Ringo strode across in 1969. That disappeared in the 1970s when a new crossing was created a few metres further along the road.

But even as EMI was losing another top act and having to deal with rumours about one of its most famous assets, there was still a record business to be run and that was always going to be hard in the face of the financial pressures facing its owners. According to Gatfield the debt and the numerous corporate rumours surrounding Terra Firma affected people both inside and outside the company. "They were incredibly unsettling for the staff and it was an issue when attracting artists and convincing acts and managers that we were solvent and going to be around."

And for the man charged with filling EMI's roster in both the US and the UK, there was another aspect that added to his problems. "It was also manna from heaven for our competitors who used it to try and kick EMI into touch during negotiations for artists."

Even though he was an outsider, having acts signed to EMI meant that Morrison noticed an ongoing problem within the company. "The uncertainty and disquiet has continued since Hands moved in. It hangs over them but the people just get on with the job although the financial needs of the company and the debt cause a lot of bad decisions over release dates and schedules."

Having had disagreements with EMI over the release date of the Gorillaz album *Plastic Beach*, Morrison suggests, "The problem is that it is an industry based on artistic talent and my phrase has always been 'schedules built round creativity not creativity built round schedules'. That's what the business people from outside the music industry fail to get."

Hands made great play of introducing a Matrix system of management into EMI whereby all the various major operations reported into a global chief who had various territorial heads. Under this system, for instance, the head of the operating EMI company in the US or the UK was not responsible for his own A&R person and, bizarrely, even Gatfield, who was employed as the global A&R chief under the system, could never see it working.

"I was one of the key people in the global Matrix system and maybe you can run a company that way in the catalogue business but with the creative side it is effectively a local business which becomes global if you are lucky with an act," he says. And the man who joined Sony Music UK in May 2011 adds, "We managed by consensus with meeting after meeting to calculate priorities by analysis and determine a strategy and a goal. I don't think anyone at Terra Firma understood how complex a business the music was and still is."

According to one unnamed former senior EMI executive adopting the Matrix system in all areas of the business was the single biggest mistake made by EMI. "We tried to resist but couldn't win. In fact we had already put the Matrix system in place in finance, business affairs, human resources and digital deals and it worked fantastically well. But where it doesn't work in is A&R, in marketing, in promotion, in video, in local deals. You cannot do it there – you cannot work it everywhere which is what Terra Firma did."

The same person further explains, "Guy thought we did not know how to sign artists so he put the Matrix system place in A&R and wanted artists to break even after just one album!"

In the first week of June 2010, BBC Radio 4 broadcast the programme *EMI: Facing The Music*, with Damian Reece as presenter, and EMI recorded music chief Charles Allen was among those interviewed. It coincided with the news that Hands had persuaded his investors to pump the further £105 million into EMI to meet the next deadline in its debt repayment programme to Citigroup.

Allen told the programme, "It buys us at least another year. Why would you write a cheque for £105 million and not look to invest in the business further? It brings stability." On the other hand analyst Enders' gave listeners an insight as to where that payment left things for EMI down the road. "The initial business plan specified a request for £360 million from the investors but they came back and said, 'We'd prefer if you were to do it in two tranches'. They raised £105 million . . . and the next tranche being the £225 million which is the sum which will ensure the future of Terra Firma's investment in EMI until 2015 according to the business plan."

In the 30-minute programme, Allen also explained that EMI had sold 15 million albums in the year and claimed they were the only major music company "showing top line growth". Acknowledging the changing face of the music industry the company's executive chairman also explained that digital was at the heart of the company's business model. "Digital is a core part of our business, 60% of our sales in America are digital."

However, within a fortnight of the programme airing, Allen was ousted from his job at the helm of EMI Recorded Music and replaced by Roger Faxon, the head of EMI's music publishing arm. For the first time since the departure of EMI Music chief executive Jim Fifield in 1998, EMI's recorded music and music publishing operations were now under the control of one man.

With the appointment of Faxon, who joined EMI in 1994 and had headed up music publishing since the departure of Marty Bandier in 2007, Allen moved to become adviser to EMI Music and Terra Firma while at the same time Stephen Alexander was named chairman of Maltby Capital in succession to Lord Birt who was moved to other assignments within Terra Firma.

In an internal memo sent to EMI staff on June 18, Faxon announced, "We must cultivate a culture of co-operation that will enable us to work better and more effectively across different geographies, functions and divisions. In other words we need to be a team."

Speaking to the music media he further explained his vision of how music reached its audience. "Music does not just reach consumers through sales or records; it gets there through radio, internet, toys etcetera . . . there is an increasing need to look at all the ways music can be found and enjoyed by consumers."

Putting recorded music and publishing under the control of one person on a global basis and naming Faxon as that person seemed to mean that Hands had made the right choice in his new senior music man. For artist manager Chris Morrison there was a sense of waiting "to see if putting the record and publishing business under one man is right" but he acknowledges Faxon's early contributions: "He's got some sense of purpose back in the company and some sort of senses that it is being run by a music man."

That said, the man whose company looks after the various recording activities of Damon Albarn reflected on a phone call he got when the new man was the appointed. "I got another call from EMI asking if I wanted to go in and meet Roger Faxon. I said that when he has been in his new role for six months then perhaps I will. He may have been with EMI since 1994 but I had never heard his name mentioned before he got the top job."

On the other hand music analyst Enders has no doubt about the validity of EMI's chief. "Hands should have appointed Faxon right from the word go. These are small businesses now so one man can run recorded music and music publishing."

In fact it was a move that she thought was a few years overdue. "I argued for EMI merging the two operations four years ago but traditionally the only reason they were kept as separate businesses was because they found themselves on then opposite sides of the negotiating tables in rights issues.

"The record industry tried to take more of the pie away from the publishers in a systematic way over 25 years and it cost either one of those organisations massive tons of money – you couldn't invent a scenario where people are suing their own sister organisation."

Over in the world of the media both *Music Week* and the *Daily Telegraph* also agreed on Faxon's qualifications. "When I saw the news I thought that it was the right thing to do," says Reece. "He's got a good track record and music publishing has always been the mainstay of EMI and I always felt the two arms were way too separate."

Music industry magazine editor Williams was equally sold on the idea. "EMI have done the bold thing of putting someone in charge who actually knows about the music industry. He is in quite a strong position to introduce his own ideas on how management should be structured and Hands' position has been weakened by the debt and the court case he brought against Citigroup."

One of Faxon's first moves was to slowly break down the Matrix management system which his boss Hands had so enthusiastically developed within EMI. Acknowledging that the Matrix structure had created "some confusion about accountability", he quickly introduced a "simpler organisational structure that promoted cross-disciplinary teamwork focused around each launch of each project, each release of each record."

For Gatfield it was the writing on the wall as far as his EMI career was concerned. "I absolutely saw the end coming as soon as Roger had been appointed. His view was that the Matrix system was wrong so I knew what was shaping up for my future." And he was right as he and his colleagues Billy Mann (president of new music/international and global artist management), Ronn Werre (COO of North America & Mexico and president of EMI Music Services and Ernesto Schmitt (EMI Music president central marketing/global catalogue) all left in August 2010.

The obvious move away from the Matrix system of management by Faxon prompted one former senior EMI executive to send an e-mail to Guy Hands, teasing him about the change in style the new man was instigating. The e-mail read; Subject: Matrix and the text said: "RIP".

This brought a reply from Hands which defiantly exclaimed: "The King Is Dead Long Live the King"

After his second stint at EMI came to end after just over two years, Gatfield could reflect on some of the problems he encountered along the way. "In the US the scale of the overhead made it bloody difficult," he says and goes on to explain that artists too where concerned about the company's situation. "I remember telling Katy Perry's management – who were concerned about the financial stability of the EMI as we were about to launch her album – that they were in the best position with this company because their record was too important and the artist was too important and the entire resources of the company would be devoted to maximise the potential of the album."

He told the same story to the manager of Coldplay but warns that for up and coming acts it was a different story. "If you were one of the giants within the organisation you're absolutely fine but if you were in that artist development process – good luck!"

The US chart statistics from Nielsen SoundScan for the first half of 2010 showed CD sales had fallen by just under 18% while digital album sales grew by 13.7% – and interestingly sales of vinyl albums also rose by 9.1%. The combined sales of albums and track equivalent albums (TEA, where 10 digital tracks equals an album) totalled 213.7 million, down 8.2% on the first half of 2009.

EMI's share of this market was 9.9% – up from a 2009 figure of 8.5% – but it still left them in fifth place behind Universal (30.3%), Sony (27%), Warner (19.8%) and the combined Indies (11.8%). They were, however, the only company to increase the number of albums sold in the first half of 2010, up from 20 million to 21.3 million and this was down to the success of Lady Antebellum's *Need You Now* album which shifted 2.3 million – over a million ahead of its nearest rival.

While Gorillaz (*Plastic Beach*) and Darius Rucker (*Learn To Live*) were featured in the top ten of the Top Rock and Top Catalog album sections, Lady Antebellum topped the Country Album section and also took sixth place with their previous album. However, the news of increased US album sales was tempered by the departure of multi-million selling Grammy award winning artist Joss Stone.

After telling the world in 2008 that she was not happy with EMI – "The industry is in a state, EMI are in a state, so I'd rather work on other things" – the British singer then seemingly negotiated her way out of EMI in August 2010.

Assessing the situation he inherited in his new role as EMI Group CEO, Faxon described Terra Firma's debt problems with Citigroup and the loan covenant as an issue that is "quite important but a narrow one". Stressing that both recorded music and music publishing were "both quite success-ful", he refused to be drawn on the subject a merger with Warner Music. "I'm just focussed on building a business going forward – that why I was put in the chair," he told US magazine *Billboard*.

In fact both EMI's recorded music and music publishing operation declared increased EBITDA for the year to March 2010 when the company's figures were published. With increased revenue of £1.6 billion

(£1.5 billion in 2009), recorded music returned earnings of £184 million, up from £160 million. At the same time publishing's revenues were up £10 million to £478 million while earnings were up to £150 million from £133 million.

Despite these increased performances and the EMI Group reporting an operating pre-tax profit of £121 million (up from the previous year's total of £7 million), overall the company showed a net loss of £512 million, down from 2009's £1.5 billion. According to Faxon the company "moved the top line a little bit . . . even better we moved the bottom line quite a lot."

The new chairman of EMI's parent company Maltby, Stephen Alexander commented that the company still faced "considerable financial challenges" and warned of possible "further equity cures" in the future to deal with banking covenants.

Also on the down side was news from Terra Firma of a projected increase in the shortfall of the EMI Group's pension fund of between £115 and £217 million, from its previous estimate of £100 to £200 million, and further cause for concern came in comments from the company's auditors. With uncertainty hanging over whether investors would inject further funds – and EMI's liabilities exceeding their assets by a massive £3.3 billion – KPMG said that conditions "may cast significant doubt on (EMI's) ability to continue as a going concern".

The situation concerning EMI's pension fund is one that has occupied the thoughts of analyst Claire Enders. "Who is going to be responsible for the pension – that is the key thing," she says. "Whoever buys the company is going to try to make it absolutely sure that they don't inherit some of those pension liabilities – they were one of the hidden poison aspects of the deal in money terms."

As the employer of the largest number of people in EMI, the recorded music division has a huge pension liability and according to Enders that might affect its value when it comes to doing a deal. "They (Citigroup) might get only £200 million for it but they'll be at least two organisations willing to pay that and cart it away with the pension obligations . . . and they'll also probably pay the £1.2 billion for publishing."

Journalist Damian Reece has similar feelings. "The pension might be the one thing that means Citi has trouble selling EMI. Quite often a pension deficit like EMI's would act as a poison pill and deter bidders if the liability is transferred to the new owner. But if you were prepared to give the pension trustees a large cheque you could ring fence the pension."

In September – the month Faxon announced his vision for the future in an e-mail to staff – EMI staffers were able to celebrate the number one success in America of Katy Perry's album *Teenage Dream* which sold over 190,000 units in its first week although rival company executives were reportedly disappointed that it didn't reach the 400,000 mark. At the same time UK heavy metal group Iron Maiden dominated the charts in Latin America as their album *The Final Frontier* reached the top spot in Argentina, Brazil, Colombia and Mexico and debuted in the US at number four.

Faxon's in-house message concluded with the six initiatives he considered essential to the future success of EMI:

* Unmatched insight into emerging consumer and market trends
* Excellence in new music, the lifeblood of our industry
* A revitalised catalogue, with a robust re-discovery and recommendation process
* Broadening the revenue base through global rights management
* Scalable, low-cost organisation and infrastructure
* Industry reform

Acknowledging that transforming EMI into "an artist-focussed global rights management business cannot be done overnight", the man who oversaw financial operations at Lucasfilms during the making of *Raiders Of The Lost Ark*, *Return Of The Jedi* and *Indiana Jones And The Temple Of Doom* and later worked at Tri-Star and Columbia Pictures before switching to EMI in 1994 as senior vice president of worldwide business development and business strategy had another message concerning the company's new chain of command – "There's one step between me and the guy on the ground."

All this, according to Enders, showed how wrong Hands had been in his management structure. "Some of his (Hands) reorganisation moves went against what was really a smart move for the company and were a bit arbitrary. Faxon is just getting back to what was there before – territorial responsibility and territorial complexity."

As Faxon was naming a former publishing colleague as the new head of the company's recorded music operations in North America, EMI music publishing in the UK was yielding its top spot to rivals Universal as the region's top publisher for the first nine months of 2010. Coming in with a reduced share of 20.3%, EMI lost top spot for the time in five successive quarters as Universal notched up a 26.9% share, according to figures produced by *Music Week*.

Former session and touring drummer with the likes of Sheryl Crow, Aimee Mann and Lloyd Cole, Dan McCarroll switched from his role as executive vice president of North American Creative at EMI's music publishing arm to take over as President of Capitol & Virgin Label Group in North America.

As the man credited with signing the likes of John Mellencamp, Toby Gad and Travie McCoy to the company, McCarroll was welcomed to his new task by Faxon with the words, "Dan has an unswerving commitment to putting artists and repertoire back into A&R." UK manager Morrison's assessment of EMI's US operations would also have brought some encouragement to the new label chief. "I think the American company has got a lot better," he says and with Gorillaz's *Plastic Beach* having hit number two in the US he had a reason to be happy. "Gorillaz had a terrific time in the States this time round – the company has got smaller and has good A&R people."

As is usual in the autumn the media began to focus their attention on the major releases lined up for the all-important fourth quarter. In a list of 18 acts with major albums set for pre-Christmas release in the US, *Billboard* chose to include just two EMI artists – country stars Keith Urban and Darius Rucker – alongside the likes of Rhianna, Kings Of Leon, Kid Rock, Black Eyed Peas, Josh Groban, Bruce Springsteen, Elton John & Leon Russell and Elvis Presley.

At the same time among the albums scheduled by EMI in the UK for the last quarter were Robbie Williams' Greatest Hits plus releases from Tinie Tempah, Deadmau5, Eliza Doolittle, Charlotte Church, Cliff Richard and Swedish House Mafia.

A significant ruling in the European Court in October 2010 brought some joy to both EMI and the rest of the record industry when it was judged that labels had been wrongly charged VAT on free CDs sent out for promotional purposes. With EMI claming that it regularly distributed between 2,500 and 3,750 promotional copies of a release, it was calculated that the company payout, including interest, could be as much as £3.3 million with a further £25 million or more due to its rival companies.

This was some consolation for EMI as it moved to plug the gap in the company's pension fund by agreeing to provide an additional £197 million in funding. After an initial payment of £16 million, EMI Group agreed to provide regular payments through to April 2016. While there was speculation that the company could afford these payments out of its operating profits, others were less positive as to where the ruling made by the Pensions Regulator would leave the company, with one pension expert suggesting the size of the deficit "could conceivably push the company into administration".

But it wasn't problems with pensions that took EMI into the headlines in late 2010 but a very public spat between two men who had once been friends but fell out over their business dealings.

CHAPTER 11

It's Not Me It's You

(Lily Allen, Regal 2009)

THE long awaited case brought by Terra Firma against Citigroup in December 2009 finally came to court in New York in October 2010 but only after the US bank had lost two motions – firstly to have the case rejected and secondly to have the lawsuit heard in the UK.

There was a deal of speculation surrounding Hands' determination to have the case heard in New York with suggestions that it was because he was unable to spend much time in the UK due to his tax exile move to Guernsey and that, in the light of the financial recession and public animosity towards banks and bankers, Citigroup would be a popular target for a jury in the US.

These arguments were coupled with the general view that if Terra Firma were to win, any punitive damages they were awarded would be far higher in the US than the UK. Either way, after attempts to reach an out of court settlement had failed, it seemed that Citigroup won their fight for any final financial ruling to be decided under English law.

In his original document filed at a New York on December 11, 2009, Hands named Citigroup dealmaker and head of UK operations David Wormsley 78 times, accusing him of making representations that were "knowingly false and deliberately and maliciously designed to fabricate a false competitive landscape that would elicit a bid from Terra Firma."

Seeking damages close to $7 billion, Hands alleged that Terra Firma was pushed to bid 265p a share for EMI in order to outbid a buyer that had already walked away and he claimed that his company could have taken a different view if it knew it was the sole bidder.

US District Judge Jed Rakoff, who had finally ruled in September 2010 that Terra Firma's claim for fraudulent misrepresentation and fraudulent concealment should proceed to trial, sat with a nine member jury in the US District Court, South District of New York on October 18 2010.

In the run up to the case the media made much of the previous close working relationship between Hands and Wormsley which began in 1997 and continued as Terra Firma built up its portfolio of businesses with help from Citigroup, its leading investment banker. Between 2000 and 2007, Terra Firma apparently paid Citigroup £136 million in fees.

As far the *Daily Telegraph*'s Reece was concerned the lawsuit might just have provided Hands with some necessary leverage in his debt negotiations with Citigroup. "I thought if he lodged a law suit against Wormsley and Citi he could bring that to the table and say, 'We can settle this one if you can agree new terms for the debt on EMI.'" When that tactic failed and the trial got nearer, Hands, according to Reece, "allowed it to get personal, emotions took over and he pursued the case – which was a big mistake."

Day One: With David Boies, one time lawyer to US Vice President Al Gore, representing Guy Hands and Theodore Wells, who represented former US Vice President Dick Cheney's chief of staff I. Lewis Libby Jnr., acting for Citigroup, the trial got under way with Boies suggesting that Wormsley and Citigroup were "playing both sides of the street at the same time" by advising both Hands and EMI.

He argued that Wormsley, in an effort to earn fees for Citigroup, had an incentive to lie to Hands that an auction was on-going and that another bidder – Cerebus Capital Management – were likely to make a bid. Boies also claimed that Wormsley had betrayed the close friendship that he had with Hands – they had spent time on holiday, at the opera and clay pigeon shooting together – and asked the question, "Why should Guy Hands have trusted Citibank?" In a dig at the bank's reversal of fortunes following the financial crisis he answered the question himself by stating, "Back in 2007 Citibank had a great reputation."

Opening on behalf of Citigroup, Wells told the court that Wormsley, who he claimed never knew Cerebus had dropped out of the chase for EMI, was "an honest person and he never lied to Guy Hands". Pointing out to the court that Hands was an experienced financier who had stints at Goldman Sachs and Nomura before stating what he described as "a large international private equity firm".

He added that Hands and his partners did due diligence and considered the deal for EMI to be a good one. "If you're going to pay $4 billion, you're going to do your homework," he said before adding that it was more than two years before Hands filed his lawsuit. "If they thought they had been lied to, you would have thought they would have picked up the phone to David Wormsley and said, 'You lied to me,'" added Wells.

Before the end of the first day, Wells told the jury, "Mr Hands thought he had the golden touch, and he did for quite a while – until he bought EMI. And he can't get a do-over by saying he was cheated or tricked."

Day Two: Cross examining Tim Pryce, a senior executive at Terra Firma who earlier confirmed that the code name for the EMI deal was "project dice", Jay Cohen, a lawyer from the team representing Citigroup, showed the jury slides that appeared to show that Terra Firma's strategy bid of 265p a share for EMI was in place before Wormsley allegedly told Hands that Cerebus was bidding 262p.

He showed a slide which indicated that Terra Firma's investment team recommended a bid of 265p on May 18, 2007, and explained, "The three calls Mr Wormsley made during which he is accused of lying to Mr Hands took place after that."

Following Pryce into the witness box, Terra Firma's chairman told the court that Wormsley was "my closest business colleague" outside his own Terra Firma staff. Adding "I believed I knew him very well", Hands said that he spoke to Wormsley on three occasions over three days before final bids for EMI were due on May 21, 2007.

Alleging that Wormlsey told him a rival bidder, Cerebus, was going to bid 265p while knowing that they had in fact dropped out, Hands explained, "If David hadn't made those statements we wouldn't have been bidding on the Monday morning at all. It wouldn't have happened."

Asked by his counsel David Boies how he would have reacted if Wormsley had not mentioned other bidders in those conversations, Hands stated, "How do I put this politely? I would have smelled a rat. If he hadn't confirmed, we would have known we were the only bidder."

Commenting that counsels for both parties had made much of the fact that both parties – Hands and Wormsley – were married with children, Judge Rakoff observed, "I congratulate them on their fertility. But I do think it's rather irrelevant to any issue in this case." In the afternoon the judge also took time out to note that some media coverage of the case suggested that it was too complicated for the jury to understand. "And that touches a sensitive chord with me," he said.

Confirming that he had become "a huge fan of the jury system", the 67-year-old Judge explained, "My experience is that most cases, including this one, come down largely to credibility contests. That a jury of everyday folks with everyday experience are supremely gifted in ascertaining who is telling the truth and who is not. And while it could, with truth, be said that some of the evidence in this case is boring, none of it, in this court's view, is remotely beyond the ken of any one of the jurors, let alone all nine."

Day Three: Cross-examining Hands, Citigroup's lead lawyer Theodore Wells, reminded the chief of Terra Firma of a speech he had made to EMI staff during which he told them that 60% to 70% of his wealth was dependant on how EMI performed.

Asked by Wells if his due diligence picked up certain problems at EMI, Hands replied, "My due diligence had no chance of picking up those items." The questions continued with counsel asking if after buying EMI, Hands was concerned that the company had too much debt. "Yes," said EMI's owner.

Pressing further Wells asked, "Did you conclude that because of the debt structure, you made a mistake in buying EMI?" Hands admitted, "We did come to that conclusion, yes." Further asked if he had concerns that his investors would lose money on EMI, Hands said, "By mid-2008 we thought that was a possibility."

Having denied that he was concerned about lawsuits from his investors who had lost money on EMI, Hands was asked, "Did you tell Mr Wormsley that you could have trouble raising money in the future from investors." He said, "I have no recollection of that" and, in answer to Wells final suggestion that brought the lawsuit "because you wanted to blame someone else for your mistake in purchasing EMI, the 51-year-old British executive told the court, "That is not correct."

Day four: The focus of attention was on two Terra Firma employees who gave evidence on behalf of their boss Guy Hands. Firstly Riaz Punja, who confirmed that he had headed up the team which did due diligence on EMI before the deal, said that Hands had called him during the weekend of May 20, 2007, and told him, "'I've just had a conversation with David Wormsley and he tells me that Cerberus is in. They will be bidding tomorrow, and they will be bidding a price of 262.'"

Punja also told the court that Terra Firma called the deal "Project Dice" after The Rolling Stones' song 'Tumbling Dice'.

Next to appear was a senior assistant who took the minutes of the company's board meetings and Kirsten Randall told the court that she had written the minutes of a meeting of the company's Investment Advisory Committee held on Sunday May 20, 2007 – the day before Terra Firma made its £4.2 billion bid for EMI.

Her handwritten notes were projected on to the wall of courtroom 14b in New York's Lower Manhattan district and among the lines was one that read "other bidders – one at 262p". She told the jurors that in her notes her hyphen separated a question that had been asked by someone at the meeting from an answer given, indicating that a rival bid at that price has been mentioned.

For Citigroup, Jay Cohen pointed to other hyphens in Randall's notes and asked whether they were also used to differentiate between questions and answers. The Australian who joined Terra Firm in 2004 said, "not necessarily" but that in the case of the line about bidders it had.

Day five: The first week of the case between Terra Firma and Citigroup came to an end with the founder of the British private equity company being cross-examined by lawyers for the US bank.

Confirming that "poking a dragon" was the last thing he wanted to do, Hands was asked why he had continued to seek an agreement with Citigroup during 2009 while believing he had been tricked into paying over the odds for the music company.

"I think fraud is a very strong word and I was trying to find a way through without destroying any relationship between us," he told the court. He explained that he thought it would have been inappropriate for him to have called Citigroup's Wormsley during the summer of 2009 before he filed his lawsuit in December of that year while pointing out that during talks about restructuring EMI's debt, he had told a Citigroup senior executive that he felt he had been misled over the deal.

On the last day of the first week of the trial, Citigroup lawyer Wells showed the court an e-mail from Hands' public relation consultant Andrew Dowler which listed points that the *Financial Times (FT)* newspaper claimed it knew about the bidding for EMI on Monday May 21, 2007. One of the four bullet points read "Cerebus is out", but Hands explained, "I don't even know if I read it" and added that "The *FT* gets things wrong on a completely consistent basis."

Day six: Giving evidence by video, Simon Borrows from the boutique investment bank Greenhill which advised EMI on it sale in 2007, told the court he had decided to bring forward the deadline for bids for the last

British major music business from May 23 to May 21 in order to "create some uncertainty in all the bidders' minds". He explained that being vague about a deadline and then suddenly announcing it to bidders was "a pretty common tactic".

The main witness was Citigroup's head of UK investment banking David Wormsley who was called by Terra Firma as a hostile witness. After Terra Firma lawyer Boies had pointed out to the court that the Citigroup executive had made strenuous efforts to cultivate the trust of Hands, Wormsley said that he had tried to convey to Hands that he could be trusted – "in my general demeanour towards him . . . to always be as truthful and honest as I could be."

The day finished with Wormsley being shown a series of e-mails he had sent to Hands and two Citigroup colleagues between October and November 2006, which according to Boies demonstrated how hard the banker and his company had worked to woo Terra Firma as clients.

In a note to the head of Terra Firma in October, Wormsley wrote, "You may be surprised to hear that within Citi, Terra Firma is one of the examples we hold up of how, as a group, we have consistently put the client before our own interests and made the whole organisation work for the client."

A second e-mail to Hands, from November, explained, "I know it may seem strange to advise you how to handle the banks but I am incapable of not trying to get you the best possible outcome" and this was followed by a further note from Wormsley to his then senior colleague Michael Klein which read, "I think we should have a Citi/Terra Firma party somewhere special to celebrate all the deals we are doing."

Also in November he wrote to then senior Citigroup banker Julian Mylchreest with this suggestion. "For reasons I won't go into, we have to show big love to Terra Firma. To that end it would be very helpful if you had an hour in London next week to sit down and meet with the Terra Firma team and hear their story." According to Boies, in this final e-mail, Wormsley was, "Trying to convince Terra Firma, by showing what you refer to as big love, to engage Citibank. Correct?" The US bank executive replied, "That's correct."

Day seven: Speaking for a second day Wormsley told the court that Hands had implied in a conversation with banker Borrows, who was heading up the sale of EMI, that he (Wormlsey) believed an offer of 240p a share would be accepted by EMI's board.

"I was furious," said Wormsley, suggesting that Hands had behaved in an "unacceptable" manner when using his name in connection with a so-called "low-ball offer" for the British music company. He added that he had received a voice mail apology from Hands which had since been deleted from his machine.

The Citigroup executive also explained that any bonus he received was not dependant on any fees that Citi earned when it lent Terra Firma money to acquire EMI. "I got no benefit in my bonus from the financing," he said. It was also explained by lawyers for Terra Firma that Citi were, in 2007, apparently angered that it had not been involved by EMI in the securitisation of its music publishing business and the bank was also concerned that another bank had been appointed as chief adviser to EMI over its sale.

"We did not wish to be pushed out, of course not," said Womsley who confirmed that Citigroup were paid both for the advice he gave to EMI as well as for the £2.6 billion loan it made to Terra Firma.

Day eight: Giving evidence for the third day Womsley explained that he been known as "the Worm" since the age of five. "I now take it (the nickname) as a sign of affection rather than anything derogatory," he said. Continuing to deny allegations made by Terra Firma that he had tricked them into buying EMI at an inflated price, the banker explained, "I played a junior role in this transaction."

Answering questions from Citigroup attorney Theodore Wells about his relationship with Guy Hands, Wormlsey described the Terra Firma boss as a man with "a big ego" while his "ability to think outside the box has been one of the reasons he has been so successful." Emphasising the minor role he claimed he played in the Terra Firma/EMI deal, he said that it was one the last before the financial crisis took hold. "It (2007) was one of the busiest times of my career. It was immediately before the banking crisis and there was a huge amount of debt available to do transactions."

Day nine: The focus switched to Judge Rakoff's ruling on the size of the damages Hands and Terra Firma might receive if they won their action against Citigroup. The method used by the British private equity form to calculate financial injury was known as "lost profits" and involved the return Hands had made on previous investments and calculating a similar return on the money spent on EMI.

The judge decided, "I really think that it is speculative and I also think the methodology is really flawed. I had a lot of problems with her (Terra Firma's expert financial witness Marianne DeMario) using the historical rate of return from a boom period that involved Terra Firma."

Despite his criticism, the judge said he was prepared to allow another method of calculating damages proposed by DeMario which was based on the difference between what Terra Firma paid for EMI and the value of the music company in May 2007, using discounted cash flow.

This calculation meant that if they lost Citigroup would still be liable for damages of around $2 billion and their lawyers argued that any figure should be calculated using EMI's share price before any bid speculation started. The judge told the two sides that "a reasonable jury could well find that the methodology proposed by the defence is preferable but that seems to me a jury question, not a question for the court."

Day ten: The case, which Judge Rakoff memorably described as "a cat fight between two rich companies", took an unexpected turn when lawyers for Citigroup asked for the removal of a jury member after it was discovered that her name appeared among the credits of American film-maker Michael Moore's documentary *Capitalism: A Love Story,* which attacked the US financial industry.

Arguing for the dismissal of balloon twister cum part-time circus performer turned "movement therapist" Donna Gianell, Citigroup lawyer Wells showed clips from the film and claimed, "This movie is so insidious. You've got to have a verdict at the end of the day that people will respect." Speaking for Terra Firma, Boies argued against her removal saying, "There are many, many personal and business relationships that we could probe (of the jury). Banks, financial institutions, private equity firms are all controversial."

However, having heard the arguments, Judge Rakoff decided to dismiss Gianell from the jury for another reason. It emerged that she had been overheard discussing the case in a court elevator with fellow jury members in contravention of court rules and then, when questioned, had lied about it. "It seems to me", said the judge, "that given that we have a juror who has lied to the court about an important matter, that we need to excuse her. So I will excuse her." According to a transcript of the judge's meeting with the juror in his robing room, Judge Rakoff considered Gianell to be someone "who wanted to make sure she stayed on this jury rather than admit to anything in the way that might possibly subject her to being excused."

Day eleven: Making his closing address to the jury Terra Firma counsel David Boies claimed that the firm had proved that Citigroup's Wormsley told Hands that the private equity firm Cerebus planned to place a 262p share bid for EMI in the final days of the auction for EMI. "If they hadn't (believed that Cerebus planned a bid) there was no reason for them (Terra Firma) to be putting a bid in on Monday, May 21." He went on to urge jurors to remember that "actions speak louder than words" before adding, "Ask yourself: why did Terra Firma bid 265p on May 21 if it did not believe that was another bidder?"

Speaking for Citigroup, Theodore Wells countered by stating that Wormsley had never told Hands about a bid from Cerebus. "There's not one single piece of paper that records that David Wormsley said Cerebus was going to in bid. If this company was going to invest £4.2 billion on that conversation, it'd be written down. This is corporate America. Someone would have written it down."

Day twelve: After close to four hours of deliberation at the end of trial running into a third week, the eight-person jury dealt Guy Hands a crushing blow and returned a verdict which cleared Citigroup of any wrong doing.

They decided that the private equity investment entrepreneur was not misled by the US bank's executive over the purchase of EMI and threw out Hands claim for damages. Outside the Manhattan court juror Dennis Posillico said he had been leaning towards Hands until Citigroup's closing arguments won him over. "There wasn't any solid evidence. It was just showing e-mails and telephone calls. To me it wasn't enough."

While confirming that the British company's reserved its right to appeal, a spokesman for Terra Firma said, "We are disappointed that the jury found that we did not prove that we relied on misrepresentation from Citi, which caused a loss to our investors."

Counsel for the US bank, Wells told reporters, "I think Mr Wormsley was put through terrible ordeal and he was totally innocent and had done nothing wrong."

With the high profile financial lawsuit at an end, it was time for the speculation as to what the future might hold for the defeated Guy Hands and his Terra Firma business. Financial journalist Reece reckoned that the days of EMI remaining an independent company "have been reduced dramatically". Describing the relationship between Hands and Citigroup as "100% ruined", he adds, "If the main shareholder in this business

(Hands) turns round and sues you, clearly the relationship ends and I can't see any way now that Citigroup will be willing to sit down and do any kind of deal that Guy Hands is involved in."

One fascinating aspect of the EMI story which the court case did expose was the identity of some of the major American investors in EMI – companies and deals which, according to *Wall St Journal* writer Dana Cimilluca, "normally stay below the radar". Among those who gave money to Terra Firma in support of EMI were Cornell University, the New York City Employee's Retirement system, a number of New York pension organisations – including both the fire and police department pension funds – and the Canadian Pension Plan.

While music analyst Claire Enders takes the view that Terra Firma will find it "impossible to persuade investors to invest any more money", she does understand why Hands took his bank to court. "I didn't think Guy Hands had anything to lose with his court case. It brought him more time and even if there was just a 5% chance of success, to get off the hook of those millions of pounds was worth every penny."

Music Week's Paul Williams took the view that the court case was Hands' "last hand at poker" which was a huge risk and "something that was very unlikely to succeed" while EMI artist manager Chris Morrison saw the writing was on the wall for Hands as he struggled to meet the terms of the loan from Citigroup. "If he won the court case it might have been a different matter but it was unlikely that he was ever going to win – especially as he chose not to hold it in Britain. Citigroup were wealthier, bigger and more powerful and they had more influence. It's not how popular you are, it's what muscle you can bring to bear."

On the back of the trial result Enders was also predicting that she would "find it hard to believe that a year from now EMI will not be in the hands of Citigroup" while EMI's CEO Roger Faxon described talk of either a break up, a merger with Warner Music or the sale of the music publishing division as "utterly idiotic".

He went on to point out that a deal with the company's competition would raise regulatory issues while adding that EMI's rival music operations were "not geared up right now to stomach the financial demands of attempting to take over another big company".

None of this of course stopped the media speculating that Warner Music or German publishing company BMG Rights were preparing bids in anticipation of a fire sale at EMI. At the same time there were rumours that EMI might be among the bidders for the publicly quoted Chrysalis

Music business which opened itself up for offers in November 2010 while Terra Firma's successful Odeon cinema chain was the subject of interest from a number of rival private equity companies.

Speaking on the back of the Terra Firma lawsuit, Warner Music boss Edgar Bronfman Jnr. did nothing to quash the rumours of a deal when he accepted that EMI "has suffered since the Terra Firma acquisition". Addressing investors and media in the US, the Warner Music CEO simply stated, "When we have something to announce – if we have something to announce – you guys will be the first to know."

One deal that did go ahead, however, was UK label Mute's decision to revert to its former independent status eight years after its acquisition by EMI in 2002 for a total of £42 million. The home to Depeche Mode, Moby, Goldfrapp and Erasure decided – according to founder Daniel Miller – "it would be more constructive if Mute became independent" but it still remained linked to EMI's distribution, sync and licensing and merchandising services in the US, UK, Canada and Ireland.

If the first decade of the millennium was dominated, from EMI's point of view, by The Beatles it came as no surprise to find that they once again made the headlines as 2010 drew to a close. After years of negotiations the Fab Four's music was finally made available through Apple's iTunes service – and sales were brisk to say the least.

Within a week of the November 16 launch, four individual tracks had entered the UK Top 75 singles chart with 'Hey Jude' at number 40 on sales of just over 7,000. It was followed by 'Let It Be' at number 46, 'Twist And Shout' (48) and 'Here Comes The Sun' (64). At the same time US digital albums sales were put at 119,000 units in the first week while Apple claimed global digital album sales of the Beatles of 450,000 with over two million individual tracks sold through iTunes.

The down-side of all this Beatles' business as far as EMI was concerned was an industry story which suggested that the iTunes deal was more beneficial to the group than the company. Sources put forward the proposition that iTunes was paying royalties from the digital downloads in the US direct to Apple Corps and paying songwriting mechanicals direct to Sony/ATV music publishing which controls virtually all the Beatles song catalogue.

If this rumour was true it would result in EMI acting as a licensee of the recordings and sharing income from the recording masters with The Beatles on a 50/50 basis, making it much more lucrative for the artist than a normal recording deal and less generous to the record company.

Unsurprisingly EMI, Apple Corps and iTunes all declined to comment on the story.

At the same time another of EMI's legendary and long standing artists – Pink Floyd – were in court to continue their argument with the record company over digital downloads. In March 2010, the group won an action that barred EMI from selling single downloads from their collection of best selling albums.

EMI's appeal against that decision was finally dismissed in December when three Court of Appeal judges accepted Pink Floyd's arguments that their record company was forbidden by contract from selling their recordings as anything but complete albums in order to "preserve the artistic integrity of the albums". EMI, who admitted it had allowed online downloads from albums and parts of tracks to be used as ringtones, were ordered to pay outstanding royalties to the group which they first signed in 1967 in addition to the costs of both the original High Court and subsequent Appeal Court hearings, which were estimated to be around £100,000.

However, within a month Floyd showed they bore their record company no ill will and signed a new five-year deal with EMI which showed that "all legal disputes between the band and the company have been settled". Under the new deal EMI will continue to market and distribute Pink Floyd's catalogue of more than 20 albums stretching back 45 years.

Around the same time established EMI artist Kate Bush took back control of four of her albums – *The Dreaming, Hounds Of Love, The Sensual World* and *The Red Shoes* – from EMI under a plan to re-issue them during 2011. The singer's relationship with the label she signed to in 1977 had apparently been stretched to near breaking point in 2008 when the company's UK chairman Tony Wadsworth left following Hands acquisition of the company.

Sources close to both Bush and EMI reported that she called up the Terra Firma chief and told him that this would be the first and last time she would ever speak to him before adding, 'The only person I have dealt with at EMI is Tony Wadsworth and now he's gone you won't be hearing from me ever again."

The end of 2010 saw EMI's share of the UK Album market, according to OCC figures, increase to 14.1% although they still lagged in fourth place behind Universal (33.9%), Sony (21.2%) and Warner (14.6%). In the list of the year's Top 100 Album Artists Robbie Williams came in number 14, one ahead of Katy Perry, with Tinie Tempah (number 29) the only other EMI act in the Top 30.

These three artists were also the only EMI acts to feature in the final British album chart of 2010 although Gorillaz and *Plastic Beach* did earn fifth place on the list of Top Selling UK-sourced albums with non-UK sales of 0.9 million and a top three chart place in the Australia, Canada, France, Germany and the USA. At number nine on the list was Robbie Williams and *In And Out Of . . .* with sales of 0.8 million. Both albums were way behind Susan Boyle's 3.7 million sales outside the UK followed by Sade's 2.3 million.

A year end calculation of the major companies' share of the European album market once again showed EMI in fourth place with an estimated 16.7% (up from 12.1%) – trailing behind Universal (36.7%), Sony (25.5%) and Warner (16.8%) – while their top selling overseas acts included Japan's Hikaru Utada, Vasco Rossi from Italy, Portuguese singer Mariza, the French duo Daft Punk and Canadian Johnny Reid.

In the USA, EMI's share of the year's music sales, according to Nielsen SoundScan figures, was up from 8.8% in 2009 to 9.6% but once again they were behind Universal (31.4%), Sony (27.4%) and Warner (19.8%) and, in line with all their competitors, their overall album sales were down. Compared with 43.1million in 2009, EMI moved 42.3 million albums plus Track Equivalent Albums. This was in a market where total CD sales fell over 19% to 237 million (294.9 million in 2009) while Digital album sales increased 13% from 76.4 million to over 86 million.

The last US album chart of 2010 featured Katy Perry at number 12 (her track 'California Girls' was the best selling digital song of the year with 4.4 million units), Lady Antebellum at 25 and Keith Urban at 27. On the list of the US charts Top Artists of 2010 Lady Antebellum took fourth spot – with Perry at number 11 – and the country trio also took third place in the list of *Billboard*'s Top 200 Albums.

However the success of these three American acts – two top country artists and a major pop star all signed to EMI's Capitol imprint – was just further proof that the company was continuing to miss out in the popular and profitable area of R&B/Hip Hop music, the second most successful genre in the world's biggest music market behind Rock.

So successful were R&B/Hip Hop acts in 2010 in the US that they took nine spots on the Top 20 Artists list – and not one of them came from EMI. While the likes of Eminem, Usher, Black Eyed Peas, Rihanna, Drake, B.O.B., Luducris, Trey Songz and Lil Wayne made their mark only Cali Swag District and Britain's Corinne Bailey Rae flew the R&B flag for Capitol.

Despite this obvious gap in EMI's artist roster, the company's performance in the face of Terra Firma's financial pressures earned praise in some quarters. Music industry journalist Paul Williams reckons that, on a day to day basis, EMI is "doing quite well" with publishing continuing to produce particularly impressive figures. "The UK was always a strong territory and they have done will in the last year at a time when all record companies are struggling to break acts."

Adding to "the long story of North America" where, despite the success of Katy Perry and Lady Antebellum, the company has had a paucity of superstar global acts "going back before Guy Hands", the writer explains, "When a Coldplay or Kylie Minogue albums comes out it *has* to sell which is not the situation at somewhere like Universal where if one superstar act doesn't do too well, they have another three coming around the corner."

Acknowledging that EMI's operating performance has always been overshadowed by the debt and corporate issues, *Daily Telegraph* columnist Reece suggests the people in the record and music publishing divisions have "worked hard and done well to turn it round from an operating point of view". He also believes that the turnover of executives at EMI since 2007 has led to a high degree of instability, suggesting, "The number of people who have gone through the business does reflect how wearing and how difficult working for Guy Hands probably is."

On the other hand Roger Ames is less than impressed with the performance of the music division over the past few years. "I don't think that what EMI has broken and achieved in the past three years has shown a good return for Terra Firma." And the former senior executive at both Warner Music and the EMI Group explains his argument. "You cannot – unless you have a miracle – turn round a record company in three years because it's unlikely that you are going to find, sign and break anything in under three years to any degree of success."

Reflecting on 2010 in terms of the overall music business, *Billboard*'s most experienced industry observer Ed Christman listed EMI at number three in the Top 10 Stories of 2010 and commented that despite being the company's third chief executive during the year, Faxon's appointment did bring "a badly needed degree of stability" although he concluded that, as a result of their on-going financial problems, Terra Firma "will have to get its investors to pony up another equity injection, just as they did last year".

The financial results of three leading major companies for the final quarter of 2010 were consistent in that they all reported a drop in income over the previous year's figures for the months ending December 31. Number one company Universal's earnings fell 27% from £263 million to £193 million although revenues were up nearly 10% to £1.29 billion compared with £1.16 billion in 2009. Second placed Sony declared a drop in income to £149 million from £176 million while revenues also dropped 14.5% to £1.08 billion. For Warner Music the quarter showed a 14% reduction in revenues from £570 million to £489 million and a £12.4 million drop in income to £16.7 million.

In the same week in early January 2011 when there was news of him receiving a dividend of £12 million from Terra Firma, Guy Hands took the business and music industry by surprise by announcing that he was intending to appeal the decision of the New York court in its lawsuit against Citigroup.

Hands, who took the dividend to support his wife's Hand Picked Hotels chain, lost his action for damages from Citigroup in November but a Terra Firma statement announced, "Boies, Schiller and Flexner, on behalf of Terra Firma, filed notice of appeal in the litigation against Citigroup. The appeal will challenge legal rulings made by the court in the litigation."

While Citigroup defended their conduct in the action as "entirely proper", sources suggested that the British private equity firm were likely to challenge technical aspects of how the trial was conducted in addition to the overall verdict.

According to respected music analyst Claire Enders there was one simple reason behind Hands' latest move. "He's just trying to keep the show on the road by buying himself more time." But, she predicted in January, it was a plan that would not work. "In March it will be the same as last year when he was pushed to raise the money to meet the loan covenants. It will go down to the wire and he will give it his all, he will not give up . . . he's going to make it painful for Citi."

With EMI's future within Terra Firma the subject of even more speculation, the focus of attention fell on BMG Rights, a joint venture between Bertelsmann and the KKR private equity firm, as potential buyers for both EMI's recorded music and publishing arms. This prediction followed hot on the heels of BMG's £107 million purchase of the Chrysalis music publishing.

Chrysalis founder Chris Wright added more fuel to the bonfire of rumours when he commented on Terra Firma's acquisition of EMI. "Terra Firma has made some mistakes. The first is the message they sent out to the creative community that the artists are all lazy and have to work harder." The man who sold his Chrysalis record company to EMI more than 20 years earlier then followed up by assessing the potential opportunities for BMG. "There are some very good assets at EMI and EMI Music is a very good company. If BMG is ever in the position to buy it then I think they should."

Chris Hufford, one half of the Courtyard Management team that guides Radiohead – and a man who has no regrets about the band's departure from EMI after their 2003 album *Hail To The Thief* – saw no future for EMI under Hand's ownership. "I don't see a great future for EMI if it is not sold," he says before adding a further thought on the music industry as a whole. "I'm not sure the record industry makes a great deal of sense working within traditional corporate structures, especially these days when there's not a great deal of money in the business."

Before the first month of the new year was over there was more news and this threw the record industry into a spin. Warner Music hired investment bankers Goldman Sachs to search out potential buyers for the whole company, seemingly at the same time as the US music group also explored the possibility of buying EMI. At this stage the smart money was on Warner selling off its Warner Chappell music publishing arm in order to fund a bid for the whole of EMI but here was the first sign that Warner's backers might just be less than enamoured with the music business and their future investment.

Bought for $2.6 billion from Time Warner in 2004, Warner Music – home to acts such as Madonna, R.E.M., Red Hot Chili Peppers, Kid Rock, Josh Groban, Michael Buble and Green Day – was backed by investors Edgar Bronfman, Bain Capital, Thomas H. Lee Partners and Providence Equity Partners and went public in 2005. Within days of the news that it was up for sale, the first interested parties were reckoned to be BMG Rights and KKR with a bid for the Warner Chappell music publishing arm which was valued at £1.5 billion. This sale would immediately wipe out Warner Music's debt of £940 million but it seemed that Sony/ATV – the music publishing business owned jointly by Sony and Michael Jackson – were also in the hunt for Warner Chappell.

There was even more surprising news to come when it seemed that Guy Hands was attempting to finds new backers for a £1.6 billion bid to buy EMI Group from Citigroup – the bank he had unsuccessfully taken to court two months earlier. With the US bank on the verge of seizing control of EMI as a result of Terra Firma's breaches of its repayment terms, it apparently invited Hands to make a bid to buy back the music operation.

With new investors who would be prepared to support him in his bid likely to be thin on the ground, the *Daily Mail* asked the simple question, "Where on earth does Guy Hands think he is going to come up with £1.6 billion?" although there were those close to the business who suggested, "Guy doesn't give up."

Acknowledging that "there are lost of permutations and partnerships possible", the businesses interested in EMI and Warner Music would, according to Enders, know exactly what to expect. "They know the future of the record business – they know it's not going to get any better and it's arguably going to get worse every year." She also warned that the days of wealthy music lovers coming along and picking up record companies on a whim were over. "There aren't many rich individuals who would want to buy EMI just because they can . . . that's inconceivable."

If Warner being put on the market and Hands bidding to buy EMI off Citigroup took people by surprise, an announcement made on February 1 2011 was a total shock . . . the US bank seized control after it decided that Terra Firma had failed a solvency test.

The take over followed the appointment of Peter Spratt and Tony Lomas from PricewaterhouseCoopers as administrators to Maltby Investments and their subsequent decision to sell Maltby and EMI to Citigroup. While it was a move that took most by surprise, music writer Williams predicted in January this year, "It's hard not to think that he (Hands) would not have met the March loan deadline – you have to ask how many times can they go back to the well of The Beatles and make it work again."

For one former EMI executive the take over of by Citigroup represented the end of an era – and only one man was to blame . . . "It took Guy Hands three years to destroy 110 years of history."

Over at the *Telegraph* Reece was suggesting that the early interest from Warner Music and BMG Rights made sense. "Putting themselves at the front of the queue reflects the fact that this asset (EMI) is still highly sought after and Citi can see that they will get a decent price for it. But in order to maximise the value it could involve the bankers breaking it up and selling it in two parts."

While predicting that EMI's music publishing arm would attract a wide range of buyers although "surely only another recording company would be mad enough to buy the recorded music business", he also reckoned the man who took over EMI in 2007 would not be involved at the death. "I'm not sure Hands will get the luxury of making the decision as to whether he could retain recorded music or publishing – Citigroup are not going to do him any favours."

How right he was as the New York-based bank stepped in and took control of the business they had kept afloat for the previous five years. On the up side Citi reduced the debt by 65% from £3.4 billion to £1.2 billion and left EMI with over £300 million in available cash.

At the same time the size of the Terra Firma's loss on EMI – estimated to be $2.7 billion – brought news that it might just be the biggest ever loss by a private equity company, according to American financial researchers who reckoned the previous highs had been a telecommunications write-off of $1.5 billion in 2002 and a $1.35 billion loss on a US bank.

One experienced and important manager saw only one outcome following Citi's take over of EMI. "Citi will want to sell fast," says Tim Clark, manager of Robbie Williams. "Neither Terra Firma or Citigroup were terribly satisfactory owners of the business and we now have to wait and see if Citi will sell to investors who understand the music industry and will fight to turn EMI into a successful company once again."

Unfortunately, the man who has been impressed by the current EMI team and their new boss – "under Faxon they have a real opportunity to build on their current success if only the money men will allow them to do so" – is not entirely optimistic about the future. "Since so very few record company executives understand what is happening to their industry, I am not overly confident that Citi will find the people who can."

However, the man left in charge of EMI looked on the move with enthusiasm. "The recapitalisation of EMI by Citi is an extremely positive step for the company," said Faxon. "It has given us one of the most robust balance sheets in the industry with a modest level of debt and substantial liquidity."

And while others made the point that, with a US bank owning EMI, none of the world's leading record labels were any longer in British hands, he stressed – from the company's headquarters in New York – "Regardless of the country of origin of our owner, EMI remains a British company – both legally and spiritually. We are not EMI because of who owns us but because of who we are – the home of the greatest artists and songwriters of the past, present and future."

With a US bank in charge and American, German and Japanese companies all listed among the potential buyers of EMI, it seemed that opinions – despite Faxon's enthusiastic patriotism – were divided over the company's British-ness.

Despite his well publicised setbacks it seemed that Hands was not put off the idea of still being in the record business. Speaking in Guernsey less than two weeks after Citigroup took control of EMI, he once again confirmed his interest in buying back the music company but admitted that valuation was an issue. "It's a question of price," he said before adding, "Terra Firma and Citigroup agreed on what EMI was worth back in 2007. We clearly both got it wrong. Now we disagree quite strongly about what's it worth."

However, sources close to the company suggested that it was "hard to see" Hands resuming his interest in music and also confirmed that Citigroup were in "no hurry" to off-load the music group, preferring to heighten the tension among any potential bidders.

For one former senior EMI executive – and a man whose departure coincided with Hands' arrival – the Terra Firma boss's plan to buy back EMI bordered on the ridiculous. "The idea that Mr Hands would buy either EMI again or Warner Music is among the most absurd I've heard in all my days. If his co-investors are persuaded to support him in such a venture then heaven help them."

And as someone who observed EMI's performance first-hand for nearly a decade he adds, "When he (Hands) claims he's doubled EMI's profits, he forgets to mention that he halved them in his first year in charge . . . EMI's profits are roughly back to where they were in 2006."

Some of what EMI had achieved under Hands and Terra Firma was highlighted when it came to the music industry's annual award season. In the US, EMI impressed with 20 wins at the 2011 Grammy Awards including five for country trio Lady Antebellum, three for EMI music publishing act Jay-Z and prizes for Iron Maiden, Keith Urban and The Beatles – yet again.

At the UK's BRIT Awards ceremony artists – Tinnie Tempah (two) and Laura Marling – and writers – Arcade Fire (two), Take That's Howard Donald and Jason Orange and Rhianna – collected a total of seven awards and shared the spotlight with EMI.

Revealing the Recording Industry in Numbers for 2010, the IFPI listing of the Top 50 Global Albums featured EMI's Lady Antebellum at number five and Katy Perry at 11. The country band also had the second best selling album in the US (following the world's top selling album from Eminem) while the American singer's track 'California Girls' was sixth in the list of Global Digital Songs – with 6.7 million units – behind Ke$ha's 'Tik Tok' on 12.8 million.

The IFPI report highlighted an 8.4% decline in global music industry revenues to a total of $15.9 billion but, while physical sales dropped 14.2% to $10.4 billion, digital sales grew 5.3% to $4.6 billion. And as America remained the world's largest music market – worth $4.1 billion but showing a 10% drop – and Japan held on to second spot (down 8.3% to $3.9 billion) so Germany overtook the UK as the third largest music market.

Germany's drop in revenues of just 4.1% (to $1.4 billion) was the smallest of the top seven markets and meant that for first time in many years they swept past the UK where business dropped by 11% to $1.3 billion. In the midst of these figures, which reflected the performance of both large and small, local and global record companies, the multi-million selling artist Moby took a swipe at the industry's biggest players.

"I truly believe, as an institution, most major labels should die," said the American musician whose British recordings for Mute went through EMI from 2002. "Signing to a major, for 99.9% of the musicians on the planet, is the worst thing they could do. They (the majors) either need to reinvent themselves or die quietly," he suggested to a Pop Music conference held in Los Angeles.

While the music industry waited in the wings to see who came up with the cash for either EMI or Warner Music, it was apparent to Faxon that Citigroup were unlikely to overstay their welcome in the business. "It's pretty clear that Citigroup will not sell CDs," he said in February 2011 before adding, "In due course we are going to get sold. But it will be an orderly and profitable process."

For media journalist Dan Sabbagh, who was at *The Times* when Hands first arrived at EMI and continued to follow the story of his departure at *The Guardian*, time was the important factor in the sale of EMI. "A quick decision remains essential for the music – any uncertainty is crippling," he says before adding a further warning. "EMI is likely to find it near impossible to sign any acts while it is unclear what the future of the company is, and it will have to work hard to keep its remaining superstars happy."

At the same time he warned that breaking-up EMI and selling it off bit by bit was not "the best answer from a value and economics point of view". This view reflected EMI's decision in 2010 to launch a single global rights management structure and further combine the recorded music and publishing divisions, making a one-off sale of the entire integrated music business the preferred option for owners Citigroup.

CHAPTER 12

Hello World

(Lady Antebellum, Capitol 2010)

W HILE nobody could put their finger on who was actually at the front of the queue, the media was having a field day listing the various scenarios that could play out in the battle for EMI and Warner Music as interested parties from far and wide came a calling.

In March 2011 the front runners for Warner Music were reckoned to be Clive Calder, who sold Zomba Music to BMG in 2001 for £2.7 billion, Access Industries, owned by Russian investor (and shareholder in Warner Music) Leonard Blavatnik, independent publishers Imagem, the private equity companies KKR, Apollo, Providence Equity, Permira, Tamares and Platinum Equity alongside US private investor Ron Burkle's Yucaipa company, a mystery bidder represented by Guggenheim Partners plus Universal and both BMG Rights (backed by KKR) and Sony Music – either separately or together.

While the bidding for Warner Music was expected to start around $3 billion mark, there was an added concern for the world's two largest music companies Universal and Sony Music as their bids would almost certainly raise anti-trust issues. Another name which would prompt serious competition scrutiny popped into the frame in April when the giant US concert promoter, ticketing and artist management group Live Nation were rumoured as potential bidders for Warner Music. This news came despite denials from chairman Irving Azoff and the tough conditions imposed on the company following its drawn out merger with Ticketmaster in 2010.

The continuing round of March madness also put a host of the same companies in the frame to buy EMI from Citigroup – the starting price was put at the same $3 billion mark for Warner Music who were, of course, put at the top of the list of possible bidders for EMI. In the words of one American banking source it was a time when both Warner and

EMI were busy "sorting the goats from the sheep" in order to draw the best bids.

According to music industry pundit Paul Williams "an EMI Warner merger is still the match made in heaven" although he adds that a link with BMG/KKR would also ensure substantial savings. Analyst Claire Enders also tipped Warner and BMG/KKR as the front runners, adding, "There will be big investors who will want to do a deal for EMI through a private equity vehicle that they trust."

For business writer Damian Reece there was always the possibility of outsiders popping up with a bid for EMI's music publishing business. "Why should just a traditional music company buy it? Why not Apple or Microsoft or someone who just wants ownership of intellectual property and has got a distribution platform to sell it through to consumers?"

And the list of those supposedly interested in buying EMI or Warner Music took a bizarre twist on April 1 2011 when singers Jay-Z and Beyonce were reported to have bought EMI for $2.5 billion and beaten off interest from railway tycoon Sir Topham Hatt and his Sodor Capital Partners fund. The April Fool's Day joke became clear as soon as people realised that Hatt is a character from the *Thomas The Tank Engine & Friends* series which is based on Sodor Island.

The joke bidder for Warner Music was an online gaming company called Zynga which supposedly had "an audacious plan to refocus WMG's business around social sharing and virtual items" and this story was blown open when people clicked on to the *Wall Street Journal* link to the story and found a bottle of ketchup with April Fool on the label.

On a more serious note Roger Ames – who has held senior positions at both Warner and EMI – refused to be drawn on his favourites in the bidding war but simply suggested that "the likely scenario is that someone puts two record companies together to make one and saves a bunch of money." At the same time he posed a question for any future owners. "But that is not going to answer the important question of whether there is a sustainable music business based around finding and developing new artists."

As a man also closely involved in the process of finding and developing talent, manager Chris Morrison admits that the uncertainty surrounding EMI does impact on the artists he looks after, including the multi-talented Damon Albarn. "He's not happy being with EMI any more, he thinks it's lost its soul and is a shell of the company it was before and he distrusts their judgement."

The UK album share figures for the first quarter of 2011 would not have made Albarn any happier with his paymasters as they came in fourth with an 11.4% of the chart, behind the 15.3% of Warner and Sony's marginally higher 15.5% share. While all three lagged well behind Universal's 30%, EMI also found themselves being hounded by leading independent Beggars Banquet who, thanks in the main to the singer Adele, racked up an impressive 11.1%.

While the speculation about EMI's future continued things took an unexpected twist when the Warner Music Group announced that the bidding round for ownership of the company came to an end at the start of the second week of April. And the US independently-owned music company was apparently now favouring selling both its recorded music and music publishing divisions to the same buyer for a combined price in excess of $3 billion.

With Platinum Equity and Access Industries appearing as the front-runners in the race, Warner Music shares peaked at a 52-week high of $8.15 in early May, which confirmed a valuation of around the $3 billion mark. Within a day speculation this had become fact with 54-year-old Russian born business man Leonard Blavatnik successfully acquiring Warner Music – the company he originally helped finance – for $3.3 billion.

With his new purchase of the world's third biggest music company, the man who, according his PR representatives is a mogul rather than an oligarch, moved from a world of oil, aluminium and chemicals into music. It prompted the *Independent* newspaper to announce that "pop is about to get a new paymaster" while business publication *The Economist* suggested that Access had overpaid for Warner. And as they speculated that he might do the same again with an inflated bid for EMI, they offered up a proposal that "Overpaying for two music firms is thus not twice as crazy as over-paying for one."

The Access acquisition of Warner Music was finally approved in July 2011 when the company's stockholders voted in favour of the deal – which brought them $8.25 per share – at a special meeting. As Access assumed an estimated $2 billion in debt from Warner, the music company was de-listed from the New York Stock Exchange.

One former Warner Music executive who acted as an advisor to Blavatnik in his pursuit of Warner said, "Len buying Warner is an incredibly positive move for Warner and a positive move for the industry as a whole – and if he bought EMI it would be equally positive."

The same man reckons that while Blavatnik understands that the music business has problems – "He has seen that is broken," says the independent advisor – he also senses that merging Warner with EMI still makes sense even in a falling market. "He recognises that there is a huge amount of value to be made by putting the two companies together and he has no problem getting access to the right people to do it.

On the shoulder of Access's successful bid for Warner Music, including its legendary Warner/Chappell music publishing division, the spotlight briefly fell on to the BMG Rights Management operation who were reported to be keen on acquiring Warner/Chappell if it became available as a result regulators forcing Access to split their latest asset.

Around the same time, Warner Music announced their figures for their third fiscal quarter up to June 2011 and they reported a 5% increase on revenue for the same period in 2010 – up to $686 million – with digital revenues up 13% to $203 million but it didn't stop a major move within the executive ranks of Warner Music. Long-time CEO Edgar Bronfman, who led the buy out of Warner Music from Time Warner, bizarrely swapped roles with company chairman Stephen Cooper in a move that led to speculation that another acquisition was in the pipeline.

While Bronfman explained that "my energies on behalf of the company would best be directed toward transformative transaction and long-term strategy" it was suggested that one such "transformative transaction" would be the purchase of EMI. On the other hand the *New York Post* carried the headline "Edgar Bronfman Bumped Upstairs" and suggested that the man who is heir to the Seagrams drinks fortune was unhappy at the prospect of working for Blavatnik. They also quoted an industry source as saying, "When was the last time you heard of billionaires working for each other?"

When world leaders Universal Music – part of the French Vivendi company – posted their year end figures for 2010 they showed a small increase in revenues, up 2% to 4,449 million, but an 18% drop in earnings, down from 508 million to 471 million despite the global sales of Eminem (6m), Lady Gaga (4.8m) and Taylor Swift (4.3m).

Rivals Sony Music's annual figures for their year to March 2011 showed a 9.9% drop in sales to £3.5 billion which the Japanese owned company put down to currency fluctuations and, trumpeting the strong performance of Michael Jackson's catalogue following his death in June 2009, they reported an 6.6% increase in operating income over the previous year, up to £285 million.

In the middle of the year EMI announced that, together with its new owners CitiGroup, they were in the hunt for a new deal. "We are off to the races," said CEO Roger Faxon in a note to staff. "We, along with Citi, intend to explore all possible alternatives, including a sale, recapitalisation or IPO of EMI – all with the aim of setting the stage for the next chapter in EMI's ownership." In the same note he forecast that by the final quarter of the year, "We will have a good idea of who our new owners are likely to be."

At the same time speculation continued as to who was going to get their hands on EMI with a suggestion that there were plenty of potential buyers in the first round of bids – which closed in early August – including a number of names from the auction for Warner Music, namely Access, Platinum Equity & the Gores Group plus Permira, previous bidders for EMI. These were all apparently interested in buying the entire EMI company while BMG Rights, Oaktree Capital & Primary Wave plus Sony were suitors for the company's music publishing arm.

Those named as chasing just the recorded music division were MacAndrew & Forbes and Universal Music while Apollo Global Management were an acknowledged interested party but nobody was sure which part of the company they were pursuing. Either way sources put the bids for the EMI Group in excess of $3.5 billion, slightly more than Access paid for Warner Music.

By the half-year regular market front runners – and potential suitors for EMI – Universal Music were announcing improved figures for the first six months of 2011 although both revenues and earnings still showed a drop. While revenues fell 1.9% to 1.86 billion – compared to a 5.4% fall in 21010 – earnings were down 17% to 132 million compared to a decline of 24.6% the previous year.

While Citigroup were being accused of delaying tactics in order to help potential suitors to raise the cash to fund a bid, EMI were reported to be lobbying singer Robbie Williams with a £40 million offer to re-sign to the label in order to impress the interested parties. Meanwhile, in the midst of all the news of bids and sales, the former owner of EMI stepped back into the spotlight.

After his defeat in New York's District Court back in October 2010, Guy Hands went back to court to dispute Citgroup's ownership of EMI. This time his Terra Firma company questioned the American bank's decision to take control of EMI based on a solvency test which saw accountants PricewaterhouseCooper put Maltby Investments, the holding company of EMI within Terra Firma, into administration and allow Citi to claim ownership.

In an application to the High Court in September 2011, Terra Firma requested access information and documents relating to the takeover in order that they could explain the situation to its investors. However, at the end of 2011, it was difficult to ascertain exactly where this action stood with analysts, commentators and court officials all unable to confirm the position.

September also saw *The Word* magazine carry a nine-page feature on Hands, Terra Firma and EMI which they headlined "The Man Who Broke The Record Business?" and illustrated it with a cartoon of Hands as an errant schoolboy plunging the charger into a canister marked TNT. While the article ran over the timetable of EMI's travails under Hands – quoting from managers, journalists and 'insiders' – they also managed to illicit some direct quotes from the man who had previously spoken to this author only on the understanding that it was 'off the record'.

"I think the main thing we did for EMI is enable it to survive," he said. "While we didn't finish what we wanted to do with EMI – we were some years away from finishing what we wanted to do – I think the momentum is there now." His final comment, when asked by *The Word* if he would do things differently second time around, Hands explained, "I'd probably worry less about the PR and do things quicker."

October saw speculation about potential new owners for EMI increase as the deadline – set for October 5 – came and went with the value of bids for recorded music being estimated at somewhere between £0.7 billion and £0.9 billion while music publishing was reckoned to be worth anywhere between £1.3 billion and £1.6 billion. An added ingredient in the mix for potential bidders was the size of EMI's pension liabilities which were put at more than £530 million – about a quarter of the company's estimated value – and likely to become part of the recorded music in the event of a split sale.

In a process described by a financial executive as "cleaning up the bids" it seemed that Citi were asking the five front runners for EMI to either fine tune their bids or confirm the financing of any offer. The handful of companies left in the mix by mid-October were Universal Music, Warner Music, Ron Perelman's MacAndrews & Forbes and Sony Music – for recorded music – plus Warner Music, Sony/ATV and BMG+KKR for music publishing.

Before the end of October, EMI's efforts to increase the value of the company by completing a new deal with the multi-million selling Robbie Williams came to nothing as the Take That star signed up with rivals

Universal, home to the boy band since 2006. The singer's long-time manager Tim Clark commented, "This great news puts Robbie Williams firmly in control of his own destiny, but with the most muscular of partners."

As the weeks rolled by so the media continued to speculate as to which company was in the driving seat when it came to buying EMI. There were reports that Warner Music were in pole position to acquire the recorded music division after Universal had pulled out of the bidding war while BMG/KKR were front runners for publishing. On the last day of October it seemed that Warner Music owner Leonard Blavatnik had also withdrawn from the race although his suggested stance was reported as "brinkmanship" after his alleged offer of around $1.5 billion for EMI's recorded music operation fell below Citigroup's valuation.

As the sale of EMI grew ever nearer so IMPALA, the organisation which represents Europe's independent music companies, confirmed their objection to the idea of either of the two existing majors buying EMI. While they expressed no concerns over world ranked number three music company Warner Music acquiring EMI, IMPALA confirmed that they would ask the European Commission to investigate if either Universal or Sony were successful.

Concerned that Universal should not be allowed to gain more market share in recorded music and that Sony acquiring music publishing would pose similar problems, IMPALA executive chair Helen Smith said, "Making such a duopoly more powerful goes completely against the basic principles of competition in cultural markets."

However, just two days after IMPALA had made their feelings known, the first deal for EMI recorded music was announced with Universal Music successfully acquiring the business for £1.2 billion ($1.9 billion) which meant that the once mighty British music major was in the hands of a French parent company with interests in video games, telecoms and pay-television, over 51,000 employees and revenues in 2010 of 28.9 billion.

The deal with EMI was about to give Universal a market share of the global music business in the region of 36% to 38% – just under the 40% figure which analysts believe would cause the regulators some concern. In the UK, the combined company could claim up to 50% of the album market with an estimated 38% of the giant American music market.

For one man, the idea of Universal rather than Warner Music getting hold of the company he formerly ran was something of a blessing. Bhaskar Menon, chairman of EMI Music until 1989, believes that placing the company's "historic business" in the hands of the French-owned con-glomerate was preferable to "burying it under a Russian autocrat who probably knows not yet the difference between rock'n'roll and Church music".

Meanwhile both *Daily Telegraph* journalist Damian Reece and another former EMI chairman, Eric Nicoli – the man who oversaw the acquisition of EMI by Guy Hands in 2007 – believed that CitiGroup pulled of a pretty good deal for themselves. "It is a reasonably good deal for Citi given that they found themselves in a very bad situation," says Reece. "They had financed what will go down as one of the worst private equity deals in history (Terra Firma acquiring EMI) and what they appear to have been able to is just about get the debt back – they seem to have just about washed their faces and got their money back."

"Citigroup," according to Nicoli, "have done pretty well to get this price, which together with the price for the publishing deal, allows them to recover a decent proportion of the debt they put in."

In a memo sent to his staff on November 11, EMI CEO Roger Faxon confirmed the deal to sell part of the company to Universal and predicted another. "Let me give you the unembroidered bottom line," he wrote before confirming, "EMI is to be split with EMI Music to be acquired by the Universal Music Group. I hope to be able to share more detail on EMI Music Publishing shortly."

He went on to explain that, "Universal won the day not only on price but also on other critical terms" and then added, "Universal will need to clear the necessary regulatory hurdles before they can take ownership. And that will take time and effort. So it is likely that EMI will remain much as it is today through and perhaps well past the end of our fiscal year (March 2010)."

In the event that the deal does go through, Faxon's new boss at Univer-sal will be fellow Englishman Lucian Grainge who was promoted from head of Universal International to chairman of Universal Music in March 2011. Fifty-one-year-old Grainge, who joined Universal in 1986, was seen an instrumental in the purchase of EMI and in a statement he con-firmed his reaction. "This is an historic acquisition for UMG and an important step in preserving the legacy of EMI Music. For me as an Englishman, EMI was the pre-eminent music company that I grew up with."

The day on which the deal to buy EMI was announced was also coinci-dentally the 80th birthday of the opening the company's iconic studios in

Abbey Road and Grainge went a stage further when asked about the future of the place The Beatles used as the title for the last album they recorded together. A year after speculation that Terra Firma was planning to sell the studios and allow them to be turned into a tourist attraction, Grainge confirmed, "It's very much our intention to keep the Abbey Road studios. It is a symbol of EMI, it is a symbol of British culture and I think it's a symbol of the creative community."

However, in order to facilitate its purchase of EMI – and ahead of potential issues with the regulators – Vivendi confirmed the sale of 500 million worth of non-core assets within the Universal Music Group including "several minority stakes" but IMPALA were seemingly unimpressed as they declared that the deal should be "blocked outright". Claiming that previous mergers had already damaged the music market, Smith said, "It's clear that Universal hopes that divestment might make regulators approve the merger, but I can't imagine that will work."

As founder of Beggars Banquet, the UK's largest remaining independent record company and home to Adele, the world's biggest selling artist in 2011, Martin Mills also holds a less than optimistic view of Universal's acquisition of EMI. "This looks like breath-taking corporate arrogance. Even greater dominance would be bad news for almost everyone involved in the art and business of music."

Head of AIM – the trade body for the UK's independent music companies – Alison Wenham also stressed her organisation's objection to the deal. "The indie position is clear. Universal is already too big, the music market is unacceptably concentrated already and Universal's acquisition of EMI is simply a hostile move against fair competition in the market place."

As an artists' manager for almost 50 years, Chris Morrison has worked with both majors and independent record companies and he has his own concerns about the sale of EMI's recorded music division. "This deal was what's best for the bankers – it's not best for the music business," he said before adding, "I'm not criticising Universal but they are too fucking big and now they are even bigger and EMI will just become another label. You will have one less place to take artists."

The former manger of Blur and Damon Albarn – their long-time association ended in 2011 – also sees the EMI Publishing deal with Sony/ATV as a disappointment. "Again it's just one less place to go for writers and there will be cut backs. But it (the cost of the two deals) does tell you how far the record company income has shrunk compared to publishing which, in the past, was always secondary."

On the other hand former EMI UK chairman Tony Wadsworth sees some hope for the 'indies' if the deal goes through and results in a trimming of the artist rosters at both Universal and EMI. "There is a chance for the independents to benefit from some of the disposals that will come," says. "They will have a chance to offer something different from the super major – the good indies will thrive by stressing their difference."

Universal's bid, which involves them paying a first instalment of £1.1 billion either when US regulators approve the deal or after 10 months, with the balance of £100 million being handed over on completion of the deal, does not involve them having any responsibility for the pensions of EMI's 21,000 employees. Under the terms of the deal Citigroup retain liability for the UK pension obligations which run at around £370 million.

In addition to adding EMI's estimated 10% share of the global music market, Universal also add EMI's last reported (March 2010) recorded music revenues of $1.8 billion to its own 2010 figure of $6 billion, taking it over $2 billion ahead of rivals Sony Music.

While EMI artists such as The Beatles, Pink Floyd, Coldplay, Katy Perry, Norah Jones, Lady Antebellum and Tinie Tempah are perhaps about to be linked with Universal's list of best sellers – including Eminem, Lady Gaga, Rhianna, Take That and Justin Bieber – life for artists such as The Rolling Stones, Queen and Robbie Williams was about to go full circle as all three had already abandoned EMI to join Universal.

According to Mick Jagger, who first signed to EMI in 1978, the new deal had very positive possibilities. "I particularly welcome the fact that EMI will once again be owned by people who really do have music in their blood," he said, while David Holmes, manager of stalwart EMI million sellers Coldplay added, "This can only be positive for the artists and executives at EMI."

And according to Andrew Lloyd Webber, whose song writing partner and musical co-creator Tim Rice joined EMI in 1966 as a management trainee, the sale simply meant, "A colossal act of faith in the future of recorded music. At last Britain's greatest record company is in safe hands."

Some observers were not so positive with Jeffrey Rabhan, an American artist manager and also chairman of the Clive Davis Institute of Recorded Music at New York University, commenting, "From a competitive standpoint it would have been better for the industry if Warner and EMI had merged. You want to have three strong players, not two and a half."

Bizarrely, within days of their acquisition of EMI, Vivendi were having to deny rumours that they planned to their sell their dominant Universal Music business including the newly added EMI with chief executive Jean-Bernard Levy explaining to the media, "We haven't grown Universal Music with two major transactions (EMI in 2011 and BMG publishing in 2006) just to spin it off."

The British national newspapers, which had been following the saga of EMI over the years through their dedicated business pages, were generally in agreement that EMI was probably in a better place with its new owners. David Wighton, writing in *The Times* – and unable to resist some song lyric clichés – reckoned, "I'm think I'm gonna be sad that EMI has finally got a ticket to ride. Living with Guy Hands and then Citigroup was clearly bringing it down. But still a great British cultural institution – the home of the Beatles – will no longer be British, whatever that means these days. Let's hope . . . that Universal can take a sad song and make it better."

His colleague Ian King firstly reminded people of two of EMI's final signings before the takeover – ". . . It is a sad commentary on the state of EMI's recorded music arm that among the last acts it signed have turned out to be Sir Bruce Forsyth and Twiggy" – before adding, "Universal, EMI Music's new owners, has done more to foster British talent in recent years than anyone."

Long-time follower of the story, and occasional commentator Damian Reece suggested in his *Daily Telegraph* column that, "Universal and Sony can probably make more sense of the EMI assets by taking out further costs but we'll probably never know if their deals create or destroy value. For EMI, however, the show is well and truly over."

Reece's reference to Sony reflected the purchase – announced later on the same day as the Universal deal – of EMI's music publishing division for a \$2.2 billion (£1.37 billion). While the news was released by Sony Corporation of America – the US arm of Japanese electronics giant – it in fact involved an investor group made up of Sony/ATV, the music publishing operation owned by Sony and the estate of Michael Jackson; Mubadala Development Company PJSC: Jynwel Capital; the Blackstone Group's GSO Capital Partners LP; and US entertainment entrepreneur David Geffen.

Jackson first forged an alliance with Sony in 1994 when he merged his ATV music publishing business – including the rights to the songs of Beatles John Lennon and Paul McCartney through Northern Songs – with Sony to create Sony/ATV while Mubadala PJSC is the wholly owned investment operation of the Government of Abu Dhabi, in the United

Arab Emirates. And alongside Jynwel and American investment company Blackstone GSO, is former record producer David Geffen, founder of Asylum and Geffen Records and co-founder of the Dreamworks film production company.

Boasting over 1.3 million copyrights in its armoury, EMI Music Publishing represents the song writing of artists such as Beyonce, Alicia Keys, Kanye West, Alan Jackson, Jay-Z and Rhianna. These artists plus Motown hits such as 'Baby Love', 'I Heard It Through The Grapevine' and 'My Girl' and the classic songs 'Over The Rainbow', 'Have Yourself A Merry Little Christmas', 'New York New York', 'Bohemian Rhapsody', 'You've Got A Friend' and 'Every Breath You Take' were now getting into bed with Sony/ATV's 750,000 song catalogue including the works of Leonard Cohen, Neil Diamond, Bob Dylan, Lady Gaga, Willie Nelson and Taylor Swift to create a company with a 33% share of the global music publishing market.

One man who was heavily involved in EMI Music Publishing's success over the years was Marty Bandier who headed up the EMI division for 17 years before leaving in 2006 and ultimately joining Sony/ATV. Understandably he was enthusiastic about the deal which put him back in charge of the EMI catalogue of songs which, it was announced, would be managed by Sony/ATV. "EMI Music Publishing is an iconic company with legendary copyrights and world class executive talent. I am excited to be reunited with the incredible songs, writers and talent of a company I helped build."

Interestingly one member of the "world class executive talent" referred to by Bandier was Faxon who was moved into EMI Publishing from his role as financial chief of the EMI Group in 2005. There he served as president and CEO under Bandier as part of what EMI chairman Eric Nicoli saw as "a smooth succession". But, while he recalled Faxon's appointment to head up EMI Publishing as one of his most satisfying achievements, it was a time when the rumours focussed on a breakdown in the relationship between Nicoli and Bandier.

With EMI recorded music moving to Universal and music publishing to Sony/ATV, the speculation continues as to what role Faxon will play down the line in the future of either of EMI's two businesses.

Whether the EMI publishing business, which in 2010 accounted for 45% of EMI's entire operating profit, is swallowed up by Sony/ATV to form one business remains unclear but European president of rivals Peermusic explained to the media that how the new company was structured was an important consideration when it came under the spot-light of the regulators. "If they can prove that the two are very much separate, competing entities, then that threat is a lot lower."

In December 2011 the likely new boss of EMI Music Publishing, Sony/ATV's Bandier announced how the new set-up would operate and he confirmed that his company intended to keep the name EMI and allow it to operate as a separate entity under their overall management. Confirming Sony/ATV's 38% control of EMI, Bandier also made a sur-prising comment on the deal, saying, "I'll let you know in about two years. It could be ranked as the greatest accomplishment or it could be the worst."

So with the global market for recorded music falling to just over $18 billion in 2010 from a high of $29.5 billion in 2005, there was specu-lation as to what exactly Universal were taking on by buying EMI's record business and merging labels such as A&M, Decca, Def Jam, Interscope, Island, Polydor, Motown and Verve with the likes of Angel, Blue Note, Capitol, Parlophone, and Virgin. "We plan to acquire EMI's recorded music division on attractive terms, adhering to our principle of total financial discipline," said Levy who, while making no reference to savings or redundancies, added tantalisingly, "They (EMI acts and staff) will find within our Group a safe, long term home, headquartered in Europe."

And when, rather than if, the deal does go through they will also find themselves in a hugely successful company which, as if to emphasise its domination of the music market, claimed five acts in the 2011 breakdown of the best selling albums in the US market by Nielsen SoundScan. Uni-versal's Lady Gaga was at number three – followed by Lil' Wayne, Drake, Justin Bieber and Jay-Z & Kanye West – while EMI boasted just Lady Antebellum in tenth place.

And Grainge, the man about to take over the helm at the helm of the world's even bigger biggest music company, summed up EMI's recent past and immediate future when he laid out the plan for EMI under Universal's leadership. "To replenish and rebuild the rosters that have lacked the level of investment that frankly a business like this should have had. You know, EMI is not a utilities company," was his prediction.

Before the end of 2011, Warner Music's long time chief executive Edgar Bronfman – the man who led the fight to buy the music company from Time Warner in 2004 – stepped down following the company's sale in May although he retained his position on the board. He made his announcement just as the company posted a full fiscal year drop in revenues of 4% to $2.8 billion which resulted in a year on year loss of $205 million, up from 2010's $143 million.

With both EMI deals out in the open and suitably analysed and assessed, the next area of speculation was how the regulator's in America and Europe would view the deal. While IMPALA made their expected objections, there was a view in 2012 that, with the traditional music industry in decline, the people who had halted EMI's earlier mergers and take-overs, might not be so hostile this time round.

Reflecting on the regulator's past decisions regarding EMI, Nicoli observes, "It's hard to see how the regulators' blocking decisions over the past several years have served consumers well," while *Music Week*'s Paul Williams suggests, "Vivendi will not be going into this without having looked seriously at the potential obstacles in terms of the competition authorities – and also the potential solutions." He also points out, "Universal/Vivendi has had an extremely good track record in getting things through the European regulators."

Menon too takes the view that the regulators should take a more favourable view of the two EMI offers which were put on the table at the end of 2011. "I tend to agree with the view that the regulators would be unwise, if not unlikely, to assume a hostile position to the Citibank sales in the prevailing economic environment and the continuing distress of the record industry."

While he accepts that Universal will almost certainly have to make some sort of offer to appease the regulators, business journalist Reece reckons that things might just be a little easier in 2012. "The regulators have been pretty hawkish in the past when it comes to consolidation in the music industry but you would have thought that now they might take a slightly more generous view," he suggests before adding, "You can't see this deal generating a huge amount of excitement in the present European climate."

Although there is no firm timetable as to how long the approval (or rejection) process will take, the US Federal Trade Commission was reported, in December 2011, to be reviewing the EMI deals in America while the European Commission carried out the same procedure for Europe. The speculation was that while Sony/ATV would have an easier ride in the US than Universal, the European regulators would be altogether tougher than their American counterparts.

At the end of 12 months, which US music magazine *Billboard* described as "a year of seismic shifts in the major-label landscape", there was the realisation that, with EMI's businesses being acquired by 'foreign' companies, Britain had finally lost its last great major player in the global music business.

In the year in which EMI celebrated its 80th birthday, the company had been sold to overseas-owned companies – and that raised the question: 'Does it matter who owns EMI in 2012?'

"We live in a global community and it's no longer to do with whose money it is but to do with the culture. EMI has a special British culture which always benefited us in the British market which is the second most important in the world in terms of repertoire. It isn't too late for that to be preserved whatever the ownership."

– Tony Wadsworth, former chairman EMI UK.

"The reason Damon (Albarn) was happy to be with EMI was because of its heritage and history. I think it's sad that there will not be a major British company."

– Chris Morrison, CMO Management

"The dominant advantage for steering this very large company record company through the challenging times ahead would lie with in its international management ability and not the nationality of its ownership."

– Bhaskar Menon, former chairman EMI Music

"It's a shame that the British independent giant is being broken up but it was always inevitable that it was going to happen. It has always been difficult to see EMI surviving on its own."

– Damian Reece, Daily Telegraph.

"I don't think it matters who owns EMI but what is important is that EMI's base and strength was in it UK repertoire. In terms of local and international talent, EMI was always strong and if that continues then that is what is important – irrespective of whether it is owned by somebody from private equity or a Russian Telecoms operator."

– Rogers Ames, former Warner Music chairman & head of EMI
North America

"I would be sorry to see EMI disappear. The last major British owned recording company with genuine global reach, it has been responsible for some of the greatest albums and artists in history of popular music. Indeed it still has an

interesting roster, including Lily Allen, Tinie Tempah and, er, Sir Cliff Richard who EMI has helped keep in the British charts for five decades."

– Neil McCormick, Chief Rock Critic *Daily Telegraph.*

"I think from a romantic patriotic point of view it's sad that there won't be a British-owned major record company anymore but then, in the harsh world of business, how much does it matter? If EMI had bought Warner a few years back it would have meant that America no longer had a major music company but nobody seemed to mention that."

– Paul Williams, Music Week.

"British ownership is in my view largely irrelevant although I understand all the emotion attaching to it. We shouldn't think of the Universal acquisition of EMI as the loss of a great British brand so much as EMI is joining a strong global company."

– Eric Nicoli, former Chairmam EMI Music.

"I don't think it matters that there isn't a British-owned record company so long as British talent is able to flourish – Universal and Sony have a good record in that respect."

– Tim Clark, manager Robbie Williams.

When EMI's financial figures up to March 2011 - the company's last year under the control of Hands and Terra Firma – were eventually announced they showed reduced revenues of £1.4 billion while both recorded music and music publishing also suffered a drop in earnings. There was, however, some consolation in that the company's net loss was cut to £324 million from a pre-audited 2010 figure in excess of £500 million.

The 2011 year-end market and chart shares figures for the major US and UK markets made no more impressive reading for EMI despite the success of acts such as Lady Antebellum, Katy Perry, Coldplay and Tini Tempah. While new owners Universal (according to Nielsen SoundScan figures) upped their share of the American album market from 31.6% to 38.7%, EMI dropped from 9.6% to 9.2%. Alongside these two, Sony increased their share by 1% to 28.4% and Warner Music fell from 19.8% to 18.7%.

In the UK, EMI's share of the overall album market dropped to 12.9% (from 14.1%) while Universal held on to the top spot with 31.7% - down from 32% in 2010. These two sets of figures only served to emphasise the size, power and potential influence of a combined Universal/EMI operation which, last year, could lay claim to a huge combined 47.9% share of the US album market and an equally impressive 44.6% piece of the UK business. And even together, rivals Sony and Warner Music (47.1% in the US and 32.6% in the UK) still lagged behind the new music giant.

As the new head of the Universal/EMI operation, Grainge now finds himself in direct competition with two other experienced and powerful stalwarts of the music industry – Doug Morris at Sony Music and Lyor Cohen at Warner Music – and for one anonymous industry observer this raises some serious concerns. "Competition is good for the industry but when it becomes an ego battle, that is not good or productive," he warned.

At the same time *Music Week*, in their summary of the major developments of 2011, reckoned the scene was all set for a significant historical development and suggested that "a successful run of the regulation gauntlet for both parties (Universal and Sony/ATV) will complete one of the biggest shifts in music history."

However, for one manager whose act blossomed at EMI before they decided to sever their links, the latest chapter in the story of the British major was anything but overwhelming. Replying to an e-mail asking for his observations on the deals, Chris Hufford, the co-manager of Radiohead, wrote, "My only comment would be 'whatever' prefaced by a bored sign. Hey ho . . . the circus continues!!!"

ACKNOWLEDGEMENTS

My thanks as ever go to Chris Charlesworth at Omnibus Press for his perseverance and enthusiasm and the 'back-room' editors and designers who make so many things happen.

There is also a whole host of people who spoke to me both on and off the record (and, in some cases, both) and many more who supplied background information essential for this book. I am most grateful to all of them for their assistance and support.

The British Library (let's keep it free), the British Newspaper Library, the BPI, the IFPI and back issues of *Billboard*, *Music Week*, *Music & Media* and *Music & Copyright* were also important sources of information as were the music industry figures published by Nielsen SoundScan, the Official Chart Company and *Music & Copyright*. I extend my thanks to all of them.

BIBLIOGRAPHY

Barfe, Louis. Where Have All The Good Times Gone?: The Rise And Fall Of The Record Industry (Atlantic Books, 2004)

Martland, Peter. Since Records Began: EMI: The First 100 Years (Batsford, 1997)

Miller, Russell & Boar, Roger. The Incredible Music Machine (Quartet /Visual Arts, 1982)

Pandit S.A. From Making to Music: The History of Thorn EMI (Hodder & Stoughton, 1996)

INDEX

By the same author . . .

POP GOES TO COURT

Rock'Roll's Greatest Court Battles

Elvis Presley, Ozzy Osbourne, George Michael, Metallica, George Harrison, The Smiths . . . they've all been involved in legal action over the past 50 years or so.

Here Comes The Judge recalls some of the most entertaining and bizarre court cases ever to take rock'n'rollers into a courtroom. Bono went all litigious over a disappearing hat, one Beatle filed suit against the other three, and 40 years after it was a hit, Procol Harum's *A Whiter Shader of Pale was suddenly the focus of bitter legal wrangling over who actually wrote it.*

Author Brian Southall digs deep into some of the most memorable music disputes ever to merit the sober deliberations of the law, and in doing so reveals much about our changing views on fame and the value of publicity.

ISBN: 978.1.84772.113.6
OP52206

By the same author . . .

NORTHERN SONGS

The True Story of The Beatles' Song Publishing Empire

From the moment Beatlemania broke out, John Lennon & Paul McCartney's publishing company Northern Songs was a potential goldmine. It would eventually become the most valuable song publishing catalogue in the world.

The history of that catalogue – how Lennon & McCartney lost it, and the complex financial and legal wranglings that took it into other hands – is the epic music industry story of the 20th century.

- How did minor singer turned publisher Dick James get to handle Lennon & McCartney's songs?
- Why did Michael Jackson's stake in the legendary catalogue cause a rift with Paul McCartney?
- And why does McCartney now own just two Beatles' songs?

This lid-lifting investigation contains interviews with: George Martin, Paul McCartney, the late Dick James' son Steven, Yoko Ono and those in the know from Apple Corp., DJM and EMI.

The hi-jacking of The Beatles' song catalogue is a staggering saga of incompetence, duplicity and music industry politics. In *Only A Northern Song* author and Beatles expert Brian Southall lays it all bare in a groundbreaking investigative book that is as compulsive as it is astounding.

ISBN: 978.1.84609.996.0
OP52030

Coming soon....

DOWNLOAD!

How Digital Destroyed The Record Industry

By Phil Hardy

Download chronicles of the making of the new record industry, from the boom years of the CD revolution of the late 1980s to the crisis of the present day, with particular stress on the last decade. It follows the actions and reactions of the major international record companies, five at the beginning of the story, now three, as they ploughed their way through the digital slough of despond, bewildered by the fleet-of-foot digital innovators far more responsive to the changing marketing conditions through which (recorded) music was consumed and valued.

Download has no substantial heroes or villains, no individual or group who shaped the transformation that the industry is undergoing. Some of these, Edgar Bronfman Jnr., Ahmet Ertegun, David Geffen, and Eric Nicoli, are known to the public. Others, Lyor Cohn, Zach Horowitz, Doug Morris and Mo Ostin, are less well known. But these characters, however powerful they may be, particularly within their companies, have been powerless to halt the loss of control that has been the key fact in the recent history of the music business. Recent years have also thrown up a new set of characters, Apple's Steve Jobs, for whom music was a way to reinvigorate a faltering computer company, and Terra Firma's Guy Hands and Access Industries' Len Blavatnik, venture capitalists bent on finding new ways of monetizing recorded music.

These all have their significant place in *Download* but the real story is the structural change that has, almost surreptitiously, taken place, within the music business. This change, for reasons author Phil Hardy explain in detail, has left the captains of the record industry as unable to act as they were unwilling to act. In effect they became little but very well paid observers of the shrinking of their domains.

ISBN: 978.1.78038.614.0
OP54846